CONTENTS

Introduction

II Multimedia Hardware

A CD-ROM accompanies this book.
Both items must be returned in order to be fully
discharged from your card.
Any late items are subject to fines.

This book is due for return on or before the last date shown below.

1 4 MAR 2001

0 5 OCT 2005

0 2 FEB 2006

2 5 OCT 2006

2 7 MAR 2008

3 0 NOV 2009

Don Gresswell Ltd., London, N.21   Cat. No. 1208   DG 02242/71

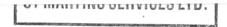

Osborne McGraw-Hill

Berkeley   New York   St. Louis   San Francisco   Auckland   Bogotá   Hamburg   London   Madrid   Mexico City
Milan   Montreal   New Delhi   Panama City   Paris   São Paulo   Singapore   Sydney   Tokyo   Toronto

Publisher
Brandon A. Nordin

Editor-in-Chief
Scott Rogers

Acquisitions Editor
Megg Bonar

Project Editor
Madhu Prasher

Editorial Assistant
Stephane Thomas

Technical Editor
Panagiotis Takis Metaxas

Copy Editor
Judith Brown

Proofreaders
Nancy Chapman and Karen Mead

Indexer
Valerie Robbins

Computer Designer
Jani Beckwith

Illustrator
Brian Wells

Series Design
Seventeenth Street Studios

Cover Design
Regan Honda

Osborne/**McGraw-Hill**
2600 Tenth Street
Berkeley, California 94710
U.S.A.

For information on translations or book distributors outside the U.S.A., or to arrange bulk purchase discounts for sales promotions, premiums, or fund-raisers, please contact Osborne/**McGraw-Hill** at the above address.

Multimedia: Making It Work, Fourth Edition

4567890 AGM AGM   019876543210

ISBN 0-07-882552-0

Multimedia Software

IV Multimedia Building Blocks

V   Multimedia and the Internet

VI   Assembling and Delivering a Project

Acknowledgments

This fourth edition of *Multimedia: Making It Work* includes the cumulated input and advice of many colleagues and friends over a seven-year period. Each time I revise and update this book, I am pleased to see that the acknowledgments section grows. Indeed, it is difficult to delete people from this (huge) list because, like the stones of a medieval castle, new and revised material relies upon the older foundation. I will continue accumulating the names of the good people who have helped me build this castle and list them here, at least until my publisher cries "Enough!" and provides substantial reason to press the Delete key.

Megg Bonar, Madhu Prasher, Judith Brown, Robin Small, Scott Rogers, and Stephane Thomas carried the Osborne/McGraw-Hill flag for this edition. As technical editor, Takis Metaxas from Wellesley College added significant value in my quest to make this work useful in the classroom. In past editions, Bob Myren, Heidi Poulin, Mark Karmendy, Joanne Cuthbertson, Bill Pollock, Jeff Pepper, Kathy Hashimoto, Marla Shelasky, Linda Medoff, Valerie Robbins, Cindy Brown, Larry Levitsky, Frances Stack, Jill Pisoni, Carol Henry, and Linda Beatty went out of their way to keep me on track. Chip Harris, Dan Hilgert, Helayne Waldman, Hank Duderstadt, Dina Medina, Joyce Edwards, Theo Posselt, Ann Stewart, Graham Arlen, Kathy Gardner, Steve Goeckler, Steve Peha, Christine Perey, Pam Sansbury, Terry Schussler, and Michael Allen have contributed to making the work more complete since its first edition. The professional and disciplined contribution of my colleague, Donna Booher, will remain always evident throughout the chapters of this work.

My very bright students and friends from the Interactive Telecommunications Program at the Helsinki School of Economics and Business Administration (Helsingen Kauppakorkeakoulu) continue to supply hands-on and practical insights into the difficulties of designing multimedia. Finland, it seems, as a country of about 5 million, ranks as the largest user of the Internet in the world on a per capita basis.

I would also like to acknowledge many friends in the computer and publishing industries who continue to make this book possible. They send me quotes and multimedia anecdotes to enliven the book; many arranged for me to review and test software and hardware; many have been there when I needed them. I would like to thank them all for the time and courtesy they afforded me on this project:

Grace Abbett, Adobe Systems
Eric Alderman, HyperMedia Group
Heather Alexander, Waggener/Edstrom
Laura Ames, Elgin/Syferd PR
Kurt Andersen, Andersen Design
Ines Anderson, Claris
David Antoniuk, Live Oak Multimedia
Yasemin Argun, Corel Systems
Cornelia Atchley, Comprehensive Technologies
Dana Atchley, Network Productions
Pamela Atkinson, Pioneer Software
Ann Bagley, Asymetrix
Patricia Baird, Hypermedia Journal
Gary Baker, Technology Solutions
Richard Bangs, Mountain Travel-Sobek
Sean Barger, Equilibrium
Jon Barrett, Dycam
Heinz Bartesch, The Search Firm
Bob Bauld, Bob Bauld Productions
Thomas Beinar, Add-On America/Rohm
Bob Bell, SFSU Multimedia Studies Program
George Bell, Ocron
Mike Bellefeuille, Corel Systems
Andrew Bergstein, Altec Lansing
Kathy Berlan, Borland International
Camarero Bernard, mFactory
Brian Berson, Diamondsoft
Bren Besser, Unlimited Access
Tim Bigoness, Equilibrium
Nancy Blachman, Variable Symbols
Dana Blankenhorn, Have Modem Will Travel
Brian Blum, The Software Toolworks
Sharon Bodenschatz, International Typeface
Michele Boeding, ICOM Simulations
Donna Booher, Timestream
Gail Bower, TMS
Kellie Bowman, Adobe
Susan Boyer, Blue Sky Software
Deborah Brown, Technology Solutions
Eric Brown, NewMedia Magazine

Russell Brown, Adobe Systems
Tiffany Brown, Network Associates
Stephanie Bryan, SuperMac
Ann Marie Buddrus, Digital Media Design
David Bunnell, NewMedia Magazine
Jeff Burger, Creative Technologies
Bridget Burke, Gryphon Software
Dominique Busso, OpenMind
Ben Calica, Tools for the Mind
Doug Campbell, Spinnaker Software
Teri Campbell, MetaCreations
Doug Camplejohn, Apple Computer
Norman Cardella, Best-Seller
Tim Carrigan, Multimedia Magazine
Herman Chin, Computer Associates International
Jane Chuey, Macromedia
Angie Ciarloni, Hayes
Kevin Clark, Strata
Cathy Clarke, DXM Productions
Frank Colin, Equilibrium
David Collier, decode communications
David Conti, AimTech
Freda Cook, Aldus
Renee Cooper, Miramar Systems
Wendy Cornish, Vividus
Patrick Crisp, Caere
Michelle Cunningham, Symantec
Lee Curtis, CE Software
Eric Dahlinger, Newer Technology
John deLorimier, Kallisto Productions
Jeff Dewey, Luminaria
Jennifer Doettling, Delta Point
Hank Duderstadt, Timestream
Mike Duffy, The Software Toolworks
Eileen Ebner, McLean Public Relations
Dawn Echols, Oracle
Dorothy Eckel, Specular International
Joyce Edwards, Timestream
Kevin Edwards, c|net
Mark Edwards, Independent Multimedia Developer

Dan Elenbaas, Amaze!

Ellen Elias, O'Reilly & Associates

Shelly Ellison, Tektronix

Kathy Englar, RayDream

Jonathan Epstein, MPC World

Jeff Essex, Audio Synchrosy

Sharron Evans, Graphic Directions

Kiko Fagan, Attorney at Law

Joe Fantuzzi, Macromedia

Lee Feldman, Voxware

Laura Finkelman, S & S Communications

Holly Fisher, MetaTools

Terry Fleming, Timeworks

Patrick Ford, Microsoft

Marty Fortier, Prosonus

Robin Galipeau, Mutual/Hadwen Imaging

Kathy Gardner, Gardner Associates

Peter Gariepy, Zedcor

Bill Gates, Microsoft

Petra Gerwin, Mathematica

John Geyer, Terran Interactive

Jonathan Gibson, Form and Function

Karen Giles, Borland

Amanda Goodenough, AmandaStories

Danny Goodman, Concentrics Technology

Howard Gordon, Xing Technology

Jonathan Graham, Iomega

Catherine Greene, LightSource

Fred Greguras, Fenwick & West

Maralyn Guarino, Blue Sky Software

Cari Gushiken, Copithorne & Bellows

Kim Haas, McLean Public Relations

Marc Hall, Deneba Software

Johan Hamberg, Timestream

Lynda Hardman, CWI - Netherlands

Tom Hargadon, Conference Communications

Chip Harris, InHouse Productions

Sue Hart, FileMaker

Trip Hawkins, 3DO/Electronic Arts

Randy Haykin, Apple Computer

Jodi Hazzan, SoftQuad

Ray Heizer, Heizer Software

Dave Heller, Salient Software

Josh Hendrix, CoSA

Maria Hermanussen, Gold Disk

Allan Hessenflow, HandMade Software

Lars Hidde, The HyperMedia Group

Dave Hobbs, LickThis

Petra Hodges, Mathematica

John Holder, John V. Holder Software

Elena Holland, Traveling Software

Mike Holm, Apple Computer

Robert Hone, Red Hill Studios

Kevin Howat, MacMillan Digital

Tom Hughes, PhotoDisc

Claudia Husemann, Cunningham Communications

Les Inanchy, Sony CD-ROM Division

Tom Inglesby, Manufacturing Systems

Carl Jaffe, Yale University School of Medicine

Farrah Jinha, Vertigo 3D

Cynthia Johnson, BoxTop Software

Scott Johnson, NTERGAID

JoAnn Johnston, Regis McKenna

Neele Johnston, Autodesk

Dave Kaufer, Waggener/Edstrom

David Kazanjian, AFTRA Actor

Jenna Keller, Alexander Communications

Helen Kendrick, Software Publishing

Benita Kenn, Creative Labs

Trudy Kerr, Alexander Communications

Gary Kevorkian, ULead Systems

David Kleinberg, NetObjects

Jeff Kleindinst, Turtle Beach Systems

Kevin Klingler, Sonic Desktop Software

Sharon Klocek, Visual In-Seitz

Christina Knighton, Play Incorporated

Lewis Kraus, InfoUse

Katrina Krebs, Micrografx

Kevin Krejci, Pop Rocket

Larry Kubo, Ocron

Howard Kwak, Multimedia SourceBook

Irving Kwong, Waggener/Edstrom

Craig LaGrow, Morph's Outpost

Kimberly Larkin, Alexander Communications

Kevin LaRue, Allegiant Technologies

Mark Law, Extensis

Nicole Lazzaro, ONYX Productions

Alan Levine, Maricopa Community Colleges

Bob LeVitus, LeVitus Productions

Steven Levy, MacWorld

Leigh-Ann Lindsey, Mathematica

Rob Lippincott, Lotus

Mark Lissick, C-Star Technology
Jason Lockhart, G3 Systems
Elliot Luber, Technology Solutions
David Ludwig, Interactive Learning Designs
Kirk Lyford, Vivid Details
Jennifer Lyng, Aladdin Systems
John MacLeod, FastForward
Philip Malkin, Passport Designs
Kevin Mallon, FileMaker
Basil Maloney, Winalysis
Kathy Mandle, Adobe
Audrey Mann, Technology Solutions
Nicole Martin, Netopia/Farallon Division
Robert May, Ikonic
Georgia McCabe, Applied Graphics Technologies
Russ McCann, Ares Software
Kevin McCarthy, Medius IV
Charles McConathy, MicroNet Technology
Carol McGarry, Schwartz Communications
Laurie McLean, McLean Public Relations
Amy McManus, Delta Point
Bert Medley, "The NBC Today Show"
Art Metz, Metz
Steve Michel, Author
Aline Mikaelian, Screenplay Systems
Nancy Miller, Canto Software
Doug Millison, Morph's Outpost
Karen Milne, Insignia Solutions
Brian Molyneaux, Heizer Software
Molly Morelock, Macromedia
Jeff Morgan, Radmedia
Rob Morris, VGraph
Glenn Morrisey, Asymetrix
Terry Morse, Terry Morse Software
Rachel Muñoz, Caere
Philip Murray, Knowledge Management Associates
Chuck Nakell, Inspiration Software
Kee Nethery, Kagi Engineering
Chris Newell, Musitek
Mark Newman, Photographer
Wendy Woods Newman, Newsbytes
Terry Nizko, AimTech
Glenn Ochsenreiter, MPC Marketing Council
Maureen O'Conell, Apple Computer
Jim O'Gara, Altsys
Eric Olson, Virtus

Karen Oppenheim, Cunningham Communications
Kim Osborne, Symantec
Nicole DeMeo Overson, GoLive Systems
Andy Parng, PixoArts
Susan Pearson, Waggener/Edstrom
Lorena Peer, Chroma Graphics
Steve Peha, Music Technology Associates
Sylvester Pesek, Optical Media International
Christiane Petite, Symantec
Paul Phelan, INESC (Portugal)
Scott Pink, Bronson
Audrey Pobre, Quarterdeck
Dave Pola, Equilibrium
JB Popplewell, Alien Skin Software
Melissa Rabin, Miramar
Shirley Rafieetary, Medius IV
Tom Randolph, FM Towns/Fujitsu
Steven Rappaport, Interactive Records
Ronelle Reed, Switzer Communications
David Reid, Author
Diane Reynolds, Graphsoft
Laurie Robinson, Gold Disk
Connie Roloff, Software Products International
John Rootenberg, Paceworks
Steve Rubenstein, San Francisco Chronicle
Jill Ryan, McLean Public Relations
Marie Salerno, AFTRA/SAG
John Sammis, DataDescription
Jay Sandom, Einstein & Sandom
Pam Sansbury, Disc Manufacturing
Richard Santalesa, R&D Technologies
Anne Sauer, Fast Electronic U.S.
Joe Scarano, DS Design
Sonya Schaefer, Adobe
Rochelle Schiffman, Electronics for Imaging
Rachel Schindler, Macromedia
Melissa Scott, Window Painters
Sandy Scott, Soft-Kat
Brigid Sealy, INESC (Portugal)
Karl Seppala, Gold Disk
Chip Shabazian, Ocron
Ashley Sharp, Virtus
Adam Silver, Videologic
Stephanie Simpson, Adaptec
Marlene Sinicki, Designer
Chris Smith, VideoLabs

Brian Snook, Visual In-Seitz
Kent Sokoloff, Timestream
David Spitzer, Hewlett-Packard
Domenic Stansberry, Author
Ann Stewart, Interactive Dimensions
Polina Sukonik, Xaos Tools
Lisa Sunaki, Autodesk
Lee Swearingen, DXM Productions
Joe Taglia, Insignia Solutions
Marty Taucher, Microsoft
Bill Tchakirides, U-Design Type Foundry
Toni Teator, NetObjects
Amy Tenderich, Norton-Lambert
Lori Ternacole, SoftQuad
Dave Terran, WordPerfect
Leo Thomas, Eastman Kodak
Terry Thompson, Timestream
Bill Thursby, Thursby Software Systems
Alexandrea Todd, McLean Public Relations
Kim Tompkins, Micrografx
Tom Toperczer, Imspace Systems
Cara Ucci, Autodesk
Ross Uchimura, GC3

David Vasquez, SFSU Multimedia Studies Program
Sally von Bargen, 21st Century Media
Helayne Waldman, SFSU Multimedia Studies Program
James J. Waldron, Visage
Arnold Waldstein, Creative Labs
Keri Walker, Apple Computer
Brad Walter, Leister Productions
Stefan Wennik, Bitstream
Chris Wheeler, TechSmith
Tom White, Roland
John Wilczak, HSC Software
Darby Williams, Microsoft
Laura Williams, Waggener/Edstrom
Mark Williams, Microsoft
Shelly Williams, Prosonus
Hal Wine, Programmer
Sara Winge, O'Reilly & Associates
Marcus Woehrmann, Handmade Software
Sandy Wong, Fenwick & West
Chris Yalonis, Passport Designs
Alexandra Yessios, auto*des*sys
Barbara Zediker, Pioneer
Frank Zellis, KyZen

About the Author...

Tay Vaughan is a recognized authority and pioneer in multimedia. He has designed and produced award-winning projects for clients such as Apple Computer, Lotus, Tandy, Sun, and Novell. He is the president of Timestream, Inc., a multimedia production company in Oakland, California, and a visiting professor at the Interactive Telecommunications Program of the Helsinki School of Economics and Business Administration.

Introduction

In a few years, multimedia computers will be an anachronism because all computers will readily deal with images, sounds, and motion video, seamlessly and smoothly integrated into what a computer is. While the specialness of multimedia computers per se may disappear when hardware and software platforms become more capable and we take sound, animation, and video features for granted, the fundamental concepts and techniques required to work with these elements will not disappear.

This is a book about the elemental parts of multimedia as much as about how to sew these parts together with current technology and tools. It is a book that shows you how to use text, images, sound, and video to deliver your messages and content in meaningful ways. It is about designing, organizing, and producing multimedia projects of all kinds and avoiding technical and legal pitfalls along the way. Above all, it is a practical guide to making multimedia, complete with tips, pointers, and answers.

The first part deals with the basic elements of multimedia. Hardware and software tools are described in detail. You will learn about the importance of text and how to make characters look pretty, about making graphic art on your computer and how to choose colors, and about how to digitize sound and video segments. You will learn about human interaction and how to design a user-friendly computer interface. Then you will be introduced to the step-by-step creative and organizing process that results in a finished multimedia project. You will even learn how to deliver your multimedia projects on the World Wide Web.

I have written this book for people who make or want to make multimedia, for people who gladly take up new challenges and are unafraid of learning curves and intensely creative work. The words and ideas of this book are the harvest of many years in the computer industry and of hands-on experience deep in the factory where multimedia is being made daily. The book is intended to be, above all, useful.

For focus, I chose two well-known computer environments to discuss in detail throughout the book: Microsoft Windows and Apple Macintosh—the most widely used platforms for making multimedia today. But multimedia is by no means limited to these platforms, and most of the ideas discussed in the book are translatable to others.

I have made a great effort to include in this book references to as much multimedia software and hardware as I could, trying not to miss any players. But because the industry is fast paced and rapidly growing, and because, while writing this book, I have rediscovered the finite limits of my own time, I am sure some have fallen into the bit bucket anyway. Immutable physical laws have prevented me from including the fine details of 40 or 50 hardware and software manuals and technical resources into the pages allowed for this book. The distillation presented here should, however, point you toward further information and study. I have also made a great effort to double-check my words and statements for accuracy; if errors have slipped past, they are mine alone.

This is the fourth edition of *Multimedia: Making It Work*. Almost seven years have passed since the first edition was published, and many changes have occurred. Today, the fastest moving wavefront in multimedia may be seen on the World Wide Web. In this edition, I have included a section about new authoring tools for creating and delivering multimedia for the Web.

Some years ago, after completing a book about HyperCard, I swore never to write another. Writing a book is much like childbirth, I believe. In the beginning, it gestates slowly, usually over a few months. Then it ramps up inexorably and quickly toward deadline, until all attention is focused upon the delivery itself and the pain and workload are great. Editors cry, "Push." Afterwards, you remember it was rough, but memories of the pain itself become diffused, and one is only too easily persuaded to do it again. I am glad to share my multimedia experiences with you, and hope that in reading this book you will become better at what you do.

Tay Vaughan
Oakland, California
May 1998

Multi

Multimedia is any combination o

> 𝒜ultimedia excites
> eyes, ears, fingertips,
> and, most importantly,
> the head.

When you **weave** together the sensual elements of multmedia -

interactive control

media

text, graphic art, sound, animation and video

part

I

Introduction

■ — dazzling
pictures
and
animations,
engaging
sounds,
compelling
video clips —
you can electrify the thought and action centers of people's minds.

in·for·ma·tion

Multi

Multimedia is any combination

[
A revolution is taking place today in the way humans access, learn, and interact with information.
]

When you **weave** together the sensual elements of multmedia -

interactive control

media

text, graphic art, sound, animation and video

chapter

1

What Is Multimedia?

■ — dazzling
pictures
and
animations,
engaging
sounds,
compelling
video clips —
you can electrify the thought and action centers of people's minds.

in·for·ma·tion

M

ULTIMEDIA is an eerie wail as two cat's eyes appear on a dark screen. It's the red rose that dissolves into a little girl's face when you press "Valentine's Day." It's a small window of video laid onto a map of India, showing an old man recalling his dusty journey to meet a rajah there. It's a catalog of fancy cars with a guide to help you buy one. It's a real-time video conference with colleagues in Paris, London, and Hong Kong on your office computer. At home, it's an algebra or geography lesson for a fifth-grader. At the arcade, it's goggle-faced kids flying fighter planes in sweaty virtual reality.

Multimedia is any combination of text, graphic art, sound, animation, and video delivered to you by computer or other electronic means. It is richly presented sensation. When you weave together the sensual elements of multimedia—dazzling pictures and animations, engaging sounds, compelling video clips, and raw textual information—you can electrify the thought and action centers of people's minds. When you give them interactive control of the process, they can be enchanted. Multimedia excites eyes, ears, fingertips, and, most importantly, the head.

This book is about creating each of the elements of multimedia and about how you can weave them together for maximum effect. This book is for computer beginners and computer experts. It is for serious multimedia producers and their clients, as well. It is for desktop publishers and video producers who may need a leg-up as they watch traditional methods for delivery of information and ideas evolve into new, technology-driven formats. This book is also for hobbyists, who want to make albums and family histories on the World Wide Web; for mainstream businesses, where word-processed documents and spreadsheets are illustrated with audio, video, and graphic animations; for public speakers, who use animation and sound on large monitors and auditorium projection systems to present ideas and information to an audience; for information managers, who organize and distribute digital images, sound, video, and text; and for educators and trainers, who design and present information for learning.

The implementation of multimedia capabilities in computers is just the latest episode in a long series: cave painting, hand-crafted manuscripts, the printing press, radio and television....
These advances reflect the innate desire of man to create outlets for creative expression, to use technology and imagination to gain empowerment and freedom for ideas.

Glenn Ochsenreiter, Director, Multimedia PC Council

If you are new to multimedia and are facing a major investment in hardware, software, and the time to learn each new tool, take a gradual approach to these challenges. Begin by studying each element of multimedia and learning one or more tools for creating and editing that element. Get to know how to use text and fonts, how to make and edit colorful graphic images and animate them into movies, and how to record and edit digital sound. Read the computer trade periodicals that contain the most up-to-date information. Your skills will be most valuable if you develop a broad foundation of knowledge about each of the basic elements of multimedia.

Producing a multimedia project or a Web site requires more than creative skill and high technology. You need organizing and business talent as well. For example, issues of ownership and copyright will be attached to some elements that you wish to use: text from books, scanned images from magazines, audio and video clips. These require permission and often payment of a fee to the owner. Indeed, the management and production infrastructure of a multimedia project may be as intense and complicated as the technology and creative skills you bring to bear in rendering it.

Definitions

Multimedia is, as described above, woven combinations of text, graphic art, sound, animation, and video elements. When you allow an end user—the viewer of a multimedia project—to control what and when the elements are delivered, it is *interactive multimedia*. When you provide a structure of linked elements through which the user can navigate, interactive multimedia becomes *hypermedia*.

We define multimedia as anything that requires more than two trips to the car.

Robert May, President, Ikonic, Inc.

Although the definition of multimedia is a simple one, making it work can be complicated. Not only do you need to understand how to make each multimedia element stand up and dance, but you also need to know how to use multimedia computer tools and technologies to weave them together. The people who weave multimedia into meaningful tapestries are *multimedia developers*.

The software vehicle, the messages, and the content presented on a computer or television screen together constitute a *multimedia project*. If the project will be shipped or sold to consumers or end users, typically in a box or sleeve, with or without instructions, it is a *multimedia title*. Your project may also be a *page* or site on the World Wide Web, where you can weave the elements of multimedia into HTML (Hypertext Markup Language) or DHTML (Dynamic Hypertext Markup Language) documents. See Chapter 15 for more about multimedia and the Web.

A multimedia project need not be interactive to be called multimedia: users can sit back and watch it just as they do a movie or the television. In such cases a project is *linear*, starting at a beginning and running through to an end. When users are given navigational control and can wander through the content at will, multimedia becomes *nonlinear* and interactive, and is a powerful personal gateway to information.

Determining how a user will interact with and navigate through the content of a project requires great attention to the message, the *scripting* or *storyboarding*, the artwork, and the programming. You can break an entire project with a badly designed interface. You can also break a project with inadequate or inaccurate content.

Multimedia elements are typically sewn together into a project using *authoring tools*. These software tools are designed to manage individual multimedia elements and provide user interaction. In addition to providing a method for users to interact with the project, most authoring tools also offer facilities for creating and editing text and images, and they have extensions to drive videodisc players, videotape players, and other relevant hardware peripherals. Sounds and movies are usually created with editing tools dedicated to these media, and then the elements are imported into the authoring system for playback. The sum of what gets played back and how it is presented to the viewer is the *graphical user interface*, or GUI (pronounced "gooey"). This interface is just as much the rules for what happens to the user's input as it is the actual graphics on the screen. The hardware and software that govern the limits of what can happen are the multimedia *platform* or *environment*.

Talking about multimedia is a lot like talking about love. Everybody agrees that it's a good thing, everybody wants it, wants to participate in it, but everybody has a different idea of what "it" really is. Right now, the industry reminds me of a bunch of teenagers dabbling in something that instinctively feels right, all the while wondering how and when they'll know for sure if they're really in "it," and what to do about it if they are.

Georgia McCabe, Director, Commercial Photo CD,
Eastman Kodak Company

CD-ROM and the Multimedia Highway

Multimedia requires large amounts of digital memory when stored in an end user's library, or large amounts of *bandwidth* when distributed over wires or glass fiber on a network.

CD-ROM and Multimedia

CD-ROM (compact disc read-only memory, see Chapter 20) has emerged during the last few years as the most cost-effective distribution medium for multimedia projects: a CD-ROM disc can be mass-produced for less than one dollar and can contain up to 72 minutes of full-screen video. Or it can contain unique mixes of images, sounds, text, video, and animations controlled by an authoring system to provide unlimited user interaction.

Discs can be stamped out of polycarbonate plastic as fast as cookies on a baker's production line. Most personal computers sold today include a CD-ROM player, and the software that drives these computers is commonly available on a CD-ROM disc—applications that required inserting as many as 16 or more disks one after another are now installed from a CD-ROM without muss or fuss. Multilayered Digital Versatile Disc (DVD) technology will supercede CD-ROM by the turn of the millenium, increasing the capacity and multimedia capability of current CD-ROM optical technology.

In the very long term, however, CD-ROM and DVD are but interim memory technologies that will be replaced by new devices that do not require moving parts. As the data highway described below becomes more and more pervasive and users become more easily "connected," copper wire, glass fiber, and radio/cellular technologies may prevail as the most commonly used delivery means for interactive multimedia.

The Multimedia Highway

Now that telecommunications networks are global, and when information providers and content owners determine the worth of their products and how to charge money for them, information elements will ultimately link up on-line as distributed resources on a data highway (actually more like a toll road), where you will pay to acquire and use multimedia-based information. In the United States, alliances are under way between the government, cable companies, telephone companies, computer companies, and existing data distribution networks such as the Internet to build a National Information Infrastructure (www.niiac-info.org/~niiac/main_doc.html).

Curiously, the actual glass fiber cables that compose much of the physical backbone of the data highway are, in many cases, owned by railroads and pipeline companies that simply buried the cable on existing rights of way where no special permits and environmental reports are necessary. One railroad in the United States invested more than a million dollars in a special cable-laying trenching car; in Great Britain, there is talk of placing a fiber-optic cable backbone along the decaying 19th-century canal and barge system. Bandwidth on these lines is leased to others, so competing retailers such as AT&T, MCI, and Sprint may even share the same cable.

Full-text content from books and magazines will be accessible by modem and electronic link; feature movies will be played at home; real-time news reports from anywhere on earth will be available; lectures from participating universities will be monitored for education credits; street maps of any city will be viewable—with recommendations for restaurants, in any language—and on-line travelogues will include testimonials and video tracks. This is not science fiction; it is being implemented now. Each of these interfaces or gateways to information is a multimedia project just waiting to be developed.

··

http://www.movielink.com
http://www.ird.net/diningout.html
http://www.nyfood.com
http://www.vacations.com

Showtimes for many major cities, restaurants, vacation trips, and current news items are quickly available on the Web

In a few years, interactive multimedia will be delivered to many homes throughout the world. Interest from a confluence of entertainment megacorps, information publishers and providers, cable and telephone companies, and hardware and software manufacturers is already driving this inevitable evolution, and profound changes in global communications strategy are on the drawing boards. What will be piped through this new system are the very multimedia elements discussed in the chapters of this book: text, graphics, animation, sound, and video. The software tools for making and editing these elements are discussed in Part 3; the methods for delivering these elements on the Internet are described in Chapter 14.

Entertainment companies that own content easily converted to multimedia projects are teaming up with cable TV companies such as QVC or Viacom (owner of MTV, Showtime, and Nickelodeon). Film studios such as Disney and Warner Brothers are creating new divisions to produce interactive multimedia, and wealthy talents like Spielberg, Katzenberg, and Geffen are forming new companies (DreamWorks) to join the action. Already, large media corporations are uniting to create huge conglomerates that will control the content of tomorrow's information. Disney has merged with Capital Cities/ABC, Time Warner has purchased Turner Broadcasting, and Microsoft has joined forces with NBC. Indeed, Microsoft's interests in the growing Internet are so pervasive that it risks breakup and reorganization by the government under antitrust and monopoly laws, as was required of AT&T, the telephone giant.

Some companies will own the routes for carrying data, other companies will own the hardware and software interfaces at the end of the line, at offices and homes. Some will knit it all together and provide supply-on-demand and billing services. Regardless of who owns the roadways and the hardware boxes, multimedia producers will create the new literature and the rich content sent along it. This is a fresh and exciting industry coming of age, but one still faced with many growing pains.

Where to Use Multimedia

Multimedia is appropriate whenever a human interface connects a human user to electronic information of any kind. Multimedia enhances traditional text-only computer interfaces and yields measurable benefit by gaining and holding attention and interest; multimedia improves information retention. When properly woven, multimedia can also be profoundly entertaining.

::::::::::::::::::::::::::::::::::

Multimedia is a very effective presentation and sales tool. If you're being driven somewhere in the back seat of a car, you may not remember how you got to your destination; but if you had been driving the car yourself, chances are you could get there again. Studies indicate that if you're stimulated with audio, you will have about a 20 percent retention rate, audio-visual is up to 30 percent, and in interactive multimedia presentations where you are really involved, the retention rate is as high as 60 percent.

::::::::::::::::::::::::::::::::::

Jay Sandom, Einstein & Sandom

Multimedia in Business

Business applications for multimedia include presentations, training, marketing, advertising, product demos, databases, catalogues, and networked communications. Voice mail and video conferencing will soon be provided on many local and wide area networks (LANs and WANs).

After a morning of mind-numbing 35 mm slide and overhead presentations delivered from the podium of a national sales conference, a multimedia presentation can make an audience come alive. Most presentation software packages let you add audio and video clips to the usual "slide show" of graphics and text material (see Chapter 7).

Multimedia is enjoying widespread use in training programs. Flight attendants learn to manage international terrorism and security through simulation. Mechanics learn to repair engines. Salespeople learn about product lines and leave behind software to train their customers. Fighter pilots practice full-terrain sorties before spooling up for the real thing. Figure 1-1 is from an animated project made with Macromedia's Director that describes the process of making steel.

Multimedia around the office has become more commonplace. Figure 1-2 shows VideoLabs' FlexCam, an inexpensive add-on video camera and stereo microphone unit. Connectix's popular QuickCam lets you add a gray-scale camera to your PC or Mac for less than $100, and Nokia sells a high-resolution Trinitron monitor (the "447K") that integrates a video camera, a microphone, and full-range stereo speakers. Such video capture hardware can be used for building employee ID and badging databases, for video annotation, and for real-time teleconferencing. Laptop computers equipped with the fastest processors come complete with CD-ROM drives and are ready for multimedia presentations on the road.

As companies and businesses catch on to the power of multimedia, and the cost of installing multimedia capability decreases, more applications will

FIGURE 1-1

Animated

instructional and

training multimedia

can simulate the

real thing, allowing

trainees to actually

turn valves and flip

switches

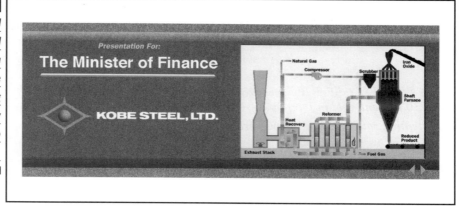

be developed both in-house and by third parties to allow businesses to run more smoothly and efficiently.

Multimedia in Schools

Schools are perhaps the most needy destination for multimedia. Many schools in the United States today are chronically underfunded and occasionally slow to adopt new technologies, but it is here that the power of multimedia can be maximized for the greatest long-term benefit to all.

FIGURE 1-2

VideoLabs'

FlexCam (neatly

implemented by

Worrell Design of

Minneapolis, MN)

can be used for

video capture and

videoconferencing

In March 1995, the White House challenged the telecommunications industry to connect every classroom, library, clinic, and hospital to the information superhighway by the year 2000. The White House has also taken steps to provide governmental support with a program of "Challenge Grants for Technology in Education," a $27-million effort to support state-of-the-art technology in about 20 low-income rural and urban school districts. Vice President Al Gore is often seen pulling wire in inner-city school labs, promoting installation of computers in schools.

Technological literacy must become the standard in our country. Preparing children for a lifetime of computer use is just as essential today as teaching them the basics of reading, writing and arithmetic.

> Bill Clinton, President, United States of America
> (president@whitehouse.gov)

http://www.bell-atl.com/wschool/about.htm
http://www.svi.org/

Bell Atlantic's WORLD SCHOOL Project is connecting more than 700 West Virginia schools to the Internet; Smart Valley, Inc., is a nonprofit Silicon Valley consortium providing advice and technical support to schools on the Internet

Multimedia will provoke radical changes in the teaching process during the coming decades, particularly as smart students discover they can go beyond the limits of traditional teaching methods. Indeed, in some instances, teachers may become more like guides and mentors along a learning path, not the primary providers of information and understanding—the students, not teachers, become the core of the teaching and learning process. This is a sensitive and highly politicized subject among educators, so educational software is often positioned as "enriching" the learning process, not as a potential substitute for traditional teacher-based methods.

An interactive episode of Wild Kingdom *might start out with normal narration. "We're here in the Serengeti to learn about the animals." I see a lion on the screen and think, "I want to learn about the lion." So I point at the lion, and it zooms up on the screen. The narration is now just about the lion. I say, "Well that's really interesting, but I wonder how the lion hunts." I point at a hunt icon. Now the lion is hunting, and the narrator tells me about how it hunts. I dream about being the lion. I select another icon and now see the world from the lion's point of view, making the same kinds of decisions the lion has to make—with some hints as I go along. I'm told how I'm doing and how well I'm surviving. Kids could get very motivated from experiencing what it's like to be a lion and from wanting to be a competent lion. Pretty soon they'd be digging deeper into the information resource, finding out about animals in different parts of the world, studying geography from maps displayed on the screen, learning which animals are endangered species....*

Trip Hawkins, Chairman & CEO, 3DO Company

Multimedia for learning takes many forms. Figure 1-3 shows Mercer Meyer's pioneering and award-winning "Just Grandma and Me," an animated story from Brøderbund, first released in 1992 and aimed at three- to eight-year-olds. Reading skills grow through word recognition: a mouse click on any word plays it back. The computer reads the story aloud, sometimes spelling words individually. Click on the mailbox and a frog jumps out; the chimney coughs smoke; the telephone rings, but nobody is home, and you hear Grandma's answering machine. Wait 'til you get to the beach! Figure 1-4, at the other end of the educational continuum, shows the title screen from an advanced electronic teaching tool prepared by Yale University School of Medicine. It provides physicians with over 100 case presentations and gives cardiologists, radiologists, medical students, and fellows an opportunity for in-depth learning of new clinical techniques in nuclear cardiac perfusion imaging. Adults, as well as children, learn well by exploration and discovery.

"Just Grandma and Me" is aimed at developing reading skills, but it also entertains with interactive sights and sounds

An interesting use of multimedia in schools involves the students them-selves. Late in 1993 in San Rafael, California, 12 Davidson Junior High School students put together perhaps the first interactive magazine for kids

This multimedia project from Yale University School of Medicine lets physicians and radiology professionals learn new technologies at their own pace

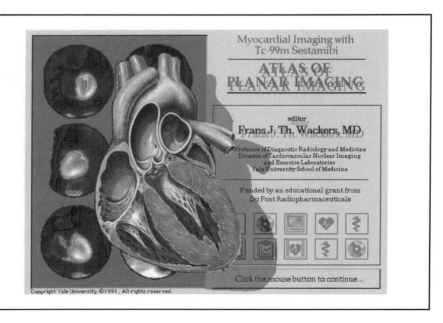

and called it the "San Rafael Community Express." They made original art using Fractal Design's Painter (see Chapter 11), interviewed students and townspeople, including the mayor, and made QuickTime movies (see Chapter 6). They wove their work into six sections on topics such as "If you're a kid, how do you get treated at local restaurants?"

* * *

http://www.elibrary.com
http://www.lib.umich.edu/chhome.html
http://sunsite.unc.edu/cisco/cisco-home.html
http://www.ucalgary.ca/~dkbrown/index.html
http://web66.coled.umn.edu/schools.html
http://ousd.k12.ca.us/joaquinmiller/joaquinmiller.html
http://gda.org

From homework helpers to literature guides to school registries to home pages and information servers, education is finding a place on the World Wide Web

At one time, laserdiscs brought the greatest amount of multimedia to the classroom—in 1994, there were more than 2,500 educational titles available on laserdisc for grades K-12, the majority aimed at science and social science curricula. Use of laserdiscs has been supplanted as schools have purchased more CD-ROM players. And, slowly, as schools become part of the National Information Infrastructure, multimedia arrives by glass fiber and network.

The technology is here to turn around the education system—all we lack is the will to make it happen.

David Bunnell, Chairman, Board of Directors, Hypermedia Communications Inc.

Multimedia at Home

From gardening to cooking to home design, remodeling, and repair to genealogy software (see Figure 1-5), multimedia has entered the home. Eventually, most multimedia projects will reach the home via television sets or monitors with built-in interactive user inputs—either on old-fashioned color TVs or on new high-definition sets (see Chapter 13). The multimedia viewed on these sets will likely arrive on a pay-for-use basis along the data highway.

In the near future we may see a new appliance become commonplace in many households—the $500 "Internet Computer." Both Oracle and Sun Microsystems envision a device connected to the Internet that offers a RISC processor, 4 to 8MB of RAM, a small hard drive, no floppy drive, and a

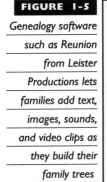

FIGURE 1-5

Genealogy software
such as Reunion
from Leister
Productions lets
families add text,
images, sounds,
and video clips as
they build their
family trees

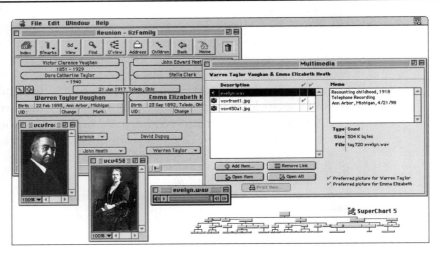

bare-bones operating system. Compaq is working on a similar device called "Webster." With such self-contained yet minimal "boxes," there will be no need for the software traditionally installed on a PC's hard disk. Instead, users will download applications as they are required.

Today, however, home consumers of multimedia either own a computer with an attached CD-ROM drive or a set-top player that hooks up to the television, such as Philips' CD-I player or Sega or Nintendo or Sony game machines. There is increasing convergence of computer-based multimedia with entertainment and games-based media traditionally described as "shoot-em-up." Nintendo alone has sold over 100 million game players worldwide and more than 750 million games.

Live Internet pay-for-play gaming with multiple players has become popular, bringing multimedia to homes on the data highway, often in combination with locally inserted CD-ROMs. By 1998, Microsoft's Internet Gaming Zone and Sony's Station Web site had more than a million registered users each—Microsoft claimed to be the most successful, with more than 6,500 people logged on and playing every evening.

The home of the future will be very different when the cost of set-top players and multimedia televisions becomes mass-market affordable and the multimedia connection to the data highway is widely available. When the number of multimedia households increases from hundreds of thousands to many millions, a vast selection of multimedia titles and material will be required to satisfy the demands of this market, and vast amounts of money will be earned producing and distributing these products.

Multimedia in Public Places

In hotels, train stations, shopping malls, museums, and grocery stores, multimedia will become available at stand-alone terminals or kiosks to provide information and help. Such installations reduce demand on traditional information booths and personnel, add value, and they can work around the clock, even in the middle of the night, when live help is off duty.

Figure 1-6 shows a menu screen from a supermarket kiosk that provides services ranging from meal planning to coupons. Hotel kiosks list nearby restaurants, maps of the city, airline schedules, and provide guest services such as automated checkout. Printers are often attached so users can walk away with a printed copy of the information. Museum kiosks are not only used to guide patrons through the exhibits, but when installed at each exhibit, provide great added depth, allowing visitors to browse through richly detailed information specific to that display.

The power of multimedia has been part of the human experience for many thousands of years: the mystical chants of monks, cantors, and shamans accompanied by potent visual cues, raised icons, and persuasive text have long been known to produce effective responses in public places. Scriabin, the 19th-century Russian composer, used an orchestra, a piano, a chorus, and a special color organ to synthesize music and color in his Fifth Symphony, *Prometheus*. Probably suffering from synesthesia (a strange condition where a sensory stimulus, such as a color, evokes a false response, such

FIGURE 1-6

Kiosks in public places can make everyday life simpler

as a smell), Scriabin talked of tactile symphonies with burning incense scored into the work. He also claimed that colors can be heard; Table 1-1 lists the colors of his color organ.

Prometheus premiered before a live audience in Moscow in 1911, but the color organ had proved technologically too complicated and was eliminated from the program. Then Scriabin died suddenly of blood poisoning from a boil on his lip, so his ultimate multimedia vision, the Mysterium, remained unwritten. He would have reveled in today's world of MIDI synthesizers (see Chapter 10), rich computer colors, and video digitizers, and, though smell is not yet part of any multimedia standard, he would surely have researched that concept, too. The platforms for multimedia presentation have much improved since Scriabin's time.

Virtual Reality

At the convergence of technology and creative invention in multimedia is virtual reality, or VR. Goggles, helmets, special gloves, and bizarre human interfaces attempt to place you "inside" a lifelike experience. Take a step forward, and the view gets closer, turn your head, and the view rotates. Reach out and grab an object; your hand moves in front of you. Maybe the object explodes in a 90-decibel crescendo as you wrap your fingers around

Frequency (Hz)	Note	Scriabin's Color
256	C	Red
277	C#	Violet
298	D	Yellow
319	D#	Glint of steel
341	E	Pearly white shimmer of moonlight
362	F	Deep red
383	F#	Bright blue
405	G	Rosy orange
426	G#	Purple
447	A	Green
469	A#	Glint of steel
490	B	Pearly blue

TABLE 1-1   *Scriabin's Color Organ*   ■

it. Or it slips out from your grip, falls to the floor, and hurriedly escapes through a mouse hole at the bottom of the wall.

VR requires terrific computing horsepower to be realistic. In VR, your cyberspace is made up of many thousands of geometric objects plotted in three-dimensional space: the more objects and the more points that describe the objects, the higher the resolution and the more realistic your view. As you move about, each motion or action requires the computer to recalculate the position, angle, size, and shape of *all* the objects that make up your view, and many thousands of computations must occur as fast as 30 times per second to seem smooth.

On the World Wide Web, standards for transmitting virtual reality worlds or "scenes" in VRML (Virtual Reality Modeling Language) documents (with the file name extension .wrl) have been developed. See Chapter 15 for more about VRML on the Internet.

Using high-speed dedicated computers, multi-million-dollar flight simulators built by Singer, RediFusion, and others have led the way in commercial application of VR. Pilots of F-16s, Boeing 777s, and Rockwell space shuttles have made many dry runs before doing the real thing. At the California Maritime Academy and other merchant marine officer training schools, computer-controlled simulators teach the intricate loading and unloading of oil tankers and container ships.

Specialized public game arcades have been built recently to offer VR combat and flying experiences for a price. From Virtual World Entertainment in Walnut Creek, California, and Chicago, for example, BattleTech is a ten-minute interactive video encounter with hostile robots. You compete against others, perhaps your friends, who share couches in the same Containment Bay. The computer keeps score in a fast and sweaty firefight. Similar "attractions" will bring VR to the public, particularly a youthful public, with increasing presence during the 1990s.

::::::::::::::::::::::::::::::::

BattleTech is pretty cool. I've played the one in Chicago. The key to winning is getting a unit where the controls work smoothly, otherwise you wind up running in circles until someone puts you out of your misery.

::::::::::::::::::::::::::::::::

Rich Santalesa, Editor, *NetGuide* Magazine

The technology and methods for working with three-dimensional images and for animating them are discussed in Chapters 12 and 13. VR is an extension of multimedia—it uses the basic multimedia elements of imagery, sound, and animation. Because it requires instrumented feedback from a wired-up person, VR is perhaps interactive multimedia at its fullest extension.

::::::::::::::::::::::::::::::::::

People who work in VR do not see themselves as part of "multimedia." VR deals with goggles and gloves and is still a research field where no authoring products are available, and you need a hell of a computer to develop the real-time 3-D graphics. Although there is a middle ground covered by such things as QuickTimeVR and VRML that gives multimedia developers a "window" into VR, people often confuse multimedia and VR and want to create futuristic environments using multimedia authoring tools not designed for that purpose.

::::::::::::::::::::::::::::::::::

Takis Metaxas, Assistant Professor of Computer Science, Wellesley College

Multi

> [You have to have a real yearning to communicate because multimedia is creating, essentially, an entirely new syntax for communication.]

good ideas

media

chapter

2

Introduction to Making Multimedia

You need hardware, software,
and good ideas to make multimedia.

To make *good* multimedia,
you need talent and skill.

I N Chapter 1, you learned what multimedia is, what it may become, and where you can experience it. In this chapter, you will be introduced to the workshop where it is made. This chapter provides guidance and suggestions for getting started. Chapters 4 through 15 deal with basic concepts and the tools required. Later, more detail is provided in Chapter 16. In Chapter 17, you will learn about producing, managing, and designing a project. In Chapter 19, you will learn about where to get material and content for your project, and in Chapter 20, you will learn how to test your work and ship it to end users. If you want to create multimedia yourself, from your own ideas and talents, check your skills against those described in Chapter 3. Chapters 15 and 18 discuss the tools and tricks for making multimedia for the Internet and the World Wide Web.

The Stages of a Project

Most multimedia and Web projects must be undertaken in stages. Some stages should be completed before other stages begin, and some stages may be skipped or combined. Here are the four basic stages in a multimedia project:

1. **Planning and costing:** A project always begins with an idea or a need that you refine by outlining its messages and objectives. Identify how you will make each message and objective work within your authoring system. Before you begin developing, plan what writing skills, graphic art, music, video, and other multimedia expertise will be required. Develop a creative graphic look and feel, as well as a structure and navigation system that will let the viewer visit the messages and content. Estimate the time needed to do all elements, and prepare a budget. Work up a short prototype or proof-of-concept.

2. **Designing and producing:** Perform each of the planned tasks to create a finished product.

3. **Testing:** Always test your programs to make sure they meet the objectives of your project, they work properly on the intended delivery platforms, and they meet the needs of your client or end user.

4. **Delivering:** Package and deliver the project to the end user.

What You Need

You need hardware, software, and good ideas to make multimedia. To make *good* multimedia, you need talent and skill. You also need to stay organized, because as the construction work gets under way, all the little bits and pieces of multimedia content—the six audio recordings of Alaskan Eskimos, the Christmas-two-years-ago snapshot of your niece, the 41 articles still to scan with your optical character recognition (OCR) program—will get lost under growing piles of paper, cassettes, videotapes, disks, phone messages, permissions and releases, cookies, Xerox copies, and yesterday's mail. Even in serious offices, where people sweep all flat surfaces of paperwork and rubber bands at five o'clock, there will be mess.

You will need time and money (for consumable resources such as disks and other memory, for telephoning and postage, and possibly for paying for special services and time, yours included), and you will need to budget these precious commodities (see Chapter 14).

You may also need the help of other people. Multimedia is often a team effort: artwork is performed by graphic artists, video shoots by video producers, sound editing by audio producers, and programming by programmers (see Chapter 3). You will certainly wish to provide plenty of coffee and snacks, whether working alone or as a team. Late nights are often involved in the making of multimedia.

You have to have a real yearning to communicate because multimedia is creating, essentially, an entirely new syntax for communication. You must have an interest in human psychology because you need to anticipate the brainwaves of all the potential end users. What will they expect from the program now? What will they want to do with the program now? How can you integrate all the multimedia elements in a really elegant and powerful way? You should adopt a strategy that allows you to prototype and test your interactive design assumptions.

Ann Marie Buddrus, President, Digital Media Design

Hardware

This book will help you understand the two most significant platforms for producing and delivering multimedia projects: the Macintosh OS from Apple and any Intel-based IBM PC or PC clone running Microsoft Windows. These computers, with their graphical user interfaces and huge installed base of many millions of users throughout the world, are the most commonly used platforms today for the development and delivery of multimedia.

Certainly, detailed and animated multimedia is also created on specialized workstations from Silicon Graphics, Sun Microsystems, and even on mainframes, but the Macintosh and the PC offer a compelling combination of affordability, software availability, and worldwide availability. Regardless of the delivery vehicle for your multimedia—whether it is destined to play on a computer, on a television set-top box such as Sega, Nintendo, or Sony, or as bits moving down the data highway—most will probably be made on a Macintosh or on a PC.

When Windows is discussed in this book, it means *Windows 95*. Microsoft introduced Windows 95 with great fanfare in August 1995 to supercede Windows 3.1, and significant enhancements were made for managing multimedia elements. While it is difficult to conceive of a million of anything (pennies in a drawer, people in a city, bytes on a floppy disk), there are tens of millions of copies of Windows 95 now in use around the world. Windows 98 provides improved networking and Internet support and a business focus but is perhaps simply a stepping stone to future broad acceptance of Windows NT (see Chapter 4).

Hardware is discussed in greater detail in Chapter 4, and hardware peripherals such as monitors, disk drives, and scanners are described in Chapter 5. Audio hardware is discussed in Chapter 10, and video hardware is discussed in Chapter 13. The workings and requisite tools of the Internet are discussed in Chapters 14 and 15.

The basic principles for creating and editing multimedia elements are the same for Macintoshes and PCs. A bitmap is a bitmap, a digitized sound is a digitized sound, regardless of the methods or tools used to make and display it or play it back. Indeed, many software tools readily convert picture, sound, and other multimedia files (and even whole functioning projects) from Macintosh to PC/Windows format, and vice versa, using known file formats or even *binary compatible* files that require no conversion at all. In this book, the icon below will flag complicated or difficult cross-platform issues that may warrant your special attention:

Software

Multimedia software tells the hardware what to do. Display the color red. Move that tiger three leaps to the left. Slide in the words "Now You've Done It!" from the right and blink them on and off. Play the sound of cymbals crashing. Run the digitized movie of Captain Hook.

In this book, the discussion of software is divided into three parts, based on what the software is designed to do for you.

Chapter 6 teaches you about the basic software tools used to work with text, images, sounds, and video; you will also learn about handy tools for capturing screen images, translating between file formats, and editing your resources.

Chapter 7 shows you how to use common tools, such as word processors, spreadsheets, and databases, for presenting instant multimedia—no special authoring systems are required.

In Chapter 8, you'll meet the increasingly wide selection of specialized multimedia authoring tools in detail.

Chapter 15 discusses techniques and methods for delivering multimedia on the World Wide Web (WWW).

You do not have to be a programmer or a computer scientist to make multimedia work for you, but you do need some familiarity with terms and building blocks; even the simplest multimedia tools require a modicum of knowledge to operate. If someone asks to borrow a metric 13 mm wrench, you should know they are probably working with a nut or a bolt. If someone sends you a file in Macintosh AIF format, you should know that you're getting digitized sound. Don't be afraid of the little things that so easily depress the uninformed. From plumbing to nuclear physics, learning is a matter of time and practice.

The CD-ROM from Macromedia that is included with this book contains examples and demonstrations of multimedia software applications and projects. Most products on this CD-ROM are "fully functioning" versions of currently shipping software. In most cases, however, the Save command is disabled, so you can experiment with these applications, but you cannot save your work.

From time to time, you will be referred to a site or a number of sites on the World Wide Web for more detailed information or for material that illustrates a point or topic in the book:

http://www.timestream.com/people/biotay/biotay1.html

The author's overly long biography

You should also know that WWW addresses are not guaranteed to be permanent, but like real people's addresses, they disappear when the house burns down or floats away in a flood.

Microsoft.com, ibm.com, sun.com, and apple.com, however, are such monoliths that it is unlikely they will float away in the river of time. If, when trying to connect to a URL, you receive a "404 - unable to find" error message, try stripping away the directories and subdirectories and file names from the URL and connecting to the domain name itself. If you can connect to the domain name, you may find a menu that will then take you to the relocated document. If, for example, you are looking for a list of tools useful to WWW service providers at *http://www.w3.org/hypertext/WWW/Tools/* and the document is not there, try to connect to *http://www.w3.org/*, then follow the hypertext menus provided. If none of these efforts brings you to your destination, you can try a search engine.

http://www.yahoo.com
http://www.lycos.com
http://www.infoseek.com
http://www.webcrawler.com
http://www.excite.com
http://www.mckinley.com
http://www.savvy.cs.colostate.edu:2000
http://www.easypage.com/all4one
http://altavista.digital.com

Some search engines for the Web

And if the search engine doesn't work, you might find a telephone number to contact the source company the old-fashioned way.

http://www.switchboard.com
http://www.yellownet.com
http://www.ypo.com
http://www.niyp.com
http://www.four11.com
http://yp.gte.net

Telephone books are also available on the Web

Creativity

Before beginning a multimedia project, you must first develop a sense of its scope and content. Let the project take shape in your head as you think through the various methods available to get your message across to your viewers.

The most precious asset you can bring to the multimedia workshop is your creativity. It's what separates run-of-the-mill and "underwhelming" multimedia from compelling, engaging, and award-winning products, whether for a short sales presentation viewed solely by colleagues within your firm or for a full-blown CD-ROM title.

You have a lot of room for creative risk taking, because the rules for what works and what doesn't work are still being empirically discovered; there are few known formulas for the success of multimedia. Indeed, companies that produce a terrific multimedia title are usually rewarded in the marketplace, but their competitors reverse engineer the product, and six months later "knock-offs" using similar approaches and techniques appear on the market.

The evolution of multimedia is evident when you look at some of the first multimedia projects done on computers and compare them to today's titles. Taking inspiration from earlier experiments, developers modify and add their own creative touches to design their own unique multimedia projects. For example, "Just Grandma and Me" (see Figure 1-3 in Chapter 1) is an extension of techniques used in an earlier HyperCard children's game (Cosmic Osmo), which in turn is an extension of experiments with interactive virtual desktops in HyperCard. Click on the telephone and up pops a dialing directory, click on the calendar and see your schedule. Click on a flower and it grows. Click on Grandma, and she may warn you about sunscreen. Click on the umbrella, and it blows away in the wind.

It is very difficult to learn creativity. Some might say it's impossible—one is born with it. But like classical artists who work in paint, marble, or bronze, the better you know your medium, the better able you are to express your creativity. For multimedia, this means you need to know your hardware and software first. Once you are proficient with the hardware and software tools, what then can you build that will look great, sound great, and knock the socks off the viewer? The rhetorical answer is simply, "How creative are you?"

---

w a r n i n g *If you are managing a multimedia project, remember that creative talent is priceless, so be certain to reward it well. If you don't, you may find that your talent takes a job elsewhere, even at lower pay!*

The Credit Alligator usually appears late in a multimedia project and has nothing to do with MasterCard or Visa. This gnarly animal typically lives unseen in the delicate fringes of workgroup politics, but can appear with great distraction during beta testing, adding moments of personal tension and occasionally destroying friendships and business relationships.

After hard cash, the most satisfying remuneration for your sweaty effort and late-night creative contributions to a multimedia project is to see your name on the credit screen. Indeed, this visible credit is a special high-value currency because it can be added to your portfolio to help you land the next job; the more of this currency, the higher your potential wage. And the more likely you will remain employed doing what you like to do.

Start building defenses against this alligator up front. When you negotiate the original contract with whoever pays the multimedia bill, be sure to include wording such as: "We shall be allowed to include a production credit display on the closing screen or in another mutually agreeable position in the finished work." If you are an individual who is contracting to a producer, be sure it is understood that if

there is a credit screen, your name will be on it.

Not all clients will stand for a credit screen. Apple Computer, for example, uses many outside contractors to produce multimedia, but as a company policy rarely allows contributors to be credited by name. Some contractors and frustrated employees develop ingenious work-arounds and indirections to bury these important intellectual credits within their work. For example, in an excellent book written by a team of skilled Apple people and published officially by Addison-Wesley (HyperCard Stack Design Guidelines by Apple Computer, Inc.), you may discover a list of talented instructional designers, illustrators, writers, and editors in Figure 3-3 of that book, an unassuming bitmapped screen grab showing an "About" box. The names of the people who wrote the book are buried there, in the "example" of a credit screen.

The Credit Alligator raises its head over the little things, too, and there are often no defenses. If your name begins with a letter that is toward the end of the alphabet, it may never appear first on the list of contributors, even if your contribution was major. Of course, if your name is Walsh or Young, you have endured this ordering system since first-grade lineups. Warning: reversing an

alphabetic credit list from last to first will only create or heighten tension; to propose such a list is, in itself, ego-driven and self-serving. Learn to live with it.

The most treacherous place where the Credit Alligator lives is in the busy time of finalizing a project and "going gold" by producing a final master. If you are not participating in the final mastering but have contributed a piece or pieces to the project, you must trust the masterer to do it right. But it doesn't always happen right.

One company recently consulted on a job where their work represented the second-greatest contribution from a group of about 15 contributors, all of whom had credit screens. Their contract required credit, but in the final version of the storyboard, they discovered their screen buried at the end of a four-minute linear sequence of all the other credits and advertisements. They asked the producer to move it up. "Sorry," said the producer, "it was an oversight." Then in the last-minute process of resequencing, the producer also switched that company's custom music to his own company's credit screen, leaving our friend's screen attached to a pretty ugly leftover sound byte. Because the company was not included in the final feedback and approval loop, they discovered this "little mistake"

First Person *continued*

only after mass replication. It's tough to change 50,000 shrink-wrapped CD-ROMs, so there was nothing to say.

Crediting creative talent is sensitive stuff. Avoid recurring bouts with the Credit Alligator by publicizing among your people your policy about credit screens. Talk about intellectual credit openly, not as a last-minute thing. Negotiate hard for inclusion of credit in all the projects you undertake for clients. Indeed, multimedia doesn't spring from the bankrolls of investors and publishers, but is the result of the hard work of talented real people.

From the monthly column "Alligators" by Tay Vaughan, first printed in Morph's Outpost, *December 1993.*

Organization

It's essential that you develop an organized outline and a plan that rationally details the skills, time, budget, tools, and resources at hand. These should be in place before you start to render graphics, sounds, and other components, and they should continue to be monitored throughout the project's execution. Chapter 16 provides planning and costing models for a multimedia project, and Chapter 17 discusses the details of multimedia project management.

Multi

[
Multimedia developers
come from all corners of
the computer, art, literary,
film, and audio worlds.
]

Are multimedia developers computer scientists?

no traditional mold

media

chapter 3

Or are they programmers, graphic artists, animators, storyboard craftspeople,

musicians,

instructional designers, or Renaissance authors?

Multimedia Skills and Training

C OMPUTER scientists, physicians, and dentists share highest honors as the most respected professions in the United States, according to a recent study of occupations. Are multimedia developers computer scientists? Or are they programmers, graphic artists, musicians, animators, storyboard craftspeople, information specialists, instructional designers, and/or Renaissance authors? However you define them, they come from all corners of the computer, art, literary, film, and audio worlds. Video producers become expert with computer-generated animations and MIDI controls for their edit suites. Architects become bored with two-dimensional drafting and create three-dimensional animated walk-throughs. Oil field engineers get tired of FORTRAN and design mouse-driven human interfaces. Classical painters learn the electronic elements of red, green, and blue and create fantastic computer-based artwork. A multimedia developer might be any or all of these and typically fits no traditional management information system (MIS) or computer science mold; many have never seen a line of COBOL code or booted up an IBM 3090 mainframe. Perhaps, in the broadest definition, multimedia developers might simply be called information technology workers.

In 1998, the Commerce Department predicted that in the United States more than 1.3 million *new* information technology workers will be needed during the next ten years. And in that same year, the Information Technology Association of America claimed that there was a severe shortage of 346,000 information technology workers—representing about 10 percent of all jobs for computer engineers, programmers, and systems analysts in the United States.

Consider Leonardo da Vinci, the Renaissance man who was scientist, architect, builder, creative designer, craftsman, and poet folded into one. To produce good multimedia, you will need a similar diverse range of skills—detailed knowledge of computers, text, graphic arts, sound, and video. These skills, the *multimedia skillset,* may be available in a single individual or, more likely, in a composite of individuals working as a team. Complex multimedia projects are, indeed, often assembled by teams of artists and computer craftspeople, where tasks can be delegated to those most skilled and competent in a particular discipline or craft. Many job titles and collaborative team roles for multimedia development are being adapted from a mix of motion picture industry, radio and television broadcasting, and computer software industry experiences.

3

warning *A multimedia expert working alone will be hard pressed to compete with a team of experts and may be overwhelmed by the sheer amount of effort required to build a complex project single handedly.*

When I was young, I started in "media" as a disc jockey and news director on radio. It was one medium. I then progressed to doing movies and slide shows with audio, calling it multiple media. When video took over from film, I moved into print media and paper, the original medium for mass communications when people knew how to read. Now, much of what I do starts out in electronic form on the PC, so I guess I'm into yet another medium. What I see being called "multimedia" seems to be all of the above displayed on a CRT, and it all looks vaguely familiar as what I was doing years ago with projectors on walls. So I guess you might say that multimedia today is the same old stuff packaged in a modern box, it just doesn't use the walls....

Tom Inglesby, Senior Editor, *Software Strategies* Magazine

The Team

A typical team for developing multimedia for CD-ROM or the Web consists of people who bring various capabilities to the table. Often, individual members of multimedia production teams wear several hats: graphic designers may also do interface design, scanning, and image processing. A project manager or producer may also be the video producer or script writer. Depending upon the scope and content of your project and the mix of people required, a team may also employ animators, art directors, composers and musicians, content developers, creative directors, digital special effects engineers, editors, photographers, researchers, videographers, programmers, and others.

Mere possession of the equipment does not make one into a videographer, film editor, set designer, scriptwriter, audio engineer, animator, and programmer. Some people do possess all of the innate talents required to produce decent multimedia, but few have mastered all the skills required to bring a major project to fruition. More typically, world-class productions are realized through the teamwork of a variety of talented people with specialized experience.

Jeff Burger, Contributing Editor, *NewMedia* Magazine

Project Manager

A project manager's role is at the center of the action. He or she is responsible for overall development and implementation of a project as well as for day-to-day operations. Budgets, schedules, creative sessions, time sheets, illness, invoices, team dynamics—the project manager is the glue that holds it together.

Mark Williams

Microsoft's Cinemania CD-ROM is a comprehensive, authoritative guide to the movies and the people who make them, designed for computer-owning film lovers (see Figure 3-1). Producing Cinemania involved a core team

FIGURE 3-1

Microsoft's Cinemania was designed and built by a team ■

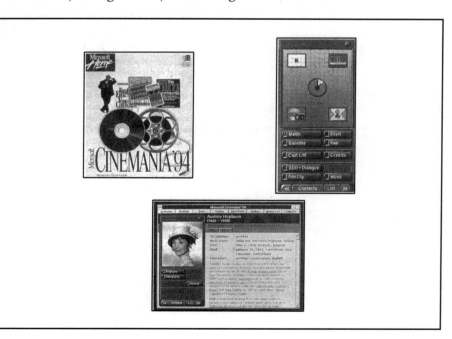

headed by project manager Mark Williams, with additional specialists, technicians, and assistants brought on board as needed.

At Microsoft, project managers are called program managers, but it means exactly the same thing. The program manager has two major areas of responsibility: design and management. Design consists of devising a vision for the product and working out the complete functionality with the design team, and then putting that into a complete functional spec and adjusting it as necessary throughout the development of the product. The management side consists of scheduling and assigning tasks, running meetings, managing milestones—essentially overseeing all aspects of product development from beginning to end.

Our core team consisted of myself, a subject matter expert—which at Microsoft we call an editor—a graphic designer, and a programmer called a software development engineer. Another important team member was the product manager—the marketing person who represents the product to the outside world. We also found that it was very valuable to get early design input from the person who creates the on-line and printed help for the product and from the person who eventually manages the testing of the product.

In the production phase we brought in additional talent for scanning images, digitizing sound, proofreading, and other production tasks. We also utilized numerous specialists along the way, such as an audio producer to secure sound track material and, crucially, acquisitions specialists.

The acquisitions folks were vital to the effort because we were trying to get a variety of media from people who really didn't understand what we were doing. The second version has been much easier because the studios and license holders saw the product and can now visualize how it works.

Speccing the right content and being able to acquire it was critical. Our pictures and content are all of the highest quality, and the design is clear and easy to use. Keeping a vision of the product in mind—making sure that the design really meets the needs of the end user—is very important. Constant usability testing gives us a way to keep the end user involved in the design process.

A good project manager must completely understand the strengths and limitations of hardware and software so that he or she can make good decisions about what to do and what not to do. Aside from that I'd say the most important skills are people skills (keeping your team happy and motivated), organizational skills, and attention to all the myriad details of a project. At the same time it's critical to keep the big picture, the vision, in mind so that everything that needs to get done does in fact get done.

Project Manager/Interface Expert

Multimedia company looking to immediately fill position on interactive television project for major telecommunications company. Project manager needed to manage production and design efforts on large-scale interactive television project for air in western United States.

- Must be adept and experienced at managing complex projects, preferably with large corporate accounts.
- Must have solid understanding of interactivity and experience with interactive media—ideally, interactive television.
- Must have several years experience with interface design or management thereof and have good design sensibilities.
- Communication skills a must; must be an articulate and effective communicator, an excellent listener, and act as a conduit for information between our team and the client's teams.
- Superior attention to detail and ability to coordinate large amounts of information a must.
- Prefer entertainment experience—ideally, television or video production.
- Solid computer or digital media experience and knowledge a must.
- Travel required to visit focus groups and gather consumer information.
- Must function well in fast-paced, team-oriented environment. Position must be filled immediately.

Multimedia Designer

The look and feel of a multimedia project should be pleasing and aesthetic, inviting and engaging. Screens should present an appealing mix of color, shape, and type. The project should maintain visual consistency, using only those elements that support the overall message of the program. Navigation clues should be clear and consistent, icons should be meaningful, and screen elements should be simple and straightforward. If the project is instructional, its design should be sensitive to the needs and styles of its learner population, demonstrate sound instructional principles, and promote mastery of subject matter. Who puts it all together?

Graphic designers, illustrators, animators, and image processing specialists deal with the visuals. Instructional designers make sure that the subject matter is clear and properly presented. Interface designers devise the navigation pathways and content maps. Information designers structure content, determine user pathways and feedback, and select presentation media based on an awareness of the strengths of the many separate media that make up multimedia.

Kurt Andersen

Kurt Andersen has been an instructional designer for the past six years. Most recently, he was a senior designer at the George Lucas Educational Foundation, where he designed multimedia prototypes for middle school math and science curricula. Currently he is a consultant in the fields of multimedia and information design and development.

A multimedia designer often wears many hats, but most importantly he or she looks at the overall content of a project, creates a structure for the content, determines the design elements required to support that structure, and decides which media are appropriate for presenting which pieces of content. In essence, the multimedia designer (sometimes called an information designer) prepares the blueprint for the entire project: content, media, and interaction.

From an interactive standpoint, many multimedia projects are too passive—you click and watch. The challenge is to get beyond what is appealing visually and design products to be activity-based. A multimedia project needs to be truly interactive, and this means you have to have a clear picture of what goes on whenever the user interacts with the program.

Advances in technology are bringing us closer to this. For example, one of the most interesting things going on is the development of adaptive systems, which accept user input and modify themselves based on this input. In training projects, they're called intelligent tutors. Right now, we're working on a medical application that will analyze a patient's history and background to present information that is personalized to that particular patient.

I was recently a member of two different teams that developed multimedia prototypes for middle school science and mathematics at the George Lucas Educational Foundation. Our approach was to develop prototypes that might be distributed as exemplars of rigorous, engaging, effective multimedia design using leading-edge technology. The real challenge was to create a program that presented mathematics so that users could play, explore, and develop their own conceptual schema around the concepts we were developing. We were also challenged to implement our ideas from a technological standpoint. For example, we wound up hooking up a high-end rendering machine so that we could do 3-D graphics on the fly.

Multimedia designers need a variety of skills. You need to be able to analyze content structurally and match it up with effective presentation methods. You need to be an expert on different media types, and a capable media integrator, in order to create an overall vision. The ability to look at information from different points of view and a willingness to shift your own point of view to be empathetic with end users are absolutely essential. So are interpersonal skills, because you spend so much of your time interacting with other team members, with clients, and extracting information from subject matter experts. You must be able to "talk the talk" with all of them. Finally, you must understand the capabilities of your resources, both technological and human, and know when to push ahead and when to stop.

3

Multimedia Designer/Producer

Seeking an experienced new media professional who loves inventing the future and enjoys the challenge of integrating complex information and media systems.

Our ideal candidate has solid experience in interface design, product prototyping, and marketing communication. A knowledge of image manipulation is critical, as well as proven skills in Lingo scripting and the use of digital time-based authoring tools. We seek a team player with excellent communication skills and grace under pressure.

• Must have experience designing large information and/or entertainment systems.
• Must have experience creating system flows and program architectures.
• Must have solid organizational skills and attention to detail.

Interface Designer

Like a good film editor, an interface designer's best work is never seen by the viewer; it's "transparent." In its simplest form, an interface provides control to the people who use it. It also provides access to the "media" of multimedia—the text, graphics, animation, audio, and video—without calling attention to itself. The elegant simplicity of a multimedia title screen, the ease with which a user can move about within a project, effective use of windows, backgrounds, icons, and control panels—these are the result of an interface designer's work.

Nicole Lazzaro
....-

Nicole Lazzaro is an interface designer with ONYX Productions in Oakland, California, and teaches interface design at San Francisco State University's Multimedia Studies Program. She spends her days thinking of new ways to design multimedia interfaces that feel more like real life.

The role of an interface designer is to create a software device that organizes the multimedia content, that lets the user access or modify that content, and that presents the content on screen. These three areas—information design, interactive design, and media design—are central to the creation of any interface, but of course they overlap.

In the real world, design responsibilities are often assigned differently depending on the project. An interface designer may also be the multimedia designer or the graphic designer. Sometimes all of the design is given to one person; sometimes it is divided among group members; and sometimes the interface springs from the group as a whole. In the best of all worlds everyone has input into the final vision, but realistically, everyone also has other responsibilities outside of interface design. The advantage of dedicating one team member experienced in a number of interface solutions to this particular task is to make sure the end user does not get left out of the equation. A good interface designer will create a product that rewards exploration and encourages use. You have to design the interface from the ground up, not just slap on some graphics and fancy icons after most of the programming is done.

A crucial skill is being familiar with a lot of multimedia interfaces so that you are able to visualize ideas as they are discussed. What is the best way to represent this function? Will this program look better using a hierarchical menu or a book metaphor? What will be the user's experience? Being familiar with film or video editing can be helpful, because telling a story with sounds and images is what most multimedia experiences are all about. From a visual perspective, cinematography and film editing are, I think, the closest parallels to what we would call interface design. These techniques can seamlessly change a point of view or tell a story more effectively, and they are being used by interface designers today. Knowing an authoring system is also crucial, so you can develop your ideas in some interactive fashion and be able to present them to your design group. Having basic drawing skills also helps, because then you can describe how a screen looks using pencil and paper. Also, know how to do user testing, and do lots of it!

> **Artist/Designer** needed to create graphics for interactive multimedia titles aimed at children. Solid experience in graphic design, including knowledge of Adobe Photoshop and Adobe Premiere. Must have superior illustration ability. Must have experience in animation. Experience in video graphics and editing (Premiere, Avid, Media100, etc.) a plus.

Writer

Multimedia writers do everything writers of linear media do, and more. They create character, action, and point of view—a traditional scriptwriter's tools of the trade—and they also create interactivity. They write proposals, they script voice-overs and actors' narrations, they write text screens to deliver messages, and they develop characters designed for an interactive environment.

Writers of text screens are sometimes referred to as content writers—they glean information from content experts, synthesize it, and then communicate it in a clear and concise manner. Scriptwriters write dialog, narration, and voice-overs. Both often get involved in overall design.

Domenic Stansberry

Domenic Stansberry is a writer/designer who has worked on interactive multimedia dramas for commercial products. He has also written for documentary film and published two books of fiction.

The role of the writer changes with each different project, depending on the people you're working with. But multimedia writing is always different from writing a film or video script. In a film or video, you're plotting a story the way a dramatist or novelist would. With multimedia, it can be more difficult: you're still thinking dramatically, but in smaller, more discrete units that have to interrelate to each other, that have to be compiled into a puzzle of sorts.

In traditional drama there are characters and an inevitability about what happens to those characters. You build circumstances that have certain significance for your characters as they go on to meet their destiny. In multimedia, we plot out stories that can go many different ways. This is inherently contradictory to the way we've thought about dramatic structure. Intelligent writers are still working hard to invent interactive dramatic structures: we see some attempts in games, which are obstacle driven. The user needs to perform a task and is presented with an obstacle—a need to overcome the obstacle and move on. This is not unlike the position a character takes in a story or movie where characters are presented with physical or psychological obstacles and must find a way to get beyond them. It's really too bad that writers are not brought in on more game projects...the quality of the interaction would be much higher.

I work best when I am involved at the conceptual level of a project, but in many projects, it is the flowcharts that are generated first. Then as the writing process unfolds, you find that the flowchart doesn't work because the material isn't what the flowchart wants it to be. When you're working on a dramatic script, you have to make the characters and the drama work first, before you start doing flowcharts. So if the writer is invited into the process at Step 7 and handed a flowchart, you're going to run into a problem. Another problem lies in working with people who are mainly from computer backgrounds. They are used to the writer as a writer of documentation—someone who comes in at the end of a project and writes a manual about how the product works. Computer people are often very uncomfortable with media people playing a role at the heart of the creative process. You need to develop a sense about where other team members are coming from when you are brought on to a project, and try to educate them if necessary.

But in the final analysis, the producer or project manager has to be the person to handle conflict in differing team members' visions. A good producer will get the most out of the team members by getting team members to work not against each other, but together toward their strengths. There are bound to be competing visions on a project, and in the best case scenario, the team members will work out their differences through a consensus process. But if they can't, the producer has to have a guiding vision.

> **Multimedia Writer** needed for multimedia kiosk in retail outlet. Must be familiar with interactive design and user interface issues. Background in marketing or copywriting a plus. Ability to work under tight deadlines in a team environment essential. Candidates will be asked to provide writing samples.

Video Specialist

A video specialist on a multimedia project may be just one person and a camcorder. Or, for projects requiring extensive amounts of sophisticated video, a video specialist may be responsible for an entire team of videographers, sound technicians, lighting designers, set designers, script supervisors, gaffers, grips, production assistants, and actors. In a multimedia project, a video specialist must be a seasoned professional, skilled in managing all phases of production, from concept to final edit. Team production of video can be very expensive and may be more than might actually be required to produce your own project.

Since the early 1990s, digital video presentation methods such as Apple's QuickTime or Microsoft's Video for Windows (see Chapter 13) have married increasingly capable hardware and software so that editing and preparing video on Macintoshes and PCs has become affordable to multimedia developers. In addition to knowing the basics about shooting good video, multimedia video specialists must also be thoroughly familiar with the tools and techniques used for digital editing on computers.

> **Video Specialist** wanted for multimedia production. Must have strong background in video direction and editing. Good understanding of shooting for interactive programming required. Strong background working with blue screen a plus.

Hank Duderstadt

Hank Duderstadt has worked as an independent video producer, director, and video editor specializing in promotions/commercials, corporate marketing, education, broadcast programming, and multimedia production.

A multimedia video specialist does much more than just shoot and edit video. He or she must understand the potentials and limitations of the medium, how these limitations affect the video production itself, and how to get the most out of the video. He or she must also understand interactivity and how it will affect the video. Shooting in traditional styles, you will end up with footage that doesn't work, and there is always a tendency to overcompensate, ending up with video that is little more than gimmicky.

With experience, you learn the tricks that make a video look larger than it really is without looking gimmicky.

When you are shooting footage that will end up on CD-ROM, you have to realize in all probability it won't be full screen, full motion. At best it could be half-screen size at 20 frames per second; or at worst, the size of a postage stamp, with 10 frames per second. Wide panoramas and complex camera moves get lost or don't work. The best shots are medium to close-ups. While video may play back in a limited screen size using today's technology, full-screen video will soon become a reality, so shoot your material on the best format available—Beta-SP is ideal—and allow time to grab library shots that also work with larger screen displays.

Another thing to decide is whether to build sets or just shoot your talent in front of a blue screen, compositing later with computer-generated environments. If this is the case, it's important to know exactly what the environment looks like before you shoot, so the talent can be easily incorporated into the scene.

Programs like Premiere, MetaFlo, Video Graffiti, and After FX equal, and often surpass, what you might find at a traditional video production facility, but don't let the ability to do all these incredible things overwhelm your vision. It's very easy to create video that loses the viewer because the editor became so thrilled with all the fancy effects!

Audio Specialist

The quality of audio elements can make or break a multimedia project. Audio specialists are the wizards who make a multimedia program come alive, designing and producing music, voice-over narrations, and sound effects. They perform a variety of functions on the multimedia team and may enlist help from one or many others: composers, audio engineers, or recording technicians. Audio specialists may be responsible for locating and selecting suitable music and talent, scheduling recording sessions, and digitizing and editing recorded material into computer files (see Chapter 11).

Multimedia Audio Specialist
Audio specialist needed for multimedia project.

Must have strong background in studio recording techniques—preferably with time spent in the trenches as an engineer in a commercial studio working on a wide range of projects. Must be comfortable working with computers and be open and able to learn new technology and make it work with high-quality results. Familiarity with standard recording practices, knowledge of music production, and the ability to work with artists a definite plus. Requires fluency in MIDI; experience with sequencing software, patch librarians, and synth programming; and knowledge of sampling/samplers, hard disk recording, and editing. In addition to having a solid technical foundation, you must be able to survive long hours in the studio riding faders and pushing buttons.

Chip Harris

Chip Harris studied trumpet and electronic music composition at the Peabody Conservatory of Music, and he has worked with the noted composer Jean Eichelberger Ivy. He has recorded releases on major and independent labels, including Atlantic, RCA, and Warner Brothers, has composed music for CD-ROM titles for Virgin Games, Accolade, and Timestream, and has created soundtracks for Clio and Joey award-winning spots.

An audio specialist working in multimedia should have a thorough understanding of the needs and requirements involved in producing a successful sound track. Most often this person will be either an engineer, technician, composer, sound designer, or any combination of the above. On the rare occasion where all of these skills are requisite for employment, the position would most likely be for an audio department manager for a good-sized and well-funded multimedia company with in-house production facilities. However, even though positions such as this are not plentiful, the skills and talents necessary for quality multimedia audio production are needed every day by companies who have opted to outsource their audio to independent contractors.

Whether it's recording voice-over talent for a business application, or composing a musical score for a shoot 'em up game, or designing sound effects that reflect the particular feel of a product, the end result will rely on knowing the medium going in. By this I mean, at what sampling rate will the audio be delivered? How much space is available for *all* audio combined? Can different sampling rates be applied to voice-over and music to save space and enhance overall quality? In composition will looping be required of individual pieces to provide a seamless score, but again, to save valuable space? And who will do the looping, the composer or the engineer? Will some voice-over talents sound presentable at higher sampling rates but not at lower? Will the producer understand the difference?

Of course, these are only a few examples of questions and problems to be dealt with in multimedia audio production. But attention to detail, listening for a cohesive presentation, and quality recording techniques are the strong glue that successfully binds the diverse audio components together.

Multimedia Programmer

A multimedia programmer or software engineer integrates all the multimedia elements of a project into a seamless whole using an authoring system or programming language (see Chapter 8). Multimedia programming functions range from coding simple displays of multimedia elements to controlling peripheral devices such as laserdisc players and managing complex timing, transitions, and record keeping. Creative multimedia programmers can coax extra (and sometimes unexpected) performance from multimedia authoring and programming systems. Without programming talent, there can be no multimedia. Code, whether written in SuperTalk, OpenScript, Lingo, Authorware, Java, or C++, is the sheet music played by a well-rehearsed orchestra.

Hal Wine

Hal Wine is a programmer familiar with both the Macintosh and Windows environments. In his many years of experience, he has worked in most of the important areas of computing and for many of the leading computing companies. He currently is a consultant in the San Francisco Bay Area.

The programmer on a multimedia team is called on to perform a number of tasks, from assisting producers in organizing their code more effectively to enhancing the production and playback tools. The most important skill a multimedia programmer can bring to a team is the ability to quickly learn and understand systems. And not just understand the various calls, but know why those calls are needed. In other words, to be able to read between the lines of the technical manuals, so that your solutions are harmonious with the philosophy and intent of the system designers.

Multimedia products are displayed on a large variety of display systems, and the enhancement needed often requires going behind the normal system safeguards to meet the objective. Such programming requires a thorough understanding of the target operating system and device capabilities to produce a robust solution.

While multimedia authoring tools are continually improving, they are still evolving. Many times a producer will want to do something slightly beyond the built-in capabilities of the tools, and the programmer will build extensions to the authoring and presentation suite in order to add the desired capability or effect.

Many of the workers on a multimedia team have come to computing from a background in another discipline such as graphic art or journalism, and while they may have strong creative skills, most can benefit from learning more about computing techniques. Often, a multimedia programmer acts as a teacher and technical coach to the team. This implies having better than average communication and comprehension skills, both verbal and written, and the ability to listen!

I often come in to handle "emergencies" in multimedia projects, rather than participate in the whole project's life cycle. This provides me with maximum variety in my own work, which really keeps me on my toes.

Sometimes, I'll be working for several clients simultaneously. The downside is that I miss out on a lot of the creative synergy, but even so, coming in at the spur of the moment, trying to understand the parameters of the problem, and producing robust solutions quickly leads to quite a bit of creativity, too! Knowing how to make your own latte is also useful.

3

> **Interactive Programmer** (Lingo, SuperTalk, Java, and C/C++) needed to work on multimedia prototyping and authoring tools for CD-ROM and interactive television projects.
>
> • Thorough knowledge of Lingo, SuperTalk, Java, and C/C++, Macintosh and Windows environments required.
> • Must have working familiarity with digital media, particularly digital video.
> • Must have a demonstrated track record of delivering quality programming on tight schedule.
> • Must function well in fast-paced, team-oriented environment.
> • Knowledge of HTML, VRML.

Producer, Multimedia for the Web

Web site producer is a new occupation, but putting together a coordinated set of pages for the World Wide Web requires the same creative process, skillsets, and often teamwork as the making of any kind of multimedia (see Chapters 17 and 18). There is a great difference, however, between putting up a simple Web page with a few links and designing, implementing, and maintaining a complex site with many areas of content and many messages. A Web site is never finished, but should, indeed, remain dynamic, fluid, and alive. Unlike a CD-ROM multimedia product replicated many times over in permanent plastic, the work product at a Web site is available for tweaking at any time.

> **Web Site Producer** Excellent full-time opportunity with a large manufacturing firm. Responsible for developing Web projects from concept through implementation for internal and external clients. Interact with all levels of management, network teams, and development teams to provide efficient project solutions. Knowledge of HTML coding of tables, frames, and forms, knowledge of CGI scripting, knowledge of Photoshop. Exciting opportunity for a self-motivated individual looking for a career in new media. This new entry-level position in the firm's national marketing department requires a team player with creative ideas who is interested in gaining experience and knowledge in every aspect of Web site development. Job responsibilities include maintaining/updating site content, managing documents, developing new site features.

Kevin Edwards

Kevin Edwards is Senior Multimedia Producer for CNET, a publicly traded media company (NASDAQ: CNWK) that integrates television programming with a network of sites on the World Wide Web. In both media, CNET provides information about computers, the Internet, and future technology using engaging content and design. CNET has about 2 million members on the Internet, and its television programming—which airs on the USA Network, the Sci-Fi Channel, and in national syndication—reaches an estimated weekly audience of more than 8 million viewers.

 Back in the summer of 1995, after graduating from NYU with a master's degree in interactive telecommunications, I headed out to San Francisco to join CNET. I've worn a lot of different hats at CNET, but my primary responsibility has been with the company's on-line foray into multimedia. For example, we recently wrapped up Mediadome, a year-long project with Intel, where I was involved from original concept through implementation. Mediadome (http:// www.mediadome.com) merges today's hottest media properties with cutting-edge technology to create a brand-new experience in Web-based entertainment, allowing users to become participants in the experience rather than just observers.

What helped me keep this project in focus was my rounded knowledge and ability to perform in all of the different roles required to produce the site, whether graphics, HTML, editorial, support, audio/video, or other. While it's a lot of fun to change hats and do many different tasks, it can be a lot of responsibility and pretty stressful. For me, building the Mediadome site meant that for a year and a half I was totally plugged into the Net, checking on our site, looking at stats, and analyzing what was going on in the entertainment/technology industries. This meant keeping Web-profession hours rather than banker's hours, so it was pretty rare for me to take a day off, even on weekends, and my office became more my living space than my apartment. To keep from burning out, you have to have a sense of ownership and a passion for what you're doing.

The best is when your team is composed of people who also turn into close friends. During Mediadome we worked incredibly well together: each knew his or her particular field 100 percent and respected the other team members. We worked hard, played hard, and were able to really rock when put to the test. In fact, there were a couple of people who started the project with very little experience, but their eagerness and ability to learn and the group's willingness to teach made it happen.

The Sum of the Parts

Successful multimedia projects begin with selecting "team players." But selection is only the beginning of a team-building process that must continue through a project's duration. Team building refers to activities that help a group and its members function at optimum levels of performance by creating a work culture incorporating the styles of its members: you should encourage communication styles that are fluid and inclusive, and you should develop models for decision making that respect individual talents, expertise, and personalities. This is not easy, but repeated studies have shown that workgroup managers with well-developed "team" skills are more successful than managers who dive headlong into projects without attention to team dynamics. While it is usually a project manager who initiates team building, all team members should recognize their role; gentle collaboration is a key element of successful projects.

3

> The environment will improve; good ideas, not hardware, will drive the multimedia industry.

Selection of the proper platform
for developing your multimedia project may be based on ▬▬▬

environment

media

part

2

Multimedia Hardware

personal preference,
budget constraints,
delivery requirements,
type of material and
content in the project.

Multi

Since its inception,
the Macintosh has
been, by definition, a
multimedia computer.

Selection of the proper platform
for developing your multimedia project may be based on ▬▬

environment

media

chapter

4

Macintosh and Windows
Production Platforms

personal preference,
budget constraints,
delivery requirements,
type of material and
content in the project.

S ELECTION of the proper platform for developing your multimedia project may be based on your personal preference of computer, your budget constraints, project delivery requirements, and the type of material and content in the project. Many developers believe that multimedia project development is smoother and easier on the Macintosh than in Windows, even though projects destined to run in Windows must then be ported across platforms. But hardware and authoring software tools for Windows have improved: today you can produce many multimedia projects with equal ease in either the Windows or Macintosh environment.

Vaughan's Rule for Keeping Up

Upgrade to proven products that lie in the calm water slightly behind the leading edge of the wave

1993

The rationale for trading in my workhorse Macintosh IIci for a Quadra 840AV in 1993 was that I will get at least three years of good use out of a computer that will remain at or near the top of the line long enough to justify its cost. Apple's RISC-based PowerMacs will begin shipping in 1994, and they will be more than twice as powerful as my Quadra. But that power will be available mainly to applications that have been written specifically for the PowerPC chip in native code. Indeed, it is rumored that some applications, until they are redesigned by their vendors, will actually run slower on the PowerPC than on my Quadra. You can capsize at the frothy leading edge of technology, where the Surf Alligators live.

1996

My Quadra 840AV continues to perform just fine and is still well supported by software vendors. While writing the third edition of this book, however, Apple kindly loaned me a top-of-the-line Power Macintosh 9500 with all the

(continued)

Vaughan's Rule for Keeping Up (continued)

bells and whistles—some heavy-duty authoring packages now *require* the PowerMac's capabilities, and I wanted to test them. My assistant uses that PowerMac; if I tried it and liked it, I know I wouldn't be able to go back (see Vaughan's One-Way Rule later in this chapter), and I know I can still get at least another year of good service out of my 840AV, on which I write these words.

1998

Too many applications just wouldn't run on my Quadra 840AV, and I was too far behind the curve. I bought a 7500 PowerMac, boosted the processor and cache, and added a second hard drive. It screams, compared to the old Quadra, which was relegated to my 10-year-old's bedroom. But now the G3 Macintosh is out, and with an entirely new operating system from Apple on the horizon, perhaps I have purchased only a year or two's grace before the leading edge of technology pinches again. However, I'm safely behind what some call the "bleeding edge."

Macintosh Versus PC

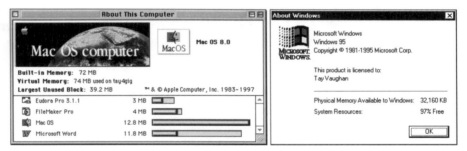

Since its inception, the Macintosh has been, by definition, a multimedia computer: at the famous rollout of the Macintosh in January 1984 at Apple's annual shareholders' meeting, the new device actually introduced itself in a crudely synthesized voice:

> Hello. I'm Macintosh. It sure is great to get out of that bag.... Unaccustomed as I am to public speaking, I'd like to share with you a maxim I thought of the first time I met an IBM mainframe: Never trust a computer you can't lift! Obviously, I can talk, but right now I'd like to sit back and listen. So it is with considerable pride that I introduce the man who's been like a father to me, Steven Jobs.

Whereas the Macintosh had good built-in audio right from the start, in 1984 IBM personal computers could not process sound without very expensive add-on components. With its focus on business computing, the PC remained for many years able to provide only system beeps and limited sound effects on a tiny (and tinny) onboard speaker. Recently, due primarily to the demands of game software, lower-cost sound boards and software have become available for PCs. Other multimedia tools and hardware, such as video digitizers, are now readily available in PC marketing channels.

When installed with Windows, a sound board, and SuperVGA graphics, the PC readily challenges the Macintosh in delivering excellent audio and visual presentations. An MPC computer, moreover, will always provide sound capability, a CD-ROM player, access to the Media Control Interface (MCI) for extensions to video overlay boards and other peripherals, and minimum CPU and memory configuration. The Multimedia Personal Computer, or MPC, is an industrywide effort begun in the late 1980s to provide a standardized and capable multimedia computing environment for PCs.

In 1997, with the Macintosh share of the personal computer market at an all-time low of about 3 percent, Gistics, Inc., a market research firm, studied the comparative advantages of Macintosh versus Windows/Intel computers and discovered that Macintosh users:

- Spend 38 fewer hours per year "futzing" with files
- Save $4,950 annually on support and training
- Use more tools (14.3 versus 8.3)
- Save $2,211 in three-year cost of ownership
- Earn $5.01 more per hour
- Earn $12.22 more revenue per hour of labor
- Create $14,550 more profits per year per person
- Earn 32 percent more net profit per project
- Achieve platform payback in 7.2 months (versus 13.9)

The Macintosh Platform

All Macintoshes can play sound. And the latest generation of Macintoshes includes hardware and software for digitizing sound without additional hardware or sound cards. For most Macintoshes, 8-bit, 16-bit, and 24-bit graphics capability is available "out of the box." The AV series of Macintoshes can digitize video as well as sound. Unlike the Windows environment, where users can operate an application with keyboard input, the Macintosh requires a mouse.

Nevertheless, there is significant variation in the ways you can set up your Macintosh hardware and software. The Macintosh computer you will need for developing a project depends entirely upon the project's delivery requirements, its content, and the tools you will need for production. Of course, the ideal production station is the newest, fastest, and most flexible computer you can get your hands on, but such a configuration may be beyond the scope of your budget. Thankfully, acceptable performance is not limited to the top-of-the-line configuration: most Macintosh models sold today are sufficient for multimedia development.

Apple introduced the first Power Macintosh computers based on reduced instruction-set computing (RISC) microprocessors during 1994. RISC technology was typically used in engineering workstations and commercial database servers designed for raw computational power, but in an alliance with IBM and Motorola, Apple designed and built this new line of RISC-based models. They supplanted earlier models based upon the Motorola 68000, 68030, and 68040 processors. In 1997, the G3 series was introduced with clock speeds greater than 233 MHz and offering higher performance than existing Pentium-based Windows machines.

Vaughan's One-Way Rule

Once you've tried it, you can't go back

In 1987, a few weeks after HyperCard was released by Apple, I went to work there, designing and building the guided tour for an information management tool used in-house by Apple. I said I didn't know the software; they said that's OK, nobody else does, either. They gave me a cubicle with my name on it, a Macintosh Plus with a 20MB hard disk, and I was up and running.

The Macintosh II had been shipping for a short while, and every department at Apple was attempting to get this latest and hottest CPU—but most units were going to the retail channel. There were about three Macintosh IIs among about 40 of us.

One afternoon, I sat at a Macintosh II, inserted my 800K disk, and ran my HyperCard stack. I couldn't believe it! The screen-to-screen dissolves and special effects I had carefully programmed on the Macintosh Plus went by so fast I couldn't see them. I had to reprogram everything, with a special test to check for CPU speed. If it was a fast machine, I programmed the visual effects to run slower; on a slow machine, faster. But the sad part was that I not only wanted this faster machine, I felt I needed it! I had had the same experience moving from a 300-baud modem to a 1200-baud modem and, later, from a 14-inch monitor to a 21-inch monitor.

The Windows Multimedia PC Platform

The MPC computer is not a hardware unit per se, but rather a standard that includes minimum specifications to turn Intel-microprocessor-based computers into multimedia computers. The standard applies not only to desktop computers but also to increasingly powerful multimedia laptops.

Because the MPC is a standard, not a computer, you can assemble your own clone with components from various suppliers and meet the standard. Upgrade kits that typically include a CD-ROM player and a sound board are available from many hardware vendors. MPC-compliant systems are available in prepackaged configurations from most manufacturers. Vendors who sell MPC computers will guarantee that software written to the MPC standard, usually labeled with the MPC mark, will play on their machines.

The Multimedia PC Marketing Council was rolled out with the support of Microsoft and major PC manufacturers in 1990 (the fanfare event is described in "First Person" in Chapter 12). Since then, oversight of the MPC specification has been transferred to the Software Publishers Association (SPA), and the Multimedia PC Marketing Council is now called the Multimedia PC Working Group (http://www.spa.org/mpc).

The original MPC Level 1 minimum standard workstation consisted of a 16 MHz 386SX microprocessor, at least 2MB of RAM, a 30MB hard disk, a CD-ROM drive, VGA video (16 colors), an 8-bit audio board, speakers and/or headphones, and Microsoft Windows software with the MultiMedia Extensions package. This minimum-configuration MPC was not powerful enough to develop serious multimedia and was hardly powerful enough to *play* multimedia at all. A more realistic MPC Level 2 minimum standard was released in 1993. This specification defined the minimum system functionality for Level 2 compliance as a 25 MHz 486SX (or compatible) microprocessor with at least 4MB of RAM (8MB recommended), a 3.5-inch high-density (1.44MB) floppy disk drive, a 160MB or larger hard drive, and a CD-ROM drive capable of sustained 300 Kbps transfer rate (double speed) with CD-DA (Red Book) outputs and volume control, 16-bit sound capability with microphone input, and a color monitor with display resolution of at least 640×480 with 65,536 (64K) colors.

In June 1995, the Multimedia PC Working Group released the Multimedia PC Level 3 specification providing for improved sound and video performance.

::::::::::::::::::::::::::::::::::

For content producers, MPC3 offers a solid set of minimum performance standards for multimedia machines. Rather than merely defining the hardware, this specification focuses on the quality of the end user experience. This quality is assured through the creation of validation suites that test each machine as a complete system, rather than as a series of individual parts. And the specification offers a number of exciting new capabilities upon which developers can depend in creating new titles, such as wavetable sound, 4× CD-ROM drives and MPEG video.

::::::::::::::::::::::::::::::::::

William Fisher, President, Quicksilver Software

4

The *big* upgrade in this MPC3 standard, following many months of meetings and negotiations within the Working Group, was the requirement for MPEG1 video playback compliance (see Chapter 13). The MPC3 platform consequently provides full motion video with TV-quality and CD-quality sound (albeit in a 352×240-pixel window). If your multimedia project will be distributed into retail consumer channels, you should consider applying to the MPC Working Group for a license to use the MPC logo on your packaging.

First Person

In November 1985, during the COMDEX trade show in Las Vegas, members of the computer press were invited to the birthing party for a new Microsoft product called Windows. A crowd of journalists and friends of Microsoft had gathered in a small, low-ceilinged hotel ballroom and were munching on hors d'oeuvres and sipping wine. Suddenly the swinging doors to the pantry opened, and Bill Gates drove a golf cart onto the floor, towing a small trailer loaded down with hundreds of blue boxes filled with the new product. A cheer went up, and the boxes disappeared into waiting hands. It was a fun party held in the time before Gates had become the richest man in the world and necessarily employed a personal security force, and before his personal income would skew by two dollars the difference between the mean and median income of all Americans. He chatted with a few of us and proudly autographed some User Guides.—Mine says, "I hope you like the product. Thanks for coming, Tay.

William H. Gates
11/20/85"

Back in my office after the show, I loaded the software onto my XT from the five 5.25-inch floppy disks in the box and ran it. Windows was a dog. Indeed, during the ensuing days and months, Windows had a very hard time in the "operating environment" popularity contest and dropped to low-visibility status. But Gates seemed to have a vision, and while we didn't hear too much about Windows during the next years, Gates and Microsoft worked on the product steadily and didn't give up. Windows 3.0, released many years later, changed the world.

Networking Macintosh and Windows Computers

If you are working in a multimedia development environment consisting of a mixture of Macintosh and Windows computers, you will want them to communicate with each other. You will also wish to share other resources among them, such as printers.

Local area networks (LANs) and wide area networks (WANs) can connect the members of a workgroup. In a LAN, workstations are usually located within a short distance of one another, on the same floor of a building, for example. WANs are communication systems spanning great distances, typically set up and managed by large corporations and institutions for their own use, or to share with other users.

LANs allow direct communication and sharing of peripheral resources such as file servers, printers, scanners, and network modems. They use a variety of proprietary technologies, most commonly Ethernet or TokenRing, to perform the connections. They can usually be set up with twisted-pair telephone wire, but be sure to use "data-grade level 5" wire—it makes a real difference, even if it's a little more expensive! Bad wiring will give you a never-ending headache of intermittent and often untraceable crashes and failures.

WANs are expensive to install and maintain, but other methods for long-distance communication are available without a dedicated telephone network: dial-up connections to the Internet through an Internet Service Provider (ISP), CompuServe, America Online, MSN, Prodigy, or MCI Mail allow messages and files to be uploaded to private electronic (e-mail) mailbox addresses and downloaded later by the recipient. You pay for a local telephone call and the length of time you are connected to the service (usually at a reasonable hourly rate or flat fee). If you are working with people in various time zones (an artist in New York, a programmer in San Francisco, and a client in Singapore), all can communicate and share information with other locations at any time of day or night.

If you are operating a cross-platform multimedia development shop, you should install an Ethernet system so your PCs can talk with your Macintoshes. This is many times more efficient than carrying removable media among your machines. Macintoshes have Ethernet networking built in; your PCs will require Ethernet cards. Ethernet is only a *method* for wiring up computers, so you still will need *client/server* software to enable the computers to speak with each other and pass files back and forth. Here you have two options: you can add software to your Macintosh to allow it to connect to a network of Windows PCs that use the Microsoft Client TCP/IP protocols, or you can add software to your Windows PC that allows it to connect to a network of Macintoshes that uses AppleTalk. Both require Ethernet as the connection method.

With DAVE from Thursby Systems (http://www.thursby.com), software is installed on the Macintosh to enable the Macintosh to connect to the Microsoft TCP/IP network. Users can then mount shared Macintosh hard drives and PostScript printers that are connected to the Macintosh's Apple-Talk network so they can be used by the PCs in the network. DAVE uses the industry standard TCP/IP protocol with a NetBIOS driver (see Figure 4-1).

To connect a PC to a network of Macintoshes, you can use MACLAN Connect from Miramar (http://www.miramarsys.com) to share the directories and files on all your computers using AppleTalk protocols—you do not have to install a dedicated server workstation (see Figure 4-2).

4

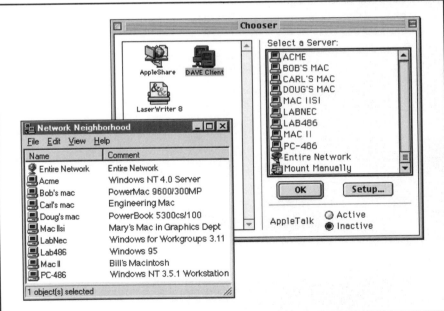

FIGURE 4-1

Thursby Software Systems' DAVE lets you network a Macintosh into a Windows workgroup using TCP/IP protocols

■

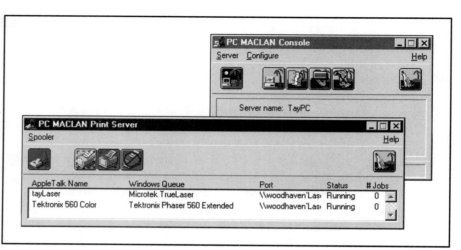

FIGURE 4-2

Miramar's MACLAN Connect lets you network a Windows PC into a workgroup of Macintoshes using AppleTalk protocols ∎

Multi

The equipment required for developing your multimedia project will depend on the content of the project, as well as its design.

Among the many devices —

communicate

media

chapter

5

COMPUTERS
MONITORS
DISK DRIVES
VIDEO PROJECTORS
LIGHT VALVES
VIDEODISC PLAYERS
VCRs
MIXERS

-there are enough wires and connections to resemble the intensive care ward of a hospital.

SOUND SPEAKERS
and POWER STRIPS

Hardware Peripherals

T H E following sections describe the hardware components necessary to translate a user's commands, queries, and responses into computer activity, to deliver and display a multimedia project, to store a project, and to communicate with co-workers and others during its production.

Connections

When you attend a conference where multimedia presentations are being shown, the human speakers usually sit facing the audience, which is treated to a view of the backside of the speakers' computers. Among the many devices—computers, monitors, disk drives, video projectors, light-valves, videodisc players, VCRs, mixers, sound speakers, and power strips—there are enough wires and connections to resemble the intensive-care ward of a hospital. Sometimes an attempt is made to drape these power and data hoses with a curtain.

The equipment required for developing your multimedia project will depend on the content of the project as well as its design. You will certainly need as fast a computer as you can lay your hands on, with lots of RAM and disk storage space. If you can find content such as sound effects, music, graphic art, clip animations, and QuickTime or AVI movies to use in your project, you may not need the extra tools for making your own. Typically, however, multimedia developers have separate equipment for digitizing sound from tapes or microphone, scanning photographs or other printed matter, and making digital still or movie images from videotape.

A few years ago I was on a flight from Dallas to Frankfurt and became involved in an unusual but gentlemanly competition. At Mach .75 and 40,000 above the sea, six of us contended for the two available 110-volt "Shavers Only" electrical outlets in the lavatories. Every hour or so we needed to charge our laptop computers, and in the manner of fellow travelers, we quietly negotiated a round-robin power schedule.

More recently, on an overnight flight across that same ocean aboard a brand-new aircraft, mine was the only seat showing its overhead light while I put the finishing touches on a multimedia presentation. After a few hours, I needed to charge batteries, and with the small charger, power cord, and batteries in hand, I went forward to the lavatory. There was no 110-volt outlet. With increasing alarm, I checked the other lavatories. No outlets anywhere.

Behind the curtain of the galley, the flight attendants had gathered to chat while their passengers slept; no, there probably weren't any outlets on this plane, they responded ambivalently. I looked furtively around the galley; none there, either.

It would seem that 110-volt conveniences for passengers with shavers and laptops have gone to that same graveyard of services where you can find Channel 12 for listening to Air Traffic Control while en route, first-person televised views from the cockpit of takeoffs and landings, a catered piano bar and lounge aft, and (in the real old days) a tiny pack of four Winston cigarettes on your dinner tray next to a matchbook proudly emblazoned with the airline's logo.

No doubt there are safety, cost, and general reduction-of-hassle-from-passengers reasons, though airlines are beginning to install special low-voltage computer power outlets for laptops at business and first-class seats. I was, in the end, better off for the extra sleep.

Small Computer System Interface (SCSI)

The Small Computer System Interface (SCSI) is built into all current models of the Macintosh and lets you add peripheral equipment such as disk drives, scanners, CD-ROM players, and other peripheral devices that conform to the SCSI standard. You can connect as many as eight devices (ID numbers from 0 to 7) to the SCSI port, but one of them must be the computer itself with ID 7, and one is usually your internal hard disk with ID 0. High-end Macintoshes have two SCSI buses, internal and external, and so can hook up twice as many devices. With Ultra SCSI, you can hook up as many as 32 devices.

SCSI cards can also be installed in PCs, and external peripheral devices such as hard disks, CD-ROM drives, tape drives, printers, scanners, rewritable cartridge drives, and magneto-optical drives can be connected to the installed card.

When a SCSI device is connected to the interface card in a PC, it is mounted to the system as another drive letter. Thus you may have floppy disk drives mounted as drives A: and B:, a hard disk as drive C:, and SCSI-based external devices as drives D:, E:, F:, G:, and so on. While usually connected to a hard disk controller card in the PC, the internal disk drive C: can also be a SCSI device, connected to a SCSI card. Specialized software such as Corel SCSI from Corel is available to maximize the flexibility of a PC-based SCSI system by providing drivers that work with hundreds of hardware devices from many different vendors.

---

cross platform   *Not all PC SCSI cards and software drivers will recognize Macintosh-formatted removable media such as Zip, Jaz, and SyQuest cartridges or magneto-optical discs. The Macintosh, however, will usually recognize PC-formatted disks and devices, so many developers working in cross-platform environments use PC formatting for their removable media.*

You will need to set up your SCSI devices carefully, because SCSI cabling is very sensitive to length and to resistance. Follow the instructions in your SCSI user's guide for proper termination and ID number assignment for SCSI devices. Having more than one external SCSI device can make your system "delicate," and even more will make it "fragile." The following configuration, which includes several external disk drives, a CD-ROM player, and a flat-bed scanner, took several hours to hook up and is fragile:

SCSIProbe Tay			
SCSIProbe 3.5			
ID Type	Vendor	Product	Version
0 DISK	QUANTUM	LP240S GM240S0...	6.3
1 DISK	SyQuest	SQ555	F9K
2 DISK	QUANTUM	P105S 910-10-9...	A.3
3 ROM	SONY	CD-ROM CDU-800...	1.9a
4 DISK	SyQuest	SQ555	EOJ
5 OPTIC	RICOH	RO-3010E	0.98
6 SCAN	MII SC31	ScanMaker II 600Z	5.08
7 CPU	APPLE	TayMac	7.1

Update | Mount | Options...

When your computer is not happy with your chain of SCSI peripherals, it is not forgiving and will refuse to boot up. Often you will need to adjust cable lengths and reconfigure terminating resistors, and try again. Make sure that IDs assigned to peripherals are neither 0 nor 7, and that the same ID number is not assigned to two different devices. If you are likely to move different peripheral devices among several computers, it is good practice to put a sticker with that device's assigned SCSI ID on each and also label all devices connected to the computer. Always connect external devices with computer and device power off. By clearly paying attention to the SCSI IDs of your peripherals, you can avoid dangerous ID conflicts (setting two devices to the same ID) when you boot up.

The hardware and the drivers for SCSI have improved over the years to provide faster data transfers across wider buses: SCSI-1 transfers data at a rate of 5MB per second and supports up to seven devices. The newer SCSI-2 is divided into two classifications: Fast SCSI (10MB per second) and Wide SCSI (with an increased bus width to 16-bit). A composite of these two (Fast/Wide SCSI) can achieve data transfer rates of 20MB per second. The latest SCSI-3 (Ultra SCSI) can support up to 32 devices and achieve speeds of 40MB per second. Unlike the less-expensive IDE scheme, a SCSI controller does not demand CPU time, and because it can support as many as 32 devices, it is preferred for network servers and situations in which writing simultaneously to two or more disks (mirroring) is required.

SCSI devices may be installed (and interchanged) on both your PC and your Macintosh: the PC will *not* read Macintosh-formatted hard disks and other data storage cartridges, but the Macintosh (usually) will read PC-formatted devices.

http://www.symbios.com/x3t10/

T10 is the Technical Committee of the National Committee on Information Technology Standards that defines SCSI standards

Integrated Drive Electronics (IDE)

SCSI connections may connect both *internal* devices, which are inside the chassis of your computer and use the computer's power supply, and *external* devices, which are outside the chassis, use their own power supply, and are plugged into the computer by cable. Integrated Drive Electronics (IDE) connections, on the other hand, are typically only internal and connect hard disks, CD-ROM drives, and other peripherals inside a PC.

A PC motherboard can support two IDE controllers, and each controller in turn can support two devices (a master and a slave). Thus, with IDE, you can install a combination of four hard disks, CD-ROM drives, or other devices in your PC. The floppy disk doesn't count because it is operated by a separate controller. The circuitry for IDE is typically much less expensive than for SCSI, but comes with limitations: IDE supports only up to 9GB drive capacity, it requires time from the main processor chip, only one drive in a master/slave pair can be active at once, and because a master drive manages the operations of both drives attached to a controller, a failure of the master drive will disable both drives.

As with SCSI, there are various flavors: plain IDE, which can transfer data at 2.5MB per second; EIDE (Enhanced IDE), which can transfer data at 16.6MB per second; and Ultra IDE (also known as Ultra DMA33), which can transfer data at 33MB per second.

The Media Control Interface (MCI)

Windows provides the Media Control Interface (MCI), a unified, command-driven method for software to talk to related multimedia peripheral devices. With MCI, any hardware (or software) device can be connected to a computer running Windows. Using the appropriate drivers (normally supplied by the device manufacturer), programmers can control the device with simple command strings or codes sent to the MCI.

Table 5-1 lists the device types supported by Windows' MCI. Applications with internal scripting languages, such as Visual Basic, Icon Author, and ToolBook, can easily be programmed to send MCI commands to these devices.

If you wish to experiment with MCI commands (the command syntax is available in the Windows Software Development Kit, or SDK), run the Media Player (C:\WINDOWS\MPLAYER.EXE), open a device, and press CTRL and F5 while it is paused. This window lets you send commands directly

Device Type	Description
animation	Animation device (for example, a player for Autodesk.flc files)
cdaudio	CD-Audio player (Red Book)
dat	Digital audio tape player
digitalvideo	Digital video in a window
other	Any undefined MCI device
overlay	Video overlay device (analog video in a window)
scanner	Image scanner
sequencer	MIDI sequencer (or .mid and .rmi files)
vcr	Videotape recorder or player
videodisc	Videodisc player
waveaudio	Waveform (digitized) audio device

TABLE 5-1 *Device Types Supported by Windows' MCI* ■

to the current device. Simple commands include close, freeze, open, pause, play, record, resume, seek, set tempo, status, and stop:

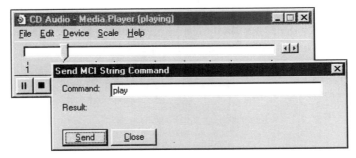

The multimedia devices and drivers are managed by the Windows SYSTEM.INI file, in the [mci] and [drivers] sections of that file, and can be added and deleted using the Multimedia Properties control panel (see Figure 5-1). In Windows, installed devices are listed in the Registry key:

HKEY_LOCAL_MACHINE\System\CurrentControlSet\control \MediaResources\mci

FIGURE 5-1

Use the Multimedia Properties control panel to add and delete multimedia devices

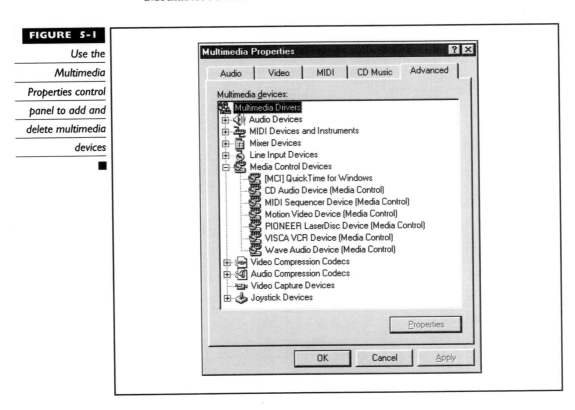

By reading the SYSTEM.INI text file when it starts up, Windows knows what multimedia devices are present in your system; this information is critical. When you install multimedia software in Windows, the setup program will actually write the appropriate lines of data into the SYSTEM.INI file for you. Typical multimedia entries in the SYSTEM.INI file might look like this:

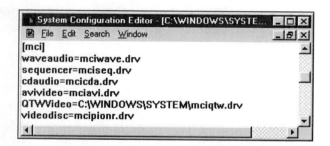

```
[mci]
waveaudio=mciwave.drv
sequencer=mciseq.drv
cdaudio=mcicda.drv
avivideo=mciavi.drv
QTWVideo=C:\WINDOWS\SYSTEM\mciqtw.drv
videodisc=mcipionr.drv
```

Memory and Storage Devices

As you add more memory and storage space to your computer, you can expect your computing needs and habits to keep pace, filling the new capacity. So enjoy the weeks that follow a memory storage upgrade or the addition of a gigabyte hard disk; the honeymoon will eventually end.

Vaughan's Law of Capacity

You never have enough memory or disk space

Somewhere in my basement is an old drive that used 256K, 8-inch floppy disks. I often carried these big floppies from workplace to workplace in a sneaker network (by tennis shoe, that is, not wire or glass fiber). I was astounded and pleased when the new 5.25-inch disks came out, and then amazed by the high technology of 3.5-inch disks that fit in a shirt pocket... The higher-density floppies kept pace with the growing sizes of my project files, until I switched to color and began including sound and animation. For a while, segmenting and joining large files across several disks worked around the constraint, but it was tedious and inadequate for large digital video files. So I went to 44MB SyQuest cartridges, then to 128MB magneto-optical disks and to Zip disks, then to 1GB Jaz cartridges. Now I burn a quick 640MB CD-R on the Philips recorder; my projects are measured in the tens and hundreds of megabytes.

To estimate the memory requirements of a multimedia project—the space required on a floppy disk, hard disk, or CD-ROM, not the random access memory (RAM) used while your computer is running—you must have a sense of the project's content and scope. Color images, text, sound bites, video clips, and the programming code that glues it all together require memory; if there are many of these elements, you will need even more. If you are *making* multimedia, you will also need to allocate memory for storing and archiving working files used during production, original audio and video clips, edited pieces, and final mixed pieces, production paperwork and correspondence, and at least one backup of your project files, with a second backup stored at another location.

It is said that when John von Neuman, often called "the father of the computer," was designing the ENIAC computer in 1945, there was an argument about how much memory this first computer should have. His colleagues appealed for more than the 2K Dr. von Neuman felt was sufficient. In the end, he capitulated and agreed to install 4K in the ENIAC, commenting "...but this is more memory than you will ever need."

Random Access Memory (RAM)

If you are faced with budget constraints, you can certainly produce a multimedia project on a slower or limited-memory computer. On the other hand, it is profoundly frustrating to face memory (RAM) shortages time after time, when you're attempting to keep multiple applications and files open simultaneously. It is also frustrating to wait the extra seconds required of each editing step when working with multimedia material on a slow processor.

On the Macintosh, the minimum RAM configuration for serious multimedia production is about 32MB; but even 64MB and 256MB systems are becoming common, because while digitizing audio or video, you can store much more data much more quickly in RAM. And when you're using some software, you can quickly chew up available RAM—for example, Photoshop (16MB minimum, 20MB recommended); AfterEffects (32MB required), Director (8MB minimum, 20MB better); Pagemaker (24MB recommended); Illustrator (16MB recommended); Microsoft Office (12MB recommended). Figure 5-2 illustrates the allocation of RAM in a Macintosh system with many applications open simultaneously.

In spite of all the marketing hype about processor speed, this speed is ineffective if not accompanied by sufficient RAM. A fast processor without enough RAM may waste processor cycles while it swaps needed portions of program code into and out of memory. In some cases, increasing available RAM may show more performance improvement on your system than upgrading the processor chip.

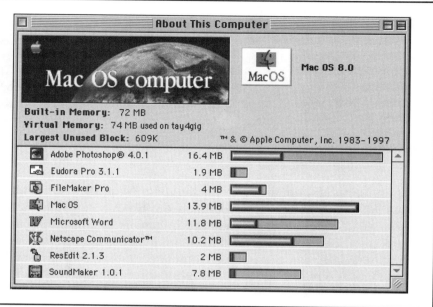

Even though the processing performance of computers has increased considerably in the last several years, input/output (I/O) devices have not kept up with this trend. While processor speed gets roughly eight times faster every ten years, main memory access speed increases by only one third in the same time period. As you realize, this widens the gap between I/O and processing times.

So our ability to efficiently use very fast computers depends on our ability to feed the processor with data sufficiently fast. This is called the parallel I/O bottleneck. *The bad news is that this problem is expected to get worse.*

From "Parallel Machines and Their Algorithms"
by Takis Metaxas

On an MPC platform, multimedia authoring can also consume a great deal of memory. You may need to open many large graphics and audio files, as well as your authoring system, all at the same time to facilitate faster copying/pasting and then testing in your authoring software. Although 8MB is the minimum under the MPC3 standard, 16MB is better, and 20MB may be required.

Read-Only Memory (ROM)

Read-only memory is not *volatile*. Unlike RAM, when you turn off the power to a ROM chip, it will not forget, or lose its memory. ROM is typically used in computers to hold the small BIOS program that initially boots up the computer, and it is used in printers to hold built-in fonts. Programmable ROMs (called EPROMs) allow changes to be made that are not forgotten. A new and inexpensive technology, optical read-only memory (OROM), is provided in proprietary data cards using patented holographic storage. Like the CD Recorders described later in the chapter, the cards are write-once. Typically, OROMs offer 128MB of storage, have no moving parts, and use only about 200 milliwatts of power, making them ideal for handheld, battery-operated devices.

Floppy and Hard Disks

Adequate storage space for your production environment can be provided by large-capacity hard disks; a server-mounted disk on a network; Zip, Jaz, or SyQuest removable cartridges; optical media; CD-R (compact disc-recordable) discs; tape; floppy disks; banks of special memory devices; or any combination of the above.

Removable media (floppy disks, compact or optical discs, and cartridges) typically fit into a letter-sized mailer for overnight courier service. One or many disks or discs may be required for storage and archiving each project, and you should plan for backups kept off-site.

Floppy disks and hard disks are mass-storage devices for binary data—data that can be easily read by a computer. Hard disks can contain much more information than floppy disks and can operate at far greater data transfer rates. In the scale of things, floppies are, however, no longer "mass-storage" devices.

A floppy disk is made of flexible mylar plastic coated with a very thin layer of special magnetic material. A hard disk is actually a stack of hard metal platters coated with magnetically sensitive material, with a series of recording heads or sensors that hover a hairbreadth above the fast-spinning surface, magnetizing or demagnetizing spots along formatted tracks using technology similar to that used by floppy disks and audio and video tape recording. Hard disks are the most common mass-storage device used on computers, and for making multimedia, you will need one or more large-capacity hard disk drives (see "Vaughan's Law of Capacity").

warning *For multimedia work, try to find a hard disk that does not offer automatic random thermal adjustments. These adjustments, OK for general purposes, can foul up the required steady data transfer to CD-R writers.*

As multimedia has reached consumer desktops, makers of hard disks have been challenged to build smaller-profile, larger-capacity, faster, and less-expensive hard disks. In 1994, hard disk manufacturers sold nearly 70 million units; in 1995, more than 80 million units. And prices have dropped a full order of magnitude in a matter of months. By 1998, street prices for 4GB drives (IDE) were less than $200. As network and Internet servers increase the demand for centralized data storage requiring terabytes (1 trillion bytes), hard disks will be configured into fail-proof redundant arrays offering built-in protection against crashes.

Zip, Jaz, SyQuest, and Optical Storage Devices

For years SyQuest's 44MB removable cartridges have been the most widely used portable medium among multimedia developers and professionals, but Iomega's inexpensive Zip drives with their likewise inexpensive 100MB cartridges have significantly penetrated SyQuest's market share for removable media. Iomega's Jaz cartridges provide a gigabyte of removable storage media and have fast enough transfer rates for audio and video development. Pinnacle Micro, Yamaha, Sony, Philips, and others offer CD-R "burners" for making write-once compact discs, and some double as quad-speed players. As blank CD-R discs become available for less than a dollar each, this write-once media competes as a distribution vehicle. CD-R is described in greater detail a little later in the chapter.

Magneto-optical (MO) drives use a high-power laser to heat tiny spots on the metal oxide coating of the disk. While the spot is hot, a magnet aligns the oxides to provide a 0 or 1 (on or off) orientation. Like SyQuests and other Winchester hard disks, this is rewritable technology, because the spots can be repeatedly heated and aligned. Moreover, this media is normally not affected by stray magnetism (it needs both heat and magnetism to make changes), so these disks are particularly suitable for archiving data. The data transfer rate is, however, slow compared to Zip, Jaz, and SyQuest technologies. One of the most popular formats uses a 128MB-capacity disk—about the size of a 3.5-inch floppy. Larger-format magneto-optical drives with 5.25-inch cartridges offering 650MB to 1.3GB of storage are also available.

Digital Versatile Disc (DVD)

In December 1995, nine major electronics companies (Toshiba, Matsushita, Sony, Philips, Time Warner, Pioneer, JVC, Hitachi, and Mitsubishi Electric) agreed to promote a new optical disc technology for distribution of multimedia and feature-length movies called DVD (see Table 5-2).

With this new medium capable not only of gigabyte storage capacity but also full-motion video (MPEG2) and high-quality audio in surround sound, the bar has again risen for multimedia developers. Commercial multimedia projects will become more expensive to produce as consumers' performance expectations rise. There are two types of DVD—DVD-Video and DVD-ROM; these reflect marketing channels, not the technology.

* * *

http://www.philips.com/pkm/laseroptics/dvd.htm
http://www.toshiba.com

DVD information

* * *

DVD can provide 720 pixels per horizontal line, whereas current televisions (NTSC) provide 240—television pictures will be sharper and more detailed. With Dolby AC-3 Digital Surround Sound as part of the specification, six discrete audio channels can be programmed for digital surround sound, and with a separate subwoofer channel, developers can program the low-frequency doom and gloom music popular with Hollywood. DVD also supports Dolby Pro-Logic Surround Sound, standard stereo, and mono audio. Users can randomly access any section of the disc and use the slow-motion and freeze-frame features during movies. Audio tracks can be programmed for as many as 8 different languages, with graphic subtitles in 32 languages. Some manufacturers such as Toshiba are already providing parental control features in their players (users select lockout ratings from G to NC-17).

* * *

DVD, like compact disc, will not boom from day one. Commercial audio and video encoding systems for MPEG2 will be available this summer, and consumer DVD-Video players will be available in Japan and the U.S. by the end of the year, beginning of next year. So the real market will only pick up next year.

In the longer term, we expect that PC software makers will welcome the increased capacity offered by DVD-ROM. Special applications for mapping and digital scanning may lead the *way, but new interactive multimedia titles and games are also hungry for space. We believe that the DVD-ROM market will develop faster than DVD-Video. There are several reasons for this. The OEM price of a DVD-ROM drive will be much lower than a complete DVD-Video player. We think a volume OEM price of approximately $200 for a DVD-ROM drive in 1997 is entirely possible. And as I already stated, the need in the PC world for more capacity and better quality moving video is also much higher than in the consumer market... Around the year 2000, approximately 10 percent of all the 250 million drives sold will be based on DVD. And of this 10 percent, the majority will probably be DVD-ROM.*

From the opening speech at CeBIT, Hanover, Germany, March 13, 1996, by Jan Oosterveld, President, Philips Key Modules

CD-ROM Players

Compact disc read-only memory (CD-ROM) players have become an integral part of the multimedia development workstation and are an impor-

Feature	Specification
Disc diameter	120 mm (5 inches)
Disc thickness	1.2 mm (0.6 mm thick disc × 2)
Memory capacity	4.7 gigabytes/single side
Track pitch	0.74 micrometer
Wave length of laser diode	650 nanometer/635 nanometer
Numerical aperture (NA)	0.6
Error correction	RS-PC (Reed Solomon Product Code)
Signal modulation	8-16
Data transfer rate	Variable speed data transfer at an average rate of 4.69 megabits/second for image and sound
Image compression	MPEG2 digital image compression
Audio	Dolby AC-3 (5.1 ch), LPCM for NTSC and MPEG Audio, LPCM for PAL/SECAM (a maximum of 8 audio channels and 32 subtitle channels can be stored)
Running time (movies)	133 minutes a side (at an average data rate of 4.69 megabits/second for image and sound, including three audio channels and four subtitle channels)
File management structure	Micro UDF and ISO-9660

TABLE 5-2 *DVD Main Specifications* ■

tant delivery vehicle for large, mass-produced projects. A wide variety of developer utilities, graphic backgrounds, stock photography and sounds, applications, games, reference texts, and educational software are available only on this medium.

CD-ROM players have typically been very slow to access and transmit data (150K per second, which is the speed required of consumer Red Book Audio CDs), but new developments have led to double-, triple-, quadruple-speed, and even 24x drives designed specifically for computer (not Red Book Audio) use. These faster drives spool up like washing machines on the spin cycle and can be somewhat noisy, especially if the inserted compact disc is not evenly balanced. See Chapter 20 for more details about CD-ROMs.

CD Recorders

With a compact disc recorder, you can make your own CDs using special CD-recordable (CD-R) blank optical discs to create a CD in most formats of CD-ROM and CD-Audio. The machines are made by Sony, Philips, Ricoh, Kodak, JVC, Yamaha, and Pinnacle. Software, such as Adaptec's Toast for Macintosh (see Figure 5-3) or Easy CD Creator for Windows, lets you organize files on your hard disk(s) into a "virtual" structure, then writes them to the CD in that order. CD-R discs are made differently than normal CDs but can play in any CD-Audio or CD-ROM player. They are available in either a "63-minute" or "74-minute" capacity—for the former, that means about 560MB, and for the latter, about 650MB. These write-once CDs make excellent high-capacity file archives and are used extensively by multimedia developers for premastering and testing CD-ROM projects and titles.

Videodisc Players

Videodisc players (commercial, not consumer quality) can be used in conjunction with the computer to deliver multimedia applications. You can control the videodisc player from your authoring software with X-Commands (XCMDs) on the Macintosh and with MCI commands in Windows. The output of the videodisc player is an analog television signal, so you must set up a television separate from your computer monitor or use a video digitizing board to "window" the analog signal on your monitor. Chapter 13 discusses this technology in greater detail.

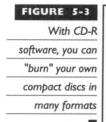

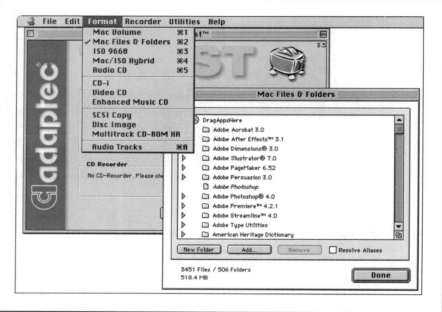

nput Devices

A great variety of input devices—from the familiar keyboard and handy mouse to touchscreens to voice recognition setups—can be used for development and delivery of a multimedia project. If you are designing your project for a public kiosk, use a touchscreen. If your project is for a lecturing professor who likes to wander about the classroom, use a remote handheld mouse. If you create a great deal of original computer-rendered art, consider a pressure-sensitive stylus and a drawing tablet.

Keyboards

A keyboard is the most common method of interaction with a computer. Keyboards provide various tactile responses (from firm to mushy) and have various layouts depending upon your computer system and keyboard model. Keyboards are typically rated for at least 50 million cycles (the number of times a key can be pressed before it might suffer breakdown).

The most common keyboard for PCs is the 101 style (which provides 101 keys), although many styles are available with more or fewer special keys, LEDs, and other features, such as a plastic membrane cover for industrial or food-service applications or flexible "ergonomic" styles. Macintosh keyboards connect to the Apple Desktop Bus (ADB), which manages all forms of user input—from digitizing tablets to mice.

Mice

A mouse is the standard tool for interacting with a graphical user interface (GUI). All Macintosh computers require a mouse; on PCs, mice are not required but recommended. Even though the Windows environment accepts keyboard entry in lieu of mouse point-and-click actions, your multimedia projects should typically be designed with the mouse or touchscreen in mind. The buttons on the mouse provide additional user input, such as pointing and double-clicking to open a document, or the click-and-drag operation, in which the mouse button is pressed and held down to drag (move) an object, or to move to and select an item on a pull-down menu, or to access context-sensitive help. The Apple mouse has one button; PC mice may have as many as three.

Trackballs

Trackballs are similar to mice, except that the cursor is moved by using one or more fingers to roll across the top of the ball. The trackball does not need the flat space required by a mouse; this is important in small confined environments and for portable laptop computers. Trackballs have at least two buttons: one for the user to click or double-click, and the other to provide the press-and-hold condition necessary for selecting from menus and dragging objects.

Touchscreens

Touchscreens are monitors that usually have a textured coating across the glass face. This coating is sensitive to pressure and registers the location of the user's finger when it touches the screen. The TouchMate system, which has no coating, actually measures the pitch, roll, and yaw rotation of the monitor when pressed by a finger, and determines how much force was exerted and the location where the force was applied. Other touchscreens use invisible beams of infrared light that crisscross the front of the monitor to calculate where a finger was pressed. Pressing twice on the screen in quick succession simulates the double-click action of a mouse. Touching the screen and dragging the finger, without lifting it, to another location simulates a mouse click-and-drag. A keyboard is sometimes simulated using an on-screen representation so users can input names, numbers, and other text by pressing "keys."

Touchscreens are not recommended for day-to-day computer work, but are excellent for multimedia applications in a kiosk, at a trade show, or in a museum delivery system—anything involving public input and simple tasks. When your project is designed to use a touchscreen, the monitor is the only input device required, so you can secure all other system hardware behind locked doors to prevent theft or tampering.

First Person

One of the more seductive rewards for working on the steep and slippery learning curves of multimedia is an occasional overwhelming introduction to a new idea or invention, the kind of encounter characterized by a neck-wrenching flash of wonderment as you stop in your tracks for a double-take. "How does that work?"

The TouchMate from Visage is just such an invention. It's about two inches high, sits under your monitor, and requires only a 12-volt power supply and a cable to the RS-232 serial port of your PC. There are no electrical or data connections between the device and the monitor, no occluding membranes glued to glass, and no LEDs buried in a protruding bezel.

So how does TouchMate work if it's not connected to the screen? It translates tiny three-dimensional changes in monitor position caused by pressure on the screen into screen coordinates. This is the same sort of awesome black-box science that enables inertial navigation systems to guide a 747 from New York to Paris, hands-free. TouchMate combines well-understood sensor hardware with the mathematics of force vectors.

The top of TouchMate, where the monitor sits, is mounted on three-dimensional springs, allowing it to move with equal freedom in all directions relative to the base. Internal sensors constantly measure the distance between the top and the base. Each sensor consists of two parallel plates that form a capacitor, one attached to the top of TouchMate and one attached to the base. Two sets of these sensor plates are located in each corner, mounted at a 45-degree angle, providing a total of eight sensors.

When the monitor (sitting on the TouchMate) is touched, the force of the touch causes a slight change in the distance between TouchMate's top and base, typically on the order of a thousandth of an inch. This causes the distance between each set of sensor plates to change slightly, changing the capacitance across the plates. TouchMate uses the change in capacitance across each sensor to determine the amount the top plate moved in the x, y, and z directions and the amount it rotated in each direction (roll, pitch, and yaw). Firmware then calculates what level of force was exerted to cause this movement and the location where the force was applied.

Magnetic Card Encoders and Readers

Magnetic (mag) card setups are useful when you need an interface for a database application or multimedia project that tracks users. You need both a card encoder and a card reader for this type of interface. The encoder connects to the computer at a serial port and transfers information to a magnetic strip of tape on the back of the card. The card reader then reads the information encoded on the card. A visitor to a museum, for example, could slide an encoded card through a reader at any exhibit station and be rewarded with a personalized or customized response from an intelligent database or presentation system. French-speaking visitors to a Norwegian museum, for instance, could hear an exhibit described in French.

---

tip *When you design a project to use mag cards or pen scanners, always provide immediate feedback to an action by the user, such as a beep response or a displayed message.*

Graphics Tablets

Flat-surface input devices are attached to the computer in the same way as a mouse or trackball. A special pen is used against the pressure-sensitive surface of the tablet to move the cursor. Graphics tablets provide substantial control for editing finely detailed graphic elements, a feature very useful to graphic artists and interface designers. Tablets can also be used as input devices for end users: you can design a printed graphic, place it on the surface of the tablet, and let users work with a pen directly on the input surface. On a floor plan, for instance, visitors might draw a track through the hallways and rooms they wish to see and then receive a printed list of things to note along the route. Some tablets are pressure sensitive and are good for drawing: the harder you press the stylus, for example, the wider or darker the line you draw. Graphic artists who try these usually fall prey to Vaughan's One-Way Rule (see Chapter 4) and never return to drawing with a mouse.

Flat-Bed Scanners

A scanner may be the most useful piece of equipment you will use in the course of producing a multimedia project; there are flat-bed and handheld scanners. Most commonly available are gray-scale and color flat-bed scanners that provide a resolution of 300 or 600 dots per inch (dpi). Professional graphics houses may use even higher resolution units. Handheld scanners can be useful for scanning small images and columns of text, but they may prove inadequate for your multimedia development.

Be aware that scanned images, particularly those at high resolution and in color, demand an extremely large amount of storage space on your hard disk, no matter what instrument is used to do the scanning. Also remember that the final monitor display resolution for your multimedia project will probably be just 72 or 95 dpi—leave the very expensive ultra-high-resolution scanners for the desktop publishers. Most inexpensive flat-bed scanners offer at least 300 dpi resolution, and most allow you to set the scanning resolution.

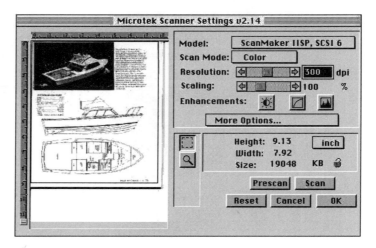

Scans let you make clear electronic images of existing artwork such as photos, ads, pen drawings, and cartoons, and can save many hours when you are incorporating proprietary art into your application. Scans also can give you a starting point for your own creative diversions.

Optical Character Recognition (OCR) Devices

Scanners enable you to use optical character recognition (OCR) software, such as OmniPage from Caere (see Figure 5-4) or Perceive from Ocron, to convert printed matter to ASCII text files in your computer. With OCR software and a scanner, you can convert paper documents into a word processing document on your computer without retyping, or *rekeying*.

Barcode readers are probably the most familiar optical character recognition devices in use today—mostly at markets, shops, and other point-of-purchase locations. Using photo cells and laser beams, barcode readers recognize the numeric characters of the Universal Product Code that are printed in a pattern of parallel black bars on merchandise labels. With OCR, or "barcoding," retailers can efficiently process goods in and out of their stores and maintain better inventory control.

An OCR terminal can be of use to a multimedia developer because it recognizes not only printed characters but also handwriting. This facility may be beneficial at a kiosk or in a general education environment where user friendliness is a goal—there is growing demand for a more personal and less technical interface to data and information.

Infrared Remotes

An infrared remote unit lets a user interact with your project while he or she is freely moving about. Remotes work like mice and trackballs, except they use infrared light to direct the cursor and require no cables to communicate. Remote mice work well for a lecture or other presentation in an auditorium or similar environment, when the speaker needs to move around the room.

Voice Recognition Systems

Voice recognition systems facilitate hands-free interaction with your project. These systems usually provide a unidirectional cardioid, noise-canceling microphone that automatically filters out background noise. Most voice recognition systems currently available can trigger common menu events such as Save, Open, Quit, and Print, and you can teach the system to recognize other commands that are more specific to your application.

Systems available for the Macintosh and Windows environments typically must be taught to recognize individual voices and then be programmed with the appropriate responses to the recognized word or phrase. The Macintosh AV and Power Macintosh computers include voice recognition capability, and add-on sound boards such as the Sound Blaster or Diamond Sonic Sound and others provide this feature for PCs.

Digital Cameras

Digital cameras such as Apple's QuickTake, the Dycam 10C, Kodak's DC40, and the Logitech Fotoman and Pixtura use the video technology described in Chapter 13. The XAPSHOT SV camera, for example, can record up to 50 images (300-line video fields) on a reusable 2-inch floppy disk. Images can be played back directly from the camera to any standard TV monitor or used with a digitizer for computer input. Software controls the image capture, image adjustment, and save functions of the digitizer. Once the image is saved in the computer environment, of course, it can easily be exported to various applications, incorporated into desktop publishing setups, used to enhance a database, or added as a graphic image to a multimedia presentation.

Output Hardware

Presentation of the audio and visual components of your multimedia project requires hardware that may or may not be included with the computer itself—speakers, amplifiers, monitors, motion video devices, and capable storage systems. The better the equipment, of course, the better the presentation. There is no greater test of the benefits of good output hardware than to feed the audio output of your computer into an external amplifier system: suddenly the bass sounds become deeper and richer, and even music sampled at low quality may sound acceptable.

Audio Devices

All Macintoshes are equipped with an internal speaker and a dedicated sound chip, and they are capable of audio output without additional hardware and/or software. To take advantage of built-in stereo sound, external speakers are required.

Digitizing sound on your Macintosh requires an external microphone and sound editing/recording software such as SoundEdit16 from Macromedia, Alchemy from Passport, or SoundDesigner from DigiDesign.

tip *Design your project to use many shorter-duration audio files rather than one long file. This simplifies the reaction of your project within your authoring system, and it may also improve performance because you will load shorter segments of sound into RAM at any one time.*

PCs are not capable of multimedia audio until a sound board is installed. Multimedia PCs (MPCs) are configured for sound from the start. The sound capabilities of both platforms are discussed in detail in Chapter 10.

tip *The quality of your audio recordings is greatly affected by the caliber of your microphone and cables. A unidirectional microphone helps filter out external noise, and good cables help reduce noise emitted from surrounding electronic equipment.*

Amplifiers and Speakers

Often the speakers you use during a project's development will not be adequate for its presentation. Speakers with built-in amplifiers or attached to an external amplifier are important when your project will be presented to a large audience or in a noisy setting. Altec Lansing's three-piece amplified speaker system, for example, is designed for multimedia presentations and is small and portable. It includes its own digital signal processing (DSP) circuitry for concert hall effects; it has a mixer for two input sources (the computer's digital output and the CD-ROM player's audio output can be blended); and it uses a subwoofer sensitive to 35 Hz.

warning *Always use magnetically shielded speakers to prevent color distortion or damage to nearby video displays.*

Monitors

The monitor you need for development of multimedia projects depends on the type of multimedia application you are creating, as well as what computer you're using. A wide variety of monitors is available for both Macintoshes and PCs. High-end, large-screen graphics monitors are available for both, and they are expensive.

Serious multimedia developers will often attach more than one monitor to their computers, using add-on graphics boards. This is because many authoring systems allow you to work with several open windows at a time, so you can dedicate one monitor to viewing the work you are creating or designing, and you can perform various editing tasks in windows on other monitors that do not block the view of your work. Figure 5-5 illustrates editing windows that overlap a work view when developing with Macromedia's authoring environment, Director, on one monitor. Developing in Director is best with at least two monitors, one to view your work, the other to view the "Score." A third monitor is often added by Director developers to display the "Cast." See Chapter 9 for more about Director. For years, one of the advantages of the Macintosh for making multimedia has been that it is very easy to attach multiple monitors for development work. Finally, with Windows 98, PCs can be configured for more than one monitor.

FIGURE 5-5

Without a second monitor, you will have difficulty editing your project and viewing it at the same time

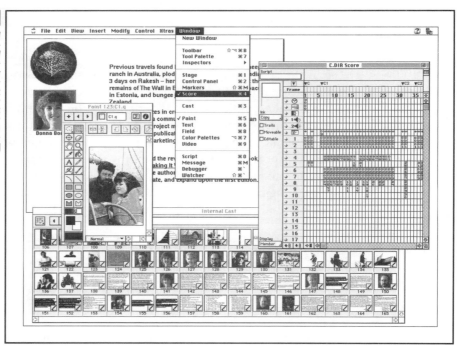

A bunch of us worked on a guided tour project destined for Sun SPARCstations. SPARCstations have large monitors with a screen resolution of 1024×768 pixels, but, because we were most proficient with Macintosh graphics tools, we created most of the bitmapped artwork on Macintosh 13-inch, 640×480-pixel, RGB monitors. Though the Macintosh software deftly managed the big image sizes, the process was very tiresome to the artists, because the 640×480 monitors provided only a window onto the larger bitmap. We had to scroll the window back and forth over the larger image to see what we were doing. Dragging and dropping was a horror show.

Finally, we installed a 19-inch monitor and set up a Macintosh with a high-resolution video card. It was better, but there were not enough of them to go around. In the end, about 75 percent of the artwork was done in scrolling windows on the Macintosh, and it turned out great.

Large monitors do not necessarily increase the real estate available to you for your graphics and information display: 35-inch monitors, or even the 50-foot projection displays common to auditoriums, may still provide just 640×480 pixels of resolution. The large monitors that do effectively increase the real estate also require higher-resolution boards in Macintosh or PC expansion slots. Again, these are expensive.

5

tip *Always develop your project using the screen resolution of the destination platform.*

It is important to develop your application on monitors of the same size and resolution as those to be used for its delivery. A variety of monitors can be used for both development and delivery.

tip *To improve performance while running in 24-bit mode, you can often convert some graphic elements to 8-bit images without degradation; this will increase the redraw speed for that image. Don't animate with very large bitmaps, no matter their color depth, and use minimal gradients or shadings.*

Video Devices

No other contemporary message medium has the visual impact of video. With a video digitizing board installed in your computer, you can display a television picture on your monitor. Some boards include a frame-grabber feature for capturing the image and turning it into a color bitmap, which can be saved as a PICT or TIFF file and then used as part of a graphic or a background in your project.

Display of video on any computer platform requires manipulation of an enormous amount of data. When used in conjunction with videodisc players, which give you precise control over the images being viewed, video cards let you place an image into a window on the computer monitor; a second television screen dedicated to video is not required. And video cards typically come with excellent special effects software.

There are many video cards available today. Most of these support various video-in-a-window sizes, identification of source video, setup of play sequences or segments, special effects, frame grabbing, digital moviemaking; and some have built-in television tuners so you can watch your favorite programs in a window while working on other things. In Windows, video overlay boards are controlled through the Media Control Interface. On the Macintosh, they are often controlled by external commands and functions (XCMDs and XFCNs) linked to your authoring software.

Good video greatly enhances your project; poor video will ruin it. Whether you deliver your video from tape using VISCA controls, from videodisc, or as a QuickTime or AVI movie, it is important that your source material be of high quality.

Projectors

When you need to show your material to more viewers than can huddle around a computer monitor, you will need to project it onto a large screen or even a white-painted wall. Cathode-ray tube (CRT) projectors, liquid crystal display (LCD) panels attached to an overhead projector, stand-alone LCD projectors, and light-valve projectors are available to splash your work onto big-screen surfaces.

CRT projectors have been around for quite a while—they are the original "big-screen" televisions. They use three separate projection tubes and lenses (red, green, and blue), and the three color channels of light must "converge" accurately on the screen. Setup, focusing, and aligning are important to getting a clear and crisp picture. CRT projectors are compatible with the output of most computers as well as televisions.

LCD panels are portable devices that fit in a briefcase. The panel is placed on the glass surface of a standard overhead projector available in most schools, conference rooms, and meeting halls. While the overhead projector does the projection work, the panel is connected to the computer and provides the image, in thousands of colors and, with active-matrix technology, at speeds that allow full-motion video and animation. Because LCD panels are small, they are popular for on-the-road presentations, often connected to a laptop computer and using a locally available overhead projector.

More complete LCD projection panels contain a projection lamp and lenses and do not require a separate overhead projector. They typically produce an image brighter and sharper than the simple panel model, but they are somewhat larger and cannot travel in a briefcase.

Light-valves compete with high-end CRT projectors and use a liquid crystal technology in which a low-intensity color image modulates a high-intensity light beam. These units are expensive, but the image from a light-valve projector is very bright and color saturated and can be projected onto screens as wide as ten meters.

Printers

With the advent of reasonably priced color printers, hard-copy output has entered the multimedia scene. From storyboards to presentations to production of collateral marketing material, color printers have become an important part of the multimedia development environment. Color helps clarify concepts, improve understanding and retention of information, and organize complex data. As multimedia designers already know (see Chapter 17), intelligent use of color is critical to the success of a project. Tektronix offers both solid ink and laser options, and their Phaser 560 will print more than 10,000 pages at a rate of 5 color pages or 14 monochrome pages per minute before requiring new toner. Epson provides lower-cost and lower-performance solutions for home and small business users; Hewlett Packard's Color LaserJet line competes with both. Most printer manufacturers offer a color model—just as all computers once used monochrome monitors but are now color, all printers will become color printers.

	Tektronix Phaser 350 (solid ink)	Tektronix Phaser 560 (laser)	HP Color LaserJet 5M (laser)	Lexmark Optra C (laser)	IBM Network Color Printer (laser)
Initial purchase cost	$3,995	$4,995	$5,199	$4,999	$4,999
Cost per page (black & white)	1.5¢	2.4¢	2.6¢	5.5¢	5.6¢
Cost per page (color)	4¢	7¢	6¢	10¢	10¢
Approx. time to print a full-color newsletter cover (8.5MB file)	2:00 min	2:20 min	4:40 min	16:00 min	2:00 min

TABLE 5-3 *Costs and Performance of Various Color Printers in 1998 (data courtesy of Tektronix)* ■

Communication Devices

Many multimedia applications are developed in workgroups comprising instructional designers, writers, graphic artists, programmers, and musicians located in the same office space or building. The workgroup members' computers typically are connected on a local area network (LAN). The client's computers, however, may be thousands of miles distant, requiring other methods for good communication.

Communication among workgroup members and with the client is essential to the efficient and accurate completion of your project. Normal U.S. Postal Service mail delivery is too slow to keep pace with most projects; overnight express services are better. And when you need it immediately, a modem or network is required. If your client and you are both connected to the Internet, a combination of communication by e-mail and by FTP (File Transfer Protocol) may be the most cost-effective and efficient solution for both creative development and project management.

In the workplace, use quality equipment and software for your communications setup. The cost—in both time and money—of stable and fast networking will be returned to you.

Modems

Modems can be connected to your computer externally at the serial port or internally as a separate board. Internal modems often include fax capability. Be sure your modem is *Hayes-compatible*. The Hayes AT standard command set (named for the ATTENTION command that precedes all other commands) allows you to work with most software communications packages.

Modem speed, measured in baud, is the most important consideration. Because the multimedia files that contain the graphics, audio resources, video samples, and progressive versions of your project are usually large, you need to move as much data as possible in as short a time as possible. Today's standards dictate at least a V.34 28,800 bps modem. Transmitting at only 2400 bps, a 350KB file may take as long as 45 minutes to send, but at 28.8 Kbps, you can be done in a couple of minutes. Most modems follow the CCITT V.32 or V.42 standards that provide data compression algorithms when communicating with another similarly equipped modem. Compression saves significant transmission time and money, especially over long distance. Be sure your modem uses a standard compression system (like V.32), not a proprietary one.

According to the laws of physics, copper telephone lines and the switching equipment at the phone companies' central offices can handle modulated analog signals up to about 28,000 bps on "clean" lines. Modem manufacturers that advertise data transmission speeds higher than that (56 Kbps) are counting on their hardware-based compression algorithms to crunch the data before sending it, decompressing it upon arrival at the receiving end. If you have already compressed your data into a .SIT, .SEA, .ARC, or .ZIP file, you may not reap any benefit from the higher advertised speeds because it is difficult to compress an already-compressed file. New high-speed/high-bandwidth technologies such as DSL (described in Chapter 14) for data transmission over telephone lines are on the horizon.

First Person

Around midnight, I got a phone call from a client in Europe. His investors were meeting later that day, and he needed the project now, not in two days by DHL courier. Compressed, the code was less than a megabyte. So I went to my office and cranked up the modem, dialed the overseas phone number, and connected. The modem software estimated a total transmission time of 73 minutes, and we started the XMODEM protocols. While the little packets of data were humming out across the continent and an ocean, I made a peanut butter sandwich and kept an eye on the Bytes Remaining counter as it worked its way down in ratchets of 1,024. It was hypnotic.

Annoying spikes and glitches in the phone system had always plagued my modem calls with intermittent transmission failures that required starting over. With about four minutes to go, I began suffering hot flashes and a pounding heart, and found myself riveted to the monitor with head in hands, cheering the system on. "Don't crash now! Just a little more... Pretty please with icing! Nice baby!" All the possible scenarios of disaster paraded in front of me: a shipping calamity in the English channel would cause the transatlantic cable to break at 30 fathoms; a street cleaning truck would take out the electric power pole on the street outside; mice would chew through the antenna leads of a lonely microwave station high in the Colorado Rockies... It all seemed suddenly so fragile. But it made it!

ISDN

For higher transmission speeds, you will need to use Integrated Services Digital Network (ISDN), Switched-56, T1, T3, DSL, ATM, or another of the telephone companies' Digital Switched Network services. Connection options are discussed in greater detail in Chapter 14.

ISDN lines are popular because of their fast 128 Kbps data transfer rate—four to five times faster than the more common 28.8 Kbps analog modem. ISDN lines (and the required ISDN hardware, often misnamed "ISDN modems" even though no modulation/demodulation of the analog signal occurs) are important for Internet access, networking, and audio and video conferencing. They are more expensive than conventional analog or POTS (Plain Old Telephone Service) lines, so analyze your costs and benefits carefully before upgrading to ISDN. Newer and faster Digital Subscriber Line (DSL) technology using copper lines and promoted by the telephone companies may overtake ISDN in popularity by the year 2002.

Cable Modems

In November 1995, a consortium of cable television industry leaders announced agreement with key equipment manufacturers to specify some of the technical ways cable networks and data equipment talk with one another. 3COM, AT&T, COM21, General Instrument, Hewlett Packard, Hughes, Hybrid, IBM, Intel, LANCity, MicroUnity, Motorola, Nortel, Panasonic, Scientific Atlanta, Terrayon, Toshiba, and Zenith currently supply cable modem products. While the cable television networks cross 97 percent of property lines in North America, each local cable operator may use different equipment, wires, and software, and cable modems still remain somewhat experimental. This was a call for interoperability standards.

This international specification will take the World Wide Web a step further, bringing broadband interconnections into homes worldwide. In the next generation of modems, we look for more commonality in cable so that vendors may enjoy mass-market sales and cable customers can be assured that their devices work on TCI systems or Time Warner cable systems or any cable systems in the world.

John C. Malone, President and CEO,
Tele-Communications, Inc.

Cable modems operate at speeds 100 to 1,000 times as fast as a telephone modem, receiving data at up to 10 Mbps and sending data at speeds between 2 Mbps and 10 Mbps. They can provide not only high-bandwidth Internet access but also streaming audio and video for television viewing. Most will connect to computers with 10baseT Ethernet connectors.

Cable modems usually send and receive data asymmetrically—they receive more (faster) than they send (slower). In the downstream direction from provider to user, the data are modulated and placed on a common 6 MHz television carrier, somewhere between 42 MHz and 750 MHz. The upstream channel, or *reverse path*, from the user back to the provider is more difficult to engineer because cable is a noisy environment—with interference from HAM radio, CB radio, home appliances, loose connectors, and poor home installation. All this noise accumulates, and the overall noise increases as the signal travels upstream in the local cable network's branching tree structure, where signals from one home become mixed with the signals of hundreds, then thousands of other homes.

....

http://www.cablemodem.com

For information about cable modems

5

Multi

[
*Making good multimedia
is picking a successful route
through the software swamp.*
]

The software in your multimedia
toolkit, and your skill at using it...

test and review

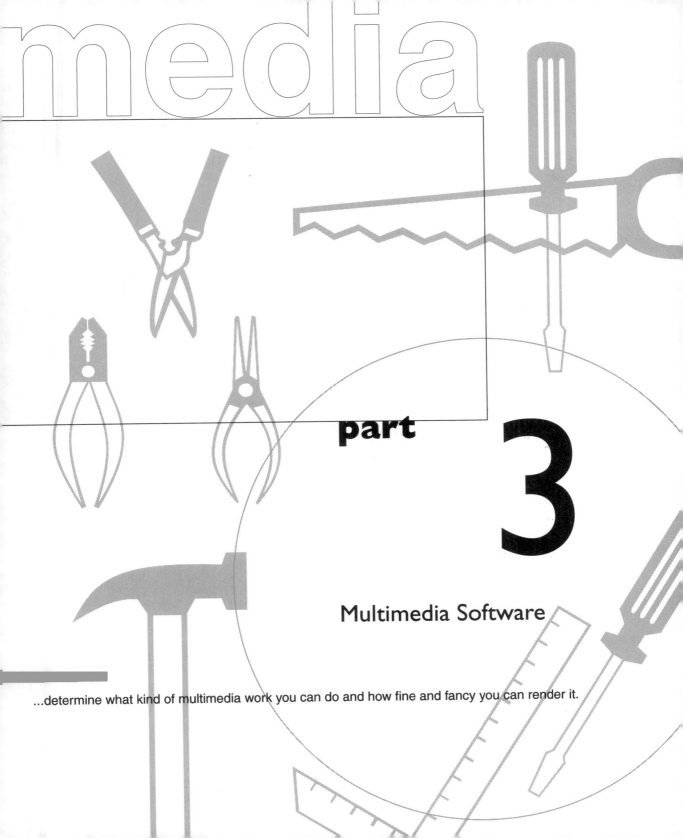

media

part

3

Multimedia Software

...determine what kind of multimedia work you can do and how fine and fancy you can render it.

Multi

Keep your software tools
sharp by upgrading them when
new features become available.

The software in your multimedia
toolkit, and your skill at using it...

test and review

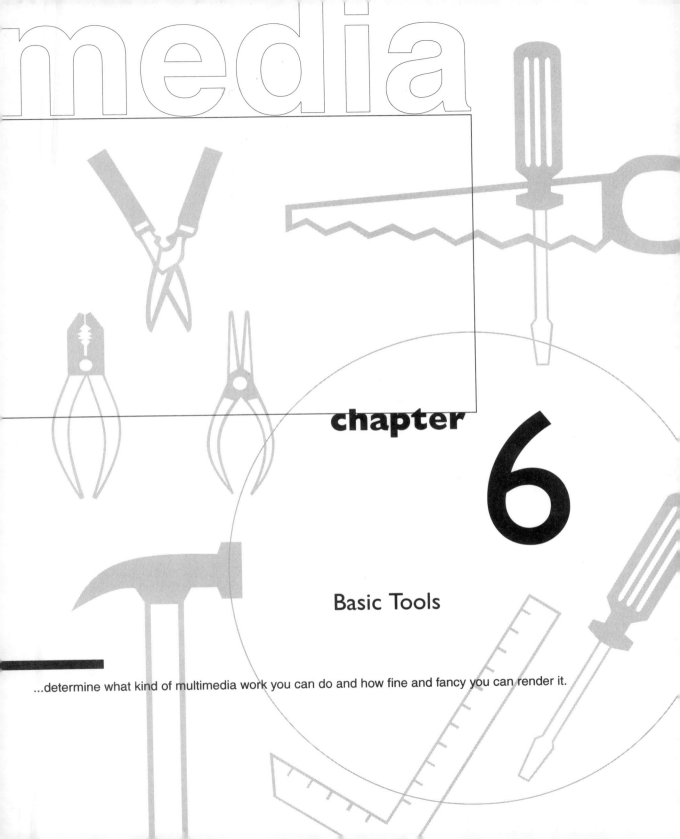

media

chapter

6

Basic Tools

...determine what kind of multimedia work you can do and how fine and fancy you can render it.

T H E basic tool set for building multimedia projects contains one or more authoring systems and various editing applications for text, images, sounds, and motion video. A few additional applications are also useful for capturing images from the screen, translating file formats, and moving files among computers when you are part of a team—these are tools for the housekeeping tasks that make your creative and production life easier. Special tools for delivering multimedia to the Internet and World Wide Web are discussed in Chapter 20.

The software in your multimedia toolkit and your skill at using it determine what kind of multimedia work you can do and how fine and fancy you can render it. Making good multimedia means picking a successful route through the software swamp. The alligators rise up out of nowhere to nip you in the knees.

Keep your tools sharp by upgrading them when new software and features become available, by thoroughly studying and learning each tool, by reading tips and tricks in the computer magazines and trade press, by keeping an eye on the conversations and FAQs (Frequently Asked Questions) files on-line and in Internet newsgroups (for example, news://comp.multimedia), and by observing the practices and products of other multimedia developers.

---

tip   *Always fill out the registration card for your new software and return it to the vendor. Or register on-line. If the vendor pays attention to product marketing, you will receive upgrade offers and often special newsletters with helpful information.*

When I left graduate school, I joined the Carpenters' Union and built highway bridges, apartment houses, and fine custom homes. The wholesale tool supply store that catered to the trade had one wall covered with more than a hundred different hammers—some for nailing big nails, some for tiny upholstery tacks, some for metal work, others with a hatchet on one side for shingles, or with a waffled striking head that would drive slick and wet nails under the roughest conditions. They all came in different weights and handle lengths and shapes. I tested a few framing hammers and chose a 24-ounce waffle-head that felt good. With it, I could drive 16d nails in a single stroke. It was a Vaughan hammer.

Next day at noon, the union steward took me aside and quietly told me that The Rules limited hammer weight to 22 ounces; the older guys couldn't keep up. My hammer was illegal, and if he saw it the next day, I'd be sent back to the hiring hall. "Sorry," I said, "jeez, I didn't know." He let me leave early so I could get to the tool store before it closed.

In producing multimedia, no tool is illegal. You should use the best tools that fit your talent, needs, and budget.

The tools used for creating and editing multimedia elements on both Macintosh and Windows platforms support the authoring systems described in Chapter 8. They do paint and image processing, image editing, drawing and illustration, 3-D and CAD, OCR and text editing, sound recording and editing, video and moviemaking, and various utilitarian housekeeping tasks.

Each new tool has a learning curve.

David Spitzer, Learning Products Engineer, Hewlett Packard

Text Editing and Word Processing Tools

A word processor is usually the first software tool computer users learn. From letters, invoices, and storyboards to project content, your word processor may also be your most often used tool, as you design and build a multimedia project. The better your *keyboarding* or typing skills, the easier and more efficient will be your multimedia day-to-day life.

Typically, an office or workgroup will choose a single word processor to share documents in a standard format. And most often, that word processor comes bundled in an "Office Suite" that might include spreadsheet, database, e-mail, Web browser, and presentation applications.

Word processors such as Word and WordPerfect are powerful applications that include spell checkers, table formatters, thesauruses, and prebuilt templates for letters, resumes, purchase orders, and other common documents. In many word processors, you can actually embed multimedia elements such as sounds, images, and video (see Chapter 7). Luckily, the population of single-finger typists is decreasing over time as children are taught typing skills in conjunction with computer lab programs in their schools.

OCR Software

Often you will have printed matter and other text to incorporate into your project, but no electronic text file. With optical character recognition (OCR) software, a flat-bed scanner, and your computer, you can save many hours of rekeying printed words, and get the job done faster and more accurately than a roomful of typists.

OCR software turns bitmapped characters into electronically recognizable ASCII text. A scanner is typically used to create the bitmap. Then the software breaks the bitmap into chunks according to whether it contains text or graphics, by examining the texture and density of areas of the bitmap and by detecting edges. The text areas of the image are then converted to ASCII characters using probability and expert system algorithms. Most OCR applications for Macintosh and Windows claim about 99 percent accuracy when reading 8- to 36-point characters at 300 dpi and can reach processing speeds of about 150 characters per second.

Figure 6-1 shows a document in the process of bitmap-to-character conversion by OmniPage Pro from Caere. Notice the small box that displays an image of the actual section of the 300 dpi bitmap currently being analyzed. With this software, the formatting and layout of the original document can be recognized and imported into Microsoft Word with styles that maintain bolding and font size.

Painting and Drawing Tools

Painting and drawing tools, as well as 3-D modelers, are perhaps the most important items in your toolkit because, of all the multimedia elements, the

FIGURE 6-1

OmniPage Pro and

other OCR

software can save

you many hours

of typing
■

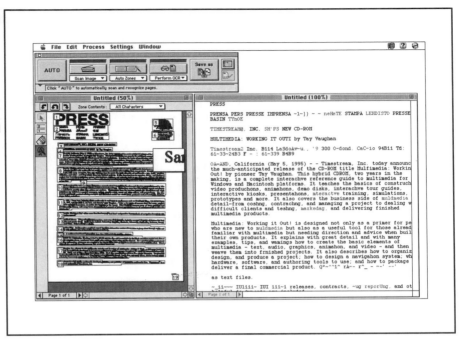

6

graphical impact of your project will likely have the greatest influence on the end user. If your artwork is amateurish, or flat and uninteresting, both you and your users will be disappointed. Look in Chapter 15 for tips on designing effective graphical screens and in Chapter 11 for more about computer graphics.

Painting software, such as Photoshop, PicturePublisher, and Fractal Design Painter, is dedicated to producing crafted bitmap images. Drawing software, such as CorelDraw, FreeHand, Illustrator, Designer, and Canvas, is dedicated to producing vector-based line art easily printed to paper using PostScript or another page markup system such as QuickDraw on the Macintosh.

Some software applications combine drawing and painting capabilities, but many authoring systems can import only bitmapped images. The differences between painting and drawing (that is, between bitmapped and drawn images) are described in Chapter 11. Typically, bitmapped images provide the greatest choice and power to the artist for rendering fine detail and effects, and today bitmaps are used in multimedia more often than drawn objects. This may change as new vector-based packages (such as Macromedia's Flash) take hold, aimed at reducing file download times on the Web. The anti-aliased character shown in the bitmap of Color Plate 5 is an example of the fine touches that improve the look of an image.

Look for the following features in a drawing or painting package.

- An intuitive graphical user interface with pull-down menus, status bars, palette control, and dialog boxes for quick, logical selection

- Scalable dimensions, so you can resize, stretch, and distort both large and small bitmaps

- Paint tools to create geometric shapes, from squares to circles and from curves to complex polygons

- Ability to pour a color, pattern, or gradient into any area

- Ability to paint with patterns and clip art

- Customizable pen and brush shapes and sizes

- Eyedropper tool that samples colors

- Autotrace tool that turns bitmap shapes into vector-based outlines

- Support for scalable text fonts and drop shadows

- Multiple undo capabilities, to let you try again

- Painting features such as smoothing coarse-edged objects into the background with anti-aliasing (see Color Plate 5); airbrushing in variable sizes, shapes, densities, and patterns; washing colors in gradients; blending; and masking

- Support for third-party special effect plug-ins.

- Object and layering capabilities that allow you to treat separate elements independently

- Zooming, for magnified pixel editing

- All common color depths: 1-, 4-, 8-, and 16-, 24-, or 32-bit color, and gray-scale

- Good color management and dithering capability among color depths using various color models such as RGB, HSB, and CMYK

- Good palette management when in 8-bit mode

- Good file importing and exporting capability for image formats such as PIC, GIF, TGA, TIF, WMF, JPG, PCX, EPS, PTN, and BMP

If you are new to multimedia and to these tools, you should take time to examine more than one graphics software package. Find someone who is already familiar with graphics applications. You will spend many days learning to use your painting and drawing software, and if it does not fit you and your needs, you will be unhappy. Many artists learn to use a single, powerful tool well.

First Person

During the early 1980s, I founded an accredited maritime school at Pier 66 in San Francisco, and we offered courses in everything from high-tech composite plastics and welding to Rules of the Road and celestial navigation. We also ran several marine trade certification programs. When I talked with Ford, General Motors, Cummins, and Caterpillar about setting up a course for marine diesel mechanics, I was surprised at their competitive interest in supporting the program. It turned out that a widely publicized survey had shown that a mechanic trained to work on a particular brand of engine will stick with it for life, loyally recommending and supporting that brand.

The same holds true for software. By the time you master an application, you have spent many hours on its learning curve. You will likely stay with that product and its upgrade path rather than change to another.

3-D Modeling and Animation Tools

3-D modeling software has increasingly entered the mainstream of graphic design as its ease of use improves. As a result, the graphic production values and expectations for multimedia projects have risen. With 3-D modeling software, objects rendered in perspective appear more realistic; you can create stunning scenes and wander through them, choosing just the right lighting and perspective for your final rendered image. Powerful modeling packages such as Macromedia's Extreme 3D, AutoDesk's 3D Studio Max, StrataVision's 3D, Specular's LogoMotion and Infini-D, and Caligari's trueSpace are also bundled with assortments of prerendered 3-D clip art objects such as people, furniture, buildings, cars, airplanes, trees, and plants. Specialized applications for creating and animating 3-D text are discussed in Chapter 9. Important for multimedia developers, many 3-D modeling applications also include export features enabling you to save a moving view or journey through your scene as a QuickTime or AVI animation file. Figure 6-2 shows a simple architectural floor plan rendered to 3-D perspective by MiniCAD.

Each rendered 3-D image takes from a few seconds to a few hours to complete, depending upon the complexity of the drawing and the number of drawn objects included in it (see Chapter 11 for more about rendering). If you are making a complex walk-through or flyby, plan to set aside many hours of rendering time on your computer.

tip *If there are small errors or things you would like to change in a rendered movie sequence, it may take less time to edit each frame of the affected sequence by hand, using an image-editing program, than to rerender the corrected original.*

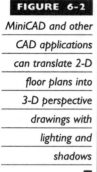

FIGURE 6-2

MiniCAD and other

CAD applications

can translate 2-D

floor plans into

3-D perspective

drawings with

lighting and

shadows

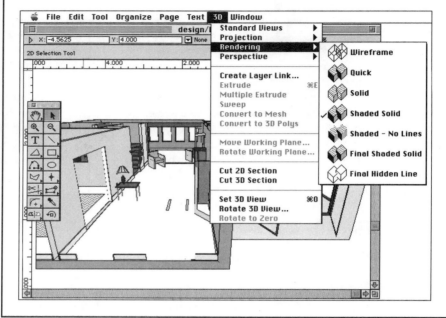

A good 3-D modeling tool should include the following features:

- Multiple windows that allow you to view your model in each dimension, from the camera's perspective, and in a rendered preview

- Ability to drag and drop primitive shapes into a scene

- Ability to create and sculpt organic objects from scratch with Bezier spline drawing tools

- Lathe and extrude features

- Color and texture mapping

- Ability to add realistic effects such as transparency, shadowing, and fog

- Ability to add spot, local, and global lights, to place them anywhere, and manipulate them for special lighting effects

- Unlimited cameras with focal length control

- Ability to draw spline-based paths for animation

Image-Editing Tools

Image-editing applications are specialized and powerful tools for enhancing and retouching existing bitmapped images. These applications also provide many of the features and tools of painting and drawing programs and can be used to create images from scratch as well as images digitized from scanners, video frame-grabbers, digital cameras, clip art files, or original artwork files created with a painting or drawing package.

---

tip *If you want to print an image to a 300 dpi laser printer for collateral reports and attractive print-matter icons, work with the image in the image-editing application at 300 dpi in black and white (every black pixel will be a very fine laser printer dot). Then resize the image to one-fourth its size (leaving the resolution set at 300 dpi), and save it as a PICT or TIFF file for importing into your word processor. The result is a finely detailed black-and-white picture printed at the highest resolution of your laser printer.*

Here are some features typical of image-editing applications and of interest to multimedia developers:

- Multiple windows provide views of more than one image at a time

- Conversion of major image-data types and industry-standard file formats

- Direct inputs of images from scanner and video sources

- Employment of a virtual memory scheme that uses hard disk space as RAM for images that require large amounts of memory

- Capable selection tools, such as rectangles, lassos, and magic wands, to select portions of a bitmap

- Image and balance controls for brightness, contrast, and color balance

- Good masking features

- Multiple undo and restore features

- Anti-aliasing capability, and sharpening and smoothing controls

- Color-mapping controls for precise adjustment of color balance

- Tools for retouching, blurring, sharpening, lightening, darkening, smudging, and tinting

- Geometric transformations such as flip, skew, rotate, and distort, and perspective changes

- Ability to resample and resize an image

- 24-bit color, 8- or 4-bit indexed color, 8-bit gray-scale, black-and-white, and customizable color palettes

- Ability to create images from scratch, using line, rectangle, square, circle, ellipse, polygon, airbrush, paintbrush, pencil, and eraser tools, with customizable brush shapes and user-definable bucket and gradient fills

- Multiple typefaces, styles, and sizes, and type manipulation and masking routines

- Filters for special effects, such as crystallize, dry brush, emboss, facet, fresco, graphic pen, mosaic, pixelize, poster, ripple, smooth, splatter, stucco, twirl, watercolor, wave, and wind (see Color Plate 7)

- Support for third-party special effect plug-ins

- Ability to design in layers that can be combined, hidden, and reordered

Plug-ins

Image-editing programs usually support powerful plug-in modules available from third-party developers that allow you to warp, twist, shadow, cut, diffuse, and otherwise "filter" your images for special visual effects. Adobe's Gallery Effects offers an assortment of special effects to transform images. Vertigo's HotTEXT lets you turn text into 3-D objects (see Figure 9-17 in Chapter 9). EyeCandy from AlienSkin Software offers a comprehensive set of filters (Figure 6-3a shows the Cutout filter in action). The PhotoTools suite from Extensis lets you quickly add drop shadows, bevels, and embossing effects. Kai's Power Tools from MetaTools (see Figure 6-3b) offers special effects and has powerful built-in algorithms for making fractal images. With Xaos Tools' Paint Alchemy (see Figure 6-3c), you can texture your images with special brushes. The special effects available in these plug-ins make image editing fun!

a

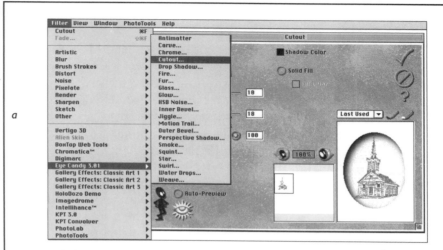

b

c

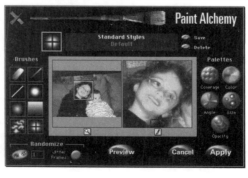

Sound Editing Tools

Sound editing tools for both digitized and MIDI sound let you see music as well as hear it. By drawing a representation of a sound in fine increments, whether a score or a waveform, you can cut, copy, paste, and otherwise edit segments of it with great precision—something impossible to do in real-time (that is, with the music playing). The basics of computerized sound for both the Macintosh and Windows environments are discussed in Chapter 10.

System sounds are shipped with both Macintosh and Windows systems (see Figure 10-1 in Chapter 10), and they are available as soon as you install the operating system. System sounds are the beeps used to indicate an error, warning, or special user activity. Using sound editing software, you can make your own sound effects and install them as system beeps, to the delight (or perhaps dismay) of colleagues and neighbors.

For digital waveform sounds, Windows ships with the Sound Recorder program, which provides some rudimentary features for sound editing. Most sound boards for PCs, however, include editing software such as Creative Labs' (makers of Sound Blaster hardware) WaveStudio, shown in Figure 6-4. The Macintosh does not ship with sound editing tools, so Macintosh users need to invest in an editor such as SoundEdit 16 from Macromedia.

FIGURE 6-4

WaveStudio is a simple waveform editor that ships with Creative Labs' Sound Blaster hardware

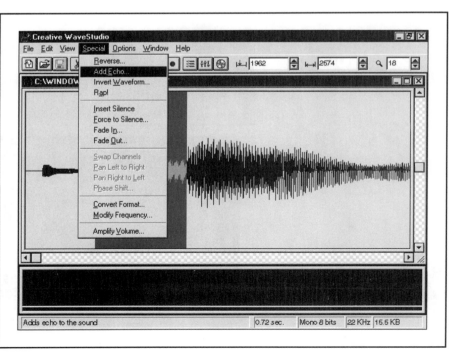

Although you can usually incorporate MIDI sound files into your multimedia project without learning any special skills, using editing tools to make your own MIDI files requires that you understand the way music is sequenced, scored, and published; see Chapter 10 for details. You need to know about tempos, clefs, notations, keys, and instruments. And you will need a MIDI synthesizer or device connected to your computer. Many MIDI applications provide both sequencing and notation capabilities, and some, such as Alchemy (see Figure 6-5) and AudioTrax, let you edit both digital audio and MIDI within the same application.

Animation, Video, and Digital Movie Tools

Animations and digital video movies are sequences of bitmapped graphic scenes (*frames*), rapidly played back. But animations can also be made within the authoring system by rapidly changing the location of *objects* or *sprites* to generate an appearance of motion. Most authoring tools adopt either a frame- or object-oriented approach to animation, but rarely both (see Chapter 12 for more about animation).

6

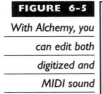

FIGURE 6-5

With Alchemy, you can edit both digitized and MIDI sound

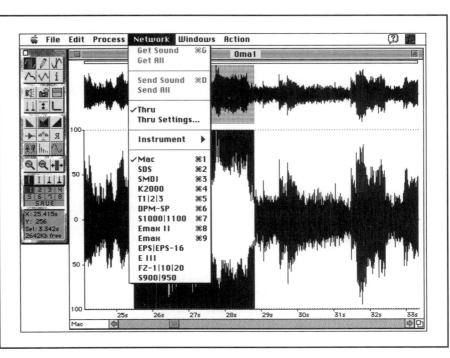

Moviemaking tools take advantage of QuickTime (Macintosh and Windows) and Microsoft Video for Windows (also known as AVI, or Audio Video Interleaved, available for Windows only) technology and let you create, edit, and present digitized motion video segments, usually in a small window in your project.

To make movies from video, you need special hardware to convert the analog video signal to digital data (see Chapter 13). Moviemaking tools such as Premiere, VideoShop, and MediaStudio Pro let you edit and assemble video clips captured from camera, tape, other digitized movie segments, animations, scanned images, and from digitized audio or MIDI files. The completed clip, often with added transition and visual effects, can then be played back—either stand-alone or windowed within your project.

Morphing is an animation technique that allows you to dynamically blend two still images, creating a sequence of in-between pictures that, when played back rapidly in QuickTime, metamorphoses the first image into the second. A racing car transforms itself into a tiger; a mother's face becomes her daughter's.

Video Formats

Formats and systems for storing and playing digitized video to and from disk files are available with QuickTime (from Apple, but QuickTime works on both Windows and Macintosh computers) and AVI (or Microsoft's Audio Video Interleaved, which works only on Windows computers). Both systems depend on special algorithms that control the amount of information per video frame that is sent to the screen, as well as the rate at which new frames are displayed. Currently, neither technology provides high-quality full-screen images at 30 frames per second (NTSC television standard) without the aid of special add-on boards; neither the PC nor the Macintosh have the processing horsepower yet.

Both technologies provide a methodology for *interleaving* or blending audio data with video data so that sound remains synchronized with the video. And both technologies allow data to stream from disk into memory in a buffered and organized manner.

QuickTime is an organizer of time-related data in many forms. Classic videotape involves a video track with two tracks of audio; QuickTime is a multitrack recorder in which you can have an almost unlimited range of tracks. Digitized video, digitized sound, computer animations, MIDI data, external devices such as CD-ROM players and hard disks, and even the potential for interactive command systems are all supported by the QuickTime format. With QuickTime, you can have a movie with five different available languages, titles, MIDI cue tracks, or the potential for interactive commands.

In Windows, the Media Control Interface (MCI) is a more traditional organizing vehicle. MCI provides a uniform command interface for managing audio and video that interleaves audio and video together in the file, hence the Audio Video Interleaved name for the technology. MCI is discussed in greater detail in Chapter 5.

The QuickTime and Microsoft Video for Windows (AVI) formats are discussed in greater detail below.

QuickTime for Windows and Macintosh

The heart of QuickTime is a software-based *architecture* for seamlessly integrating sound, text, animation, and video (data that changes over time) on Macintosh and Windows platforms. QuickTime is also used to deliver multimedia to the World Wide Web as a plug-in for Netscape and Internet Explorer. On the Web, QuickTime can deliver 3-D animation, real-time special effects, virtual reality, and streaming video and audio. QuickTime is discussed in this chapter about tools because, while it is not an "authoring tool," nor a video, image, sound, or text editor, its role as a powerful cross-platform integrator of multimedia objects and formats makes it a tool upon which multimedia developers depend. The QuickTime file format is the starting point for the new MPEG-4 Intermedia Format (see Chapter 13).

QuickTime Building Blocks

Three elements make up QuickTime:

■ QuickTime movie file format
■ QuickTime Media Abstraction Layer
■ QuickTime media services

The movie file format is a container that provides a standard method for storing video, audio, and even text descriptions about a media composition. The Media Abstraction Layer describes how your computer should access the media that is included in the QuickTime movie. The media services part of QuickTime not only has built-in support for over 35 media file formats, including most major video, still image, audio, animation, and MIDI formats, but also allows developers to plug in their own new or custom media formats. Remember, QuickTime is an architecture, a system for multimedia delivery, and is extensible.

QuickTime 3 Pro is a necessary upgrade to the free QuickTime package so you can do more than simply play back movies. The upgrade contains two applications. Movie Player (see Figure 6-6) lets you import and combine over 30 different file formats. You can compress them into deliverable multimedia projects using the Sorenson Video and QDesign audio compressors so they will stream from any Internet-ready Web server. With built-in filters in Movie Player, you can adjust colors, contrast, and brightness, and you can apply special effects to your composition, such as film noise and edge detection. The Picture Viewer application is used for viewing and converting images among many standard image-file formats, including Photoshop's native format.

QuickTime includes built-in support for ten different media types (video, audio, text, timecode, music/MIDI, sprite/animation, tween, MPEG, VR, 3D) and offers a comprehensive set of "services," such as:

- Timing and synchronization
- Audio and image data compression and decompression
- Image blitting, format conversion, scaling, composition, and transcoding
- Audio mixing, sample rate conversion, and format conversion
- Audio and video effects and transitions
- Synchronized storage read and write
- Media capture
- Media import and export
- Standard user interface elements, such as movie controllers, media previewers, and media capture dialogs

QuickTime Embedded Commands for HTML

When delivering QuickTime projects on the World Wide Web, you can embed powerful commands into your HTML documents that control and fine-tune the display of your QuickTime file:

- AUTOPLAY starts a movie playing automatically
- BGCOLOR sets a background color for the movie display
- CACHE indicates whether the movie should be cached (Netscape Navigator 3.0 or later)
- CONTROLLER specifies whether to display the QuickTime movie controller bar

- HEIGHT and WIDTH specify size of the movie in Web pages
- HIDDEN allows sound-only movies to play in the background without affecting the look of a Web page
- HREF indicates which URL to link to when the movie is clicked
- LOOP loops movie playback automatically
- SCALE scales the movie display automatically
- TARGET provides a frame target for the URL specified in an HREF tag
- VOLUME sets the default playback volume

In addition, QuickTime has the following VR commands:

- CORRECTION specifies an image correction mode
- FOV sets the initial field-of-view angle
- NODE sets the initial node
- PAN sets the initial pan angle
- TILT sets the initial tilt angle

Microsoft Video for Windows

Audio Video Interleaved (AVI) is a Microsoft-developed format for playing full-motion interleaved video and audio sequences in Windows, without specialized hardware, at about 15 frames per second in a small

FIGURE 6-6

QuickTime's Movie Player for Windows and AVI's Media Player can play back video clips

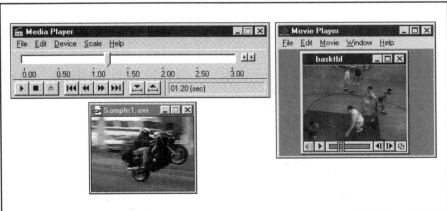

window. Video data are interleaved with audio data within the file that contains the motion sequence, so the audio portion of the movie remains synchronized to the video portion. With acceleration hardware, you can run AVI video sequences at 30 frames per second.

The AVI file format is not an extensible, "open" environment and lacks features needed for serious video editing environments. To improve this situation, a group of interested companies recently created the OpenDML file format to make AVI more useful for the professional market. But because QuickTime works with OpenDML files and delivers on both Macintosh and Windows platforms and across the Web, look for a growing number of neat multimedia projects housed in a QuickTime container.

Like Apple's QuickTime, AVI provides the following features:

- Playback from hard disk or CD-ROM

- Playback on computers with limited memory; data are streamed from the hard disk or CD-ROM player without using great amounts of memory

- Quick loading and playing, because only a few frames of video and a portion of audio are accessed at a time

- Video compression to boost the quality of your video sequences and reduce their size

AVI includes two tools to capture and edit video sequences and play them back: VidCap and VidEdit, respectively. AVI also includes data preparation tools (BitEdit, PalEdit, and WaveEdit); MCIAVI.DRV, the MCI driver for AVI; Media Player (see Figure 6-6); and sample video sequences.

Movie Editors

With the invention of QuickTime and Video for Windows, desktop video publishing (DVP) on Macintoshes and PCs became a digital process (see Chapter 13 for a discussion of the analog process). Improved compression and decompression techniques allow quarter-, half-, and full-screen/full-motion movies instead of the small, 160×120-pixel-sized movies characteristic of earlier digital video experiments.

With desktop editing software and an appropriate video digitizing board, you can digitize video clips, edit the clip off-line, add special effects and titles, mix sound tracks, and save the finished product as a digital file on magnetic or optical media.

Video digitizing boards for making Macintosh QuickTime movies from videotape are available from RasterOps, Radius, Fast, and others. The Targa board from TrueVision, VideoBlaster from Creative Labs, Super Video Windows SL from New Media Graphics, and other boards are available for making AVI movies for Windows.

Specialized video editors have been designed around this technology for both the Macintosh and PC environments—for example, AVID's VideoShop, Fast's VideoMachine, Adobe's Premiere, Asymetrix's Digital Video Producer, and Ulead's Media-Studio Pro (see Chapter 13). These applications let you mix video clips, audio recordings, animation, still images, and graphics to create QuickTime or AVI movies. You arrange your clips linearly, cutting and pasting and layering them into transitions with special effects such as dissolves, page turns, spins, tinting, distorting, and replicating. A familiar push-button control panel is used for stop, rewind, play, fast-forward, record and single-stop, and these applications display time references, frame counts, and audio and transparency levels.

Figure 6-7 shows a movie being edited in Premiere, with visual effects and sounds. Adobe's After Effects is a powerful addition to the video editing suite, with sophisticated tools for combining digital video, audio, and images into fully controlled time-based projects. Special video plug-ins for After Effects that will make your movies look truly professional are available from AlienSkin.

6

---

warning   *Digital video editing and playback requires an immense amount of free disk space, even when the video files are compressed.*

---

tip   *Because digital movie data must stream rapidly and without interruption from your disk drive, be sure that you defragment and optimize your disk with a utility such as Norton's Speed Disk before recording and playing back your movie files. If your movie file is fragmented, the read head of the disk drive may need to pause sending data while it physically moves to wildly different locations on the disk; a defragmented file lets the head read sequentially from one adjoining sector to the next.*

Compressing Movie Files

Image compression algorithms are critical to the delivery of motion video and audio on both the Macintosh and PC platforms. Without compression, there is simply not enough bandwidth on the Macintosh or PC to transfer the massive amounts of data involved in displaying a new screen image every 1/30 of a second. A compression ratio of 5:1 allows use of CD-ROM players to deliver streamed images at transfer rates of 150K per second (see Chapter 13); higher ratios allow transmission of video images over telephone lines.

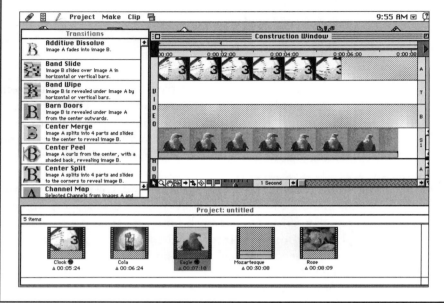

To understand compression, consider these three basic concepts:

■ *Compression ratio*: The compression ratio represents the size of the original image divided by the size of the compressed image—that is, how much the data are actually compressed. Some compression schemes yield ratios that are dependent on the image content: a busy image of a field of multicolored tulips may yield a very small compression ratio, and an image of blue ocean and sky may yield a very high compression ratio. Video compression typically manages only the part of an image that changes from image to image (the *delta*).

■ *Image quality*: Compression is either lossy or lossless. *Lossy* schemes ignore picture information the viewer may not miss, but that means the picture information is in fact lost—even after decompression. And as more and more information is removed during compression, image quality decreases. *Lossless* schemes preserve the original data precisely—an important consideration in medical imaging, for example. The compression ratio typically affects picture quality because, usually, the higher the compression ratio, the lower the quality of the decompressed image.

■ *Compression/decompression speed:* You will prefer a fast compression time while developing your project. Users, on the other hand, will appreciate a fast decompression time to increase display performance.

Helpful Accessories

No multimedia toolkit is complete without a few indispensable utilities to perform some odd, but oft-repeated, tasks. These are the comfortable and well-worn accessories that make your computer life easier.

On both the Macintosh and in Windows, a screen-grabber is essential. Because bitmapped images are so common in multimedia, it is important to have a tool for grabbing all or part of the screen display so you can import it into your authoring system or copy it into an image-editing application. Screen-grabbing to the Clipboard, for example, lets you move a bitmapped image from one application to another without the cumbersome steps of first exporting the image to a file and then importing it back into the destination application. Figure 6-8 shows dialog boxes from Capture (for the Macintosh) and SnapPro and Hijaak 95's Capture (for Windows). These tools let

6

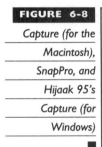
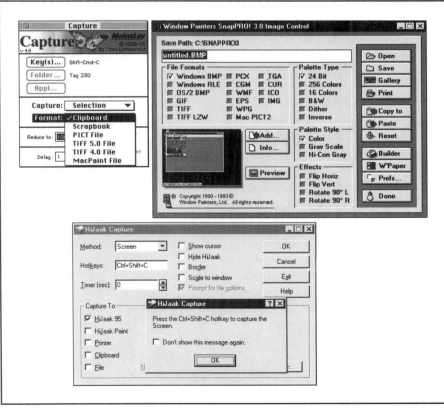

FIGURE 6-8

Capture (for the Macintosh), SnapPro, and Hijaak 95's Capture (for Windows)

you grab screen images and save them on the Clipboard or in optional PICT, TIFF, or other file formats.

Format converters are another indispensable tool for projects in which your source material may originate on Macintoshes, PCs, Unix workstations, Amigas, or even mainframes. This is an issue particularly with image files, because there are many formats and many compression schemes. Figure 6-9 illustrates deBabelizer, an image converter and editor from Equilibrium Technologies that also automates batch processing. For the PC, two image converters include Image Alchemy from Handmade Software and HiJaak 95's Convert from Quarterdeck.

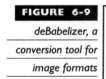

FIGURE 6-9

deBabelizer, a conversion tool for image formats

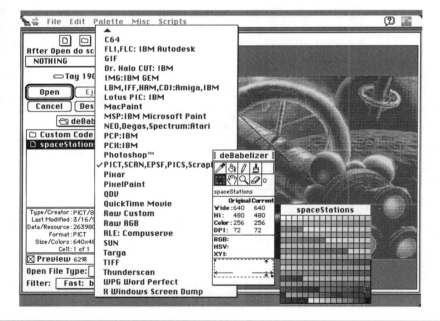

Multi

[
Common desktop presentation
tools are becoming more
multimedia powerful ...
]

sound and **animation**

media

In another few years,

most personal computers sold will be able to
produce at least the sound and animation elements of multimedia.

chapter

7

Making Instant Multimedia

T HERE is no reason to buy a dedicated multimedia authoring package if your current software (or an inexpensive upgrade) can do the job. Indeed, not only can you save money by doing multimedia with tools that are familiar and already at hand, but you also save the time spent on arduous and sometimes lengthy learning curves involved in mastering many dedicated authoring systems. Common desktop presentation tools have become multi-media powerful, while dedicated multimedia authoring systems are offering simplified, easy-to-use versions (see Chapter 8).

Most personal computers sold today are able to produce at least the sound and animation elements of multimedia. Manufacturers of popular software for word processing, spreadsheets, database management, graphing, draw-ing, and presentation have added capabilities for sound, image, and anima-tion to their products. You can call a voice annotation, picture, or QuickTime or AVI movie from most word processing applications. You can click a cell in a spreadsheet to enhance its content with graphic images, sounds, and animations. Your database can include pictures, audio clips, and movies. Your presentation software can easily generate interesting titles, visual effects, and animated illustrations for your product demo. With these multimedia-enhanced software packages, you get many more ways to effec-tively convey your message than just a slide show.

To enliven your material and provide interesting illustrations, you can add multimedia elements to familiar tools such as word-processed docu-ments, spreadsheets, presentation aids, and even HTML documents. But where do you get these elements? You can either make your images, sounds, and animations from scratch, or you can import them from collections of clip media. You can also license rights to use resources or content, such as pictures, songs and music, and video, from their owners. Importing from stock material limits you somewhat, but it may be all you need, and these collections can yield quick and simple multimedia productions. If you make your multimedia elements from scratch or edit existing material, you'll need to have special software and hardware tools to customize the images, sounds, and animations, but the results are more spectacular and dramatic.

---

warning   *You need special multimedia tools for digitizing your sounds and creating animations and movies before you can attach these objects to your word, data, or presentation documents. These tools are discussed in Chapter 6.*

Some multimedia projects may be so simple that you can cram all the organizing, planning, rendering, and testing stages into a single effort, making "instant" multimedia.

Here is an example: The topic at your weekly sales meeting is sales force performance. You want to display your usual spreadsheet so the group can see real names and numbers for each member of the team; then you want to show a multicolored 3-D bar graph for visual impact. Preparing for your meeting, you annotate the cell containing the name of the most productive salesperson for the week, using sounds of applause taken from a public-domain CD-ROM, or a recording of your CEO saying "Good job!" or a colleague's "Wait till next week, Pete!" At the appropriate time during the meeting, you click that cell and play the annotation. And that's it—you have just made and used instant multimedia.

The following overviews do not include all products in each category of software tools, but they will give you a good sense of how multimedia might be applied in your everyday life working with computers. You will also find some tips and advice on using them in your multimedia projects.

Linking Multimedia Objects

The elements of multimedia (and other digitized information) are often treated as discrete *objects* that have particular characteristics or *properties*. With objects described in a common format using object-oriented programming systems (OOPs), text, bitmapped images, sounds, and video clips can be dynamically linked among applications and documents or even embedded in them. This object-oriented approach to information management is supported on both Macintosh and Windows platforms and is utilized at the core of some multimedia authoring systems (see Chapter 8).

AppleEvents

On the Macintosh, AppleEvents lets applications communicate with each other, sharing data and commands. InterApplication Communication (IAC) works with AppleEvents to automatically update documents that are linked with the "publish-and-subscribe" features of AppleEvents.

When you *publish* an application and then edit the data in it, the changes you make are copied to all of the *subscribers* to that data, even across a network. Publish-and-subscribe uses a transition file called the *edition file*.

You can *subscribe* to a spreadsheet table in a word processing document, for example, and when you change the spreadsheet, the word processing document gets changed automatically. Or you can embed a PICT image or QuickTime file in one application and change it in another, and the changes will appear in both applications—the two applications talk directly to each other.

To use publish-and-subscribe, follow these steps:

1. Select data that you want to place into another application or document.

2. From the Edit menu, choose Create Publisher. This brings up a dialog box asking you to name the edition file that will connect the publisher to the other documents subscribing to the data.

3. After you have created the edition file, go to the document or application where you want to use the data and select Subscribe To... from the Edit menu.

Now you have placed a *live* copy of the data in your document; whenever you modify the original publisher data, the subscriber is automatically updated, too.

DDE and OLE

Dynamic Data Exchange (DDE) and *Object Linking and Embedding* (OLE, pronounced "olay") are two methods for linking data objects among Windows applications. For example, let's say you want to advertise your new mousetrap design with a flashy graphic—an illustration showing your mousetrap compared to other mousetraps on the market—and some text describing its extraordinary features. First, you make a colorful picture in a graphics application such as Micrografx Designer, then you create a bar chart comparing the number of mice in a spreadsheet program such as Excel, and finally, you paste all your elements into a word processor such as Microsoft Word.

---

cross platform   *QuickTime for Windows supports OLE, so QuickTime movies made on the Macintosh can be integrated into Windows applications that support OLE.*

When two applications share data through DDE, they are in a *conversation*. DDE allows data to be transmitted between a *client* (the application that initiates the conversation) and a *server* (the application responding to the client). Data can be transmitted as a *hot link* so that modifications in the server application are also updated in the client application, or as a *cold link* so that data in the client application remain independent of the server after it has been imported.

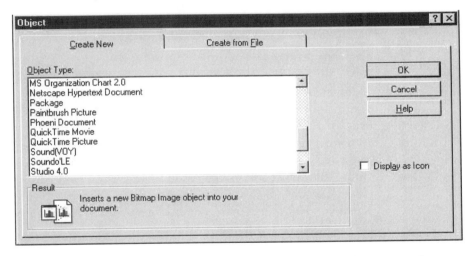

OLE lets you embed or link data objects created in different Windows or Macintosh applications. An *embedded* object becomes a part of the file into which it is pasted, independent of the original application where it was created. A *linked* object, on the other hand, is changed automatically in a *container* file that *points* to the original file when the original file is updated. Linking is a useful feature for data that may be modified after it has been placed into other files.

---

warning   *Using OLE, make sure that your linked files aren't moved to other directories, or the links may be broken. OLE 2.0 (and later versions) have improved the ability to track links between containers and objects, but the best way to ensure that your object isn't "lost" is to embed it in a file.*

Office Suites

Office suites integrate into a single package the various productivity tools essential to running a business. Suites offer the convenience of a common interface with similar menus, commands, and toolbars, and they also allow you to share data among the applications in that suite using OLE and DDE. Suites also provide compatibility across the Macintosh and Windows platforms. Microsoft Office, for example, contains Word for word processing; Excel, a spreadsheet program, PowerPoint for creating presentations; and for Windows, a database manager (Access) and a scheduler. Each program is a stand-alone application, but all are interlinked through OLE and DDE. Claris's ClarisWorks for Macintosh and Windows provides a word processor, spreadsheet program, database manager, presentation tool, drawing/painting tool, and communications software in one application. Works offers seamless cross-platform file sharing between Macintosh and Windows platforms.

Word Processors

Many word-processed documents are ultimately printed to paper, but many are also delivered on a server or floppy disk, to an electronic mailbox, or as HTML documents on the World Wide Web. If others will be viewing your document on a computer, consider attaching multimedia voice notes, pictures, or animated illustrations to emphasize your point or to clarify something that is difficult to express in words. The "First Person" in this chapter illustrates the use of multimedia elements (in this case, QuickTime graphics) embedded into the working draft of a manuscript. The manuscript is shown, as are the graphics, along with a note to the editor.

Word

Microsoft's Word for Macintosh and Windows provides essentially the same user interface on both platforms and offers special multimedia features. You can make and import various image formats, including PICT, TIFF, BMP, and EPS, to place them in your document. You can add QuickTime movies to your document (see Figure 7-1); control the movie's playback characteristics (forward, backward, start, and stop); and perform simple editing with cut, copy, and paste commands. In the Windows version, AVI movies can also be played within your Word document. You can import digitized sounds, and you can record voice comments from an internal microphone, saving the recording (with a portion of the text or an icon as an identifier) for playback. Annotations can be searched for sound effects and content, edited, and even saved as separate files in any of four formats. With Word for Windows, you can also create links to other programs using OLE. Figure 7-2 demonstrates graphic chart information derived from an Excel spreadsheet linked to a Word document.

First Person

Working draft of Chapter 4, revision 2, reads:

My father said that Mommy was still in a coma and my little brother was sleeping. We should go home now. So we went out the back way to the physician's parking lot: down the elevator and past the noisy kitchen with its racks of trays, white-uniformed cooks, piles of canned goods, and the steamy smells of institutional stew. The green screen door slammed indelibly into my five-year-old memory, and the attendant waved to my dad; he probably didn't know we were there on family business. It was all pretty serious.

We found Mommy's car behind the police station. I stayed in my seat while my father got out and walked very slowly around the twisted metal. He was calculating the impact forces, visualizing the accident in slow-motion freeze frames, and at one point, he leaned in through the broken glass and ran his hand across the dent in the steel glove compartment where my brother had smashed his face. He went around only the one time, then got back in. "She must have been doing about forty when she hit the pole," he offered as if I were an adult, and we drove out the narrow circular drive alongside the station house. It was a crisp, clear, football-and-pumpkins Saturday afternoon in October.

Editorial note to Sally: Per your comment last week, pick a good illustration from the file of images that I have attached. One of them should fit the bill.... Thanks! See you next week.

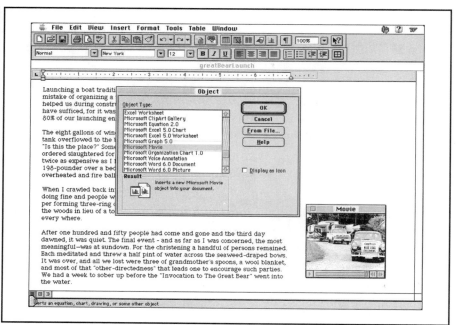

FIGURE 7-1

Microsoft Word

imports multimedia

elements

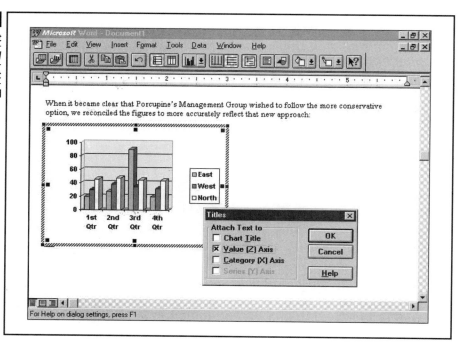

FIGURE 7-2

An Excel chart

linked into a Word

document

WordPerfect

In Corel's WordPerfect Macintosh version, a tool palette and drawing commands allow you to create and edit graphics with the standard Macintosh drawing tools, as well as create Bezier curves and polygons; there's also a free rotation tool. A color editor lets you blend, rainbow, and complement colors. You can edit, size, scale, and crop graphic images, and then click and drag them anywhere in your document while text automatically reformats around them.

WordPerfect for Macintosh offers a QuickTime movie-playing facility (see Figure 7-3). The movie is represented by its poster, usually the first frame of the movie. You can represent your movie as a character, anchor it to a page or paragraph, move it, add a caption, or put a frame around it, just as you can with graphics. There is a movie controller that gives you many options, such as custom playback or changing the poster.

7

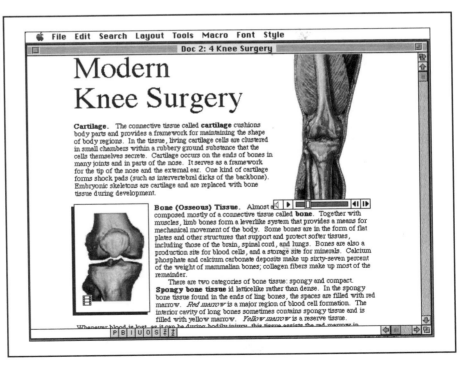

FIGURE 7-3

WordPerfect for Macintosh provides a QuickTime player

tip   *For voice annotation in WordPerfect, you can put sounds and voice into the audio track of a QuickTime movie, and they will play back just fine.*

Using DDE, WordPerfect for Windows can share data with other DDE-compatible programs that use DDE links. If the data changed in a linked program, they are automatically updated in the WordPerfect document. A figure editor makes it easy to add graphics to your documents. You can view, retrieve, create, modify, and size figures, and save or import them into your document. WordPerfect for Windows works with the common graphic formats for DOS, as well as Windows metafiles and bitmaps.

Word Pro

With its Windows DDE and OLE capabilities, Word Pro (formerly Ami Pro) from Lotus can link to other applications and embedded objects, such as sounds and AVI movies. Using DDE, you can paste a link in Windows bitmap or metafile format into an empty selected frame. You can even create a macro to control another application through DDE. With OLE, you can link or embed objects into a frame in a Word Pro document (see Figure 7-4).

FIGURE 7-4

Word Pro from Lotus is multimedia enhanced

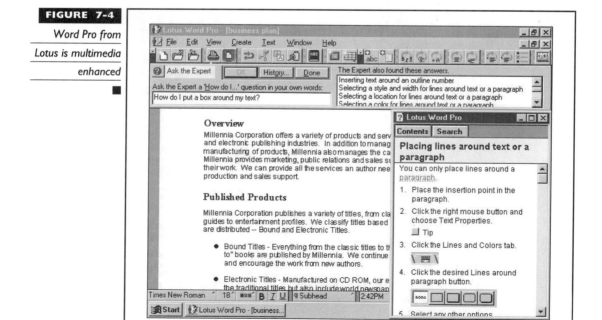

Spreadsheets

Spreadsheets have become the backbone of many users' information management systems. A spreadsheet organizes its data in columns and rows. Calculations are made based on user-defined formulas for, say, analyzing the survival rates of seedlings, or the production of glass bottles in Russia, or a household's consumption of energy in ergs per capita. Spreadsheets can answer what-if questions, build complex graphs and charts, and calculate a bottom line. From Alaska to Zimbabwe, spreadsheets have become a ubiquitous computer tool.

Most spreadsheet applications provide excellent chart-making routines; some allow you to build a series of several charts into an animation or movie, so you can dramatically show change over time or under varying conditions. Full-color curves that demonstrate changing annual sales, robbery and assault statistics, or birth rates may have a far greater effect on an audience than will a column of numbers.

The latest spreadsheets let you attach special notes and drawings, including full multimedia display of sounds, pictures, animations, and video clips.

Lotus 1-2-3

Lotus 1-2-3 lets you rearrange graph elements by clicking and dragging and using a menu to access data objects from the outside world. You can place bitmapped pictures and other objects such as QuickTime movies anywhere in your spreadsheet. There is a complete color drawing package for placing lines, circles, arrows, and special text on top of the spreadsheet to help illustrate its content (see Figure 7-5).

Excel

Using a special template document, you can create a slide show with Microsoft Excel (in both the Macintosh and Windows versions) to present worksheets, charts, and graphics. You can apply video and audio transition effects between slides, adjusting speed and the method of slide advance. The SLIDES.XLA file must be installed in the Windows version, and the Slide-show Add-In file for the Macintosh. QuickTime and AVI movies can be linked to Microsoft Excel documents. Figure 7-6 shows the Windows version of Excel's Edit Slide dialog box being used to embed material from Word Pro, an OLE-capable word processor. Notice the transition effects and speed controls available for placement between slides.

FIGURE 7-5

*Lotus 1-2-3
spreadsheets can
contain images
and movies* ■

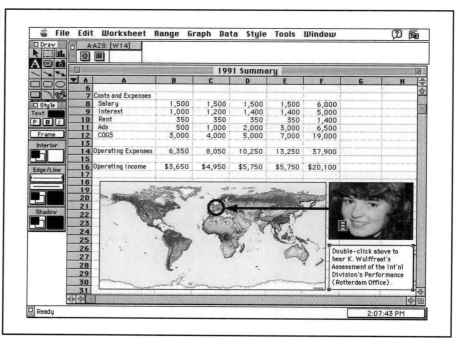

FIGURE 7-6

*Microsoft Excel
can create and
present slide shows* ■

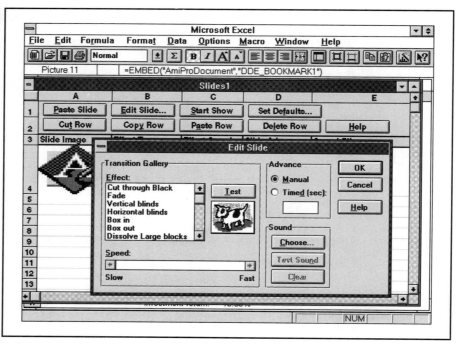

Databases

A database program can store, sort, retrieve, and organize many types of information. Like spreadsheets, databases can exist in a digital environment without ever needing to be printed to paper. Images, sounds, and movies are treated as objects and can be stored, retrieved, and played by many databases.

During the coming years, it is likely that multimedia databases will become a primary method by which corporate users interact with multimedia elements.

FileMaker Pro

Claris's FileMaker Pro, a relational database, rates high in ease of use and cross-platform capability with both Windows 95 and Macintosh PowerPC versions (see Figure 7-7). FileMaker Pro has a relatively simple interface, yet it is powerful enough to handle moderately complex operations through scripting capabilities. You can use the built-in graphics tools and record sound within the application, or you can import images, sounds, and QuickTime movies from other applications. Although you can design layouts from scratch, there are now 40 customizable templates from which to choose for business, education, or home use. FileMaker Pro supports Apple-Events in the Macintosh version and OLE/DDE in the Windows version.

Access

Microsoft Access (Windows only; see Figure 7-8) is a relational database application available on its own or as part of the Microsoft Office Professional bundle of products. With a relational database, you input and store data only once, but you can view data in various ways. With Access, you can view the data in tables that show data from many records at once, forms that show data from each individual record, and reports from which to summarize and print data. The Database Wizard automatically builds tables, queries, forms, and reports with common business and personal database templates, including ones for asset management, order entry, and music collection tracking. It even adds sample data to help you get started. Or, if you already have a flat-file list or spreadsheet, use the Table Analyzer Wizard to import the data into an Access database. Access supports OLE objects and allows you to import images into forms and reports.

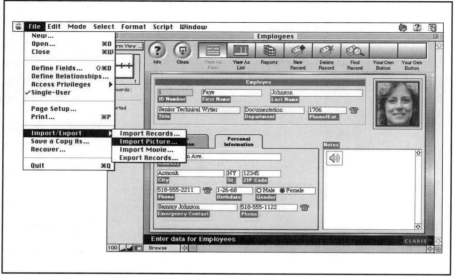

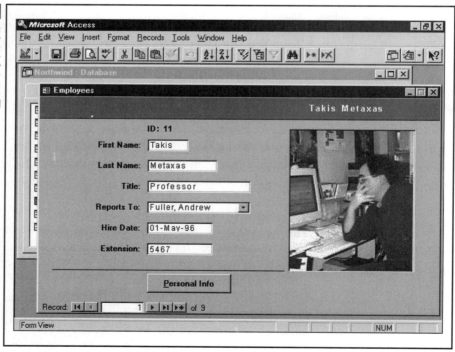

Visual dBASE

Visual dBASE from Borland provides a desktop interface for working with tables, queries, forms, reports, and labels. It is part of a three-product family of object-oriented, event-driven relational database tools for Windows, and it works with multimedia elements using OLE and DDE. Also part of this database family (available separately) are a Compiler for application distribution and a Client/Server tool. Note the graphic image containing the customer's signature and the inserted video clip in Figure 7-9.

Presentation Tools

Presentation software was originally developed to computerize the creation and delivery of presentations to audiences and conferences–as printed output that could be distributed on paper or shown on large screens by overhead projector, or digitally produced as 35 mm color slides. As direct connections from computer monitor outputs to projectors became commonplace, these

7

FIGURE 7-9

Borland's Visual dBASE manages images and video clips

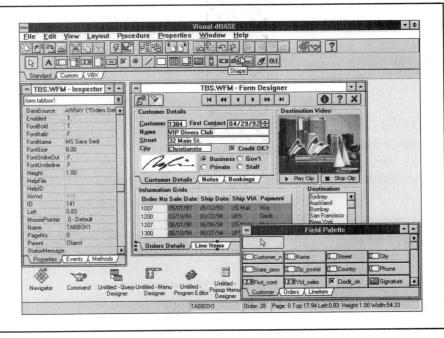

same tools became useful for live computer-driven (interactive) presentations with or without printed handouts.

A gray area is emerging between presentation tools and multimedia authoring systems, as software publishers develop methods to accommodate the needs of computer-based presenters and as large-scale video and LCD panel projection systems become more affordable. Presentation software might, indeed, be considered authoring software, because the publishers of these tools have made their products multimedia capable.

The line between multimedia authoring and desktop presentation software is already a wide gray area. As system tools make multimedia easier to understand and implement, it will become more common in mainstream applications. The same thing happened in desktop publishing. Initially, people were buying Pagemaker to dress up office memos. Now, virtually all word processors have basic page layout capabilities, and the dedicated "publishing" products are targeted at professionals. Multimedia authoring is headed the same way.

Karl Seppala, Macintosh Product Line Manager, Gold Disk, Inc.

Magicians use live props that often run across the stage or fly out of hats as well as other attention-grabbing effects to direct viewers' attention away from tricks and sleight of hand. In contrast, multimedia presenters use the same delivery techniques (the smoke and mirrors of computerized visual effects) to focus their viewers' attention on presentation content, so that the content will be remembered even when it's competing with a heavy lunch or a dimly lit conference room.

Presentation tools add synchronized audio, self-running animations, and video to the slide show presentation armamentarium. The applications described in this section include tools from the classic genre of presentation software.

Astound

Astound from Gold Disk, available for both Macintosh and Windows, lets you create attention-getting presentations that combine text, images, sound effects, video, and animated movies. Astound lets you combine objects from different applications, and with its built-in editors, you can edit objects, sounds, and QuickTime movies within the application. You can also create animated effects using built-in transition options and a timeline feature that lets you control when objects enter and leave the screen. As shown in Figure 7-10, Astound can add interactive responses to clicks on buttons, text blocks, and pictures. You can save the presentation as a stand-alone, self-running file for playing on either Macintosh or Windows platforms.

Persuasion

Persuasion is available from Adobe for both Macintosh and Windows environments. It's a complete desktop presentation toolkit for producing overhead transparencies, 35 mm slides, and printed materials, including speaker notes and audience handouts (see Figure 7-11). Persuasion includes tools for outlining, word processing, drawing, charting, and formatting, and it works in either black and white or color. Persuasion supports OLE-embedded objects for editing of text, graphics, and spreadsheets. Persuasion will also present in various slide show formats for on-screen viewing. This slide show feature lets you move manually or automatically through an entire presentation using the computer screen, which is useful for creating self-running demos. In slide show mode, users can choose from many transition effects, such as wipes and dissolves, that can be assigned either to whole slides or to layers within individual slides. The Persuasion Player for Windows and Macintosh lets you show your presentation regardless of the platform on which you created it.

7

FIGURE 7-10

Gold Disk's Astound

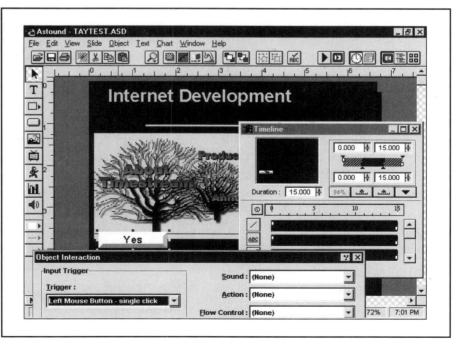

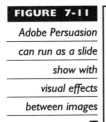

FIGURE 7-11

Adobe Persuasion

can run as a slide

show with

visual effects

between images

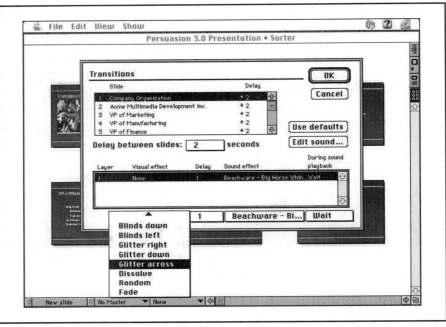

PowerPoint

PowerPoint from Microsoft, for both Macintosh and Windows, offers a complete drawing and text package with an automatic or manual slide show feature. You can embed graphics and data from other applications into PowerPoint, and you can embed bitmapped images, slides, and presentations from PowerPoint into other applications. You can build live links between PowerPoint and other applications. The Windows version supports Multimedia Extensions for Windows by using OLE in conjunction with the Media Control Interface (MCI) command set; it lets you link objects such as AVI files and embedded sound. In the Macintosh version, you can link and embed data and objects with the Publish and Subscribe commands. PowerPoint includes two Wizards (the Auto Content Wizard and the Pick-A-Look Wizard) to guide you through the creation of a presentation.

DeltaGraph Professional

DeltaGraph Professional from DeltaPoint is a comprehensive and flexible charting, graphics, and presentation application for Macintosh and Windows platforms (see Figure 7-12). Large data sets can be organized over multiple pages using the Data Notebook feature. Text outlining makes it

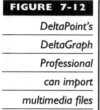

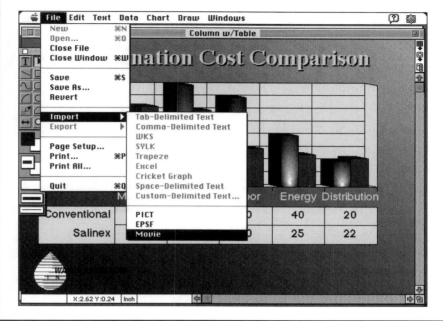

easy to create organization and bullet charts. Data can be imported from and linked to many third-party file formats. You can adjust axis scaling, tick marks, legends, labels, perspective, and 3-D rotations. You can create fully customized presentations with the slide show feature, and you can add sound effects and visual transition effects as well as QuickTime movies. The Windows version supports OLE-embedded objects, while the Macintosh version has Publish and Subscribe support. The Chart Gallery makes it easy to find one of the 60 chart types, and the Chart Advisor will examine your data and recommend the best chart to use.

Harvard Graphics

Harvard Graphics from Software Publishing Corporation includes features that guide users through the creation of a presentation. The Advisor Design Checker interactively analyzes a user's single slide or entire presentation against various design guidelines developed by presentation experts. With the Quick Advice feature, users can obtain advice regarding the selection and most effective use of specific presentation styles, output devices, and chart types. Harvard Graphics is a full-featured presentation tool that lets you add images, movies, animation, sound, and interactivity to each slide (see Figure 7-13).

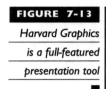

FIGURE 7-13

*Harvard Graphics
is a full-featured
presentation tool*

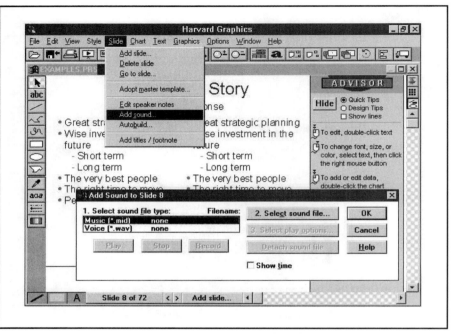

ASAP WordPower

ASAP WordPower from Software Publishing Corporation (for Windows; see Figure 7-14) is an inexpensive and basic presentation tool for those with limited graphic creation ability. It does not include a drawing or a painting tool. Made by the same people who make Harvard Graphics (discussed above), users can create simple slide presentations that include images, movies, sounds, and transitions.

MediaStudio Pro

MediaStudio Pro for Windows from Ulead Systems includes a suite of integrated video, audio, and image editing tools as well as a morphing tool, thumbnail album, and PhotoCD browser. The multimedia converter handles batch processing of images, graphics, waveform files, animation, and video files. MediaStudio Pro supports QuickTime for Windows and Video for Windows (see Figure 7-15).

MediaWrangler

The MediaWrangler for Windows from Alta Vista Technologies (shown in Figure 7-16) combines a multimedia presentation tool with a multimedia

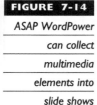

FIGURE 7-14

ASAP WordPower can collect multimedia elements into slide shows ■

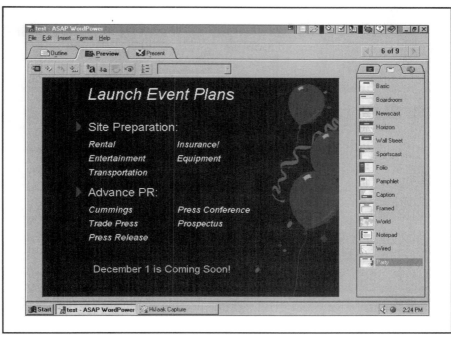

FIGURE 7-15

MediaStudio Pro is a powerful tool for managing and presenting multimedia elements ■

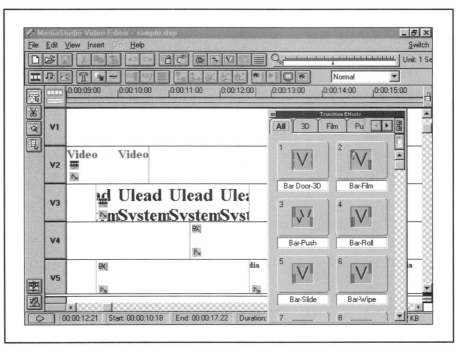

7

FIGURE 7-16

Alta Vista's

MediaWrangler

converts slide show

presentations into

Internet Web pages

■

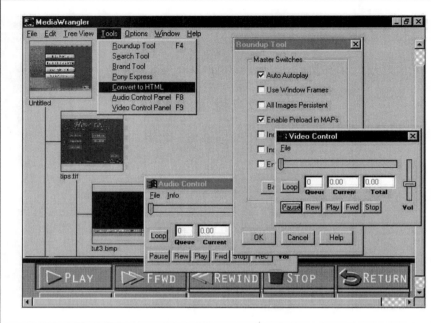

database. This inexpensive tool supports 35 image file formats as well as AVI and MPEG, WAV, and MIDI. To view presentations on the Internet, MediaWrangler converts slides into HTML documents. An extensive collection of clip media includes 41 premade WWW buttons.

SST 3.0

Super Show and Tell from Midisoft (Windows only; see Figure 7-17) is a visually intensive multimedia presentation tool. SST lets you integrate text, images, sound, video, and animation files with point-and-click, drag-and-drop functions and play them back in sequence.

FIGURE 7-17

Midisoft's SST

gathers together

multimedia

elements for

playback as

slide shows

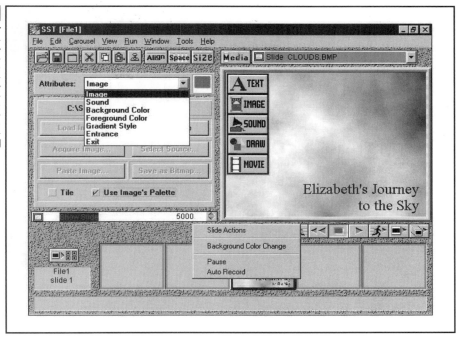

http://www.adobe.com
http://www.altavista.com
http://www.apple.com
http://www.borland.com
http://www.claris.com
http://www.corel.com
http://www.deltapoint.com
http://www.lotus.com
http://www.macromedia.com
http://www.microsoft.com
http://www.midisoft.com
http://www.spco.com
http://www.ulead.com

Here's where to find more information about software products for instant multimedia

7

Multi

[
Authoring tools are used
for designing interactivity
and the user interface ...
]

Multimedia authoring tools provide the
important framework for organizing and editing
the elements of your multimedia project ⎯⎯⎯

interactivity

media

START

STOP

chapter

8

Multimedia Authoring Tools

including
graphics,
sounds,
animations,
and
video clips.

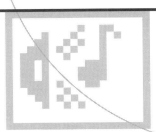

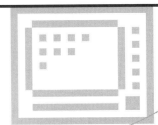

M ULTIMEDIA authoring tools provide the important framework you need for organizing and editing the elements of your multimedia project, including graphics, sounds, animations, and video clips. Authoring tools are used for designing interactivity and the user interface, for presenting your project on screen, and for assembling multimedia elements into a single, cohesive project.

Authoring software provides an integrated environment for binding together the content and functions of your project. Authoring systems typically include the ability to create, edit, and import specific types of data; assemble raw data into a playback sequence or cue sheet; and provide a structured method or language for responding to user input. With multimedia authoring software, you can make

- Video productions
- Animations
- Games
- Demo disks and interactive guided tours
- Presentations
- Interactive kiosk applications
- Interactive training
- Simulations, prototypes, and technical visualizations

Types of Authoring Tools

This chapter arranges the various authoring tools into groups based on the metaphor used for sequencing or organizing multimedia elements and events:

- Card- or page-based tools

- Icon-based, event-driven tools

- Time-based and presentation tools

- Object-oriented tools

Card- or page-based tools: In these authoring systems, elements are organized as pages of a book or a stack of cards. Thousands of pages or cards may be available in the book or stack. These tools are best used when the bulk of your content consists of elements that can be viewed individually, like the pages of a book or cards in a card file. The authoring system lets you link these pages or cards into organized sequences. You can jump, on command, to any page you wish in the structured navigation pattern. Card- or page-based authoring systems allow you to play sound elements and launch animations and digital video.

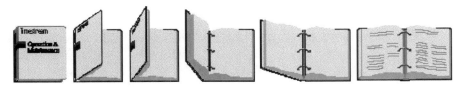

Icon-based, event-driven tools: In these authoring systems, multimedia elements and interaction cues (events) are organized as objects in a structural framework or process. Icon-based, event-driven tools simplify the organization of your project and typically display flow diagrams of activities along branching paths. In complicated navigational structures, this charting is particularly useful during development.

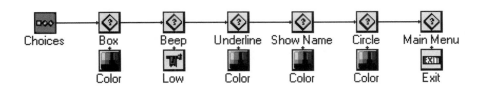

Time-based tools: In these authoring systems, elements and events are organized along a timeline, with resolutions as high as 1/30 second. Time-based tools are best to use when you have a message with a beginning and an end. Sequentially organized graphic frames are played back at a speed that you can set. Other elements (such as audio events) are triggered at a given time or location in the sequence of events. The more powerful time-based tools let you program jumps to any location in a sequence, thereby adding navigation and interactive control.

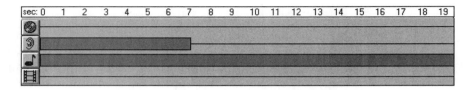

Object-oriented tools: In these authoring systems, multimedia elements and events become *objects* that live in a hierarchical order of parent and child relationships. Messages passed among these objects order them to *do* things according to the *properties* or *modifiers* assigned to them. In this way, for example, Suzie (a teenager object) may be programmed to take out the trash every Friday evening, and does so when she gets a message from Dad. Spot, the puppy, may bark and jump up and down when the postman arrives. Spot is defined by barking and jumping modifiers; Suzie by hauling-trash modifiers or child objects (groan, sit up, stand up, saunter slowly, get bag, carry bag, slam door, etc.). Objects typically take care of themselves. Send them a message and they do their thing without external procedures and programming. Object-oriented tools are particularly useful for games, which contain many components with many "personalities," and for simulating real-life situations, events, and their constituent "objects."

The Right Tool for the Job

Each multimedia project you undertake will have its own underlying structure and purpose and will require different features and functions. In the best case, you must be prepared to choose the tool that best fits the job; in the worst case, you must know which tools will at least "get the job done." Authoring tools are constantly being improved by their makers, who add new features and increase performance with upgrade development cycles of six months to a year. It is important that you study the software product reviews in computer trade journals, as well as talk with current users of these systems, before deciding on the best ones for your needs.

---

warning   *Because multimedia authoring systems are constantly being updated, make sure you purchase and use the latest version of software.*

Editing Features

The elements of multimedia—images, animations, text, digital audio and MIDI music, and video clips—need to be created, edited, and converted to standard file formats, and the specialized applications described in Chapters 6, 9, 10, 11, 12, and 13 provide these capabilities. Also, editing tools for these elements, particularly text and still images, are often included in your authoring system. The more editors your authoring system has, the fewer specialized tools you will need. In many cases, however, the editors that come with an authoring system will offer only a subset of the substantial features found in dedicated tools. According to Vaughan's Law of Multimedia Minimums (see Chapter 10), these features may very well be sufficient for what you need to do; on the other hand, if editors you need are missing from your authoring system, or if you require more power, it's best to use one of the specialized, single-purpose tools.

Organizing Features

The organization, design, and production process for multimedia (described in Chapters 16 and 17) involves storyboarding and flowcharting. Some authoring tools provide a visual flowcharting system or overview facility for illustrating your project's structure at a macro level. Storyboards or navigation diagrams, too, can help organize a project. Because designing the interactivity and navigation flow of your project often requires a great deal of planning and programming effort, your storyboard should describe not just the graphics of each screen, but the interactive elements as well. Features that help organize your material, such as those provided by Super-Edit, Authorware, IconAuthor, and other authoring systems, are a plus.

Programming Features

Multimedia authoring systems offer one or more of the following approaches, which are explained in the paragraphs that follow.

- Visual programming with cues, icons, and objects
- Programming with a scripting language

- Programming with traditional languages, such as Basic or C
- Document development tools

Visual programming with icons or objects is perhaps the simplest and easiest authoring process. If you want to play a sound or put a picture into your project, just drag the element's icon into the playlist. Or drag it away to delete it. Visual authoring tools such as Authorware and IconAuthor are particularly useful for slide shows and presentations.

Authoring tools that offer a scripting language for navigation control and for enabling user inputs—such as SuperCard, Macromedia Director, Hyper-Card, and ToolBook—are more powerful. The more commands and functions provided in the scripting language, the more powerful the authoring system. Once you learn one of these languages, you will be able to learn other scripting languages relatively quickly; the principles are the same, regardless of the command syntax and keywords used. Many scripting languages on both platforms are similar to HyperTalk, the underlying scripting language of HyperCard.

A scripted handler to generate a system beep may be very similar, regardless of platform. In HyperTalk (Macintosh), SuperTalk (Macintosh), and Lingo (Macintosh and Windows), a script that makes the computer beep one time reads:

```
on mouseUp
  beep
end mouseUp
```

In OpenScript, used by ToolBook (Windows), a similar script reads:

```
to handle buttonUp
  beep 1
end buttonUp
```

As with traditional programming tools, look for an authoring package with good debugging facilities, robust text editing, and on-line syntax reference. Other scripting augmentation facilities are advantages, as well. In complex projects, you may need to program custom extensions of the scripting language for direct access to the computer's operating system. On the Macintosh, this means being able to use external commands and functions (XCMDs and XFCNs) written in C or Pascal. In Windows, you will need to call Dynamic Link Libraries (DLLs) and the Windows Media Control Interface (MCI) device drivers.

A powerful document reference and delivery system is a key component of some projects. Some authoring tools offer direct importing of preformatted text, indexing facilities, complex text search mechanisms, and hypertext linkage tools. These authoring systems are useful for development of CD-ROM information products, on-line documentation and help systems, and sophisticated multimedia-enhanced publications.

Interactivity Features

Interactivity empowers the end users of your project by letting them control the content and flow of information. Authoring tools should provide one or more levels of interactivity:

- *Simple branching,* which offers the ability to go to another section of the multimedia production (via an activity such as a keypress, mouse click, or expiration of a timer)

- *Conditional branching,* which supports a go-to based on the results of IF-THEN decisions or events

- A *structured language* that supports complex programming logic, such as nested IF-THENs, subroutines, event tracking, and message passing among objects and elements

8

Performance Tuning Features

Complex multimedia projects require exact synchronization of events—for example, the animation of an exploding balloon with its accompanying sound effect. Accomplishing synchronization is difficult because performance varies widely among the different computers used for multimedia development and delivery. Some authoring tools allow you to lock a production's playback speed to a specified computer platform, but others provide no ability whatsoever to control performance on various systems. In many cases, you will need to use the authoring tool's own scripting language or custom programming facility to specify timing and sequence on systems with different (faster or slower) processors. Be sure your authoring system allows precise timing of events.

Playback Features

As you build your multimedia project, you will be continually assembling elements and testing to see how the assembly looks and performs. Your authoring system should let you build a segment or part of your project and then quickly test it as if the user were actually using it. You will spend a great deal of time going back and forth between building and testing as you refine and smooth the content and timing of the project.

Delivery Features

Delivering your project may require building a run-time version of the project using the multimedia authoring software. A *run-time* version allows your project to play back without requiring the full authoring software and all its tools and editors. Often, the run-time version does not allow users to access or change the content, structure, and programming of the project. If you are going to distribute your project widely, you should distribute it in the run-time version. Because the World Wide Web has become a significant delivery medium for multimedia, authoring systems typically provide a means to convert their output so that it can be delivered within the context of HTML, either with special plug-ins or by embedding Java or other code structures in the HTML document. Make sure your authored project can be easily distributed: Chapter 20 discusses delivery in general; Chapter 18 discusses delivery of multimedia on the Web.

Cross-Platform Features

It is also increasingly important to use tools that make transfer across platforms easy. For many developers, the Macintosh remains the multimedia authoring platform of choice, but 80 percent of that developer's target market may be Windows platforms. If you develop on a Macintosh, look for tools that provide a compatible authoring system for Windows or offer a run-time player for the other platform.

Card- and Page-Based Authoring Tools

Card- and page-based authoring systems provide a simple and easily understood metaphor for organizing multimedia elements. Because graphic images typically form the backbone of a project, both as navigation menus and as content, many developers first arrange their images into logical sequences or groupings similar to the chapters and pages of a book, or cards in a card catalog. Navigation routines become, then, simply directives to go to a page or card that contains appropriate images and text, and associated sounds, animations, and video clips.

Page-based authoring systems contain media objects: the objects are the buttons, text fields, graphic objects, backgrounds, pages or cards, and even the project itself. The characteristics of objects are defined by properties (highlighted, bold, red, hidden, active, locked, and so forth). Each object may contain programming script, usually a property of that object, that is activated when an event (such as a mouse click) related to that object occurs. Events cause messages to pass along the hierarchy of objects in your project; for example, a mouse-click message can be sent from a button to the background, to the page, and then to the project itself. As the message travels, it looks for handlers in the script of each object; if it finds a matching handler, the authoring system then executes the task specified by that handler.

Most page-based authoring systems provide a facility for linking objects to pages or cards (by automatically programming branching go-to statements for navigating by mouse clicks), but learning to write your own scripts and understanding the message-passing nature of these authoring tools is essential to making them perform well. Following are some typical messages that might be passed along the object hierarchy of the HyperCard, Super-Card, and ToolBook authoring systems:

HyperCard, SuperCard, and MediaTalk Message	ToolBook Message
closeCard	leavePage
closeStack	leaveBook
idle	idle
mouseDown	buttonDown
mouseStillDown	buttonStillDown
mouseUp	buttonUp
newBackground	newBackground
openCard	enterPage
openStack	enterBook

Now let's look at specific examples. To go to the next card or page when a button is clicked, you would place a message handler into the script of that button. (In the languages demonstrated below, handlers begin with "on" or "to handle.") Here is an example in HyperTalk:

```
on mouseUp
  go next card
end mouseUp
```

Here is an example in OpenScript (ToolBook):

```
to handle buttonUp
  go next page
end buttonUp
```

The handler, if placed in the script of the card or page, will execute its commands upon receiving a "mouseUp" or "buttonUp" message occurring at any location on the card or page—not just while the cursor is within the bounds of a button.

Most card- or page-based authoring systems require a special intermediate file that also receives scripted message handlers and acts as a repository for special routines and resources that are available to all projects being executed by the application. In HyperCard, this file is called Home; in SuperCard, this is the Shared File; in ToolBook, you may have one or more System Books.

HyperCard (Macintosh)

HyperCard is the most widely available programming system and multimedia authoring tool for the Macintosh. Since 1991, however, only a run-time version of HyperCard is bundled with new Macintoshes; the fully functional version for authoring must be purchased from Apple. HyperCard comes with ready-to-use template stacks (including an address book, datebook, graph maker, phone dialer, and scanned art) to shorten the learning curve for novice multimedia developers.

With Apple's HyperCard, you create projects called *stacks* that are made up of cards. *Cards* can share the same background graphics, buttons, and text; and cards and shared backgrounds, as well, may contain graphic images, buttons, and text fields. HyperCard offers various card sizes (ranging from 64×64 pixels to 1280×1280 pixels); multiple windows (up to 18 at a time); styled text; AppleEvents support for links to programs running locally or across a network; hypertext support; support for black-and-white, gray-scale, or color PICT-based resources; QuickTime animation; and a powerful scripting language, HyperTalk, with user-definable menus and shared code libraries.

HyperCard includes an editor for bitmapped graphics. Color PICT images can be edited and placed into HyperCard stacks. HyperCard provides graphics tools for drawing, filling, and editing rectangles, ovals, polygons, lines, and text. Five styles of text fields (transparent, opaque, rectangle, shadow, and scrolling) can contain text in various fonts and styles. The program offers several methods for printing images and text reports.

You can organize your content by linking a card to any other card using scripts attached to buttons, fields, or other HyperCard objects. HyperTalk scripts, however, can do more than just link information. You can perform computational tasks, sense and respond to user input, create character, icon, and motion animations, launch other applications, and control external multimedia devices.

Figure 8-1 demonstrates the use of HyperCard's card and background layers: when the gray foreground cover is wiped away with an "eraser," the background graphic image is revealed. This requires programming in HyperTalk to remove the cover beneath the special eraser cursor and to post elapsed time. The program handlers are in a transparent button over the image; they are as follows:

```
on mouseEnter
   global showFlag, totTime
   if showFlag is "True" then exit to HyperCard
   set cursor to "Eraser"
   put 0 into thisTime
   repeat while the mouseLoc is within the rect of bg btn "Frame"
     set cursor to "Eraser"
     if the mouse is down then
        lock screen
        choose eraser tool
        unlock screen
        put the ticks into startTime
        subtract 60 from startTime
        repeat
           click at the mouseLoc
           if the mouse is up then exit repeat
        end repeat
        put the ticks - startTime into thisTime
        put round((thisTime + totTime)/60) into bg fld "Timer"
        add thisTime to totTime
        lock screen
        choose browse tool
        unlock screen
     end if
   end repeat
   set cursor to hand
end mouseEnter

on mouseLeave
   set cursor to hand
   choose browse tool
end mouseLeave
```

8

FIGURE 8-1

The globe and the cat are animated in HyperCard, as the foreground cover is erased to reveal the image beneath

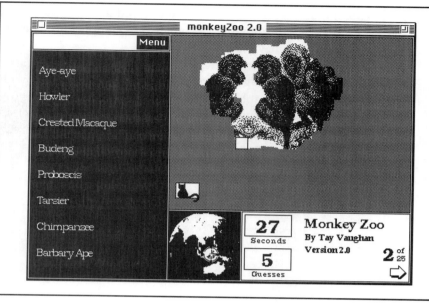

An animated earth is made up of 18 characters and rotates underneath a marker to point out the habitat of the monkey species that is hidden below the cover. When enough of the cover is erased so the user can recognize the monkeys, the user releases the mouse button and chooses a name from a menu. If the name is incorrect, a sound plays and a cat appears and wags its tail (the cat is a button icon), and the user can continue. If the user selects the correct monkey, an encyclopedia of information about that species is presented, and a pull-down menu (see Figure 8-2) provides access to a sound bite or video clip before going on. There are 25 monkeys, and the program keeps score.

SuperCard (Macintosh/Windows)

Allegiant Technologies' SuperCard is an authoring application for the Macintosh used to produce sophisticated multimedia presentations, front ends to databases, and computer-based education and training projects. SuperCard also offers a Windows run-time player so that projects designed and built on the Macintosh can be delivered in the Windows environment.

With SuperCard, you can build integrated, stand-alone applications that include multiple windows of any type, full-color graphic objects with attached scripts, and a wide variety of other standard Macintosh interface elements. Unlike HyperCard, a SuperCard project contains windows, and

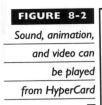

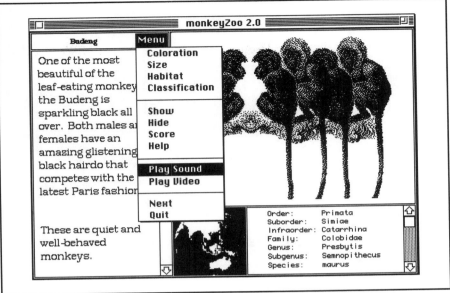

windows contain backgrounds and cards that in turn contain drawn and bitmapped graphics, buttons, and text fields. SuperCard can convert Hyper-Card stacks to SuperCard format.

SuperCard is shipped as two applications: SuperCard and SuperEdit. SuperCard is optimized for running the projects you create in SuperEdit. SuperEdit is optimized for assembling applications. SuperCard, however, does have a powerful run-time editor built in, so developers typically design their screens and content layout first in SuperEdit and then fine-tune the project and its scripts using SuperCard's editor.

SuperCard lets you create any of the seven standard types of Macintosh windows and can contain many different custom windows that can be opened at any time and in any combination. A scrolling window may accommodate cards as large as 32,767×32,767 pixels—virtually 30 feet by 30 feet; if you make your window, say, 640×480 pixels, you can then scroll across the "geography" of the larger card. Custom windows from other projects can also be open at the same time, so you can move among applications with ease. You can create custom menus and add scripts to provide them with functionality. Figure 8-3 shows a SuperCard project with many custom windows being edited in SuperEdit.

SuperCard supports both drawn and bitmapped graphics—both can be created in SuperCard or in other Macintosh applications and imported into SuperCard. Graphic objects can have scripts attached to them, so you can

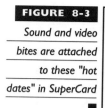

FIGURE 8-3

Sound and video bites are attached to these "hot dates" in SuperCard ∎

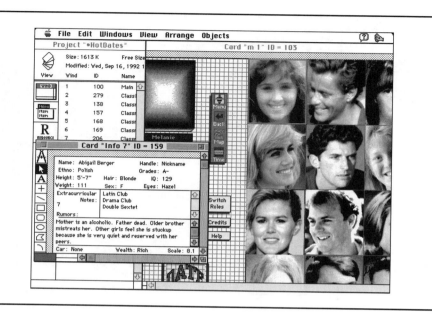

create buttons of any shape. With an AutoTrace tool, bitmaps can be converted to drawn object polygons and to irregularly shaped buttons.

SuperCard provides animation commands within its scripting language and can generate PICS and STEP animation files. The program will run at all color depth monitor settings, but it cannot import images with color depths greater than 8 bits (256 colors).

ToolBook (Windows)

ToolBook from Asymetrix offers a Windows graphical user interface and programming environment for building multimedia projects, called *books*, to present information graphically as drawings, scanned color images, text, sounds, and animations. A book is divided into pages and is stored as a Windows/DOS file. Pages can contain text fields, buttons, and both drawn and bitmapped graphic objects. You assemble a book from pages and link the pages together; ToolBook's OpenScript programming then performs interactive and navigational tasks and defines how objects behave.

Hot words in text fields can have a script attached; these hot words provide a hypertext feature in ToolBook to connect related information that appears in different places throughout a book, or in other books that can be opened. Clicking a hot word makes the word respond like a button.

ToolBook has two working levels: Reader and Author. You run a book's scripts at Reader level. At Author level, you use commands to create new books, create and modify objects on pages, and write scripts. ToolBook offers linking options for buttons and hot words, so you can create navigation scripts by identifying the page to go to. There is also a script recorder feature to record actions and translate them into OpenScript statements. ToolBook provides built-in tools for debugging, and if you are an experienced programmer, you can extend OpenScript by writing additional functions and Dynamic Link Libraries (DLLs). Scripts may be as large as 64K. With Shared Scripts, you can assign the same behavior to multiple objects. To extend your ToolBook project, ToolBook offers Visual Basic Controls (VBX), which lets you import standard VBX windows objects such as enhanced fields and list boxes, clocks and timers, gauges, and grid controls.

You can control image-drawing and display speed, and you can paste or import large bitmaps, device-independent bitmaps (DIBs), and graphics from other applications. Graphics filters allow importing of DRW, EPS, TIF, BMP, DIB, and Windows metafile files. You can store 16- or 256-color palettized bitmaps outside of the ToolBook application and display them in child, pop-up, or overlapped windows. You can create Windows-style buttons, list boxes, and dialog boxes, and you can translate Windows messages into OpenScript messages. You can also import RTF (Rich Text Format) text files into your project for fully formatted text from any word processor.

With ToolBook, developers have access within OpenScript to the Windows MCI for controlling external devices. ToolBook provides more than 250 prescripted graphic objects to copy and paste into your own project to control multimedia devices. These widgets look and feel similar to the controls on CD players, VCRs, and other consumer electronic devices. From OpenScript, you also have access to the timer services of Windows, as well as object notification when a particular multimedia task is complete so that you can trigger other actions. You can link to and control any multimedia hardware or software that has a Windows DLL or a Windows driver. Devices supported by ToolBook include CD-ROM (for both digital data and Red Book Audio), laserdisc players, animation software, waveform audio cards, video overlay boards, and MIDI sequencers. ToolBook also supports .WAV and .MIDI files.

Multimedia ToolBook allows you to integrate your project into databases and includes built-in Paradox and dBASE database engines. For more extensive connectivity with other databases, the ToolBook Database Connection allows easy access and integration with all ODBC-compliant databases.

ToolBook supports Windows' multiple instance capability, so you can open two or more ToolBook windows at the same time, and the books can interact under script control. In this way you can, for example, display a control panel in one window and show the controlled animation, video, or bitmap in another. In Figure 8-4, four ToolBook windows are open at one time.

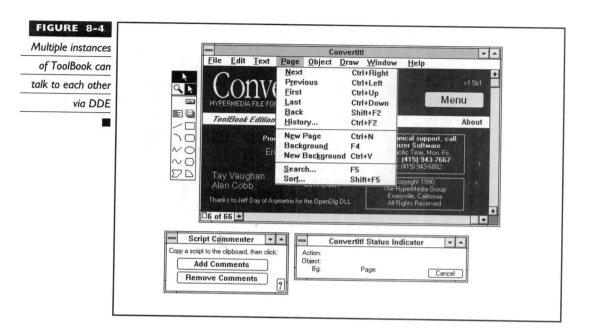

FIGURE 8-4

Multiple instances
of ToolBook can
talk to each other
via DDE

ToolBook supports Dynamic Data Exchange (DDE), so you can open other Windows applications and control them within your own project. Windows callback support and message translation, as well as support for any standard DLL, are available in OpenScript.

Visual Basic (Windows)

Visual Basic is a programming system for Windows that is often used to organize and present multimedia elements. It is made up of *controls* (objects) that reside on *forms* (or windows). Visual Basic uses language code syntactically similar to BASICA or GW-BASIC. The program is *event driven*—that is, code is attached to objects and remains idle until called to respond to user- or system-initiated events, such as a mouse click or system timeout. You use controls to create the user interface of an application, including command buttons, option buttons, check boxes, list boxes, combo boxes, text boxes, scroll bars, frames, file and directory selection boxes, timers, and menu bars.

Visual Basic provides flexible response to mouse and keyboard events (including drag and drop), can show and hide objects, and provides access to the Windows Clipboard, DDE, and OLE facilities (see Chapter 7 for more about DDE and OLE). There are also powerful debugging commands to help isolate and correct code errors. When your Visual Basic project is complete, you can convert it into an executable EXE file to run as a stand-alone Windows application.

Multimedia enhancements to Visual Basic are available with the Professional Toolkit extensions. These offer additional custom controls: a Grid control for adding tables with rows and columns; a Child control for multiple document interfaces (MDI) child windows; a Graph control for creating graphs; and a Windows MCI control for incorporating audio, video, and animation elements using Windows MCI. Controls can be stored as special files with the extension VBX.

The MCI.VBX lets you control CD players, VCRs, music files, laserdiscs, and full-motion video, using a control panel containing Play, Pause, Stop, Rewind, Next, Record, Eject, and other buttons drawn on a Visual Basic form. Figure 8-5 shows a Visual Basic controller for audio CD with a sample of code. At the left of this code sample is the Visual Basic Toolbox palette for creating controls.

Icon-Based Authoring Tools

Icon-based, event-driven tools provide a visual programming approach to organizing and presenting multimedia. First you build a structure or flow-chart of events, tasks, and decisions, by dragging appropriate icons from a

8

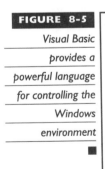

FIGURE 8-5

Visual Basic provides a powerful language for controlling the Windows environment

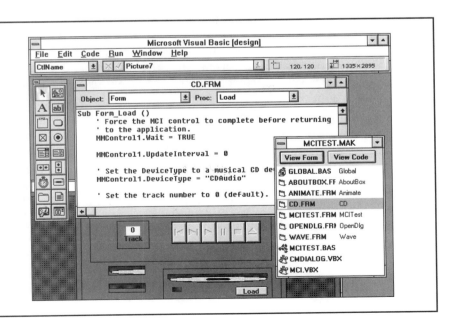

library. These icons can include menu choices, graphic images, sounds, and computations. The flowchart graphically depicts the project's logic. When the structure is built, you can add your content: text, graphics, animation, sounds, and video movies. Then, to refine your project, you edit your logical structure by rearranging and fine-tuning the icons and their properties.

Authorware (Macintosh/Windows)

With Authorware from Macromedia, nontechnical multimedia authors can build sophisticated applications without scripting. By placing icons on the flow line, you can quickly sequence events and activities, including decisions and user interactions. Authorware is useful as a design tool for storyboarding, because it lets you change sequences, add options, and restructure interactions by simply dragging and dropping icons. You can print out your navigation map or flowchart, an annotated project index with or without associated icons, design and presentation windows, and a cross-reference table of variables. Developers who use both Macintoshes and PCs can work with almost identical interfaces, authoring functions, media-editing capabilities, and data management on both platforms. A demo version of Authorware is available on the Macromedia CD-ROM, found behind the back cover of this book.

Authorware offers more than 200 system variables and functions for capturing, manipulating, and displaying data, and for controlling the operation of your project. Variables include interaction, decision, time, video, graphics, general, file, and user; functions include math, string, time jump, video, graphics, general, file, and user. You can paste variables and functions into calculation windows, option slots, or presentation windows, and you can control the format of variables embedded in selected display text. Authorware provides links to external user functions written as DLLs in Windows, or XCMDs and XFCNs on the Macintosh.

Authorware has a complete set of tools for incorporating and editing multimedia elements (graphic images, sounds, animations, and movies) created with other software. For text, you can mix fonts, styles, sizes, modes, and colors, and you can draw graphic objects (polygons, ovals, rectangles, rounded rectangles, and lines) and fill them with up to 36 patterns. Authorware will import files in PICT, DIB, TIFF, EPSF, Windows metafile, and Windows bitmap formats. Graphics can be displayed with numerous transition effects. Authorware provides its own waveform sound editor, Sound-Wave, and it supports AIFF, SND, PCM, and Windows Waveform and MIDI formats. Path animation routines and QuickTime movies can be fine-tuned, and multiple layering is supported to govern which animated object overlaps another. Video can be displayed in still or motion in resizable, moveable video windows with variable-speed playback.

In Authorware, design icons (1 through 8 in the illustration that follows) denote a special function that is performed when the icon is encountered during interaction with a user. Start/Stop Flag icons (9 and 10) are used while testing and debugging in the authoring mode. Multimedia icons (11 through 13) control playback of graphic animations, sound, and video. All the icons in the illustration are described next.

- Display icons (1) put text and/or graphics on the screen.

- Animation icons (2) move the objects of a preceding Display icon from one point to another in a given amount of time or at a specified speed.

- Erase icons (3) erase the text and/or graphics displays.

- Wait icons (4) interrupt file flow until the user presses a key or clicks the mouse, or until a specified amount of time elapses.

- Decision icons (5) select which icons (from a set of attached icons) to use next.

- Interaction icons (6) present options or questions and then, based on the user's response, select and branch to attached icons for feedback to the user.

- Calculation icons (7) perform arithmetic or special control functions, execute user-written code, jump to other files, or jump to other applications.

- Map icons (8) organize and modularize the file by providing space to put more icons. Each Map icon provides its own flow line on which you can place other icons, including additional Map icons.

- Start Flag icons (9) begin running a file from an intermediate location.

- Stop Flag icons (10) stop a file from running.

- Movie icons (11) provide for playing PICS, FLI, and FLC frame animations.

- Sound icons (12) provide many options for loading sounds and controlling their playback.

- Video icons (13) provide control of video players and playback of video segments and their sound tracks.

Figure 8-6 shows the layout of an on-line magazine published on CD-ROM using Authorware for Macintosh as the authoring system. Note that Interaction icons branch to other topics.

IconAuthor (Windows)

From AimTech, IconAuthor's visual programming environment enables nonprogrammers to create applications by building structures and then adding content to the building blocks. To build the structures, icons representing functions or tasks are moved from an icon library and connected to a flowchart (see Figure 8-7). You combine the icons into a logical sequence that depicts the flow of your project.

When you have built your structure, you can then add content, including text, graphics, animation, and/or full-motion video. IconAuthor provides an integrated set of graphic, text, animation, and video editors to let you create screens as well as special effects such as wipes, zooms, and fades. With Rezolution, the graphic editing utility in IconAuthor, you can display graphic

---

FIGURE 8-6

Authorware provides a structural and navigational overview of your entire project, using icons

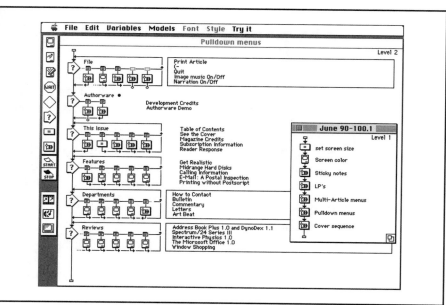

FIGURE 8-7

Icons are the

building blocks in

IconAuthor's visual

programming

environment
■

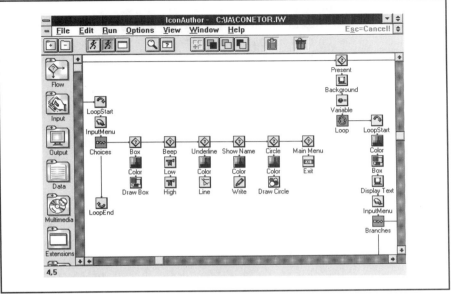

images in various resolutions for CGA, EGA, VGA, and SuperVGA monitors. Rezolution can also convert between palettes of 2, 8, 16, and 256 colors.

IconAuthor uses the Windows MCI for management of videodisc and videotape devices, can read and write to dBASE database files, and supports DDE and access to DLLs.

Quest (Windows)

Quest from Allen Communication is a Windows-based authoring tool designed especially for building computer-based training (CBT) applications. In Quest, postage-stamp representations of modules and frames are placed in a work-flow organization with arrows delineating branching paths. Frames in Quest contain "live" objects; you can "talk to" and modify object properties during both development and run time. Once a live object has been named, you can select actions and conditions for it, request data from it, and let an end user manipulate it.

Quest includes two levels of development: the Design Level and the Frame Level. At the Design Level, instructional designers can map out overall structure and set up links between frames. A QuickFrames feature lets you make customized frame groups to insert into a project on the fly. With FastTracks, you can use prebuilt screen layouts, menus, templates, borders, buttons, question/answer frames, and interactions—even a whole series of prelinked frames that allow you to quickly build a prototype. FastTracks libraries allow developers to group commonly used objects and images for use in current or future titles.

At the Frame Level, graphics, audio/video options, controls, interactions, branching, and animations are created and manipulated with toolbars. Quest supports any standard Windows MCI device and accepts over 25 bitmap file formats, including GIFs and JPEGs. Quest also supports .FLI, .FLC, and .CEL animation file formats and any MCI-compliant overlay board or video player for digital video, including Video for Windows, QuickTime, JPEG, Intel's Indeo, and MPEG. For audio, Quest supports .WAV and .MIDI file formats, CD-Audio, and any standard Windows MCI device driver.

Quest includes several hundred special effects features, such as 3-D, fade in, and wipe out, as well as six types of animation: path, cycle, bounce, drag, dissolve, and file. The *style* feature defines text styles for reuse throughout a project. Quest supports up to 24-bit color, has a fixed color palette for 256-color mode, and provides dithering to 16-color imaging. The Smart-Spots Editor provides pixel-by-pixel control of answer areas.

Because Quest is oriented toward computer-based training situations, interactive features include answer analysis wild-carding for multiple correct and incorrect answers; and a Text Answer Analysis Wizard for single-word answers, phrases, numbers, and nonexact answer variations and answer-specific feedback, scoring, and branching. You can set up multiple path criteria between frames, including paths by colors and random branching.

Quest includes an embedded authoring language called Quest C, which makes all the power of the ANSI standard C programming language available within the system. The Quest C Coach lets novices select options from dialog boxes to create C code. Through a simple dialog box, you can access programming functions, variables, and command statements to control and manipulate live objects. Quest C programs can be written and compiled without going to an external editor.

Time-Based Authoring Tools

Time-based systems are popular multimedia authoring tools. Each uses its own distinctive approach and user interface for managing events over time. Many use a visual timeline for sequencing the events of a multimedia presentation, often displaying layers of various media elements or events alongside the scale in increments as precise as one second. Others arrange long sequences of graphic frames and add the time component by adjusting each frame's duration of play.

Director (Macintosh/Windows)

Macromedia's Director is a powerful and complex multimedia authoring tool from Macromedia with a broad set of features to create multimedia presentations, animations, and interactive multimedia applications. It requires a significant learning curve, but once mastered, it is among the most powerful of multimedia development tools. In Director, you assemble and sequence the elements of your project using a Cast and a Score. A demo version of Director is available on the Macromedia CD-ROM, found behind the back cover of this book.

Cast

The Cast is a multimedia database containing still images, sound files, text, palettes, QuickDraw shapes, programming scripts, QuickTime movies, and even other Director files. As shown in Figure 8-8, not only can you import a wide range of data types and multimedia element formats directly into this Cast, but you can also create multimedia elements from scratch using Director's own tools and editors.

A full-featured painting tool lets you create bitmapped artwork in any color depth. You can create gradients, tile patterns, and animated transfor-

8

FIGURE 8-8

Director's Cast feature contains all the multimedia elements of your project

mations (such as rotations and skews) of artwork. Other tools edit and create QuickDraw shapes, text, QuickTime movies, palettes, and scripts.

Score

Once you have imported or created the multimedia elements for your project and placed them into your Cast, you tie these Cast members together using the Score facility. Score is a sequencer for displaying, animating, and playing Cast members, and it is made up of frames that contain Cast members, tempo, a palette, timing, and sound information in up to 24 channels. Each frame is played back on a "stage" at a rate specified in the tempo channel. The Score provides elaborate and complex visual effects and transitions, adjustments of color palettes, and tempo control. In Figure 8-9, the frames are the vertical bands, and the channels are the horizontal bands.

Animations, for example, are made by placing a graphic or *sprite* onto the stage and changing its location slightly over several or more frames. When the frames are played back at tempo, the sprite moves. You can synchronize animations with sound effects by highlighting a range of frames and selecting the appropriate sound from your Cast.

FIGURE 8-9

Director's Score feature sequences and sets the tempo for playback

Lingo

Director utilizes Lingo, a full-featured scripting language, to enable interactivity and programmed control. A built-in script editor offers Lingo debugging facilities. Because you can attach scripts to individual elements of the Cast, you can copy and paste complete interactive sequences. Lingo also uses Xtras, which are special code segments used to control external sound and video devices. Several Xtras and extensive examples of their use are shipped with Macromedia Director. You can also use many HyperCard XCMDs and XFCNs to extend the program's functionality for special purposes.

Using Lingo scripts, you can chain together separate Director documents and call other files as subroutines. You can also import elements into your Cast using pointers to a file. This allows you to share the same elements among many Casts; when your Score calls for that element, it is loaded into RAM from the file. Chaining and sharing let you create Director projects as large or complex as your storage medium will accommodate. Maricopa College supports a comprehensive Web site containing a wealth of up-to-date Director tips and resources at http://www.mcli.dist.maricopa.edu/director/.

QuickTime Support

Director provides extensive support for QuickTime. You can import existing QuickTime movies directly into the Cast and have them play as part of your production at any time. A special QuickTime window lets you use the standard QuickTime controller to preview and perform simple editing with imported QuickTime movies. There are also special Lingo commands and functions that provide specific interactive control of many aspects of the QuickTime movies, including their location, playback rate, and audio volume.

With Director, you can also create animations and save them in Quick-Time format. Export options provide control of the exported QuickTime movie's size and frame rate.

Object-Oriented Authoring Tools

mTropolis (Macintosh/Windows)

mTropolis from Quark provides an object-oriented environment in which objects (images, animations, videos, text, or sounds) are assigned properties.

These objects respond to external events, send messages to each other, and inherit behaviors from other objects. Unlike other authoring tools such as SuperCard, ToolBook, or Director, there are no timelines or stacks of cards to form a core authoring paradigm. Indeed, you begin a project by building elements in empty space—this makes mTropolis a true object-oriented authoring system.

A project consists of a hierarchy of sections, subsections, and scenes; a *shared scene* contains common elements and modifiers. New objects (including sections and scenes) are dragged and dropped from a palette (see the lower left of Figure 8-10) into the project. The design interface is visual, so you can drag and drop icons and double-click to set properties from dialog boxes. Objects and families of objects can be saved in libraries for repeated use.

Like many multimedia authoring tools, mTropolis is a message- or event-based application. Messages are broadcast to the entire project or are targeted to specific object destinations. When in a parent-child relationship, objects can respond to messages as a family.

FIGURE 8-10

mTropolis is a true object-oriented authoring system

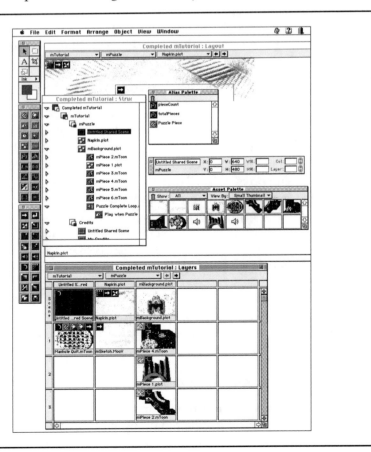

When modifiers (*Effect* modifiers, *Variable* modifiers, *Messenger* modifiers, and *Special* modifiers) are dropped onto an object, that object takes on the properties carried by the modifier, and the properties can be switched on and off with messages.

Effect modifiers change the visible characteristics of the elements on which they are placed. Variable modifiers store integers, strings, and other values. Messenger modifiers are used to conditionally send specific kinds of information, such as messages and commands, to elements and other modifiers. Thus *collision* (a Messenger modifier) sends a message when an element collides with another; the *if* modifier sends a message when a specified condition is true; and the *timer* modifier sends a message when a specified time has elapsed. A *behavior* modifier can encapsulate groups of modifiers and other behaviors to create "super modifiers," which provide recursively complex operations.

mTropolis offers a layout view (to directly manipulate the graphic aspects of your project) and a structure view (for an outline of logical hierarchy showing which objects are contained within others). You can edit these views by dragging and dropping objects. mTropolis also provides an animation editor to work with "mToon" files, a proprietary mTropolis file format that can contain PICT, PICS, and QuickTime movies. Using the MovieTrax editor, you can build multitrack QuickTime movies. QuickTime VR features (including pan, tilt, zoom, and current node) are supported using mTropolis's Panorama Messenger.

Miniscript is mTropolis's natural language scripting environment for mathematical calculations, comparisons, and conditional branching. With it, you can set and get the values of variables and the properties of objects, and you can send messages. The mFactory Object Model (MOM) is a C/C++ API for 3GL programmers to extend and customize projects with user-built modifiers.

Completed mTropolis projects are built into stand-alone executable applications for 68K and Power Macintoshes, Windows 3.1, and Windows 95/NT.

8

QuarkImmedia (Macintosh/Windows)

March 23, 1998 — Denver — Quark Inc. announced this week that it will ship mTropolis™ 2.0 for free to registered mTropolis customers, but it will not continue selling the product to new customers. Instead, Quark™ will incorporate much of the technology into future multimedia products and is also considering licensing mTropolis in its current form to other companies.

From a Quark press release

As the powerful object-oriented mTropolis tool is further developed and integrated into Quark's long-term multimedia strategies, Quark's page layout tool, QuarkXPress, will become more presentation and network capable. Currently available for object-oriented programming is QuarkImmedia, which works in conjunction with QuarkXPress for building multimedia projects for CD–ROM, Internet/intranet, or disk distribution. QuarkImmedia consists of the QuarkImmedia Design Tool and QuarkImmedia Viewer. The Design Tool works as an Xtra with QuarkX-Press to stitch together multimedia objects in a playlist (see Figure 8-11). QuarkImmedia Viewer then allows users to run and view projects on both Mac and Windows platforms.

MediaForge (Windows)

MediaForge from Strata provides a Flexible Authoring Metaphor Environment so developers can choose to work within an object-based authoring system, or write scripts, or use a combination of both. Like the interface for mTropolis, MediaForge's object-based authoring system lets you drag and drop graphic files, movies, and sound objects in your presentation. For the scripting approach, the MediaBasic Editor is the scripting engine for Strata's Visual MediaBasic scripting language.

MediaForge's objects live in a hierarchical metaphor, which assigns

FIGURE 8-11

With QuarkImmedia, you can stitch together multimedia objects for presentations

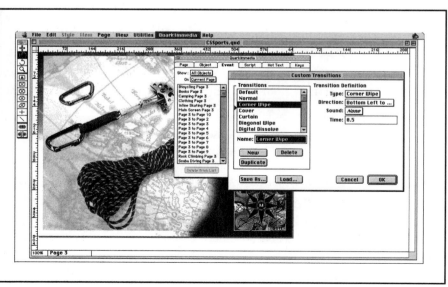

parent-child-grandchild relationships. You can view and edit the hierarchy in a List Editor, which displays the family tree. A project is the parent in the chain, and background elements become children to the project; *scene elements* comprise the project's grandchildren at the bottom of the chain. There can be any number of background and scene elements in your project, but each must be linked into the hierarchy. A scene, for example, cannot exist unless it is linked to a background.

You build your project on MediaForge's WYSIWYG editing *stage*, where you drag and drop objects using customizable toolbars and tool palettes. There are also integrated media editors for text, images, and sound. You can create animated *sprites* that will follow a path, and with the Sprite Import Wizard, you can build Framed Sprite Sequence (FSS) files and include them in your project. During editing, a *player palette* provides standard VCR-type controls for viewing your work and fine-tuning before final assembly. Over 160 transitional special effects in 8-, 16-, 24-, and 32-bit color are supported.

MediaForge supports RTF, ASCII, .BMP, .WMF, .PCX, .TIF, .TGA, .PCT, .JPG .WAV, .MIDI, CD-Audio, .MOV, .AVI, QuickTime, and Intel's Indeo formats as well as MCI-compliant overlay boards and video players. A Windows 95/NT player and a Web player with URL and http support are available.

Cross-Platform Authoring Notes

You face two major hurdles when you move multimedia projects across platforms; these hurdles have to do with the different schemes Macintosh and Windows computers use to manage text and colors.

If your project uses only bitmapped images and sounds, the text issue is moot. But if you use text in fields or require user entry of text, you will face size and shape issues (see Chapter 9). The Macintosh and Windows environments each use different fonts (even when the fonts have the same name), so you may wish to experiment with your fonts before designing or converting a project.

Each platform also uses its own character set; some special characters may appear as different characters on the other platform. The following Macintosh characters do not map across platforms, and you will have to use a substitute character:

Macintosh Character	Suggested Substitute
• (bullet)	* (asterisk)
" " (smart quotes)	" (normal quote)
≠ (does not equal)	<>

Macintosh Character	Suggested Substitute
≤ (less than or equal to)	<=
≥ (greater than or equal to)	>=
…(ellipsis)	... (three periods)

Here are some important tips for working with text in cross-platform applications:

- For text in boxes, center the text, leaving plenty of space or margin to avoid possible word-wrap on the other platform.
- Avoid outline and shadow styles on the Macintosh. They are not currently supported in Windows and may default to boldface.
- When the look of a larger-size font is extremely important, turn it into a bitmap, by screen capturing before you convert.
- If you use TrueType fonts or Adobe ATM, the fonts must be installed and available on both platforms.

Colors can also be difficult to manage in cross-platform projects, because both computer platforms employ different palette-mapping systems. The colors you use on the Macintosh, for example, may not appear the same on the PC. When you convert a Macintosh 256-color graphics file to Windows, all colors are mapped to their nearest equivalents, so the results you get will depend on the color palettes used on each platform. The results of converting a Macintosh 256-color palette to a Windows 16-color palette are usually disappointing. Color palettes are discussed in detail in Chapter 11.

---

tip *Rather than dithering a 256-color bitmap to 16 colors with unattractive results, try using gray-scale images instead.*

Multi

[Today's poets and songwriters concentrate text by distilling prose into a very few words heavy with meaning.]

6,000 years ago.....................................

words have
meaning

media

SUMERIA

MESOPOTAMIA

Babylonia

part

4

Multimedia Building Blocks

...........................meaningful marks were scraped onto mud tablets and left to harden in the sun.

EGYPT

Multi

Words and symbols in any form, spoken or written, are the most common system of communication.

6,000 years ago......................................

words have
meaning

media

SUMERIA

MESOPOTAMIA

Babylonia

chapter

9

Text

.........................meaningful marks were scraped onto mud tablets and left to harden in the sun.

EGYPT

USING text and symbols for communication is a very recent human development that began about 6,000 years ago in the Mediterranean Fertile Crescent—in Mesopotamia, Egypt, Sumeria, and Babylonia—when the first meaningful marks were scraped onto mud tablets and left to harden in the sun. Only members of the ruling classes and the priesthood were allowed to read and write the pictographic signs and cuneiforms.

The earliest messages delivered in written words typically contained information vital to the management of people, politics, and taxes. Because this new medium did not require rote memorization by frail human gray matter, written messages became popular among the elite. Unlike their human counterparts, these new messages were less likely to perish due to dysentery, acts of God, or amnesia. Even if a message were intercepted by foes or competitors, it would still be indecipherable except by those few who had acquired reading skills.

In fact, because those who could read probably attended the same private school together, reading, writing, and power politics in those days were naturally intertwined. In some former eras it was a capital offense to read unless you belonged to the proper social class or possessed a patent granted by your rulers.

Today, text and the ability to read it are doorways to power and knowledge. Reading and writing are expected and necessary skills within most modern cultures. Now, depending upon your proficiency with words, you may be awarded a doctorate instead of the death penalty. And, as has been the case throughout history, text still delivers information that can have potent meaning.

With the recent explosion of the Internet and the World Wide Web, text has become more important than ever. Indeed, the native language of the Web is HTML (Hypertext Markup Language), originally designed to display simple text documents on computer screens, with occasional graphic images thrown in as illustrations (see Chapter 14 for more history about the Internet). Academic papers, magazine articles, complex instruction manuals, and even the contents of entire books are now available for reading with a Web browser. Add a built-in function that links, with a click of the mouse, selected words and phrases to other related and perhaps more-detailed material (the "hypertext" part of HTML discussed later in this chapter), and you can surf the Net in a medium much richer than the paper pages of a book.

First Person

In the 15th century, when the Church was a strong power throughout Europe, Johann Gensfleisch zum Gutenberg, a trained goldsmith from Mainz, Germany, invented moveable type for printing presses. And he began producing religious literature, indulgence slips, and the Holy Bible. In the case of the Bible, he sold his copies to people who could read Latin and pay the equivalent of three years of a clerk's wage to own a personal copy of this Great Work. Other printers, including the Estienne family in France and Aldus Manutius in Italy, soon entered the publishing marketplace to compete, and

they changed the fabric of society. The mass production of identical copies of text enabled an information-based paradigm shift that changed the human universe in a substantial way. Lots of scribes and illuminators were put out of business.

By way of pointing out that some elements of the human equation may be constant throughout history, I would remark that Gutenberg, like many adventurers surfing the waves of today's revolution, took on a financial investor, Johann Fust. Gutenberg, who was a visionary craftsman perhaps better suited to lab and shop work, defaulted on a payment to Fust in 1455, was sued, and

lost his press and all its profits. Toward the end of his life, it is said that he was granted a place as courtier to the archbishop of Mainz, a position perhaps better remunerating than the diminishing social security plan rewarding today's surfer who wipes out while hanging ten at the leading edge of the business world.

—From a speech by Tay Vaughan to the jointly held World Conference on Educational Multimedia and Hypermedia and World Conference on Educational Telecommunications, Freiburg, Germany, June 1998

The social impact of this text-biased medium on the way people access and use information will be profound as the Web matures. In contrast to today's television medium, which consists of sound and images with a few text headlines "dumbed down" to a perceived lowest-common denominator of passive audience, the Web offers an active experience laden with enough choices to challenge even bright people who can read. More than television, with its 5 or 50 or even 100 channels, the Web offers an explorer's paradise of millions of HTML documents. As bandwidth improves and more multimedia elements are successfully embedded within these documents, developers of content will not escape the difficult design issues discussed in Chapters 17 and 18. Who is the audience? What words should I use?

With its penchant for interactivity, multimedia too often ignores the power of narrative, of stories. There's really something to be said for documents with a beginning, middle, and end.

Steven Levy, author of *Hackers* and *Artificial Life*,
editor/columnist for *MacWorld*

The Power of Meaning

Even a single word may be cloaked in many meanings, so as you begin working with any medium it is important to cultivate accuracy and conciseness in the specific words you choose. In multimedia, these are the words that will appear in your titles, menus, and navigation aids.

Today's poets and songwriters concentrate text by distilling lengthy prose into few words heavy with meaning. Advertising wordsmiths render the meaning of entire product lines into an evocative single word, logo, or tag line. Multimedia authors weave words, symbols, sounds, and images, and then blend text into the mix to create integrated tools and interfaces for acquiring, displaying, and disseminating messages and data, using computers.

"Barbie," "green," and "lite" may each easily trigger a rush of different meanings. A piercing cry in the night, the sight of fire engines leaving your street as you steer your car into your neighborhood, the scent of drying kelp along the seashore, the feel of rough pine bark against your chest as you climb, fingernails on a chalkboard—all these raw sensory messages are important only because of what they mean to you. Indeed, you alone know the words that will stop you dead in your tracks with anger, or, better, soothe you seductively over a quiet dinner for two. These words have meaning.

All of these examples demonstrate the following multimedia principle: It's important to design labels for title screens, menus, and buttons using words that have the most precise and powerful meanings to express what you need to say. Understand the subtle shadings. GO BACK! is more powerful than *Previous*; QUIT is more powerful than *Close*. TERRIFIC! may work better than *That Answer Was Correct*.

Experiment with the words you plan to use by letting others try them. If you have the budget, set up a focus group to have potential users experience your words. Watch them work. See if users flinch, balk, or click the Help button in confusion. See if they can even find Help.

Words and symbols in any form, spoken or written, are the most common system of communication. They deliver the most widely understood meaning to the greatest number of people—accurately and in detail. Because of this, they are vital elements of multimedia menus, navigation systems, and content. You will reward yourself and your users if you take the time to use excellent words. Let your poet loose!

tip *Browse through a thesaurus. You will be surprised at the number of synonyms and related words that are closely associated to the word you start with, and you will certainly find the one word that most perfectly fits your need. The majority of today's popular word processors ship with a bundled electronic thesaurus.*

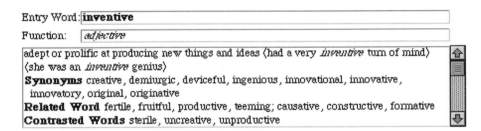

If you are reading this book in English, you might consider yourself lucky. A recent study by the British Council concluded that 1 billion people will speak English by the year 2000 as a first, second, or "foreign" language. English is the official or joint official language of more than 75 countries, and Algeria recently dumped French in favor of English as the second language in schools, irritating a great many Parisian intellectuals. More than two thirds of the world's scientists read English, and three quarters of the world's mail is written in English. Eighty percent of the world's information that is stored on computers is written in English.

When we have a technical meeting with engineers coming from Germany, France, Spain, Sweden, Japan, and other countries, people say "Hello!" when they walk into the room; English is clearly the international common language of business and commerce and science. Sometimes the etiquette of polite speech is even more fascinating: when you have a room with a group of Germans talking to each other in German and suddenly a foreign visitor comes in, from one sentence to the other, they seamlessly switch to English.

Dipl.-Ing. Roland Cuny, Product Division Emerging
Technologies, Siemens Nixdorf Informationssysteme AG,
Paderborn, Germany

About Fonts and Faces

A *typeface* is a family of graphic characters that usually includes many type sizes and styles. A *font* is a collection of characters of a single size and style belonging to a particular typeface family. Typical font *styles* are boldface and italic. Other style attributes, such as underlining and outlining of characters, may be added by your computer software. Type sizes are usually expressed in points; one *point* is .0138 inches or about 1/72 of an inch. The font's size is the distance from the top of the capital letters to the bottom of the descenders in letters such as *g* and *y*. Helvetica, Times, and Courier are typefaces; Times 12-point italic is a font. In the computer world, the term "font" is commonly used when typeface or face would be more correct.

A font's size does not exactly describe the height or width of its characters. This is because the *x-height* (the height of the lowercase letter *x*) of two fonts may vary, while the height of the capital letters of those fonts may be the same (see Figure 9-1). Computer fonts automatically add space below the descender (and sometimes above) to provide appropriate line spacing, or *leading* (pronounced "ledding," named for the thin strips of lead inserted between the lines by traditional typesetters). There can be significant variation among fonts.

Leading can be adjusted in most programs on both the Macintosh and in Windows. Typically you will find this fine-tuning adjustment in the Text menu of image editing programs or the Paragraph menu of word processing programs, though this is not an official standard. No matter where your application has placed the controls for leading, you will need to experiment with them to achieve the best result for your font. Figure 9-2 illustrates common methods of adjusting leading for both the Macintosh and Windows.

With a font editing program like Fontographer from Macromedia (you'll see an example of it in Figure 9-12 later in the chapter), adjustments can also

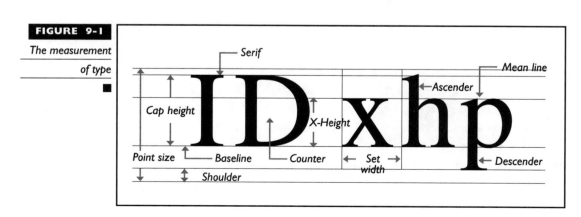

FIGURE 9-1

The measurement of type

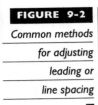

FIGURE 9-2

Common methods
for adjusting
leading or
line spacing

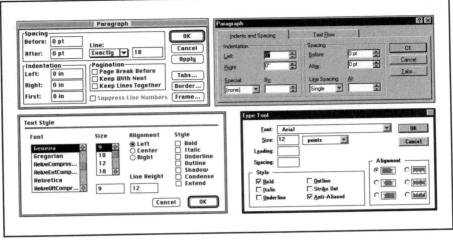

be made along the horizontal axis of text: the *character metrics* of each character and the *kerning* of character pairs can be altered. Character metrics are the general measurements applied to individual characters; kerning is the spacing between character pairs. Working with PostScript, TrueType, and Master fonts, but not bitmapped fonts (see "Computers and Text" later in this chapter), the metrics of a font can be altered to create interesting effects. For example, you can adjust the body width of each character from *regular* to *condensed* to *expanded*, displayed in the Sabon font used in this book:

Regular

Condensed

Expanded

Or you can adjust the spacing between characters (*tracking*) and the kerning between pairs of characters:

Tighter Track

Looser Track

Av Av

Kerned   Unkerned

When it draws or *rasterizes* the letter *A* on the screen or in printed output, the computer must know how to represent the letter using tiny square pixels or dots. It does this according to the hardware available and according to your specification from a choice of available typefaces and fonts. High-resolution monitors and printers can make more attractive-looking and

9

varied characters. And today's broad selection of software fonts makes it easier to find the right typeface and font for your need. Here are some examples of the same letter displayed using different fonts:

Cases

In centuries when type was set by hand, the type for a single font was always stored in two trays, or *cases*; the upper tray held capital letters, and the lower tray held the small letters. Today a capital letter is called *uppercase,* and a small letter is called *lowercase.*

tip *Studies have shown that words and sentences with mixed upper- and lowercase letters are easier to read than words or sentences in all caps.*

In some situations, such as for passwords, a computer is *case sensitive.* But nowadays, in most situations requiring keyboard input—on the Macintosh or in Windows—the computer recognizes both the upper- and lowercase forms of a character to be the same. In that manner, the computer is said to be *case insensitive.*

warning *The directory and file names used in Uniform Resource Locator (URL) addresses on the Internet are case sensitive! Thus,* http://www.timestream.com/people/ biotay.html *points to a different directory and file than* http://www.timestream.com/ People/bioTay.html. *On the other hand, the record type (HTTP) and the domain name (www.timestream.com), and e-mail addresses (tay@timestream.com) as well, are case insensitive. Read more about addresses on the Internet in Chapter 14.*

Recently, company and product names such as EveryWare, AirWorks, PhotoDisc, PageMaker, LogoMotion, FileMaker, and WebStar have become popular. Placing an uppercase letter in the middle of a word, called an *intercap,* is a trend that emerged from the computer programming community where coders discovered they could better see the words they used for variables and commands.

Serif Versus Sans Serif

Typefaces can be described in many ways, just as a home advertised by a realtor, a wine described by a food critic, or a political candidate's platform can all be described in many ways. Type has been characterized as feminine, masculine, delicate, formal, capricious, witty, comic, happy, technical, newsy—you name it. But one approach for categorizing typefaces is universally understood, and it has less to do with the reader's response to the type than it does with the type's mechanical and historical properties. This approach uses the terms *serif* and *sans serif*.

Serif versus sans serif is the simplest way to categorize a typeface; the type either has a serif or it doesn't (*sans* is French for without). The serif is the little decoration at the end of a letter stroke. Times, New Century Schoolbook, Bookman, and Palatino are examples of serif fonts. Helvetica, Arial, Optima, and Avant Garde are sans serif. Notice the difference between serif and sans serif in the following illustration:

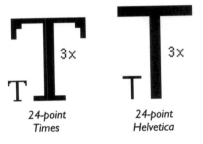

24-point Times *24-point Helvetica*

On the printed page, serif fonts are traditionally used for body text because the serifs are said to help guide the reader's eye along the line of text. Sans serif fonts, on the other hand, are used for headlines and bold statements. But the computer world of standard, 72-dpi monitor resolution is not the same as the print world, and it can be argued that sans serif fonts are far more legible and attractive when used in the small sizes of a text field on a screen. Indeed, careful selection of a sans serif font designed to be legible in the small sizes (such as Geneva on the Macintosh or Small Fonts in Windows) makes more sense when you are presenting a substantial amount of text on the screen. The Times font at 9-point size may look too busy and actually be difficult and tiring to read. And a large, bold serif font for a title or headline can deliver a message of elegance and character in your graphic layout. Use what is right for your delivery system, which may not necessarily be the same as what is right when you print the material to paper—

WYSIWYG (*What You See Is What You Get*) when printing out what you create on a computer monitor is more of a goal than absolute fact.

Using Text in Multimedia

Imagine designing a project that used no text at all. Its content could not be at all complex, and you would need to use many pictures and symbols to train your audience how to navigate through the project. Certainly voice and sound could guide the audience, but users would quickly tire of this—greater effort is required to pay attention to spoken words than to browse text.

A single item of menu text accompanied by a single action (a mouse click, keystroke, or finger pressed to the monitor) requires little training and is clean and immediate. Use text for titles and headlines (what it's all about), for menus (where to go), for navigation (how to get there), and for content (what you see when you get there).

---

tip   *In designing your navigation system, bring the user to a particular destination with as few actions and as short a wait as possible. If the user never needs the Help button to get there, you are doing everything right!*

Designing with Text

Computer screens provide a very small workspace for developing complex ideas. At some time or another, you will need to deliver high-impact or very concise text messages on the computer screen in as condensed a form as possible. From a design perspective, your choice of font size and the number of headlines you place on a particular screen must be related both to the complexity of your message and to its venue.

If your messages are part of an interactive project or Web site where you know the user is seeking information, you can pack a great deal of text information onto the screen before it becomes overwhelmingly busy. Seekers want dense material, and while they travel along your navigational pathways, they will scroll through relevant text and study the details. Here is where you must strike a balance, however. Too little text on a screen requires annoying page turns and unnecessary mouse clicks and waits; too much text can make the screen seem overcrowded and unpleasant.

On the other hand, if you are providing public-speaking support, the text will be keyed to a live presentation where the text accents the main message. In this case, use large fonts and few words with lots of white space. Let the audience focus on the speaker at the podium, rather than spend its time reading fine points and subpoints projected on a screen.

---

tip   *A lengthy text document read by a Web browser may scroll for hundreds of lines without annoying the user; it's expected. As a rule of thumb, however, try to make your Web pages no longer than one-and-a-half to two screenfuls of text. Many "standard" pages are 600 pixels in height (about one-and-a-half screens on a VGA monitor). For pages intended to get people's attention, make your page about 400 pixels high so there will be no scrolling at all. For printing text documents, provide a separate link to a complete document in either text, word processor, or Adobe PDF format instead of relying on a browser's print facilities. It is often more convenient to print and read a document than scroll through many pages of text on a monitor.*

Choosing Text Fonts

Picking the fonts to use in your multimedia presentation may be somewhat difficult from a design standpoint. Here again, you must be a poet, an advertising psychologist, and also a graphic designer. Try to sense the potential reaction of the user to what is on the screen. Here are a few design suggestions that may help:

- For small type, use the most legible font available. Decorative fonts that cannot be read are useless:

    Can you read me?

- Use as few different faces as possible in the same work, but vary the weight and size of your typeface using italic and bold styles where they look good. Using too many fonts on the same page is called ransom-note typography.

- In text blocks, adjust the leading for the most pleasing line spacing. Lines too tightly packed are difficult to read.

- Vary the size of a font in proportion to the importance of the message you are delivering.

- In large-size headlines, adjust the spacing between letters (kerning) so that the spacing feels right. Big gaps between large letters can turn your title into a toothless waif. You may need to kern by hand, using a bitmapped version of your text.

9

■ To make your type stand out or be more legible, explore the effects of different colors and of placing the text on various backgrounds. Try reverse type for a stark, white-on-black message.

■ Use anti-aliased text where you want a gentle and blended look for titles and headlines. This can give a more professional appearance. *Anti-aliasing* blends the colors along the edges of the letters (called *dithering*) to create a soft transition between the letter and its background. Color Plate 5 shows an example of anti-aliased type.

■ Try DropCaps and InitialCaps to accent your words. Most word processors and text editors will let you create dropCaps and SMALLCAPS in your text. Adobe and others make InitialCaps (such as the one shown below from Adobe, called "Gothic"). The letters are actually carefully drawn artwork and are available in special libraries as encapsulated PostScript files (EPSF).

■ If you are using centered type in a text block, keep the number of lines to a minimum.

■ For attention-grabbing results, try graphically altering and distorting the text. Wrap your word onto a sphere, bend it into a wave, or splash it with rainbow colors. Font editing tools such as ResEdit, Fontographer, FontMonger, and FontChameleon are discussed later in this chapter. Also, paint and drawing packages for customizing text and bitmaps are discussed in Chapter 7.

■ Experiment with drop shadows. Place a copy of the word on top of the original and offset the original up and over a few pixels. Then color the original gray (or any other color). The word may become more legible and provide much greater impact. At Web sites, shadowed text and graphics on a plain white background add depth to a page. See Chapter 11 for tips on making shadows.

■ Surround headlines with plenty of white space. *White space* is a designer's term for roomy blank areas; programmers call the invisible character made by a space (ASCII 32) or a tab (ASCII 9) white space.

- Pick the fonts that seem right to you for getting your message across, then double-check your choice against other opinions. Learn to accept criticism.

- Use meaningful words or phrases for links and menu items.

- Text links (*anchors*) on Web pages can accent your message: they stand out by color and underlining. Use link colors consistently throughout a site, and avoid iridescent green on red or purple on puce.

- Bold or emphasize text to highlight ideas or concepts, but do not make text look like a link or a button when it is not.

- On a Web page, put vital text elements and menus in the top 320 pixels. Studies of surfer habits have discovered that only 10 to 15 percent of surfers *ever* scroll *any* page.

---

cross platform *Characters identified in a particular font (say, Courier 12-point) do not look the same on a Macintosh as they do on Windows display monitors. Typically, what is called 12-point on a Macintosh will be a 10- or 9-point size in Windows. And the actual shape of the characters will be different (see Figure 9-3).*

Menus for Navigation

An interactive multimedia project or Web site typically consists of a body of information or *content* through which a user navigates by pressing a key, clicking a mouse, or pressing a touchscreen. The simplest menus consist of text lists of topics. Users choose a topic, click it, and go there. As multimedia and graphical user interfaces become pervasive in the computer community, certain intuitive actions are being widely learned.

For example, if there are three words on a computer screen, the typical response from the user, without prompting, is to click one of these words to evoke activity. Sometimes menu items are surrounded by boxes or made to look like push buttons. Or, to conserve space, text such as Throw Tomatoes, Play Video, and Press to Quit is often shortened to Tomatoes, Video, and Quit. Regardless, the intention remains clear to the user.

Text is helpful to users to provide perpetual cues about their location within the body of content. When users must click up and down through many layers of menus to reach their goal, they may not get lost, but they may feel transported to the winding and narrow streets of a medieval city where only the locals know the way. This is especially true if the user moves

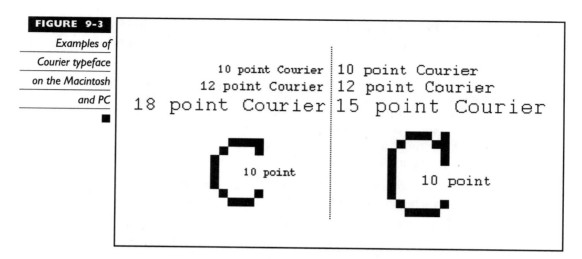

FIGURE 9-3

Examples of Courier typeface on the Macintosh and PC

slowly from screen to screen en route to that goal. If Throw Tomatoes leads to Red or Green, then to California or Massachusetts, then to President or Vice President, then to Forehead or Chest, then to Arrested or Got Away, and so on, the user can end up tangled in the branches of a navigation tree without cues or a map. However, if an interactive textual or symbolic list of the branches taken (all the way from the beginning) is continuously displayed, the user can at any time skip intervening steps in a nonlinear manner or easily return to one of the previous locations in the list.

> Tomatoes
> > Red
> > > Massachusetts
> > > > President
> > > > > Chest
> > > > > > Arrested

The more locations included in the menu list, the more options available for navigation. On the Web, designers typically place on every page at least a Main Menu of links that offers the user a handhold and mechanism for returning to the beginning. Navigation methodologies and navigation maps are discussed in greater detail in Chapter 17 and, in the case of surfing the World Wide Web, in Chapter 18.

tip *Avoid using more than a few levels of GO BACKs or RETURNs if you do not provide a map. Too much tunneling in and out with repetitive mouse clicks will frustrate users and discourage exploration. Display a perpetual menu of interactive text or symbolic cues, so users can always extricate themselves from any place in the tunnel. In a Web browser, this is handled by a Back button containing a history of places visited.*

Buttons for Interaction

In most modern cultures a doorbell is recognized by its context (next to the door itself, possibly lit); but if you grew up in a high-rise apartment, you may have seen 50 or more buttons at the entrance. Unless you knew that yours was the third from the top on the left, you could find your button only by reading the printed or scrawled name beside it. And certainly your Aunt Barbara needed this text cue to avoid having to push the Help button, which in this case rang in the building superintendent's apartment.

In multimedia, *buttons* are the objects, such as blocks of text, a pretty blue triangle, or a photograph, that make things happen when they are clicked. They were invented for the sole purpose of being pushed or prodded with cursor, mouse, key, or finger—and to manifest properties such as highlighting or other visual or sound effects to indicate that you hit the target. On the Web, text and graphic art may be buttons. Buttons and the art of button design and human interaction are discussed in detail in Chapter 17. For now, remember that the rules for proper selection of text and fonts in your projects apply to buttons as well as headlines, bullet items, and blocks of text.

When I was four years old, a button was the little plastic knob mounted in brass next to the front door. When I pushed it, a muffled ringing sound worked its way through the house from the kitchen. Sometimes I would push the button a lot and somebody would always come to the door. As an adult, I'm still pushing buttons to make things happen.

Ann Stewart, Genesys Telecommunications Laboratories, Inc.

9

The automatic button-making tools supplied with multimedia and HTML page authoring systems are useful, but in creating the text for you, they offer little opportunity to fine-tune the look of the text. Character- and word-wrap, highlighting, and inverting are automatically applied to your buttons, as needed, by the authoring system. These default buttons and styles may seem overused or trite, but by using common button styles, shapes, borders, and highlights, you increase the probability that users will know what to do with them—especially when they are also labeled.

warning *The text that labels your predesigned buttons is typically generated by the same routines that draw text into fields. So make sure that the fonts you select for your buttons are available in the environments in which you will run your software. Your button fonts will need to travel with your project. See Table 9-1 for a list of fonts shipped with Windows 95 and Macintosh System 8. These are perhaps safest for button labeling.*

Fonts Installed in Macintosh System 8	Fonts Installed in a VGA System in Windows 95
Charcoal (TrueType)	Algerian (ALGER.TTF)
Chicago (TrueType)	Arial (ARIAL.TTF)
Courier (TrueType)	Arial Bold (ARIALBD.TTF)
Courier Bold (TrueType)	Arial Bold Italic (ARIALBI.TTF)
Courier 9, 10, 12, 14, 18, 24 (Bitmap)	Arial Italic (ARIALI.TTF)
Geneva (TrueType)	Arial Rounded MT Bold (ARLRDBD.TTF)
Geneva Italic 9 (Bitmap)	Bookman Old Style Bold (BOOKOSB.TTF)
Geneva 10, 14, 18, 20, 24 (Bitmap)	Braggadocio (BRAGGA.TTF)
Helvetica (TrueType)	Britannic Bold (BRITANIC.TTF)
Helvetica Bold (TrueType)	Brush Script MT Italic (BRUSHSCI.TTF)
Helvetica 10, 12, 14, 18, 24 (Bitmap)	Century Gothic (GOTHIC.TTF)
Monaco (TrueType)	Colonna MT (COLONNA.TTF)
Monaco 12 (Bitmap)	CorelBook View (chkview.fon)
New York (TrueType)	Courier 10, 12, 14 (coure.fon)
New York 9, 10, 12, 14, 18, 20, 24 (Bitmap)	Courier New (COUR.TTF)
Palatino 12, 14, 18, 24 (Bitmap)	Courier New Bold (COURBO.TTF)
Symbol (TrueType)	Courier New Bold Italic (COURBI.TTF)
Symbol 9, 10, 12, 14, 18, 24 (Bitmap)	Courier New Italic (COURI.TTF)
Times (TrueType)	Desdemona (DESDEMMON.TTF)
Times Bold (TrueType)	Footlight MT Light (FTLTLT.TTF)
Times Bold Italic (TrueType)	Impact (IMPACT.TTF)
Times 9, 10, 14, 24 (Bitmap)	Kino MT (KINO.TTF)
	Matura MT Script Capitals (MATURASC. TTF)
	Modern (MODERN.FON)
	MS LineDraw (LINEDRAW.TTF)
	MS Sans Serif 8, 10, 12, 14, 18, 24 (serife.fon)
	Playbill (PLAYBILL.TFF)
	Roman (ROMAN.FON)
	Script (SCRIPT.FON)
	Small Fonts (smalle.fon)
	Symbol (SYMBOL.TTF)

TABLE 9-1   *Fonts Included in Windows 95 and System 8* ■

Fonts Installed in Macintosh System 8	Fonts Installed in a VGA System in Windows 95
	Symbol 8, 10, 12, 14, 18, 24 (symbole.fon)
	Times New Roman (TIMES.TTF)
	Times New Roman Bold (TIMESBD.TFF)
	Times New Roman Bold Italic (TIMESBI.TTF)
	Times New Roman Italic (TIMESI.TTF)
	V1 Lucida Sans (v1sp.fon)
	V2 Lucida Sans (v2sp.fon)
	V3 Lucida Sans (v3sp.fon)
	V4 Lucida Sans (v4sp.fon)
	V5 Lucida Sans (v5sp.fon)
	V6 Lucida Sans (v6sp.fon)
	V7 Lucida Sans (v7sp.fon)
	Wide Latin (LATINWD.TTF)
	WingDings (WINGDING.TTF)

TABLE 9-1   *Fonts Included in Windows 95 and System 8 (continued)* ∎

Pick a font for buttons that is, above all, legible; then adjust the text size of the labels to provide adequate space between the button's rim and the text. You can choose from many styles of buttons and several standard methodologies for highlighting. You will want to experiment to get the right combinations of font, spacing, and colors for just the right look.

In most authoring platforms, it is easy to make your own buttons from bitmaps or drawn objects. In a message-passing authoring system, where you can script activity when the mouse button is up or down over an object, you can quickly replace one bitmap with another highlighted or colored version of the bitmap to show that the button has been "pushed" or that the mouse is over it. Making your own buttons from bitmaps or drawn objects gives you greater design power and creative freedom and also ensures against the missing font problem. On the other hand, this custom work may require a good deal more time. Interesting text and graphic buttons for the Web can be created as .GIF or .JPG bitmaps that, when clicked, link to other pages. There is no easy provision in HTML for highlighting or animating these graphic images, but typically the destination address (URL) is displayed in the status window of the browser when the mouse is over a linked image or text element. So users know first if the mouse is over an active button and second, where that button will take them if they click. If you take a short step beyond vanilla HTML, with a few lines of JavaScript you *can* program your button image to switch with another when the mouse is over it or "pushing down" (see Chapter 17 for sample code to do this).

Whether default or custom, treat the design and labeling of your buttons as an industrial art project: buttons are the part of your project the user touches.

Fields for Reading

You are already working uphill when you design text to be read on the screen. Experiments have shown that reading text on a computer screen is slower and more difficult than reading the same text in hard copy or book form. Indeed, many users, it seems, would rather print out their reports and e-mail messages and read them on paper than page through screens of text. Reading hard copy is still more comfortable.

---

warning *Research has shown that when people read text on a computer screen they blink only 3 to 5 times per minute, but they blink 20 to 25 times per minute when reading text on paper. This reduced eye movement may cause dryness, fatigue, and possibly damage to the eyes. Research also suggests that monitors should be placed lower than eye level.*

Unless the very purpose of your multimedia project or Web site is to display large blocks of text, try to present to the user only a few paragraphs of text per page. Use a font that is easy to read rather than a prettier font that is illegible. Try to display whole paragraphs on the screen, and avoid breaks where users must go back and forth between pages to read the entire paragraph.

---

cross platform *The amount of text that will fit in a field is commonly limited by memory constraints. In most authoring systems on the Macintosh, this limit is 32K; under Windows, it is often 64K. If your text exceeds this limit (32K allows about 4,000 eight-character words), you will need to provide another mechanism for document paging. In some authoring systems, there is significant degradation of performance when scrolling through large amounts of text in a scrolling field.*

---

warning *Although in HTML 4 you can specify a base font size, color, and face for displaying text on a Web page, you have no guarantee that that font is installed in the user's system. If it is missing, a browser will attempt to substitute a similar font, but the look is not guaranteed to be the same as the one you have designed. Provide a way to download the font to the end user's computer if the right look is important to you.*

Portrait Versus Landscape

Traditional hard copy and printed documents in the taller-than-wide orientation are simply not readable on a standard VGA monitor with 640×480 pixel resolution and a wider-than-tall aspect ratio. The taller-than-wide orientation used for printed documents is called *portrait*; this is the 8.5-by-11-inch size unique to the United States or the internationally designated standard A4 size, 8.27 by 11.69 inches. The wider-than-tall orientation normal to monitors is called *landscape*. Shrinking an 11-inch-tall portrait page of text into 480 pixels of monitor height yields illegible chicken tracks. As discussed in Chapter 5, the 640×480, square-pixel screen with its 4×3 aspect ratio has become the most prevalent display screen in the world (there are millions of them). While we wait for wider use of monitors displaying 1024×768 pixels and even 1280×1024 (where a full page of text is readable in portrait mode), there are four possible solutions if you are working with a block of text that is taller than what will fit:

- Put the text into a scrolling field. This is the solution used by Web browsers.

- Put the text into a single field or graphic image in a project window and let the user move the whole window up or down upon command. This is most appropriate when you need to present text with page breaks and formatting identical to the printed document.

- Break the text into fields that fit on monitor-sized pages, and design control buttons to flip through these pages.

- Design your multimedia project for a special monitor that is taller than it is wide (portrait). Such "page view" monitors are expensive; they are used for print-based typesetting and layout.

HTML Documents

The standard document format used for pages on the World Wide Web is called Hypertext Markup Language (HTML). In a HTML document you can specify typefaces, sizes, colors, and other properties by "marking up" the text in the document with *tags*. The process of marking up documents is simple: Where you want text to be bold, surround it with the tags <B> and

</B>; the text between the tags will then be displayed by your browser application in bold type. Where you have a header, surround it with <H1> and </H1>; for an ordered list of things (1, 2, 3, ... or a, b, c, ..., etc.), surround your list with <OL> and </OL>. There are many tags you can use to lay out a page. How HTML works is discussed in greater detail in Chapters 15 and 18. There are also many good HTML learning guides and references available on the Web.

----

http://www.p-pub.com
http://www.stars.com
http://www.ncsa.uiuc.edu/demoweb/html-primer.html
http://union.ncsa.uiuc.edu:80/HyperNews/get/www/html/guides.html
http://webreference.com

Check out these Web sites for more information about HTML

The remarkable growth of the World Wide Web is straining the "old" designs for displaying text on computers. Indeed, while marked-up text files (HTML documents) remain at the foundation of Web activity, when you visit a well-designed Web site, you often discover graphic images, animations, and interactive work-arounds contrived to *avoid* displaying text. The neat paragraphs, indented lists, and formats for text documents for which HTML was originally intended are evolving into multimedia documents, not text documents, and the HTML method and standard are consequently suffering great stress.

As features and tags and plug-ins and special scripts are tacked onto or embedded into HTML to satisfy the demand for multimedia interfaces, at some point HTML will need to be redesigned from the ground up—as a multimedia delivery tool, not just a text display tool with assorted attachments. Indeed, this redesign is currently under way in the form of Dynamic HTML (See Figure 9-4).

HTML doesn't provide you with much flexibility to make pretty text elements, but you may be able to lay out pleasing documents using block-quote indents, tables, frames, and horizontal rules. Pretty text in HTML documents is typically done as graphical bitmaps that are placed within the HTML document's layout with image tags (<IMG SRC= >). Indeed, using plain HTML, you do not know what font a reader will use to view your document—the default display font is a preference that can be set in the browser and is one known to be available on the viewer's machine. So some viewers may read your words in serif Times Roman, others in sans serif

Helvetica or Arial. Designing documents in HTML for the World Wide Web is discussed in Chapter 18.

http://www.futuretense.com
http://www.adobe.com
http://www.tumbleweed.com
http://www.netscape.com

Software companies are working to increase the power of HTML

Symbols and Icons

Symbols are concentrated text in the form of stand-alone graphic constructs. Symbols convey meaningful messages. The Macintosh trash can symbol, for instance, tells you where to throw away old files; the Windows hourglass cursor tells you to wait while the computer is processing. Though you may think of symbols as belonging strictly to the realm of graphic art, in multimedia you should treat them as text—or visual words—because they carry meaning. Symbols such as the familiar trash can and hourglass are more properly called *icons*; these are symbolic representations of objects and processes common to the graphical user interfaces of many computer operating systems.

FIGURE 9-4

Web pages written in Dynamic HTML and displayed by DHTML-capable browsers allow greater creative flexibility than vanilla HTML

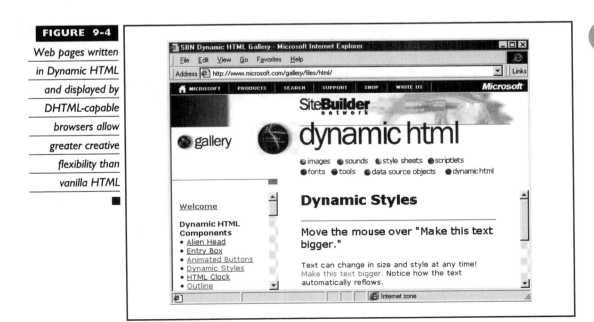

Certainly text is more efficient than imagery and pictures for delivering a precise message to users. On the other hand, pictures, icons, moving images, and sounds are most easily recalled and remembered by viewers. With multimedia, you have the power to blend both text and icons (as well as colors, sounds, images, and motion video) to enhance the overall impact and value of your message.

Word meanings are shared by millions of people, but the special symbols you design for a multimedia project are not; these symbols must be learned before they can be useful message carriers. Some symbols are more widely used and understood than others, but readers of even these common symbols had to grow accustomed to their meanings. Learning a system of symbols can be as difficult as lessons in any foreign language.

---

warning   *Do not be seduced into creating your own language of symbols and icons.*

Here are some symbols you may already know:

And here are some astronomer's symbols from the days of Kepler and Galileo that you may not have learned—still in heavy use by astrologers, they represent the 12 constellations of the zodiac:

$$♀\ ♈\ ♉\ ♊\ ♋\ ♌\ ♍\ ♎\ ♏\ ♐\ ♑\ ♒\ ♓$$

But why are there 13 icons in the illustration above? Or did you notice? Find the sign for the planet Venus among the constellations. Not easy if you are unfamiliar with the meaning of these symbols.

When HyperCard was first introduced in 1987, there was a flurry of creative attempts by graphic artists to create interesting navigational symbols to alleviate the need for text. The screens were pure graphic art and power—all lines and angles and stunning shadows. But many users were frustrated because they could not get to the data right away and had to first wade through help and guidance material to learn the symbols. In this context, it is clearly safer, from a product design point of view, to combine symbols with text cues. This ensures the graphic impact of the symbols but allows prompting the user on their meaning. The Macintosh trash can icon, incidentally, also has a text label, "Trash," just in case people don't get the idea from the symbol.

Nonetheless, a few symbols have emerged in the interactive multimedia world as an accepted lexicon of navigation cues that do not need text. These symbols are by no means universal, but Figure 9-5 shows some that have roots from the days of teletypewriters, others from early HyperCard and videodisc development, and yet others from the consumer electronics world. Even for these common symbols, text labels are often added to the graphic icons to avoid uncertainty.

Animating Text

There are plenty of ways to retain a viewer's attention when displaying text. For example, you can animate bulleted text and have it "fly" onto the screen. You can "grow" a headline a character at a time. For speakers, simply highlighting the important text works well as a pointing device. When there are several points to be made, you can stack keywords and flash them past the viewer in a timed automated sequence (as in the roadside Burma Shave ads—signs placed every half mile or so along the highway, each offering the motorist just a few more words toward a complete slogan). You might fly in some keywords, dissolve others, rotate or spin others, and so forth, until

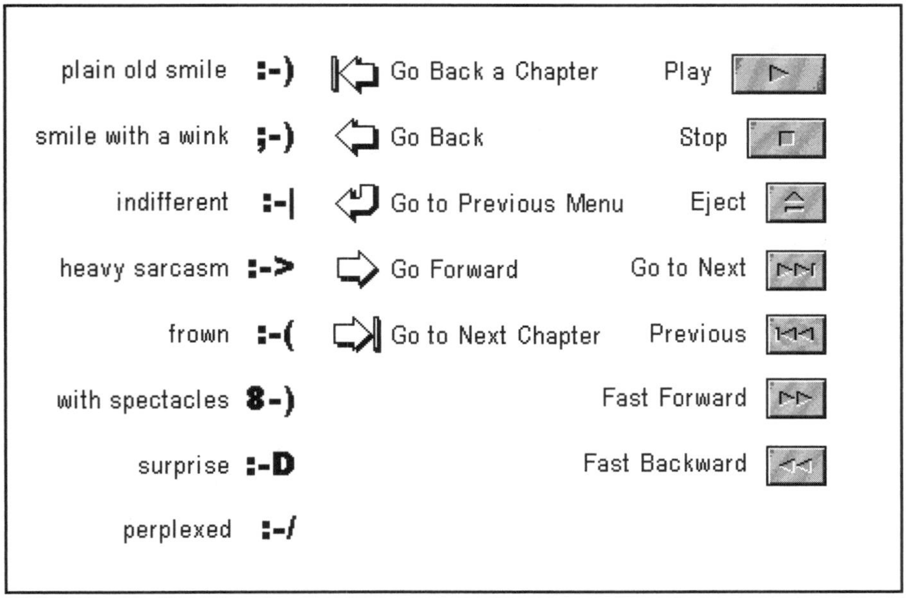

FIGURE 9-5

Some symbols are easily recognized but may still require text titles; "smiley" symbols, or emoticons, used in Internet conversation to express mood, are made up entirely of text and punctuation characters

plain old smile :-)	Go Back a Chapter Play
smile with a wink ;-)	Go Back Stop
indifferent :-|	Go to Previous Menu Eject
heavy sarcasm :->	Go Forward Go to Next
frown :-(	Go to Next Chapter Previous
with spectacles 8-)	Fast Forward
surprise :-D	Fast Backward
perplexed :-/	

you have a dynamic bulleted list of words that is interesting to watch. But be careful—don't overdo the special effects or they will become boring.

••

http://www.specular.com
http://www.xaostools.com
http://www.macromedia.com
http://www.metatools.com

Special tools offer 3-D impact and plug-ins for creating cool text graphics

Powerful but inexpensive applications such as Specular's LogoMotion and Xaos Tools' TypeCaster (see "Making Pretty Text" later in this chapter) let you create 3-D text using both TrueType and Type 1 Adobe fonts. You can also use Illustrator or FreeHand EPS (Encapsulated PostScript) outline files to create still images in 3-D and then animate the results to create QuickTime movies with broadcast-quality rendering.

Computers and Text

Very early in the development of the Macintosh computer's monitor hardware, Apple chose to use a resolution of 72 picture elements (*pixels*) per inch. This matches the standard measurement of the printing industry (72 *points* per inch) and allows desktop publishers and designers to see on the monitor what their printed output will look like (called "What You See Is What You Get," or WYSIWYG). In addition, Apple made each pixel square shaped, providing even measurements in all directions. Until the Macintosh was invented, and the VGA video standard set for the PC (at 96 pixels per inch), pixels were typically taller than they were wide. The aspect ratio for older EGA monitors, for example, is 1.33:1, taller than wide. VGA monitor resolutions for both Macintosh and Windows display 640 pixels across the screen and 480 pixels down the screen (called 640×480 resolution), and the pixels themselves have an aspect ratio of 1:1 (square).

The Font Wars

In 1985, the desktop publishing revolution was spearheaded by Apple and the Macintosh computer, in combination with word processing and page layout software products that enabled a high-resolution 300-dpi laser printer using special software to "draw" the shapes of characters as a cluster of tiny square pixels computed from the geometry of the character. This special software was Adobe's PostScript page description and outline font language. It was licensed by Apple and included in the firmware of Apple's LaserWriter laser printer.

PostScript is really a method of describing an image in terms of mathematical constructs (Bezier curves), so it is used not only to describe the individual characters of a font but also to describe entire illustrations and whole pages of text. Because each PostScript character is a mathematical formula, it can be easily scaled bigger or smaller so it looks right whether drawn at 24 points or 96 points, whether the printer is a 300-dpi LaserWriter or a high-resolution 1200-, 2400-, or even 3600-dpi image setter suitable for the finest print jobs. And the PostScript characters can be drawn much faster than in the old-fashioned way. Before PostScript, the printing software looked up the character's shape in a bitmap table containing a representation of the pixels of every character in every size. PostScript quickly became the de facto industry font and printing standard for desktop publishing and played a significant role in the early success of Apple's Macintosh computer.

There are two kinds of PostScript fonts: Type 3 and Type 1. Type 3 font technology is *older* than Type 1 and was developed for output to printers; it is rarely used by multimedia developers. There are currently over 6,000 different Type 1 typefaces available. Type 1 fonts also contain *hints,* which are special instructions for grid-fitting to help improve resolution. Hints can apply to a font in general or to specific characters at a particular resolution. For displaying PostScript fonts on both Macintosh and Windows monitors, Adobe developed Adobe Type Manager (ATM, described in the next section). Type 3 fonts do not work with ATM.

Other companies followed Adobe into the desktop publishing arena with their own proprietary and competitive systems for scalable outline fonts. In May 1989, Apple and Microsoft announced a joint effort to develop a "better and faster" quadratic curves outline font methodology, called True-Type. In addition to printing smooth characters on printers, TrueType would draw characters to a low-resolution (72-dpi or 96-dpi) monitor. Furthermore, Apple and Microsoft would no longer need to license the PostScript technology from Adobe for their operating systems. Today, TrueType fonts ship with the Windows and Macintosh computers. Microsoft licensed a set of fonts from Monotype, a font "foundry," which became the fonts that ship with Windows.

9

---

t i p   *On the Macintosh, if you have installed multiple bitmapped, TrueType, and PostScript versions of the same font, the system will attempt first to use the bitmaps, then the TrueType version, then a PostScript Type 1 version. If the selected font is not available, the system will use a default font.*

Though the PostScript-versus-TrueType war continues to reverberate through the computer and publishing industries, multimedia developers really need to be concerned only about how these scaled fonts look on monitors, not about how they are printed to paper; unless, of course, you are printing perfect proposals, bids, storyboards, reports, and above all, invoices :-). TrueType and PostScript (with ATM) outline fonts allow text to be drawn at any size on your computer screen without *jaggies*:

The Jaggies

Adobe Type Manager

Adobe Type Manager (ATM) is required to display Type 1 PostScript fonts at all sizes without jaggies. This software is available for both the Macintosh and Windows. Once it's installed, ATM works automatically with word processing, page layout, spreadsheet, and graphics applications, including multimedia authoring systems.

In Windows, the ATM software requires about 450K of disk space, and each Type 1 PostScript outline font will take up another 40K. Using the ATM Control Panel (see Figure 9-6), you can add to and take away from your list of installed fonts. PostScript fonts typically are placed in a directory called PSFONTS in the root of your hard disk. TrueType fonts are stored in the C:\Windows\Fonts directory. Adding and deleting fonts is a simple procedure using the special options in the pull-down File menu of this directory. Neither TrueType nor PostScript fonts require bitmap representations in Windows.

On the Macintosh, fonts are stored in *suitcases* (see Figure 9-7). For PostScript fonts, the suitcase must contain at least one bitmap representation of the font, while the outline font, sometimes called the *printer font*, is stored outside of the suitcase in the Fonts folder. For TrueType fonts, the suitcase contains the outline font and optional bitmapped representations. Three-dimensional and drawing applications will use the outline font, not the bitmap information in the font suitcase, to make letters. To make PostScript fonts display without jaggies when there is no bitmap available for the size you desire, you need to install Adobe's ATM desk accessory into your Control Panel folder in the System folder.

FIGURE 9-6

Adobe Type

Manager (ATM)

Control Panel

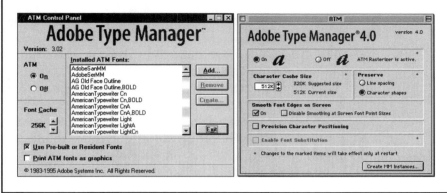

Small Typefaces

In the early days of both Macintosh and Windows, a bitmap for the font and size was always required in the system in order to display text without

FIGURE 9-7

Macintosh and

Windows manage

fonts differently,

but both handle

TrueType and

PostScript

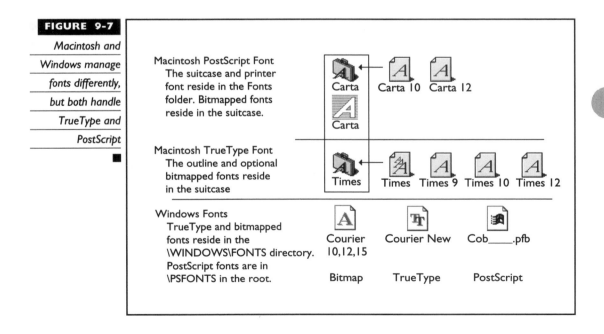

jaggies. A collection of special, memory-hungry bitmaps was required to display fonts outside the normal range installed on the computer. TrueType and PostScript/ATM, using mathematical formulas, allow you to display smooth-edged type of any size and style on your monitor without requiring a collection of bitmap files.

Unfortunately, this helpful innovation does not come without a penalty. The smaller fonts (12-point and less) are not as legible on your monitor when drawn by mathematical formula as they are when drawn from bitmaps. TrueType and PostScript/ATM do their best to render the small sizes, but they are hard pressed to compete with the clarity of font bitmaps. These were carefully hand-tweaked by type designers to provide optimum legibility at monitor resolutions. Moving a single pixel in a small letter can make a subtle but critical difference.

warning *Bitmapped, TrueType, and PostScript fonts do not display (or print) exactly the same, even though they may share the same name and size. The three technologies use different formulas. This means that word-wrapping in a text field may change. Text fields created under ATM, for example, will look different after ATM is disabled. So if you build a field or a button that precisely fits text displayed with PostScript, be aware that if you then display it with the same font in TrueType, the text may be truncated or wrapped, wrecking your layout.*

Installed Fonts in Windows and Macintosh

Before you can use a font, it must be recognized by the computer's operating system. If you want to use other fonts, you will need to install them into your system. TrueType fonts delivered as core fonts for Windows are four weights and styles of Arial, four weights and styles of Courier New, four weights and styles of Times New Roman, Symbol, Wingdings, and Marlett. With Macintosh System 8 are TrueType fonts Charcoal, Chicago, Courier, Geneva, Helvetica, Monaco, Palatino, Symbol, Times, and ZapfDingbats. When you install applications, other fonts are often added to your collection.

Font Foundries

Collections of fonts are available through retail channels or directly from their manufacturers. Typefaces are created in a *foundry*, a term much like *case*, that has carried over from times when lead was poured into molds to make letter faces. There is also a special interest group (SIG) at America Online (go to Computing:Software Libraries:Desktop & Web Publishing Forum:Fonts) where people who enjoy designing and making interesting fonts post them for others to download—hundreds and hundreds of them with names like Evil of Frankenstein, CocaCola, Kerouac, LED, PonchoVia (sic), Spaghetti, TreeFrog, and Sassy.

http://www.adobe.com
http://www.esselte.com
http://www.bitstream.com
http://www.monotype.com
http://www.YandY.com
http://www.dol.com

Commercial type foundries display their wares on the World Wide Web

Adobe ships a CD-ROM named Type On Call bundled in the box with Photoshop, Premiere, and other products. This disc contains "unlockable" fonts: you pick from a menu containing fonts and other Adobe products (see Figure 9-8), then call a toll-free telephone number and speak with an order taker. When you have paid your money by credit card, the order taker provides you passwords, and the fonts you purchased are copied to your hard disk. When you purchase some applications, such as Corel Draw, Adobe Illustrator, or Micrografx Publisher, many extra fonts are included for free.

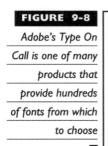

FIGURE 9-8

Adobe's Type On Call is one of many products that provide hundreds of fonts from which to choose

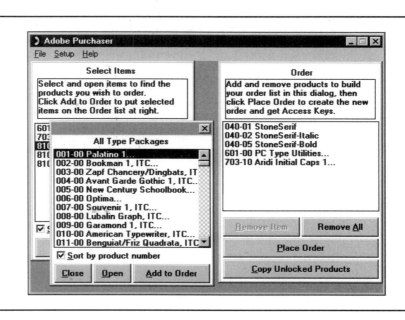

• •

http://jasper.ora.com:80/comp.fonts/index.html
http://www.cs.purdue.edu/homes/gwp/dtp/fonts.html
http://www.will-harris.com/type.htm

These gateways lead to a discussion of fonts and where to find them. With Esperfonto, Will Harris provides an interesting tool for making font decisions: Casual or Formal: Body or Display: Friendly or Serious: Cool or Warm: Modern or Traditional

---

warning: *It is easy to spend hours and hours downloading neat and interesting fonts; they are like the midnight snack table on a Mediterranean cruise liner—ice carvings and delectable goodies laid out as far as the eye can see.*

Managing Your Fonts

Never assume that the fonts you have installed on your computer will also be installed on a user's computer. Choose a system of type management and stick with it so that you will never face the nightmare of your carefully picked fonts being replaced by an ill-suited default font (see the next "First Person"). If your work is being distributed to sites that may not have the fonts you are using, or if you do not license these fonts for distribution with your work, be sure to bitmap the special font text you use for titles, headlines, buttons, and so forth. For text to be entered by users, it is safest to stay with the installed Windows or Macintosh fonts, because you know they are universally available on that platform. In Windows, use the TrueType fonts installed during the Setup procedure.

When you have lots of fonts you want to work with in a project, DiamondSoft's Font Reserve for the Macintosh (see Figure 9-9) and Font-Minder from Ares Software (see Figure 9-10) are useful font management utilities. These programs allow you to open and close fonts without "installing" them in your system during startup when they would take up memory. These utilities are used widely in the desktop publishing world where smart management of thousands of fonts is essential.

FIGURE 9-9

On the Macintosh, you can organize and manage large collections of fonts with DiamondSoft's Font Reserve

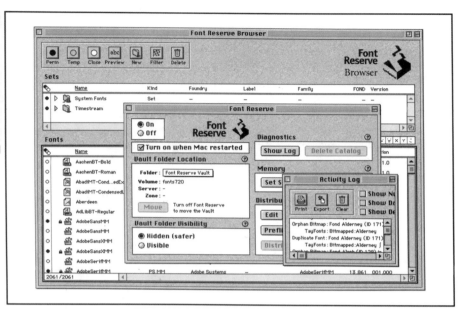

FIGURE 9-10

FontMinder for Windows 95 lets you "install" fonts without having to restart

9

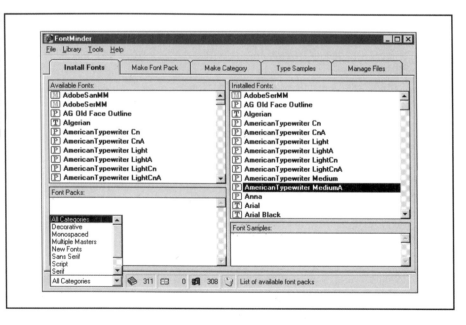

We had a short break between sessions to install the software for a panel discussion about multimedia. Four of us brought disks with discussion material. Our moderator installed her HyperCard stack first, and we heard her wail, "Something's wrong with my fonts!" We all looked at her ugly 48-point Geneva and felt sorry for her; we knew her mistake. The beautiful fonts she had installed on her home system were not installed on the Macintosh used for the presentation, and she had failed to bring the fonts along, separately or in the resource fork of her stack. By then, it was too late, anyway.

 You won't be able to print with Helvetica or stroke its characters because the font's outline file is missing or ATM is turned off.

OK

tip   *Always be sure your fonts travel with your application when you are delivering software to run on a hardware platform other than the one you used to create the application. To avoid many font display problems, particularly for menus and headlines, you may wish to snap a picture of your text with a screen capture utility and use this image, or bitmap, instead of text that you type into a text field. (Chapter 12 describes bitmaps and how to capture and edit images.) This will ensure that the screen always looks right, regardless of what hardware platform you use or what fonts are installed.*

Character Sets and Alphabets

Knowing that there is a wide selection of characters available to you on your computer and understanding how you can create and use special and custom-made characters will broaden your creative range when you design and build multimedia projects.

The ASCII Character Set

The American Standard Code for Information Interchange (ASCII) is the 7-bit character coding system most commonly used by computer systems in the United States and abroad. ASCII assigns a number or value to 128 characters, including both lower- and uppercase letters, punctuation marks, Arabic numbers, and math symbols. Also included are 32 control characters used for device control messages, such as carriage return, line feed, tab, and form feed.

ASCII code numbers always represent a letter or symbol of the English alphabet, so that a computer or printer can work with the number that represents the letter, regardless of what the letter might actually look like on the screen or printout. To a computer working with the ASCII character set, the number 65, for example, always represents an uppercase letter A. Later, when displayed on a monitor or printed, the number is turned into a typeface.

ASCII was invented and standardized for analog teletype communication early in the age of bits and bytes. The capabilities of the technology have now moved far beyond the original intent of the standard, but because millions of installed computers and printers use ASCII, it is difficult to set any new standards for text without the expense and effort of replacing existing hardware. At least, for these 128 characters, most computers and printers share the same values.

tip *On the Macintosh, use KeyCaps, a desk accessory delivered with the system and found in the Apple menu, or use John Holder's shareware program, ViewFont, to examine the fonts available to your Macintosh system. In Windows, use the Character Map accessory (CHARMAP.EXE) to view and access characters, especially those not on the keyboard.*

The Extended Character Set

A byte, which consists of eight bits, is the most commonly used building block for computer processing. ASCII uses only seven bits to code its 128 characters; the eighth bit of the byte is unused. This extra bit allows another 128 characters to be encoded before the byte is used up, and computer systems today use these extra 128 values for an extended character set. The extended character set is most commonly filled with ANSI (American National Standards Institute) standard characters, including often-used symbols, such as ¢ or ∞, and international diacritics or alphabet characters, such as ä or ñ. This fuller set of 256 characters is also known as the ISO-Latin-1 character set; it is used when programming the text of HTML Web pages.

cross platform *The rules for encoding extended characters are not standardized. Thus ASCII value 165, for example, may be a bullet (•) character on the Macintosh; the character for Japanese yen (¥) in Windows (ANSI); or a capital N with tilde (Ñ) in DOS.*

Unicode

As the computer market has become more international in the past ten years, one of the resulting problems has been handling the various international language alphabets. It was at best difficult, and at times impossible, to translate the text portions of programs from one script to another. For example, the differences between the Roman script used by western European writers and the Kanji script used by Japanese writers made it particularly challenging to transfer innovative programs from one market to another.

http://www.unicode.org

The Unicode organization supports standards for managing the characters of all known languages in the world

Since 1989, a concerted effort on the part of linguists, engineers, and information professionals from many well-known computer companies has been focused on a 16-bit architecture for multilingual text and character encoding. Called *Unicode*, this new standard can accommodate up to about 65,000 characters and will ultimately include the characters from all known languages and alphabets in the world. In version 2.0, the Unicode standard contains 38,885 distinct coded characters covering the principal written languages of the Americas, Europe, the Middle East, Africa, India, Asia, and the Pacific islands.

Where several languages share a set of symbols that have a historically related derivation, the shared symbols of each language are unified into collections of symbols (called *scripts*). A single script can work for tens or even hundreds of languages (for example, the Latin script used for English and most European languages). Sometimes, however, only one script will work for a language (such as the Korean Hangul). Here are the 25 supported scripts of Version 2.0 of the Unicode standard:

Arabic	Cyrillic	Gujarati
Armenian	Devanagari	Gurmukhi
Bengali	Georgian	Han
Bopomofo	Greek	Hangul

Hebrew	Latin	Telugu
Hiragana	Malayalam	Thai
Kannada	Oriya	Tibetan
Katakana	Phonetic	
Lao	Tamil	

Unicode also contains collections of symbols and special characters in secondary scripts:

Numbers	General diacritics	General punctuation
General symbols	Mathematical symbols	Technical symbols
Dingbats	Arrows, blocks, box drawing forms, and geometric shapes	Miscellaneous symbols
		Presentation forms

The Unicode standard includes more than 18,000 Han characters (ideographs for Japanese, Chinese, and Korean), and future releases will include obsolete alphabets such as cuneiform, hieroglyphs, and ancient Han characters. In addition, character space will be reserved for users and publishers to create their own scripts, designed especially for their own applications. For example, a carpenter might develop a script that included a character meaning "half-inch Sheetrock," another character meaning "three-quarter-inch plywood," and so forth. HTML 4.0 allows access to the Unicode characters by numeric reference. Thus 水 (in hexadecimal) represents the Chinese character for water.

Microsoft, Apple, Sun, IBM, Xerox, NeXT, Lotus, and Novell (among others) are participating in the creation of this standard, and both Microsoft and Apple have incorporated Unicode into their operating systems.

Mapping Text Across Platforms

If you build your multimedia project on a Windows platform and play it back on a Macintosh platform (or vice versa), there will be subtle (and sometimes not-so-subtle) differences. Fonts are perhaps the greatest cross-platform concern, because they must be *mapped* to the other machine. If a specified font doesn't exist on the target machine, a substitute must be provided that does exist on the target. This is *font substitution*. Windows and Macintosh provide default fonts for this substitution.

In many cross-platform-savvy applications, you can explicitly define the mapping of your fonts. In Director, for example, you can control font-mapping behavior by altering the FONTMAP.TXT file; Director remaps those fonts that the target system cannot provide. Table 9-2 shows the default font mapping for Macromedia's Director.

It is not just fonts that are problematic; characters, too, must be mapped across platforms. Character mapping allows bullets, accented characters, and other curious characters that are part of the extended character set on one platform to appear correctly when text is moved to the other platform. Curly quotation marks, for example, rarely, if ever, map successfully across platforms.

To solve font and character uncertainties when working across platforms, many multimedia developers convert the text of their projects into bitmaps. These bitmaps may also be converted to 1-bit images that do not require great memory for storage in a project. Once converted to bitmaps, however, text cannot be easily edited or reworked.

Mac→Win	Win→Mac
Mac:Chicago→Win:System	Win:Arial→Mac:Helvetica
Mac:Courier→Win:Courier New	Win:Courier→Mac:Courier
Mac:Geneva→Win:Sans Serif	Win:Courier New→Mac:Courier
Mac:Helvetica→Win:Arial	Win:MS Serif→Mac:New York
Mac:Monaco→Win:Terminal	Win:MS Sans Serif→Mac:Geneva
Mac:New York→Win:MS Serif	Win:Symbol→Mac:Symbol Map None
Mac:Symbol→Win:Symbol Map None	Win:System→Mac:Chicago
Mac:Times→Win:Times New Roman (sizes: 14→12, 18→14, 24→18, 30→24)	Win:Terminal→Mac:Monaco
	Win:Times New Roman→Mac:Times (sizes: 12→14, 14→18, 18→24, 24→30)

TABLE 9-2 *Typical Mappings for Standard Macintosh and Windows Fonts Used by Macromedia's Director* ■

First Person

While we were in the early phases of producing my CD-ROM, Multimedia: Working It Out! (see the last page of this book), I sold the rights to distribute it into Korea and Mainland China. Nobody on the production team had ever seen a computer that typed short-form Mandarin, and we knew that even when the English was localized, we would be hard pressed to recognize any of the text, much less edit or alter it in its new form.

멀티미디어 : Making It Work, 제2판

멀티미디어는 텍스트, 그래픽 아트, 사운드, 에니메이션 및 비디오의 조화로운 산물이다.

– Tay Vaughan –

So we devised a structured system of labels and names for multimedia: Working It Out! and converted all the text in the project (about 600 "pages" of about a paragraph each) into 1-bit bitmaps in a Director movie. Donna Booher edited and formatted the text in Microsoft Word, Dan Hilgert bitmapped and screen-captured each page with Capture and Photoshop, and Peter Wolf imported the PICT files into Director (by the hundreds) as cast members. Each cast member had a unique (but systematic) name associated with a Director movie, a heading, and various icons. It took awhile.

The localizers across the Pacific, then, would simply translate a page or a series of pages using their own native-language word processor, capture their own bitmaps, and we would substitute the new bitmaps for the old using the unique identification labels. No language skills required!

When we started, Terry Thompson devised a color-coded master filing system and database so that all the word-processed text and the screen-captured bitmaps would remain neatly side-by-side and concurrent. This is called version control. By the time this project shipped, Donna's computer was crashing four or five times a day and we had lost files, Dan had gone back to school, Peter and I were slapping miscellaneous text elements into the project without tracking where they came from, and we were changing labels and moving cast members around as we streamlined performance, debugged, and staggered toward a golden master and the Federal Express drop-off. We had converted Terry's neatly organized system into chaos.

9

**First
Person**
continued

After the CD-ROMs were pressed, and there wasn't anything anybody could change anymore anyway, we did a tricky thing with Lingo programming, DeBabelizer, and OmniPage Pro to convert the final project's bitmapped text back into word processor text.

First we collected all the bitmapped text into a single Director movie (we weren't interested in pretty pictures, QuickTime, sounds, or other types of cast members, just text). Then we placed each page of bitmapped text into a movie frame (Cast to Time), neatly labeled that frame at the top with the identifying code of the image using a Lingo handler, and saved all of the frames as PICT images (an automatic command in Director's Export menu). With DeBabelizer, we batch-converted these hundreds of PICT images from 72 dpi (screen capture resolution) to 300 dpi (printer resolution) and saved each as a 1-bit TIFF image. The process was automatic.

OmniPage Pro is a powerful optical character recognition (OCR) program that usually reads documents on a flatbed scanner and turns them into nicely formatted word processing documents. OmniPage (ah ha!) allows batch processing of TIFF (and more recently, PICT) images at 300 dpi, so we ran all of these TIFFs (automatically) through OmniPage, and bingo! they came out as archival word processing files. Then we sent the word files to Guido Mozzi in Italy so his team of translators could begin localizing there.

Some efforts are cyclical, we have discovered. The trick is to learn something and improve the process each time the task comes around!

Languages in the World of Computers

In modern Western languages, words are made up of symbols or letters strung together, representing as a whole the sounds of a spoken word. This is not so for Eastern languages such as Chinese, Japanese, and Korean (and the ancient languages of Sumeria, Egypt, and Mesopotamia). In these languages, an entire concept might be represented by a single word symbol that is unrelated to a specific phonetic sound.

The letters or symbols of a language are its alphabet. In English, the alphabet consists of 26 Roman or Latin letters; in Japanese, the Kanji alphabet comprises more than 3,000 kanas, or whole words. The Russian alphabet, made up of Cyrillic characters based on the ancient Greek alphabet, has about the same number of letters as a Roman alphabet. All languages, from Navajo to Hebrew, have their own unique alphabets.

::::::::::::::::::::::::::::::::::::

The written Japanese language consists of three different types of character sets, namely: kanji, katakana, and hiragana. Kanji was originally taken from the Chinese language and is essentially a pictographic representation of the spoken word. Each kanji has two different readings, "on-yomi" and "kun-yomi," respectively the "Chinese rendering" and the "Japanese rendering." Both are used depending on the conjugation of the kanji with other kanji.

Due to certain incompatibilities between the Japanese spoken word and kanji, two sets of kana or phonetic syllabary (alphabet) were developed. Katakana is the "square" kana and is used today for writing only foreign words or onomatopoeic expressions. Hiragana is the "cursive" kana and can be used alone to represent a certain word or combined with kanji to form other words and sentences. Romaji, a more recent addition to the alphabets of Japan, allows for the phonetic spelling of the Japanese language using the Roman characters familiar to the Western world.

::::::::::::::::::::::::::::::::::::

Ross Uchimura, Executive Vice-President, GC3 Ltd.,
a cross-cultural expert

Most modern alphabets share one very important attribute: the graphic shapes and method for writing the Arabic numbers 0 1 2 3 4 5 6 7 8 9. This is a simple system for representing decimal numbers, which lends itself to easy reading, writing, manipulation, and calculation. Expressing and performing

$$16 + 32 = 48$$

is much easier in Arabic numbers than in Roman or Greek numerals:

$$XVI + XXXII = XLVIII$$

$$\iota\varsigma + \lambda\beta = \mu\eta$$

Use of Arabic notation has gradually spread across the world to supplant other systems, although Roman numerals are still used today in Western languages in certain forms and contexts.

Translating or designing multimedia (or any computer-based material) into a language other than the one in which it was originally written is called *localization.* This process deals with everything from the month/day/year order for expressing dates to providing special alphabetical characters on keyboards and printers. Even the many Western languages that share the Roman alphabet have their own peculiarities and often require special characters to represent special sounds. For example, German has its umlaut (¨); French its various accents (é), the cedilla (ç), and other diacritics; and Spanish its tilde (ñ). These characters are typically available in the extended character set of a font.

First Person

When I was in Germany some years ago, I read a curious report in the Frankfurter Allgemeine about a fellow who was suing the local electric utility for not correcting the spelling of his name to its proper form in the German alphabet. His name had an umlaut in it (Wörm), but his bill always read Woerm. In German, the letter ö sounds different from the letter o, so I can't say I blamed him. At first he didn't pay his bill, claiming that he wasn't that person; then the courts told him to pay anyway. So he initiated a civil suit to protect his name.

It seems the utility was using a new IBM system with a high-speed chain printer to produce the monthly bills, and none of the umlaut characters were available on the ASCII-based chain. By long-standing convention, when you are limited to the English alphabet, the letter e immediately follows any umlautless vowel, to indicate that the umlaut should be there but isn't. Today, with high-speed laser printers and special fonts, the problem has probably gone away.

More recently, there are reports that the California Department of Motor Vehicles cannot handle blank spaces in the name fields of its massive database, so Rip Van Winkle's name was changed to Rip VanWinkle without his permission. Expect a lawsuit.

SPECIAL CHARACTERS IN HTML   In HTML, *character entities* based upon the ISO-Latin-1 standard make up the alphabet that is recognized by browser software on the World Wide Web. All of the usual characters of an English keyboard are included (the 7-bit ASCII set is built in), but for the extended character set that includes tildes, umlauts, accents, and special symbols, you must use an escape sequence to represent them in an HTML document. A character entity is represented either by a number or by a word and is always prefixed by an ampersand (escape) and followed by a semicolon. For example, the name for the copyright symbol is "copy" and its number is 169; it may be inserted into a document either as © or as ©—either way, the character © is generated by the browser. The list of character entities allowed in standard HTML is growing and will soon include mathematical symbols and even icons to represent things like trash cans, clocks, and disk drives. Word processors for languages other than English automatically insert the necessary character entities when a document is saved in HTML format.

http://www.w3.org/TR/REC-html40/sgml/entities.html

An encyclopedic discussion and reference for HTML character entity references

Font Editing and Design Tools

Special font editing tools can be used to make your own type, so you can communicate an idea or graphic feeling exactly. With these tools, professional typographers create distinct text and display faces. Graphic designers, publishers, and ad agencies can design instant variations of existing typefaces.

Typeface designs fall into the category of industrial design and have been determined by the courts in some cases to be protectable by patent. For example, design patents have been issued for Bigelow & Holmes' Lucida, ITC Stone, and for Adobe's Minion.

warning *If your commercial project includes special fonts, be sure that your license agreement with the font supplier allows you to distribute them with your project.*

9

Occasionally in your projects you may require special characters. With the tools described in the paragraphs that follow, you can easily substitute characters of your own design for any unused characters in the extended character set. You can even include several custom versions of your client's company logo or other special symbols relevant to your content or subject right in your text font.

ResEdit

ResEdit is a resource editor available from Apple that is useful for creating and changing graphic resources such as cursors, icons, dialog boxes, patterns, keyboard maps, and bitmapped fonts on the Macintosh. It can be used to edit or create new FONT resources for storing the bitmaps of screen fonts. If you need to make small adjustments to a screen font or create special characters, as illustrated in Figure 9-11, try ResEdit.

Fontographer

Fontographer, supplied by Macromedia, is a specialized graphics editor for both Macintosh and Windows platforms. You can use it to develop PostScript, TrueType, and bitmapped fonts for Macintosh, Windows, DOS, NeXT, and Sun workstations. Designers can also modify existing typefaces, incorporate PostScript artwork, automatically trace scanned images, and create designs from scratch. A sample Fontographer screen is shown in Figure 9-12, and a working version is included on the Macromedia Showcase CD-ROM included with this book.

Fontographer's features include a freehand drawing tool to create professional and precise inline and outline drawings of calligraphic and script characters, using either the mouse or alternative input methods (such as Wacom pressure-sensitive pen systems, Kurta digitizing tablets, and Cal-Comp DrawingBoard). Fontographer allows the creation of multiple font designs from two existing typefaces, and you can design lighter or heavier fonts by modifying the weight of an entire typeface.

Fontographer for Windows opens any PostScript Type 1 or TrueType font for the PC and lets you create condensed, expanded, and oblique versions of the same font or modify any of those fonts to suit your design needs. One character, several characters, or entire fonts can be scaled, rotated, and skewed to create new and unique typefaces. A metric window provides complete control over character width, spacing, offset, and kerning. The

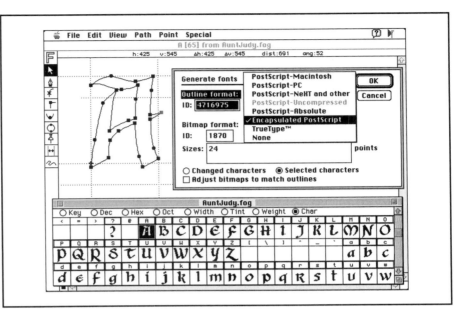

FIGURE 9-12

Fontographer is a powerful font editor for Macintosh and Windows

current Windows version of Fontographer does not make Multiple Master fonts (PostScript fonts that allow you to adjust a range of certain characteristics for a set of characters, for example, serif to sans serif or condensed to extended) or Type 3 PostScript fonts, and it does not have an Option-Copy, Paste feature for bringing drawings through the Clipboard from FreeHand or Illustrator. Nor can the current version read a Macintosh Fontographer database; font transfer is accomplished through Type 1 PostScript.

Type-Designer

Type-Designer for Windows from DS Design (see Figure 9-13) is a font editor that lets you create, convert, and manipulate PostScript Type 1 and TrueType fonts as well as EPS file format illustrations. An extensive palette of editing tools allows you to make changes to a font's outline. With Type-Designer you can open up to eight typefaces simultaneously and cut and paste characters between them.

FontMonger

FontMonger (for Macintosh) from Ares Software offers a proprietary hinting technology (see "The Font Wars," earlier in the chapter) to ensure that your fonts will look good regardless of size. FontMonger converts

FIGURE 9-13

Type-Designer for

Windows is a

vector-based

font editor

■

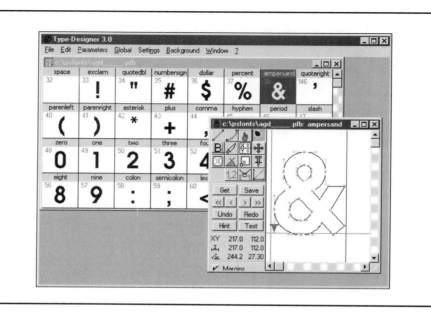

Macintosh or PC fonts to either platform, as well as in any direction between PostScript Type 1, Type 3, and TrueType formats. A range of preset type modifications allows you to edit and expand your type library by generating a new font composed of small caps, obliques, subscript, or superscript characters (see Figure 9-14). To create new fonts or to manipulate existing ones, FontMonger includes a freehand drawing tool, a scissors tool, and a gizmo tool that rotates, slants, and skews character outlines.

FontChameleon

FontChameleon from Ares Software for both the Macintosh and Windows platforms (see Figure 9-15) builds millions of different fonts from a single master font outline. The program provides a number of preset font descriptors, which you build into a PostScript Type 1 or TrueType font. With slider bars you can manipulate various aspects of the font, including its weight, width, x-height, ascenders and descenders, and the blend of the serifs. Although you have an indefinite number of possibilities to manipulate the font descriptors of a master outline font, you cannot create new master fonts because drawing tools or import capabilities are not included. The fonts you do build from the master outline can be used on the Macintosh, Windows, or OS/2 platforms.

FontMonger lets you design logos, characters, or an entire font

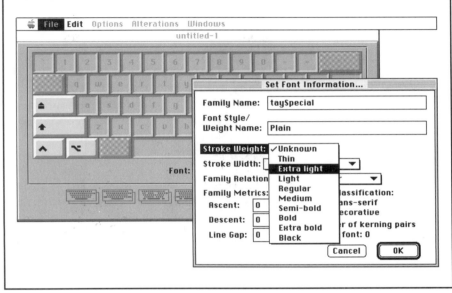

Making Pretty Text

To make your text look pretty, you need a toolbox full of fonts and special graphics applications that can stretch, shade, shadow, color, and anti-alias

9

In FontChameleon, the Font Descriptors on the right are manipulated with slider bars

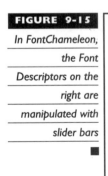
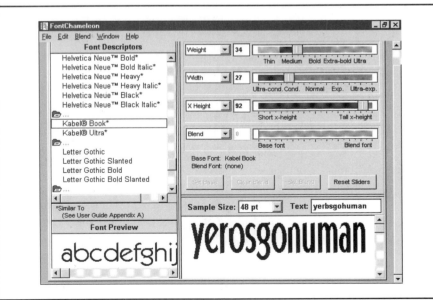

your words into real artwork. Pretty text is typically found in bitmapped drawings where characters have been tweaked, manipulated, and blended into a graphic image. Simply choosing the font is the first step. Most designers find it easier to make pretty type starting with ready-made fonts, but some will create their own custom fonts using font-editing and design tools such as Fontographer, Type-Designer, and FontMonger, described above.

With the proper tools and a creative mind, you can create endless variations on plain-old type, and you not only choose but also customize the styles that will fit with your design needs.

When they first invented typesetting there were variants cut of each character so text would look as if it had been handwritten by a monk! Desktop designers have been fighting so hard to get their setting to look like it's come from a Berthold system, that most of the new potential of desktop typography has been overlooked.

David Collier, Author of *Collier's Rules for Desktop Design and Typography* (Addison-Wesley, 1990)

Most image-editing and painting applications let you make text using the fonts available in your system. You can colorize the text, stretch, squeeze, and rotate it, and you can filter it through various "plug-ins" to generate wild graphic results.

Figure 9-16 is an image with text created in Photoshop. The rose was scanned from a photograph, separated from its background (1), and placed onto black (2). A 200-point word, "Rose," was typed in bold black Peignot Light onto a white background without anti-aliasing (3). Then a rainbow of hues was "stolen" from the little strip on Photoshop's color wheel by screen-capturing, and the strip was duplicated horizontally until it would be large enough to cover the entire word (4). Selecting and dragging the rainbow of colors on top of the word, the rainbow was laid onto the black letters by removing white from the underlying image using Photoshop's Composite Controls—note the lower slider is moved one value to the left, from 255 to 254 (5). The characters of the word were then selected along their edges by selecting all the white background with the Magic Wand tool, then "inverting" that selection (Invert in the Select menu). The rainbow word was dragged on top of the red rose (6), and a two-pixel border around it was selected (Border in the Select menu). Then the word was finally "anti-aliased" onto the background using the Blur filter, blurring just the border of the word (7).

Three-dimensional modeling programs allow you to create a character, add depth to it or extrude it, shade and light it, and manipulate it into other

FIGURE 9-16

Image-editing

applications let you

make pretty text

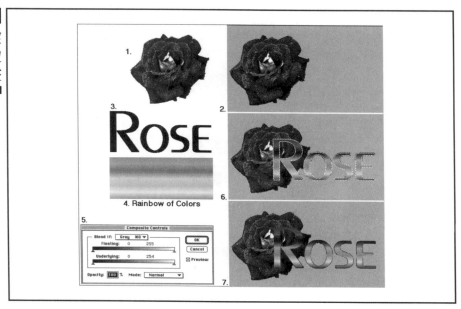

shapes. The character here was generated in just this way and, when animated using Macromedia's Director, spins in place:

Inexpensive applications such as Brøderbund's TypeStyler, RayDream's addDepth 2, COOL 3D from U-Lead, and plug-ins for Photoshop from Xaos Tools (TypeCaster) and Vertigo (HotTEXT) are designed to manipulate typefaces in a graphical way. Figure 9-17 shows text being drawn and manipulated using COOL 3D and HotTEXT. The custom-tortured characters can be captured as a bitmap and incorporated into your project. Figure 9-18 shows TypeCaster's easy to use interface working in Photoshop with drag-and-drop textures. These 3-D programs let you put together interesting still and animated titles and headlines for Web pages, documents, presentations, reports, videos, and multimedia titles. You can rotate the text, adjust style, color, texture, camera angle and background, and even map images onto the surface. There are many sources of support for GIF animations with transparency and interlacing. Working in 3-D space takes some practice until you become intuitively comfortable with the notion of roll, pitch, and yaw and familiar with the application's controls for adjusting lights, textures, and views.

9

FIGURE 9-17

COOL 3D and
HotTEXT let you
extrude, warp,
twist, and rotate
characters and
adjust lighting and
texture effects for
high-impact
3-D titles

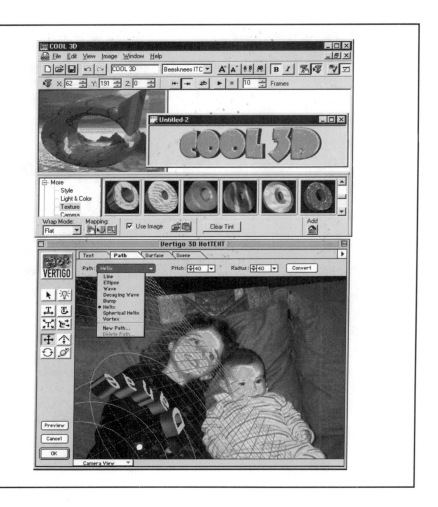

Hypermedia and Hypertext

Multimedia—the combination of text, graphic, and audio elements into a single collection or presentation—becomes *interactive multimedia* when you give the user some control over what information is viewed and when it is viewed. Interactive multimedia becomes *hypermedia* when its designer provides a structure of linked elements through which a user can navigate and interact.

When a hypermedia project includes large amounts of text or symbolic content, this content can be indexed and its elements then linked together to afford rapid electronic retrieval of the associated information. When words are keyed or indexed to other words, you have a *hypertext system*; the text part of this term represents the project's content and meaning, rather than

FIGURE 9-18

Use the
TypeCaster plug-in
to create pretty
text in Photoshop,
Illustrator,
FreeHand, and
other applications

■

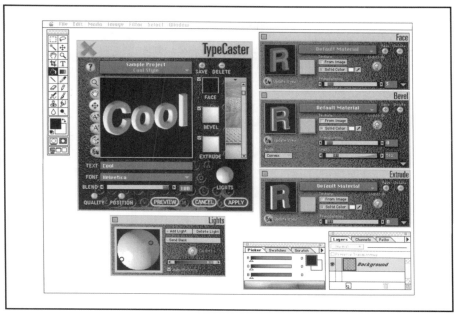

the graphical presentation of the text. Hypertext is what the World Wide Web is all about.

When text lives in a computer instead of on printed pages, the computer's powerful processing capabilities can be applied to make the text more accessible and meaningful. The text can then be called *hypertext*; because the words, sections, and thoughts are linked, the user can navigate through text in a nonlinear way, quickly and intuitively.

Using hypertext systems, you can electronically search through all the text of a computer-resident book, locate references to a certain word, and then immediately view the page where the word was found. Or you can create complicated Boolean searches (using terms such as AND, OR, NOT, and BOTH) to locate the occurrences of several related words, such as "Elwood," "Gloria," "mortgage," and "happiness" in a paragraph or on a page. Whole documents can be linked to other documents. Figure 9-19 shows Master-View from TMS, a searchable full-text and image retrieval database.

http://www.tmsinc.com

TMS hypertext and image retrieval software

A word can be made *hot,* as can a button, thus leading the user from one reference to another. Click on the word "Elwood," and you may find

FIGURE 9-19

A hypertext query dialog from the TMS MasterView search engine for Windows

■

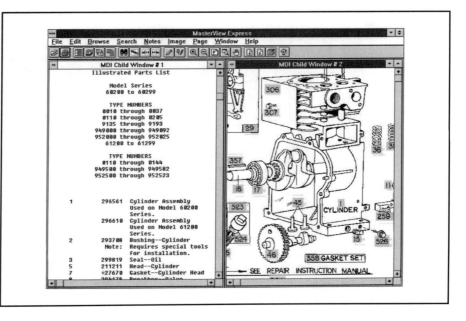

yourself reading a biography or resume; click on "mortgage," and a calculator pops up. Some authoring systems (HyperCard and ToolBook, for example) incorporate a hypertext facility that allows you to identify words in a text field using a bold or colored style, then link them to other words, pages, or activities, such as playing a sound or video clip related to that hot word. You cannot do this kind of nonlinear and associative navigation in a sequentially organized book. But on a CD-ROM, where you might have more than 100,000 pages of text to investigate, search, and browse, hypertext is invaluable.

Because hypertext is the organized cross-linking of words not only to other words but also to associated images, video clips, sounds, and other exhibits, hypertext often becomes simply an additional feature within an overall multimedia design. The term "hyper" (from the Greek word υπερ— "over") has come to imply that user interaction is a critical part of the design, whether for text browsing or for the multimedia project as a whole. When interaction and cross-linking are then added to multimedia, and the navigation system is nonlinear, multimedia becomes hypermedia.

In 1945, Vannevar Bush wrote a seminal eight-page article, "As We May Think," for the *Atlantic Monthly* (http://www2.TheAtlantic.com/atlantic/atlweb/flashbks/computer/bushf.htm). This short treatise, in which he discusses the need for new methodologies for accessing information, has become the historic cornerstone of hypertext experimentation. Doug Englebart (inventor of the mouse) and Ted Nelson (who coined the term "hypertext" in 1965) have actively championed the research and innovations required of computer technology for implementing useful hypertext systems, and they have worked to combat the historic inertia of linear thought. Nelson would claim that the very structure of thought is neither sequential nor linear and that computer-based hypertext systems will fundamentally alter the way humans approach literature and the expression of ideas during the coming decades.

The argument against this theory of associative thought is that people are, indeed, more comfortable with linear thinking and are easily overwhelmed by too much freedom, becoming quickly lost in the chaos of nonlinear gigabytes. As a practical reminder, it is important always to provide location markers, either text-and-symbol menus or illustrative maps, for users who travel the threads of nonlinear systems.

Bush identified the problem—and the need to provide new ways to access information—but was he right about how the mind works? I suspect a purely associative model of human memory and mental processes is too simplistic.

Philip Murray, *From Ventura to Hypertext*, Knowledge Management Associates, Danvers, MA, 1991

The Power of Hypertext

In a fully indexed hypertext system, all words can be found immediately. Suppose you search a large database for "boats," and you come up with a whopping 1,623 references or *hits*—among them, Noah's Ark (open boat in water), television situation comedies (*The Love Boat*), political criticisms of cabinet members who challenged the status quo (rocked the boat), cabinet members who were stupid (missed the boat), and Christmas dinner trimmings (Grandmother's gravy boat). So you narrow your search and look for "boats" and "water" when both words are mentioned on the same page; this time you get 286 hits. "Boats," "water," and "storms" gets you 37; "boats," "water," "storms," and "San Francisco," one single hit. With over a thousand hits, you are lost. With one hit, you have something! But you still may not find what you are looking for, as you can see in this fictional example:

> The *storm* had come and gone quickly across the Colorado plains, but *water* was still puddled at the foot of the house-high bank of mud that had slid into town when the dam burst. In front of the general store, which had remained standing, four strong men carefully lifted a tiny *boat* onto the large dray wagon borrowed from the woodcutters. On a layer of blankets in the bilge of the *boat*, the undertaker had carefully

laid out the remains of both the Mayor and his paramour. The Mayor had not drowned in the flood, but died of a heart attack in the midst of the panic. Children covered the *boat* with freshly cut pine boughs while horses were quickly harnessed to the wagon, and a strange procession began to move slowly down *San Francisco* Street toward the new cemetery.

The power of such search and retrieval systems provided by a computer for large volumes of data is immense, but clearly this power must be channeled in meaningful ways. Links among words or clusters of information need to be designed so that they make sense. Judgments must be made about relationships and the way information content is organized and made available to users. The lenses through which vast amounts of data are viewed must necessarily be ground and shaped by those who design the access system.

::::::::::::::::::::::::::::::::::

The hype about hypertext may be justified. It can provide a computer-supported information environment which can add to our appreciation of the text, can go some way towards aping the mental agility of the human mind, can allow navigation along patterns of association, can provide a non-linear information environment. But the problems of constructing non-linear documents are not few and can prove to be very complex.

::::::::::::::::::::::::::::::::::

> Patricia Baird, editor of *Hypermedia*, a scientific journal published in the United Kingdom

The issue of who designs the lenses and how the designers maintain impartial focus is troubling to many scientists, archivists, and students of cognitive thinking. The scientists would remain "hermeneutically" neutral, they would balance freedom against authority and warn against the epistemological unknowns of this new intellectual technology. They are aware of the forces that allow advertising and marketing craftspeople to intuitively twist meanings and spin events to their own purposes, with actions that can affect the knowledge and views of many millions of people and thus history itself. But these forces remain poorly understood, are not easily controlled by authority, and will express themselves with immeasurably far-reaching, long-term impact on the shape of human culture.

::::::::::::::::::::::::::::::::::

Hypermedia on its own simply functions as a reference tool. But when it is integrated within a goal-based activity, it becomes a powerful learning resource.

::::::::::::::::::::::::::::::::::

> Brigid Sealy & Paul Phelan, INESC, Porto, Portugal (conclusions from research funded by the European Commission's Human Capital and Mobility Program)

The multimedia designer controls the filtering mechanisms and places the lenses within the multimedia project. A manufacturer, for instance, that presents its products using interactive multimedia can bring abundant information and selling power within reach of the user, including background information, collateral marketing material, pricing statistics, and technical data. The project design will be, of course, biased—to sell more of the manufacturer's products and generate more profit; but this bias is assumed and understood in these circumstances. When the assumptions and understandings of inherent bias in any information base break down, when fiction or incomplete data are presented as full fact, that is when the powerful forces of multimedia and hypermedia can have their greatest deleterious effect.

---

warning *Bad multimedia projects will not alter the collective view of history; really bad projects might.*

Using Hypertext

Special programs for information management and hypertext have been designed to present electronic text, images, and other elements in a database fashion. Commercial systems have been used for large and complicated mixtures of text and images, for example, a detailed repair manual for a Boeing 747 aircraft, a parts catalog for Pratt & Whitney jet turbine engines, an instant reference to hazardous chemicals, and electronic reference libraries used in legal and library environments. Such searchable database engines are widely used on the Web, where software *robots* visit millions of Web pages and index entire Web sites (see Figure 9-20). Hypertext databases rely upon proprietary indexing systems that carefully scan the entire body of text and create very fast cross-referencing indexes that point to the location of specific words, documents, and images. Indeed, a hypertext index by itself can be as large as 50 to 100 percent the size of the original document. Indexes are essential for speedy performance.

Commercial hypertext systems were developed historically to retrofit gigantic bodies of information. Licenses for use and distribution of these commercial systems are expensive, and the hypertext-based projects typically require the large mass-storage capability of one or many CD-ROMs and/or dedicated gigabyte hard disks. Simpler but effective hypertext indexing tools are available for both Macintosh and Windows, and they offer fairly elaborate features designed to work in concert with many multimedia authoring systems. Server-based hypertext and database engines designed for the Web are now widely available and competitively priced.

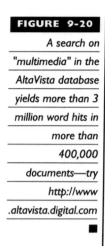

FIGURE 9-20

A search on "multimedia" in the AltaVista database yields more than 3 million word hits in more than 400,000 documents—try http://www .altavista.digital.com
■

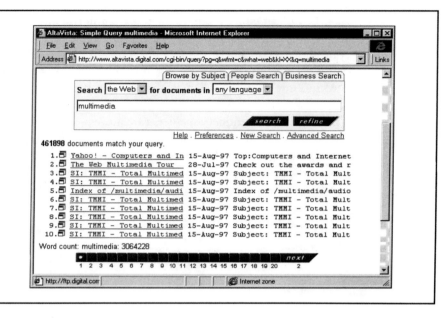

tip   *Rather than designing an elaborate, fully cross-referenced hypertext system for your multimedia project, you can "hardwire" the links between the most salient words (highlight them in your text) so that a mouse click leads to a topic menu specific to the chosen word. Though this constrains the user's movement through the text, the user will not perceive it as such, and you can thus maintain strict control over your navigation pathways and design.*

Searching for Words

While the designer of a hypermedia database makes assumptions, he or she also presents users with tools and a meaningful interface to exercise the assumptions. Employing this interface, users can tailor word searches to find very specific combinations. Following are typical methods for word searching in hypermedia systems:

■ Categorical: Selecting or limiting the documents, pages, or fields of text within which to search for a word or words.

■ Word relationship: Searching for words according to their general proximity and order. For example, you might search for "party" and "beer" only when they occur on the same page or in the same paragraph.

- Adjacency: Searching for words occurring next to one another, usually in phrases and proper names. For instance, find "widow" only when "black" is the preceding adjacent word.

- Alternates: Applying an OR criterion to search for two or more words, such as "bacon" or "eggs."

- Association: Applying an AND criterion to search for two or more words, such as "skiff," "tender," "dinghy," and "rowboat."

- Negation: Applying a NOT criterion to search exclusively for references to a word that are not associated with the word. For example, find all occurrences of "paste" when "library" is not present in the same sentence.

- Truncation: Searching for a word with any of its possible suffixes. For example, to find all occurrences of "girl" and "girls," you may need to specify something like **girl#**. Multiple character suffixes can be managed with another specifier, so **geo*** might yield "geo," "geology," and "geometry," as well as "George."

- Intermediate words: Searching for words that occur between what might normally be adjacent words, such as a middle name or initial in a proper name.

- Frequency: Searching for words based on how often they appear: the more times a term is mentioned in a document, the more relevant the document is to this term.

Hypermedia Structures

Two buzzwords used often in hypertext systems are link and node. *Links* are connections between the conceptual elements, that is, the *nodes* containing text, graphics, sounds, or related information in the knowledge base. Links connect Caesar Augustus with Rome, for example, and grapes with wine, and love with hate. The art of hypermedia design lies in the visualization of these nodes and their links so that they make sense, not nonsense, and can form the backbone of a knowledge access system. More recently, with the popularization of HTML for the World Wide Web, the term *anchor* is used for the reference from one document to another document, image, sound, or file on the Web (see Chapter 15).

Links are the navigation pathways and menus; nodes are accessible topics, documents, messages, and content elements. A *link anchor* is where you come from; a *link end* is the destination node linked to the anchor. Some hypertext systems provide unidirectional navigation and offer no return pathway; others are bidirectional.

The simplest way to navigate hypermedia structures is via buttons that let you access linked information (text, graphics, and sounds) that is contained at the nodes. When you've finished examining the information, you return to your starting location.

HyperWriter!, a powerful multimedia linking system from NTERGAID, makes use of Windows' left and right mouse buttons for this navigation. The left button activates a link (takes you to the information node), and the right button brings you back. A typical navigation structure might look like the following:

Pages of text with hot words linked to InfoBites only

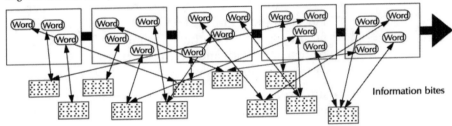

Information bites

Navigation becomes more complicated when you add associative links that connect elements not directly in the hierarchy or sequence. These are the paths where users can begin to get lost if you do not provide location markers. A link can lead to a node that provides further links, as shown here:

Pages of text with hot words linked to InfoBites linked to pages and to other InfoBites

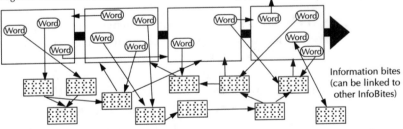

Information bites (can be linked to other InfoBites)

When you offer full-text search through an information base, there may be links between any number of items at your current node and any number of other nodes with items that meet your relationship criteria. When users are browsing freely through this system, and one page does not follow the next (as expected in the linear metaphor of books and literature), users can get lost in the associative maze of the designer's content:

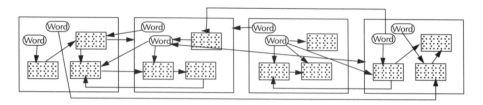

One publisher of hypermedia products claims that becoming lost in "hyperspace" may not be all that bad. The struggle to find your way back can be valuable in itself, and is certainly a learning experience.

Hypertext Tools

Two functions are common to most hypermedia text management systems, and they are often provided as separate applications: building (or authoring) and reading. The builder creates the links, identifies nodes, and generates the all-important index of words. The index methodology and the search algorithms used to find and group words according to user search criteria are typically proprietary, and they represent an area where computers are carefully optimized for performance—finding search words among a list of many tens of thousands of words requires speed-demon programming.

Hypertext systems are currently used for electronic publishing and reference works, technical documentation, educational courseware, interactive kiosks, electronic catalogs, interactive fiction, and text and image databases. Today these tools are used extensively with information organized in a linear fashion; it still may be many years before the majority of multimedia project users become comfortable with fully nonlinear hypertext and hypermedia systems. When (and perhaps if) they do, the methodology of human thought and conceptual management—indeed, the way we think—will be forever changed.

9

:::::::::::::::::::::::::::::::::::::

Hypermedia can take advantage of powerful capabilities that are becoming clearer as the new multimedia medium matures—a greater choice in exploration, if not in outright plot definition, for example. From my experiences with "Playa Sirenas," the real challenge facing storytellers in this new medium is allowing readers appropriate choices (some authorship of the story, really) while they navigate through the hypermedia experience, without destroying the successful and basic patterns that have been part of storytelling since people first gathered around campfires.

There is something organic about these time-proven storytelling patterns. As an author in the new medium, you must first design the DNA or template of your story, then allow (and promote) mutation along evolutionary lines that you, as the author, have created as part of the template.

:::::::::::::::::::::::::::::::::::::

Hermann Steffen, Hypermedia Novelist, San Jose, Costa Rica

Multi

How you use the power of sound can make the difference between an ordinary multimedia presentation and a professionally spectacular one.

the power of sound

media

chapter

10

Sound

These waves spread like the ripples from a pebble tossed into a still pool and when they reach your eardrums, you experience the changes of pressure, or vibrations, as sound.

S

OUND is perhaps the most sensuous element of multimedia. It is meaningful "speech" in any language, from a whisper to a scream. It can provide the listening pleasure of music, the startling accent of special effects, or the ambience of a mood-setting background. Some feel-good music powerfully fills the heart, generating emotions of love or otherwise elevating listeners closer to Heaven. How you use the power of sound can make the difference between an ordinary multimedia presentation and a professionally spectacular one. Misuse of sound, however, can wreck your project.

The Power of Sound

When something vibrates in the air by moving back and forth (such as the cone of a loudspeaker), it creates waves of pressure. These waves spread like the ripples from a pebble tossed into a still pool, and when they reach your eardrums, you experience the changes of pressure, or vibrations, as sound. In air, the ripples propagate at about 750 miles per hour, or Mach 1 at sea level. Sound waves vary in sound pressure level (amplitude) and in frequency or pitch. Many sound waves mixed together form an audio sea of symphonic music, speech, or just plain noise.

Acoustics is the branch of physics that studies sound. Sound pressure levels (loudness or volume) are measured in decibels (dB); a decibel measurement is actually the ratio between a chosen reference point on a logarithmic scale and the level that is actually experienced. When you quadruple the sound output power, there is only a 6 dB increase; when you make the sound 100 times more intense, the increase in dB is not hundredfold, but only 20 dB. This scale makes sense because humans perceive sound pressure levels over an extraordinarily broad dynamic range. The decibel scale, with some examples, is shown in Table 10-1; notice the relationship between power (measured in watts) and dB.

DB	Watts	Example
195	25-40 million	Saturn rocket
170	100,000	Jet engine with afterburner
160	10,000	Turbojet engine at 7,000 pounds thrust
150	1,000	
140	100	
130	10	75-piece orchestra, at fortissimo
120	1	Large chipping hammer
110	0.1	Riveting machine
100	0.01	Automobile on highway
90	0.001	Subway train; a shouting voice
80	0.0001	Inside a 1952 Corvette at 60 mph
70	0.00001	Voice conversation; freight train 100 feet away
60	0.000001	Large department store
50	0.0000001	Average residence or small business office
40	0.00000001	Residential areas of Chicago at night
30	0.000000001	Very soft whisper
20	0.0000000001	Sound studio

TABLE 10-1   *Typical Sound Levels in Decibels (dB) and Watts* ■

10

Sound is energy, like the waves breaking on a sandy beach, and too much volume can permanently damage the delicate receiving mechanisms behind your eardrums, typically dulling your hearing in the 6 kHz range. In terms of volume, what you hear subjectively is not what you hear objectively. The perception of loudness is dependent upon the frequency or pitch of the sound: at low frequencies, more power is required to deliver the same perceived loudness as for a sound at the middle or higher frequency ranges. You may feel the sound more than hear it. For instance, when the ambient noise level is above 90 dB in the workplace, people are likely to make increased numbers of errors in susceptible tasks—especially when there is a high-frequency component to the noise. When the level is above 80 dB, it is quite impossible to use a telephone. Experiments by researchers in residential areas have shown that a sound generator at 45 dB produces no reaction from neighbors; at 45 to 55 dB, sporadic complaints; at 50 to 60 dB, widespread complaints; at 55 to 65 dB, threats of community action; and at more than 65 dB, vigorous community action. This research from the 1950s continues to provide helpful guidelines for practicing rock musicians and multimedia developers today.

There is a great deal more to acoustics than just volume and pitch. If you are interested, there are many texts that discuss why middle C on a cello does not sound like middle C on a bassoon; or why a five-year-old can hear a 1,000 Hz tone played at 20 dB while an older adult with presbycusis (loss of hearing sensitivity due to age) cannot. Your use of sound in multimedia projects will not likely require highly specialized knowledge of harmonics, intervals, sine waves, notation, octaves, or the physics of acoustics and vibration, but you do need to know the following:

■ How to make sounds

■ How to record and edit sounds

■ How to incorporate sounds into your work

Multimedia System Sounds

You can use sound right off the bat on both the Macintosh and on a multimedia PC running Windows because system beeps and warnings are available as soon as you install the operating system.

On the Macintosh, you can choose one of several sounds for the system beep to indicate an error or warning: Droplet, Indigo, Quack, Simple Beep, Sosumi, and Wild Eep.

In Windows, system sounds are .WAV files, and they reside in the Windows\Media subdirectory; available system sounds include Chimes, Chord, Ding, Tada, and the Microsoft Sound. As Figure 10-1 shows, you can assign these sounds to system events such as Windows startup, warnings from other applications, or clicks outside an open dialog box (which causes the default beep in Windows). And you can create *schemes* of sounds and select a particular scheme according to your mood. You can add your own sound files and install them so they play when system events occur: place the .WAV sound files in your Windows\Media directory and use the Sound control panel to select them.

If you are new to either platform (Mac or PC/Windows), your first multimedia sound experience might be simply finding one of these system sounds in the appropriate control panel (the Sound dialog box) and testing it. To play sound with Windows, you need to have a sound board with the correct drivers installed in your PC. Figure 10-1 shows the Sound control panels in both Macintosh and Windows.

Using Macintosh models with a connected microphone or any older Macintosh with a sound digitizing device like MacRecorder, you can record and label new system sounds. This recording software is built into the system: just click on the Sound control panel's Add... button:

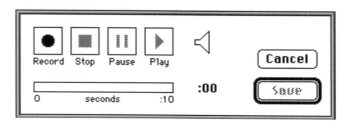

MIDI Versus Digital Audio

MIDI (Musical Instrument Digital Interface) is a communications standard developed in the early 1980s for electronic musical instruments and computers. It allows music and sound synthesizers from different manufacturers to communicate with each other by sending messages along cables connected to the devices. MIDI provides a protocol for passing detailed descriptions of a musical score, such as the notes, sequences of notes, and what instrument will play these notes. But MIDI data are not digitized sound; they are shorthand representations of music stored in numeric form. Digital audio is a recording, MIDI is a score—the first depends on the capabilities of your sound system, the other on the quality of your musical instruments *and* the capabilities of your sound system.

A MIDI file is a list of time-stamped commands that are recordings of musical actions (the pressing down of a piano key or a sustain pedal, for example, or the movement of a control wheel or slider) that, when sent to a MIDI playback device, results in sound. A concise MIDI message can cause a complex sound or sequence of sounds to play on an instrument or synthesizer, so MIDI files tend to be significantly smaller (per second of sound delivered to the user) than equivalent digitized waveform files.

In contrast to MIDI data, *digital audio* data are the actual representations of sound, stored in the form of thousands of individual numbers (called samples). The digital data represent the instantaneous amplitude (or loudness) of a sound at discrete slices of time. Because it is not device dependent,

10

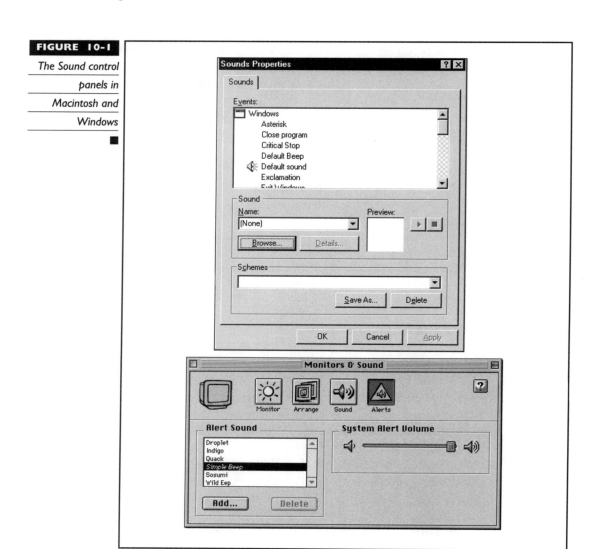

FIGURE 10-1

The Sound control panels in Macintosh and Windows

digital audio sounds the same every time it is played. But that consistency comes at a price: large data storage files. Digital sound is used for music CDs.

MIDI data are to digital audio data what vector or drawn graphics are to bitmapped graphics. That is, MIDI data are device dependent; digital data are not. Just as the appearance of vector graphics differs depending on the printer device or display screen, the sounds produced by MIDI music files depend on the particular MIDI device used for playback. Similarly, a roll of perforated player-piano score played on a concert grand would sound different than if played on a honky-tonk piano. Digital data, on the other hand, produce sounds that are more or less identical regardless of the playback system. The MIDI standard is like PostScript, letting instruments communicate in a well-understood language.

MIDI has several advantages over digital audio and two huge disadvantages. First, the advantages:

- MIDI files are much more compact than digital audio files, and the size of a MIDI file is completely independent of playback quality. In general, MIDI files will be 200 to 1,000 times smaller than CD-quality digital audio files. Because MIDI files are small, they don't take up as much RAM, disk space, and CPU resources.

- Because they are small, MIDI files embedded in Web pages load and play more quickly than their digital equivalents.

- In some cases, MIDI files may sound better than digital audio files if the MIDI sound source you are using is of high quality.

- You can change the length of a MIDI file (by varying its tempo) without changing the pitch of the music or degrading the audio quality. MIDI data are completely editable—right down to the level of an individual note. You can manipulate the smallest detail of a MIDI composition (often with submillisecond accuracy) in ways that are impossible with digital audio.

Now for the disadvantages:

- Because MIDI data do not represent sound but musical instruments, you can be certain that playback will be accurate only if the MIDI playback device is identical to the device used for production. Imagine the emotional humming chorus from *Madame Butterfly* sung by a chorus of Budweiser frogs—same score, wrong instrument. Even with the General MIDI standard (see the General MIDI table of instrument sounds in Table 10-3), the sound of a MIDI instrument varies according to the electronics of the playback device and the sound generation method it uses.

- Also, MIDI cannot easily be used to play back spoken dialog, although expensive and technically tricky digital samplers are available.

In general, the most important advantage of digital audio is its consistent playback quality, but this is where MIDI is the least reliable! With digital audio you can be more confident that the audio track for your multimedia project will sound as good in the end as it did in the beginning when you

10

created it. For this reason, it's no surprise that digital audio is used far more frequently than MIDI data for multimedia sound tracks.

There are two additional and often more compelling reasons to work with digital audio:

■ A wider selection of application software and system support for digital audio is available for both the Macintosh and Windows platforms.

■ The preparation and programming required for creating digital audio do not demand a knowledge of music theory; working with MIDI data usually does require a modicum of familiarity with musical scores, keyboards, and notation as well as of audio production.

Choosing Between MIDI and Digital Audio

In general, use MIDI data in the following circumstances:

■ Digital audio won't work because you don't have enough RAM, hard disk space, CPU processing power, or bandwidth.

■ You have a high-quality MIDI sound source.

■ You have complete control over the playback hardware.

■ You don't need spoken dialog.

In general, use digital audio in the following circumstances:

■ You don't have control over the playback hardware.

■ You have the computing resources and bandwidth to handle digital files.

■ You need spoken dialog.

***

t i p   *It is possible to use both MIDI and digital audio together in the same project. There are even software tools, such as Macromedia's DeckII, E-Magic's Logic Audio, and Opcode's Digital Performer, that allow you to work with both types of data at the same time.*

Digital Audio

You can digitize sound from a microphone, a synthesizer, existing tape recordings, live radio and television broadcasts, popular CDs, and your favorite long-playing records. In fact, you can digitize sounds from any source, natural or prerecorded. The hardware and software requirements for digitizing sound are discussed in Chapters 4 and 7.

Digitized sound is *sampled sound*. Every *n*th fraction of a second, a sample of sound is taken and stored as digital information in bits and bytes. How often the samples are taken is the *sampling rate*, and the amount of information stored about each sample is the *sample size*. The more often you take a sample and the more data you store about that sample, the finer the resolution and quality of the captured sound when it is played back.

The three sampling frequencies most often used in multimedia are CD-quality 44.1 kHz (kilohertz), 22.05 kHz, and 11.025 kHz. Sample sizes are either 8 bits or 16 bits. The larger the sample size, the better the data describe the recorded sound. An 8-bit sample size provides 256 equal units to describe the dynamic range or amplitude—the level of sound at that time—of the slice of sound captured. A 16-bit sample size, on the other hand, provides a staggering 65,536 equal units to describe the dynamic range. As you can see in Figure 10-2, slices of analog waveforms are sampled at various frequencies, and each discrete sample is then stored either as 8 or 16 bits of data.

The value of each sample is rounded off to the nearest integer (quantization), and if the amplitude is greater than the intervals available, clipping of the top and bottom of the wave occurs (see Figure 10-3). Quantization can produce an unwanted background hissing noise, and clipping may severely distort the sound.

FIGURE 10-2

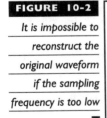

It is impossible to reconstruct the original waveform if the sampling frequency is too low

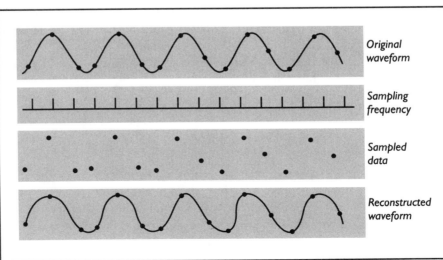

Original waveform

Sampling frequency

Sampled data

Reconstructed waveform

10

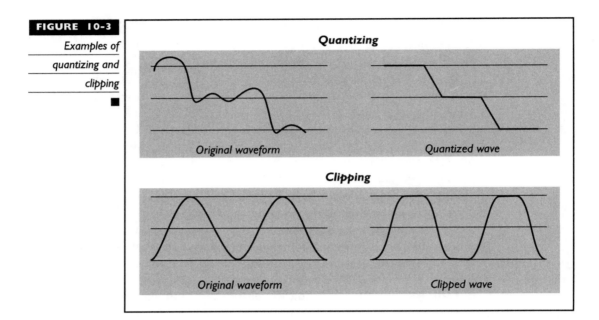

FIGURE 10-3

Examples of

quantizing and

clipping

Preparing Digital Audio Files

Preparing digital audio files is fairly straightforward. If you have analog source materials—music or sound effects that you have recorded on analog media such as cassette tapes—the first step is to digitize the analog material by recording it onto computer-readable digital media. In most cases, this just means playing sound from one device (such as a tape recorder) right into your computer, using appropriate audio digitizing software.

You want to focus on two crucial aspects of preparing digital audio files:

- Balancing the need for sound quality with your available RAM and hard disk resources

- Setting proper recording levels to get a good, clean recording

File Size Versus Quality

Remember that the sampling rate determines the frequency makeup of the recording. Sampling at higher rates more accurately captures the high-frequency content of your sound. *Audio resolution* determines the accuracy with which a sound can be digitized. Using more bits yields a recording that sounds more like its original.

warning *The higher the sound quality, the larger your file will be.*

Stereo recordings are more lifelike and realistic, because human beings have two ears. Mono recordings are fine, but tend to sound a bit "flat" and uninteresting when compared with stereo recordings. Stereo sound files require twice as much storage space as mono files for the same length of time.

Table 10-2 provides some commonly available sampling rates and resolutions, with resulting file sizes.

Here are the formulas for determining the size (in bytes) of a digital recording. For a monophonic recording:

sampling rate * duration of recording in seconds * (bit resolution / 8) * 1

For a stereo recording:

sampling rate * duration of recording in seconds * (bit resolution / 8) * 2

Thus the formula for a 10-second recording at 22.05 kHz, 8-bit resolution would be

22050 * 10 * 8 / 8 * 1

which equals 220,500 bytes. Sampling rate is measured in kHz, or thousand samples per second, while resolution is measured in bits per sample (remember, there are 8 bits in a byte). A 10-second stereo recording at 44.1 kHz, 16-bit resolution (meeting the CD-quality Red Book Audio standards—an international recording standard discussed later in this chapter) would be

44100 * 10 * 16 / 8 * 2

which equals 1,764,000 bytes. A 40-second mono recording at 11 kHz, 8-bit resolution would be

11000 * 40 * 8 / 8 * 1

which equals 440,000 bytes.

Mmm..Music, Mmm..Motion, Mmm..Megabytes!

Sharon Klocek, Producer, Visual In-Seitz, Inc., while clearing off her hard drive

Sampling Rate	Resolution	Stereo or Mono	Bytes Needed for 1 Minute	Comments
44.1 kHz	16-bit	Stereo	10.5MB	CD-quality recording; the recognized standard of audio quality.
44.1 kHz	16-bit	Mono	5.25MB	A good trade-off for high-quality recordings of mono sources such as voice-overs.
44.1 kHz	8-bit	Stereo	5.25MB	Achieves highest playback quality on low-end devices such as most of the sound cards in Windows PCs.
44.1 kHz	8-bit	Mono	2.6MB	An appropriate trade-off for recording a mono source.
22.05 kHz	16-bit	Stereo	5.25MB	Darker sounding than CD-quality recording because of the lower sampling rate, but still full and "present" because of high bit resolution and stereo.
22.05 kHz	16-bit	Mono	2.5MB	Not a bad choice for speech, but better to trade some fidelity for a lot of disk space by dropping down to 8-bit.
22.05 kHz	8-bit	Stereo	2.6MB	A popular choice for reasonable stereo recording where full bandwidth playback is not possible.
22.05 kHz	8-bit	Mono	1.3MB	A thinner sound than the choice just above, but very usable. Any Macintosh or any MPC can play back this type of file. About as good as listening to your TV set.
11 kHz	8-bit	Stereo	1.3MB	At this low a sampling rate, there are few advantages to using stereo.
11 kHz	8-bit	Mono	650K	In practice, probably as low as you can go and still get usable results; very dark and muffled.
5.5 kHz	8-bit	Stereo	650K	Stereo not effective.
5.5 kHz	8-bit	Mono	325K	About as good as a bad telephone connection.

TABLE 10-2   *One-Minute Digital Audio Recordings at Common Sampling Rates and Resolutions*   ■

Consumer-grade audio compact discs are recorded in stereo at a sampling rate of 44.1 kHz and a 16-bit resolution. Fortunately, for hard disk storage requirements at least, user expectations of audio quality are somewhat lower for computer-based multimedia presentations than they are for Grammy Award-winning recordings (see Vaughan's Law of Multimedia Minimums in the "Production Tips" section of this chapter). Particularly on the Macintosh, 8-bit, 22 kHz recordings are typical. Even lower rates are used for sound effects in many games.

---

tip *The only reason to digitize audio at a higher specification than can be used by the target playback device is for archiving it. As playback technologies and bandwidth improve over time, you may wish (someday) for higher-quality original files when you upgrade a product.*

Setting Proper Recording Levels

A distorted recording sounds terrible. If the signal you feed into your computer is too "hot" to handle, the result will be an unpleasant crackling or background ripping noise. Conversely, recordings that are made at too low a level are often unusable because the amount of sound recorded does not sufficiently exceed the residual noise levels of the recording process itself. The trick is to set the right levels when you record.

Any good piece of digital audio recording and editing software will display digital meters to let you know how loud your sound is. Watch the meters closely during recording, and you'll never have a problem. Unlike analog meters that usually have a 0 setting somewhere in the middle and extend up into ranges like +5, +8, or even higher, digital meters peak out. To avoid distortion, do not cross over this limit. If this happens, lower your volume (either by lowering the input level of the recording device or the output level of your source) and try again. Try to keep peak levels between -3 and -10. Any time you go over the peak, whether you can hear it or not, you introduce distortion into the recording.

Editing Digital Recordings

Once a recording has been made, it will almost certainly need to be edited. Figure 10-4 shows WaveStudio sound editing software, and Figure 10-5

10

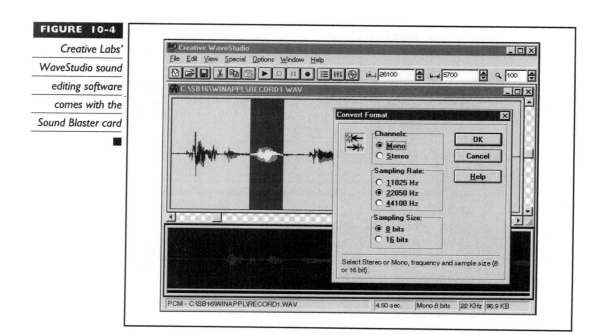

FIGURE 10-4

Creative Labs'

WaveStudio sound

editing software

comes with the

Sound Blaster card
■

illustrates SoundEdit 16-2's special effects menu. The basic sound editing operations that most multimedia producers need are described in the paragraphs that follow.

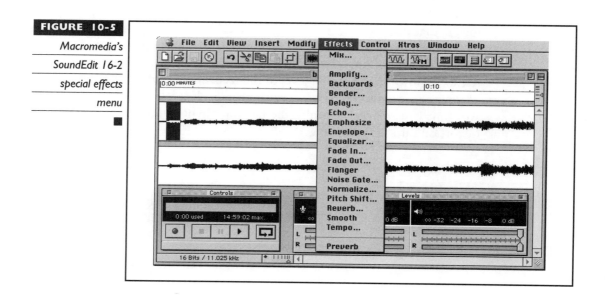

FIGURE 10-5

Macromedia's

SoundEdit 16-2

special effects

menu
■

TRIMMING   Removing "dead air" or blank space from the front of a recording and any unnecessary extra time off the end is your first sound editing task. Trimming even a few seconds here and there might make a big difference in your file size. Trimming is typically accomplished by dragging the mouse cursor over a graphic representation of your recording and choosing a menu command such as Cut, Clear, Erase, or Silence.

SPLICING AND ASSEMBLY   Using the same tools mentioned for trimming, you will probably want to remove the extraneous noises that inevitably creep into a recording. Even the most controlled studio voice-overs require touch-up. Also, you may need to assemble longer recordings by cutting and pasting together many shorter ones. In the old days, this was done by splicing and assembling actual pieces of magnetic tape.

VOLUME ADJUSTMENTS   If you are trying to assemble ten different recordings into a single sound track, there is little chance that all the segments will have the same volume. To provide a consistent volume level, select all the data in the file, and raise or lower the overall volume by a certain amount. Don't increase the volume too much, or you may distort the file.

FORMAT CONVERSION   In some cases, your digital audio editing software might read a format different from that read by your presentation or authoring program. Most Macintosh sound editing software will save files in SND and AIF formats, and most authoring systems will read these formats. In Windows, most editing software writes .WAV files.

RESAMPLING OR DOWNSAMPLING   If you have recorded and edited your sounds at 16-bit sampling rates but are using lower rates and resolutions in your project, you must resample or downsample the file. This process will save considerable disk space.

FADE-INS AND FADE-OUTS   Most programs offer enveloping capability, useful for long sections that you wish to fade in or fade out gradually. This enveloping is important to smooth out the very beginning and the very end of a sound file.

EQUALIZATION   Some programs offer digital equalization (EQ) capabilities that allow you to modify a recording's frequency content to sound brighter or darker.

TIME STRETCHING   More advanced programs let you alter the length (in time) of a sound file without changing its pitch. This feature can be very useful, but watch out: most time-stretching algorithms will severely degrade the audio quality of the file if the length is altered more than a few percent in either direction.

DIGITAL SIGNAL PROCESSING (DSP)   Some programs allow you to process the signal with effects such as reverberation, multitap delay, chorus, flange, and other special effects.

Being able to process a sound source with effects can greatly add to a project. To create an environment by placing the sound inside a room, hall, or even a cathedral can bring depth and dimension to a project. But a little can go a long way—do not overdo the sound effects! Once a sound effect is processed and mixed onto a track, it cannot be further edited, so always save the original so you can tweak it again if you are not happy with the results.

REVERSING SOUNDS   Another simple manipulation is to reverse all or a portion of a digital audio recording. Sounds, particularly spoken dialog, can produce a surreal, otherworldly effect when played backward.

Making MIDI Audio

Composing your own original score can be one of the most creative and rewarding aspects of building a multimedia project, and MIDI is the quickest, easiest, and most flexible tool for this task. Yet creating an original MIDI score is hard work. Knowing something about music, being able to play the piano, and having a lot of good ideas are just the prerequisites to building a good score; beyond that, it takes time and musical skill to work with MIDI.

Happily, you can always hire someone to do the job for you. In addition to the talented MIDI composers who charge substantial rates for their services, many young composers who want to get into multimedia are also available. With a little research, you can often find a MIDI musician to work for limited compensation. Remember, however, that you often get what you pay for.

To make MIDI scores, you will need sequencer software (such as Midisoft Studio for Windows, illustrated in Figure 10-6), and a sound synthesizer (typically built into the sound board on PCs, but an add-on board or peripheral for the Macintosh). A MIDI keyboard is also useful to simplify the creation of musical scores. The MIDI keyboard is not, however, necessary for playback unless the keyboard has its own built-in synthesizer (most do) that you wish to specify for playback. Sequencer software lets you record and edit MIDI data and quantizes your score to adjust for timing inconsistencies (a great feature for those who can't keep the beat). The sequencer software records your actions on the MIDI keyboard (or another MIDI device) in real-time, and will play back exactly the notes you played on the keyboard; the software may also print a neatly penned copy of your score to paper. Sound boards and other hardware components of MIDI are discussed in Chapter 5.

- -

http://www.midisoft.com
http://www.rain.org/~bain/midi30.html
http://www.midi-classics.com

You'll find information about MIDI and music files for downloading

Instruments that you can synthesize are identified by a General MIDI numbering system that ranges from 0 to 127 (see Table 10-3). Until this system came along, there was always a risk that a MIDI file originally composed with, say, piano, electric guitar, and bass, might be played back with piccolo, tambourine, and glockenspiel if the ID numbers were not precisely mapped to match your original hardware setup. This was usually the case when you played a MIDI file on a MIDI configuration different from the one that recorded the file.

tip *Making MIDI files is as complex as recording good sampled files, so often it pays to find someone already set up with the equipment and skills to create your score, rather than investing in both the hardware and learning curve.*

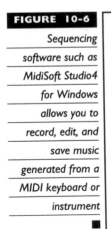

FIGURE 10-6

Sequencing software such as MidiSoft Studio4 for Windows allows you to record, edit, and save music generated from a MIDI keyboard or instrument

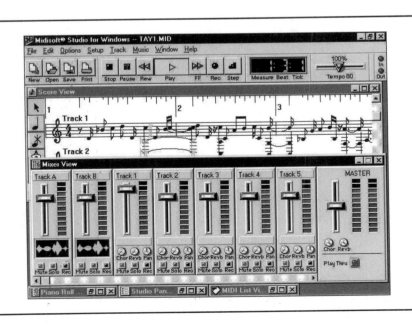

ID	Sound	ID	Sound
0	Acoustic grand piano	31	Guitar harmonics
1	Bright acoustic piano	32	Acoustic bass
2	Electric grand piano	33	Electric bass (finger)
3	Honky-tonk piano	34	Electric bass (pick)
4	Rhodes piano	35	Fretless bass
5	Chorused piano	36	Slap bass 1
6	Harpsichord	37	Slap bass 2
7	Clarinet	38	Synth bass 1
8	Celesta	39	Synth bass 2
9	Glockenspiel	40	Violin
10	Music box	41	Viola
11	Vibraphone	42	Cello
12	Marimba	43	Contrabass
13	Xylophone	44	Tremolo strings
14	Tubular bells	45	Pizzicato strings
15	Dulcimer	46	Orchestral harp
16	Hammond organ	47	Timpani
17	Percussive organ	48	String ensemble 1
18	Rock organ	49	String ensemble 2
19	Church organ	50	SynthStrings 1
20	Reed organ	51	SynthStrings 2
21	Accordion	52	Choir aahs
22	Harmonica	53	Voice oohs
23	Tango accordion	54	Synth voice
24	Acoustic guitar (nylon)	55	Orchestra hit
25	Acoustic guitar (steel)	56	Trumpet
26	Electric guitar (jazz)	57	Trombone
27	Electric guitar (clean)	58	Tuba
28	Electric guitar (muted)	59	Muted trumpet
29	Overdriven guitar	60	French horn
30	Distortion guitar	61	Brass section

TABLE 10-3 *General MIDI Instrument Sounds* ■

ID	Sound	ID	Sound
62	Synth brass 1	93	Pad 6 (Metallic)
63	Synth brass 2	94	Pad 7 (Halo)
64	Soprano saxophone	95	Pad 8 (Sweep)
65	Alto saxophone	96	FX 1 (Rain)
66	Tenor saxophone	97	FX 2 (Soundtrack)
67	Baritone saxophone	98	FX 3 (Crystal)
68	Oboe	99	FX 4 (Atmosphere)
69	English horn	100	FX 5 (Brightness)
70	Bassoon	101	FX 6 (Goblins)
71	Clarinet	102	FX 7 (Echoes)
72	Piccolo	103	FX 8 (Sci-Fi)
73	Flute	104	Sitar
74	Recorder	105	Banjo
75	Pan flute	106	Shamisen
76	Bottle blow	107	Koto
77	Shakuhachi	108	Kalimba
78	Whistle	109	Bagpipe
79	Ocarina	110	Fiddle
80	Lead 1 (Square)	111	Shanai
81	Lead 2 (Sawtooth)	112	Tinkle bell
82	Lead 3 (Calliope lead)	113	Agogo
83	Lead 4 (Chiff lead)	114	Steel drums
84	Lead 5 (Charang)	115	Wood block
85	Lead 6 (Voice)	116	Taiko drum
86	Lead 7 (Fifths)	117	Melodic Tom
87	Lead 8 (Bass + lead)	118	Synth drum
88	Pad 1 (New Age)	119	Reverse cymbal
89	Pad 2 (Warm)	120	Guitar fret noise
90	Pad 3 (Polysynth)	121	Breath noise
91	Pad 4 (Choir)	122	Seashore
92	Pad 5 (Bowed)	123	Bird tweet

10

TABLE 10-3   *General MIDI Instrument Sounds* (continued) ■

ID	Sound	ID	Sound
124	Telephone ring	57	Crash cymbal 2
125	Helicopter	58	Vibraslap
126	Applause	59	Ride cymbal 2
127	Gunshot	60	High bongo
	Percussion Keys	61	Low bongo
35	Acoustic bass drum	62	Mute high conga
36	Bass drum 1	63	Open high conga
37	Side stick	64	Low conga
38	Acoustic snare	65	High timbale
39	Hand clap	66	Low timbale
40	Electric snare	67	High agogo
41	Low-floor tom	68	Low agogo
42	Closed high-hat	69	Cabasa
43	High-floor tom	70	Maracas
44	Pedal high-hat	71	Short whistle
45	Low tom	72	Long whistle
46	Open high-hat	73	Short guiro
47	Low-mid tom	74	Long guiro
48	High-mid tom	75	Claves
49	Crash cymbal 1	76	High wood block
50	High tom	77	Low wood block
51	Ride cymbal 1	78	Mute cuica
52	Chinese cymbal	79	Open cuica
53	Ride bell	80	Mute triangle
54	Tambourine	81	Open triangle
55	Splash cymbal		
56	Cowbell		

TABLE 10-3   *General MIDI Instrument Sounds* (continued) ■

Once you have gathered your audio material, you will need to edit it to fit your multimedia project precisely. As you edit, you will continue to make creative decisions. Because it is so easy to edit MIDI data, you can make many fine adjustments to your music.

MIDI's true place in multimedia work may be as a production tool rather than a delivery medium. MIDI is by far the best way to create original music for multimedia projects, so use MIDI to get the flexibility and creative control you want. Then, once the music is completed and fits your project, lock it down for delivery by turning it into digital audio data, as discussed below.

---

t i p   *Test your MIDI files thoroughly by playing them back on a variety of hardware devices before you incorporate them into your multimedia project.*

Audio File Formats

When you create multimedia, it is likely that you will deal with file formats and translators for text, sounds, images, animations, or digital video clips. A sound file's format is simply a recognized methodology for organizing the digitized sound's data bits and bytes into a data file. The structure of the file must be known, of course, before the data can be saved or later loaded into a computer to be edited and/or played as sound. Table 10-4 shows some of the common sound formats used for multimedia.

On the Macintosh, digitized sounds may be stored as data files (for example, .AIF or .SDII), or they may be stored as resources in the resource fork of the system or application as SNDs. The Macintosh uses a unique dual-fork file structure, and you will need to know whether the file resides in a resource fork or as a stand-alone file.

In Windows, digitized sounds are most commonly stored as wave (.WAV) files. For the Internet, new formats are emerging as companies develop solutions for streaming and playing sound on the World Wide Web. These solutions are discussed in detail in Chapter 15.

There are many ways to store the bits and bytes that describe a sampled waveform sound. The method used for Red Book Audio data files on consumer-grade music CDs is Linear Pulse Code Modulation. An audio CD can provide up to 76 minutes of playing time, which is enough for a slow-tempo rendition of Beethoven's Ninth Symphony. Incidentally, being able to contain Beethoven's Ninth is reported to be Philips's and Sony's actual size criterion during early research and development for determining the length of the sectors and ultimately the physical size of the compact disc format itself.

The CD-I (compact disc-interactive) format, developed by Philips as a variant of the Red Book standard, uses Adaptive Delta Pulse Code

10

Extension	MIME Type	Platform	Use
Aif	Audio/x-aiff	Mac, SGI	Audio
Aifc	Audio/x-aiff	Mac, SGI	Audio (compressed)
AIFF	Audio/x-aiff	Mac, SGI	Audio
Aiff	Audio/x-aiff	Mac, SGI	Audio
Au	Audio/basic	Sun, NeXT	ULAW audio data
Mov	Video/QuickTime	Mac, Win	QuickTime video
Mpe	Video/mpeg	All	MPEG video
Mpeg	Video/mpeg	All	MPEG video
Mpg	Video/mpeg	All	MPEG video
Qt	Video/QuickTime	Mac, Win	QuickTime video
Ra, ram	Audio/x-pn-realaudio	All	RealAudio Sound
Snd	Audio/basic	Sun, NeXT	ULAW Audio Data
Vox	Audio/	All	VoxWare Voice
Wav	Audio/x-wav	Win	WAV Audio

TABLE 10-4 *Common File Types Used for Digitized Sounds (Internet MIME Types)* ∎

Modulation (ADPCM) to deliver 2 hours of high-fidelity stereo music or as many as 20 hours of voice-quality monaural audio, per compact disc. This CD-I format provides for interleaving ADPCM audio data with screen graphics or video to allow synchronization of audio and image without extensive data buffering. It requires, however, a special CD-ROM/XA (extended architecture) player.

The AIFF format (or AIFC when supporting MACE compression schemes of 3:1 and 6:1) is preferred for Macintosh sound files, where all the sound data reside in the data fork. The wave format (.WAV) was introduced by Microsoft and IBM with the introduction of Windows.

Both Macintosh and Windows can make use of MIDI files. A MIDI interface is built into many sound boards on the PC (and is a requirement for MPC computers). On the Macintosh, a MIDI adapter is required for MIDI instrument input and output. On both platforms, MIDI sounds are typically stored in files with the .MID extension.

Sound for the World Wide Web

In the early days of the Internet, when machines typically ran in a Unix environment, the common file format for sounds (.au) was the international telephone format (CCITT G711) of *uLaw* (also known as *Mu-law* or *µ-law*, nicknamed the "TalkRadio" or "Geek of the Week" format and pronounced "mew-law"). It provided meager 8 kHz sampling rates at 8-bit mono, but produced very small file sizes. Today, the uLaw format supports 8 kHz at 16 bits in 2:1 compression. *aLaw* is the European equivalent of uLaw. Many more sound file types are now commonly found on the Web (see Table 10-4).

There are two methods for playing either digital or MIDI sound on the Web. First, you can wait for the entire sound file to download to your computer, then play it back with a helper application. Second, you can begin to play a downloading sound as soon as enough of the sound is cached on your computer such that there will always be more sound waiting to be played than still needs to be downloaded. The sound file *streams* into your computer in the background, keeping ahead of what has already been played so the playback doesn't pause or break up. Streaming files are dependent upon connection speed: you must wait longer (*streaming latency*) before the streamed sound begins to play when using a 28.8 Kbps modem (low bandwidth) than when using a high-speed T1 connection (high bandwidth).

Chapter 15 discusses in greater detail the browser plug-ins and techniques used to deliver sound and motion video on the Web.

I am still making two-measure loops and fighting file size constraints. Nothing has changed....
Full quote due in February....

Chip Harris, Composer and Musician, In-House Productions

10

Working with Sound in Windows

Windows includes standardized support for both digital audio and MIDI. All MPC machines now support digital audio (wave audio), standardized MIDI playback, and CD-Audio. The MPC standard also requires manufacturers to provide a digital mixing system (albeit a simple one), so that all audio outputs (MIDI, wave audio, and CD-Audio) can be mixed together and directed to a single pair of stereo outputs.

In April 1992, Microsoft rolled out its new version of Windows 3.1 with speeches and a live MIDI performance at the spring COMDEX/Windows World Trade Show in Chicago.

Tracy Hurst played the piano and Steve Peha worked the electronic interface. As Tracy played "Striving for Glory: The Windows 3.1 Theme" on his Roland HP-5700, the music was instantaneously transcribed by Midisoft Studio, and the notes ran real-time across the 50-foot big screen, like sing-along bouncing balls. The show worked perfectly, and Windows magazine later called it a tour de force for Windows multimedia. It was slick.

But I knew these people who looked so professional and confident. I knew about the late nights, the crashed disk drives, the long drive from Boston, and the hurried runs to the nearest Radio Shack. This performance was not just about MIDI; it was about multimedia development in general. Hard work and technology are the substantial invisible part of the iceberg supporting multimedia's visible leading edge.

MIDI in Windows

Microsoft's approach to MIDI has two parts: One part is MIDI mapping (see Figure 10-7), which directs the flow of MIDI data from application software to MIDI hardware devices. The second part is a set of MIDI file-authoring guidelines for creating MIDI files that play back properly and on the widest possible variety of hardware devices.

Windows splits all MIDI devices into two categories: base-level MIDI devices and extended-level MIDI devices.

- *Base-level MIDI devices* can play back at least three melodic instrument parts with at least six notes playing at one time and a percussion track with at least three notes playing at one time. Most FM-based sound cards, such as Sound Blaster Pro or Pro Audio Spectrum, are considered base-level devices. Older versions of FM-based sound cards were 8-bit and are now obsolete.

- *Extended-level MIDI devices* can play back at least nine melodic instrument parts with at least 16 notes playing at one time and a percussion track with at least 16 notes playing at one time. Most sample-based sound cards, such as Roland SCC-1 and Turtle Beach Daytona and Maui, are extended-level devices.

General MIDI devices, such as the Roland SC-55 Sound Canvas and the Sound Blaster cards, are considered extended-level devices—even though they have only 24-voice polyphony. *Polyphony* allows for more than one note to be played simultaneously (for example, a chord).

FIGURE 10-7

With the Windows Multimedia Properties control panel, you can map devices to the 16 MIDI channels

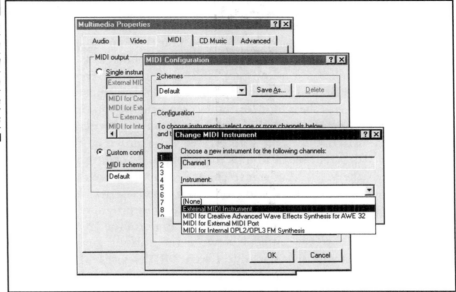

MIDI device manufacturers typically supply a MIDI driver to work with Microsoft's system-level MIDI commands. This frees software developers from having to write individual drivers for each piece of MIDI hardware.

MIDI Mapping

MIDI files created to adhere to Microsoft's guidelines are called device-independent MIDI files. Each file stores two arrangements of each piece. One arrangement is intended for extended-level devices, in MIDI channels 1 to 10, and a second arrangement is intended for base-level devices, in channels 13 to 16. (There are 16 different MIDI channels to work with. Each channel can be sent, or mapped, to a different hardware device.)

With the Multimedia Properties control panel (see Figure 10-7), you can set up a configuration that allows channels 13 to 16 to be sent to your device, for example, while the other channels are sent elsewhere or ignored. If you have an extended-level device, you can filter out the base-level channels. Ready-made MIDI maps may be supplied with your MIDI device. When Windows sees a MIDI message coming its way, it checks to see on which MIDI channel that message is being transmitted, and then it sends the message to the appropriate MIDI hardware device. For example, if you have a sound card in your PC that has an on-board synthesizer as well as a MIDI output, you can tell Windows to send certain MIDI channels to the

10

synthesizer and other MIDI channels to the MIDI output, where they are sent to an external MIDI device.

In addition to the simple channel mapping just described, Windows also provides patch mapping and key mapping. But you will need a small add-on application (see Figure 10-8) that does not come with Windows 95 but is distributed by Microsoft and available at most online services: idfedit.exe. This is the editor for the "Instrument Definition File."

Patch mapping is useful when you want to play, on a General MIDI device, MIDI files that were created on a different type of device containing a different set of sounds (or patches). By creating an appropriate patch map, the MIDI Mapper can change any patch from the source file into the correct patch on the destination MIDI playback device. *Key mapping* is similar to patch mapping. Instead of mapping program change numbers from one device to another, key maps map notes (or "piano keys"). This is intended to resolve conflicts between the various key-based percussion mapping systems used on many different MIDI devices. MIDI channel 10 usually maps to the percussion sounds, in which each key plays the sound of a different instrument.

Table 10-5 shows the channel and polyphony assignments that are part of the Microsoft guidelines for MIDI file authoring. By setting up your instrument definition file to correspond to this arrangement of channels, you can ensure that the MIDI file you create will sound as intended when played on another MPC system.

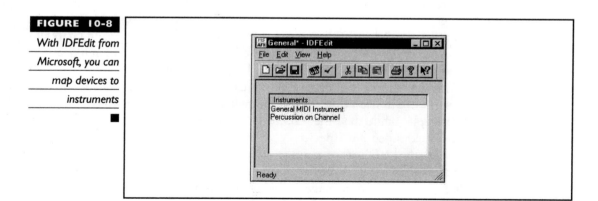

FIGURE 10-8

With IDFEdit from Microsoft, you can map devices to instruments

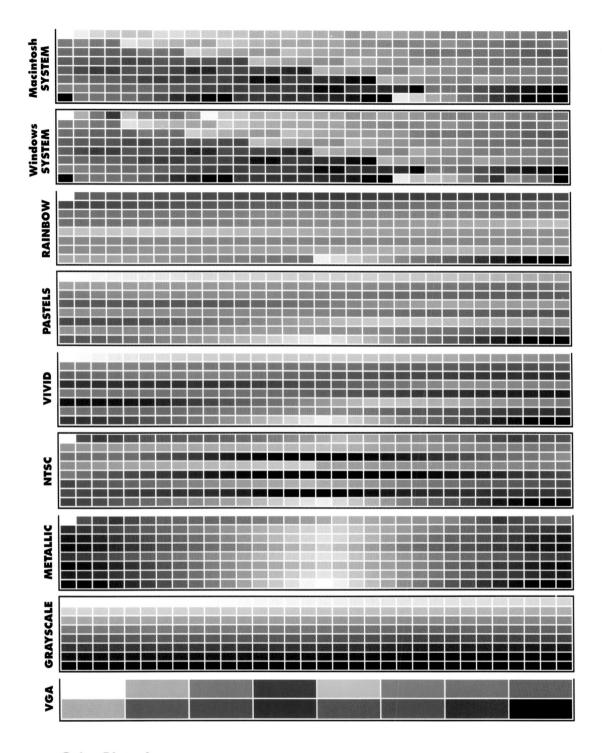

Color Plate 1:

These palettes of 256 colors (8-bit color depth) are provided in Macromedia's Director.
Note the VGA palette: these are the colors available in 16-color VGA mode in Windows.

Color Plate 2:

The RGB (red, green, blue) color space model is used to specify the intensity of each color dot on a computer monitor. See Chapter 11 to learn about color on computers.

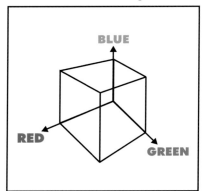

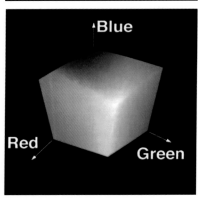

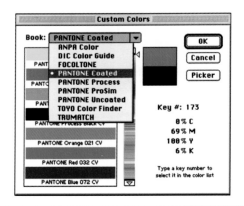

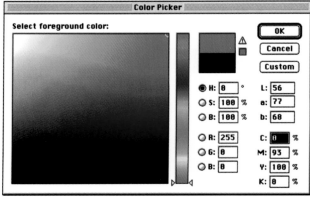

Color Plate 3:

Color pickers allow you to select a color using one or more different models of color space. The Photoshop picker (above) shows color data in four color space models: RGB (red, green, blue), HSB (hue, saturation, brightness), Lab (lightness, green-red axis, and blue-yellow axis) and CMYK (cyan, magenta, yellow, black). Also shown (top) is the proprietary Pantone picker. Color models are described in Chapter 11.

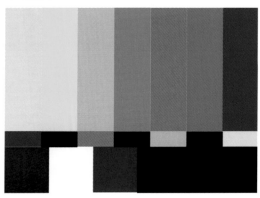

R: 204	R: 255	R: 0	R: 0	R: 255	R: 255	R: 0
G: 204	G: 255	G: 255	G: 255	G: 0	G: 0	G: 0
B: 204	B: 0	B: 255	B: 0	B: 255	B: 0	B: 255
R: 0	R: 19	R: 255	R: 19	R: 0	R: 19	R: 204
G: 0	G: 19	G: 0	G: 19	G: 255	G: 19	G: 204
B: 255	B: 19	B: 255	B: 19	B: 255	B: 19	B: 204

R: 8	R: 255	R: 58	R: 19	0	19	38	R: 19
G: 62	G: 255	G: 0	G: 19	0	19	38	G: 19
B: 89	B: 255	B: 126	B: 19	0	19	38	B: 19

Color Plate 4:

This SMPTE color bar pattern can be used at the beginning of a video tape for calibration. The RGB values of each bar are included so you can make your own screen using an image editing application. See Chapter 13.

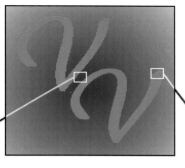

Color Plate 5:

Type and graphics that are anti-aliased into the background show softer edges.

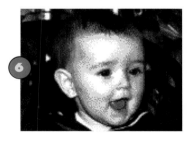

Color Plate 6:

These pictures illustrate color depth.
Image 1 is 24-bits deep (millions of colors);
Image 2 is dithered to 8-bits using an adaptive palette (the best 256 colors to represent the image);
Image 3 is also dithered to 8-bits, but uses the Apple Macintosh system palette (an optimized standard mix of 256 colors);
Image 4 is dithered to 4-bits (16 colors);
Image 5 is dithered to 8-bit grayscale (256 shades of gray);
Image 6 is dithered to 4-bit grayscale (16 shades of gray); and
Image 7 is dithered to 1-bit (two colors - in this case, black and white). Refer to Chapter 11.

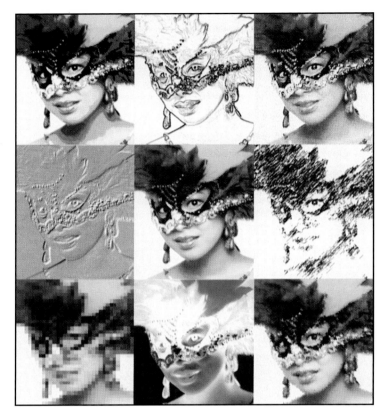

Color Plate 7:
Special effects for enhancing, altering, and manipulating bitmapped images are provided by most image editing applications, such as Picture Publisher (shown here, courtesy of Micrografx, Inc.), or as special plug-ins such as Kai's Power Tools for Photoshop.

Color Plate 8:
Both of these images were created on a computer using Fractal Design Painter with a pressure-sensitive stylus and special electronic watercolor effects. The lake scene is by Peter McCormick and the penguin by Peter and Caitlin Mitchell-Dayton.

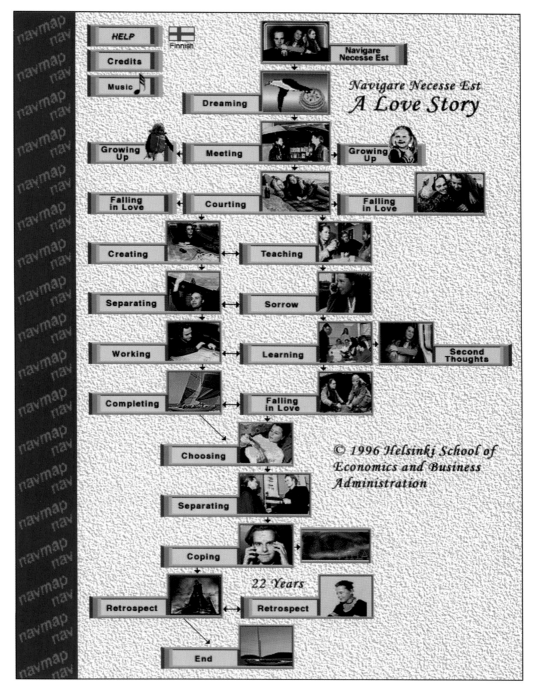

Color Plate 9:

A simplified navigation map can not only provide an overview of a multimedia project, but it can contain active links to documents using "hot" areas of the graphic (Chapter 18 explains ISMAPs and USEMAPs in World Wide Web documents). This is the navMap page from *Navigare Necesse Est*, a love story found at http://www.hkkk.fi/mmedia/. Clearly, the linking of information in such easy-to-make graphical user interfaces (see also Color Plate 11-1) demonstrates the power of multimedia on the Web.

Other HEX Values

216 Netscape Non-dithering Colors

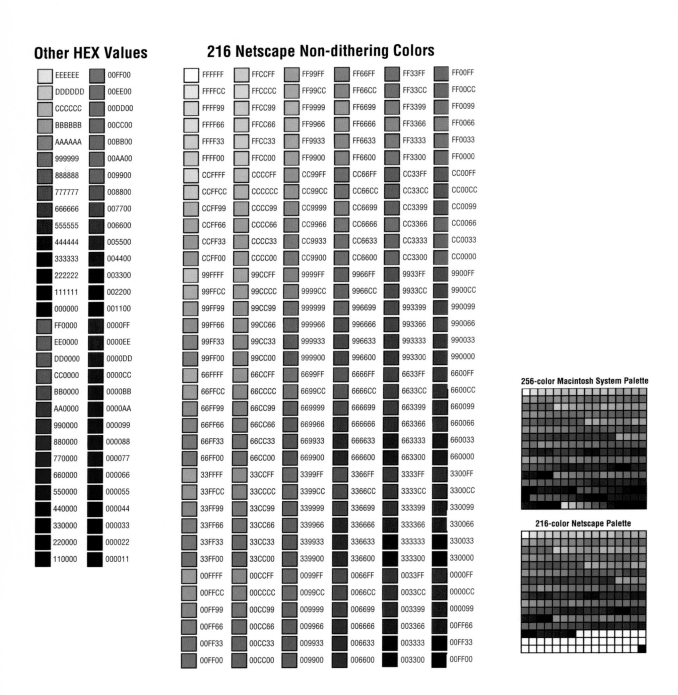

Color Plate 10:

Netscape Navigator uses 216 "non-dithering" colors on a Windows platform running in 256 color mode (8-bit color depth). Here are the colors and their associated hexadecimal values. Tricks for making your World Wide Web images look good on both Macintosh and Windows platforms are discussed in Chapter 18.

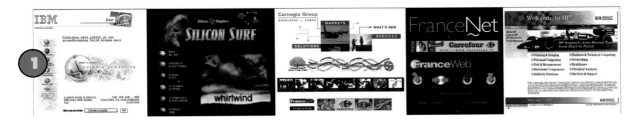

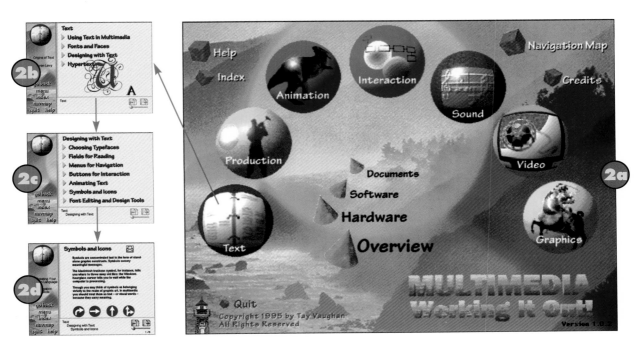

Color Plate 11:
There are many design approaches for buttons and interactive hot spots. Screen 1 is a collective of World Wide Web pages that combine graphic and text buttons (see Chapter 18); screens 2a, 2b, 2c, and 2d show a typical hierarchical menu system from *Multimedia: Working It Out*, the CD-ROM version of this book (available from Timestream, see the last page of this book); screen 3 is from an Osborne/McGraw-Hill CD-ROM Catalog; screen 4 shows the author and a few friends–click on any face for small-town secrets.

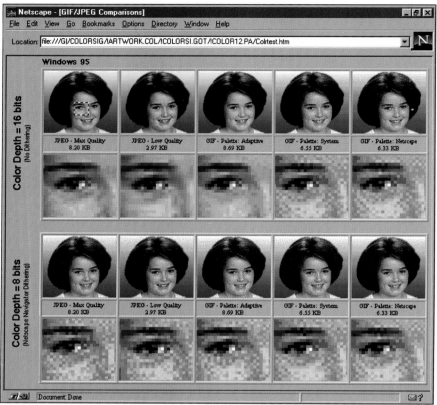

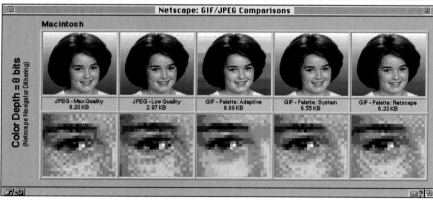

Color Plate 12:

These images were dithered in Photoshop to best fit the 8-bit palettes of GIF files (Adaptive, System, or Custom 216 Netscape). Also shown are JPEG files compressed with highest and lowest quality and their actual file sizes. The files were then displayed using Netscape Navigator at 16-bit and then 8-bit color depth. Note the subtle differences among palettes and systems, especially in the gradient blue background. Gradients do not usually dither well into 8-bit palettes. Chapters 11 and 18 provide more detail about making images for the World Wide Web.

Color Plate 13:

Morphing software (explained in Chapter 12) was used to seamlessly transform the images of sixteen kindergartners. When a sound track of music and voices was added to the four-minute piece, it made a compelling QuickTime video about how similar children are to each other.

Channels	Assignment	Polyphony
1 to 9	Reserved for extended-level melodic (nonpercussion) parts	16 notes
10	Reserved for extended-level percussion parts	16 notes
11	Unused	
12	Unused	
13 to 15	Reserved for base-level melodic (nonpercussion) parts	6 notes
16	Reserved for base-level percussion parts	3 notes

TABLE 10-5 *MIDI Channel and Polyphony Assignments* ■

General MIDI Standard

Microsoft's guidelines also specify that device-independent MIDI files should be created to conform to the new General MIDI hardware standard for MIDI playback devices. This standard accomplishes the following:

- Dictates a standardized program change mapping system and a standardized set of sounds. This means, for example, that all General MIDI devices have a bassoon sound mapped to patch number 70, and that sound can be called up by transmitting a MIDI program change command with a value of 70 to any General MIDI device. In fact, all General MIDI devices have the same set of 128 orchestral sounds, synthesizer sounds, and special effects. The actual timbres may vary from instrument to instrument, but the types of sound (piano, bass, guitar, and so forth) are the same.

- Provides minimum polyphony and channel requirements. All General MIDI devices must be capable of playing 24 notes simultaneously and of receiving MIDI messages simultaneously on all 16 MIDI channels.

- Provides standardized percussion and instrument channel assignments and patch mapping. All General MIDI devices play instrument sounds on channels 1 to 9; channel 10 is for percussion instruments. All General MIDI devices use the same percussion sounds on the keyboard keys (MIDI note numbers) of MIDI channel 10.

10

Digital Audio Under Windows

Developing digital audio under Windows is much simpler than working with MIDI, but that's to be expected because it is much simpler in general to deal with digital audio data than MIDI data. Microsoft has established a common file format called the wave audio format (.WAV files), a standardized method for storing digital audio information. You can play a MIDI file with the Media Player installed by Windows:

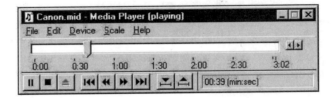

Though every Macintosh provides at least 8-bit audio (and more recently, 16-bit), in the PC world only MPC computers are guaranteed to have sound capability. Indeed, many millions of PCs have no digital audio capabilities at all. The component that gives a Windows PC its digital audio capabilities is the add-in sound card (see Chapter 5), and today, virtually every home PC ships with a sound card. In addition to wave audio playback under Windows, Microsoft has also standardized tools for the playback of CD-Audio (also called Red Book Audio). And through Microsoft's Media Control Interface (MCI) command set, multimedia programmers can control the playback of audio data from a compact disc.

Working with Sound on the Macintosh

The original 128K Macintosh, released in January 1984, was technically a capable multimedia machine. It displayed bitmapped graphics (albeit in black and white) and, more significantly, boasted 8-bit digital audio capability right on the motherboard. In fact, the very first Macintosh actually introduced itself by voice when it was first unveiled by Steve Jobs (see Chapter 4 to read what it said).

Here's a little history: In order to use the Apple moniker, the original founders of Apple Computer, Inc., worked out an arrangement with the Beatles (yes, *those* Beatles). One part of that agreement stipulated that Apple Computer, Inc., would never venture into the music business. To Steve Jobs and Steve Wozniak, working out of their garage in the late 1970s on a machine that could barely manage a convincing system beep, that clause probably seemed a harmless one. Little did they know that less than ten years later their computer would become the most popular music computer in the world.

Over the years, many people have speculated that the agreement with the Beatles has kept Apple out of the music business and delayed development of system software for audio applications. Although Apple would doubtless deny this, the company did recently pay representatives of the Beatles about $30 million to settle the issue once and for all.

Sound Manager

The Sound Manager (consisting of the Sound control panel and the Sound Manager extension) allows applications to play and record sound using Macintosh built-in sound hardware. Sound Manager supports 16-bit CD-quality audio, redirection of sound to third-party hardware cards, plug-in audio compression/decompression software (*codecs* for MACE, IMA, and uLaw formats), integration with QuickTime (see "Sound with QuickTime," below), and asynchronous alert sounds (so alert dialogs and other interface elements can continue processing while an alert sound is playing).

MIDI on the Macintosh

In the Windows environment, almost every major publisher of music and audio software has supported Microsoft's approach to MIDI. In contrast, many Macintosh developers are still not supporting Apple's MIDI Manager, the Macintosh software counterpart to the Windows MIDI Mapper, so many programs still rely exclusively on their own proprietary drivers. In fact, while Apple MIDI Manager version 2.0.2 works with System 7.5, it is not supported by Apple because it is considered a development tool.

10

---

warning   *Be sure the components of your Macintosh MIDI software and hardware are designed to work with each other.*

MIDI Manager

MIDI Manager is not a stand-alone application or utility, but a group of tools: Apple MIDI Driver, MIDI Manager, PatchBay Help, PatchBay, Patch-Bay DA, and Serial Switch.

While use of the MIDI Manager is being supplanted by QuickTime (see the next section), Apple's MIDI Manager is still in wide use because it represents an easy method for multitasking with MIDI. It may not possess MIDI mapping capabilities, but MIDI Manager does have additional features for interapplication communication and synchronization that are lacking in the Windows MIDI Mapper. Apple's software is, true to its name, a true manager of MIDI data and not just a data "mapper"; on the other hand, Microsoft's MIDI Mapper was designed to facilitate playback of MIDI data for multimedia. Thus the MIDI Manager is a more serious tool for synchronization as well as for multiple MIDI bus capabilities. (MIDI Manager supports both the Macintosh modem and printer ports, simultaneously.)

Apple's MIDI Manager interface is called PatchBay. With PatchBay you "patch" (route) the input and output of any number of MIDI applications to or from the Macintosh's serial ports and even to or from other MIDI applications running at the same time. Communication among the various clients is established by dragging "patch cords" (lines) between pairs of devices. Connections can be made between inputs and outputs and to clock sources (for synchronization) as well. PatchBay is shipped with most MIDI applications. See Figure 10-9.

Many non-MIDI programs can now play back MIDI data from within the context of a multimedia presentation using QuickTime (see the following section). It is even possible to use MIDI Manager's synchronization features to put visual events from one program in sync with MIDI events in another.

Sound with QuickTime

Apple broke new ground, outpacing Microsoft's Audio/Video Interleaved technology, with the release of QuickTime. QuickTime is a standard file format for displaying digitized motion video from hard disk or CD-ROM

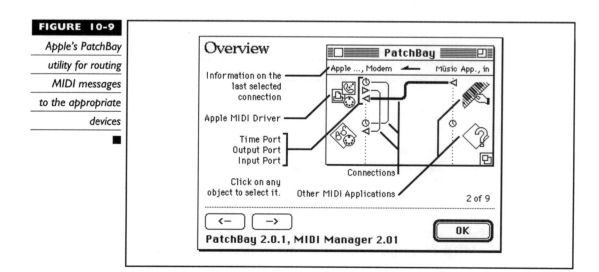

FIGURE 10-9

Apple's PatchBay utility for routing MIDI messages to the appropriate devices without special hardware. Digital audio data is interleaved with video information in the file, and when it is played back, the audio stays synchronized to the motion picture. You can use QuickTime just to play stereo sounds and MIDI; the video part of QuickTime is not required.

MIDI Music in QuickTime

QuickTime can play MIDI music from a "music track" embedded within a QuickTime movie file. This music track can store sampled sounds and a playback list for these sounds. The scheme for playing music in QuickTime is called the Macintosh Music Architecture, and it consists of a Note Allocator, a Tune Player, and other sound-playing devices and software components such as General MIDI.

The Note Allocator maintains a database of MIDI components attached to the Macintosh. But because many users may not have external MIDI devices attached to their computer, there is a built-in software-only playback component. The Tune Player then plays a time-ordered list of events (your MIDI file) into the MIDI component, negotiating with the Note Allocator. The result is music.

To convert a standard MIDI file (known as a *SMF*, with Type = Midi and Creator = ttxt or Moov) to QuickTime format, you need to have the QuickTime Musical Instruments extension installed. Then you can use Apple's SimpleText or MoviePlayer applications to convert the file by simply opening or importing it. You can change MIDI instrument settings during the transition from SMF to QuickTime format.

---

tip   *If your MIDI file has a period or "dot" (.) in its file name, it will cause QuickTime to open it as a Text Track instead of a Music Track. Rename the file so it doesn't contain a period.*

10

Notation Interchange File Format (NIFF)

ftp://blackbox.cartah.washington.edu/pub/NIFF

The NIFF standard is a collaborative work

Over the centuries, music notation has developed as its own complex language.

The NIFF file format was created in the mid-1990s from input from many commercial music software developers, publishers, and experienced music software users who were frustrated by lack of a standard format for sending and receiving this intricate language of notes, rests, accents, and squiggles.

For years, MIDI files have been the only way musical information could be shared between different software applications. Notation attributes are often lost when MIDI files are imported from one program into another because everything but pitches and durations requires guessing. Stems may point in the "wrong" direction, notes may beam differently, separated voices may become joined into chords. Even rests are "implied" in MIDI files. NIFF files describe a score's layout and object attributes as well as its underlying MIDI data. NIFF is to music notation files what Adobe Acrobat is to formatted text files.

Chris Newell, President, Musitek (that shipped the world's first NIFF-writing module in 1996 with its Midiscan product)

NIFF allows linking of MIDI data and notation as well as inclusion of Encapsulated PostScript (EPS) files and fonts. Its designers recognized that NIFF files will likely be transmitted electronically over low-bandwidth lines, and they deliberately kept the file format as compact as possible. The format complies with the design rules of Microsoft's Resource Interchange File Format (RIFF), so the same NIFF format files can be used by software running on any type of machine.

The NIFF logical structures were designed to handle situations like the following: In a Mahler symphony score there are three trumpet parts. In one system, the trumpets appear on three separate staves (labeled "Tpt. 1," "Tpt. 2," "Tpt. 3"), because they are playing a complex canon. In another system, they appear all together on one staff, called "Tpts. 1, 2, 3," because they are playing homophonic music. They are written as chords, with three notes on one stem.

In the logical view, the notes played by the trumpets belong to three separate parts. In the physical view of the canonic system, each trumpet part is assigned its own staff. Each staff is labeled with its own name.

In the physical view of the homophonic system, the three parts are combined onto a single staff, labeled "Tpts. 1, 2, 3." The simultaneous notes of each chord played by the three trumpet parts appear together with a single stem within each time-slice. Each note indicates the part to which it belongs.

Adding Sound to Your Multimedia Project

Whether you're working on a Macintosh or in Windows, you will need to follow certain steps to bring an audio recording into your multimedia project. Here is a brief overview of the process:

1. Decide what kind of sound is needed (such as background music, special sound effects, and spoken dialog). Decide where these audio events will occur in the flow of your project. Fit the sound cues into your storyboard, or make up a cue sheet.

2. Decide where and when you want to use either digital audio or MIDI data.

3. Acquire source material by creating it from scratch or purchasing it.

4. Edit the sounds to fit your project.

5. Test the sounds to be sure they are timed properly with the project's images. This may involve repeating steps 1 through 4 until everything is in sync.

When it's time to import your compiled and edited sounds into your project, you'll need to know how your particular multimedia software environment handles sound data. Each program handles it a bit differently, but the process is usually fairly straightforward: just tell your software which file you want to play and when to play it. This is usually handled by an importing or "linking" process during which you identify the files.

cross platform *Not all presentation software can play digital audio and/or MIDI files. In most sophisticated animation environments, better support is often available. You can often count on being able to work with digital audio, but you may not be able to work very effectively with MIDI, especially on the Macintosh.*

Multimedia authoring tools and environments are discussed in Chapter 8. Presentation, word processing, and spreadsheet applications that allow you to import sounds are discussed in Chapter 9. Here is some advice about using sound with various multimedia software.

---

cross platform *SuperCard imports a sound file but stores it in the data fork of the project. The sound cannot be exported or edited again without special tools. Be sure to archive your original SND or resource files before you import them.*

....

Conventional audio speakers were never designed with computer users in mind. Hooking up regular speakers to a PC is OK for low-quality mono signals, but now, with high-quality stereo audio cards coming onto the market, you need high-quality speakers to do your sound justice.

....

Andrew Bergstein, Marketing Director of Altec Lansing,
manufacturers of patented computer audio systems and speakers

Scripting languages such as OpenScript (ToolBook), the Media Control Interface (Windows), HyperTalk (HyperCard), SuperTalk (SuperCard), and Lingo (Director) provide a greater level of control over audio playback, but you'll need to know about the programming language and environment. Here's an example of OpenScript programming to control MIDI play:

```
on buttonDown
    midiOpen ("midifile.mid", 0, 1, notError)
    play it
    if notError<>nil
        send midiPlayError
    else
        wait until the file is done
        send done
    endIf
end buttonDown
```

In authoring environments, it is usually a simple matter to play a sound when the user clicks a button, but this may not be enough. If the user changes screens while a long file is playing, for example, you may need to program the sound to stop before leaving the current screen. If the file to be played cannot be found on the hard disk, you may need to code an entire section for error handling and file location. Sample code is generally provided in both printed and disk-based documentation for software that includes sound playback.

Toward Professional Sound: The Red Book Standard

The method for digitally encoding the high-quality stereo of the consumer CD music market is an international standard, ISO 10149. This is also known as the Red Book standard (derived simply from the color of the standard's book jacket). Developers of this standard claim that the digital audio sample size and sampling rate of Red Book Audio (16 bits at 44.1 kHz) allow accurate reproduction of all sounds that humans can hear. Until recently, dedicated professional sound-studio equipment was used for this high-fidelity recording; today high-end sound boards are available that will record and play 16-bit sampled sound at 44.1 kHz and at 48 kHz. These boards are available for both Macintosh and PC platforms. Software is also available to translate the digital files of Red Book Audio found on consumer compact discs directly into a digital sound editing file on your computer (see Figure 10-10).

Space Considerations

The substantial amount of digital sound information required for high-quality sound takes up a lot of disk storage space, especially when the

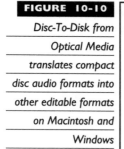

FIGURE 10-10

Disc-To-Disk from Optical Media translates compact disc audio formats into other editable formats on Macintosh and Windows

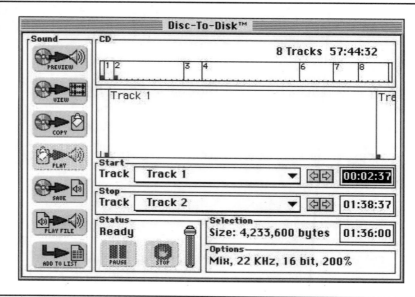

quantity is doubled for two-channel stereo. It takes about 1.94MB to store 11 seconds of uncompressed Red Book stereo sound.

If monaural sound is adequate for your project, you can cut your storage space requirement in half or get double the play time in the same memory space. With compression techniques, you might be able to store the sound in one-eighth the space, but you will lose some fidelity due to the rounding-off effects of quantization. Further, to conserve space you can try downsampling, or reducing the number of sample slices you take in a second. Many multimedia developers use 8-bit sample sizes at 22.05 kHz sampling rates because they consider the sound to be good enough (about the quality of AM radio), and they save immense amounts of digital real estate by not using the Red Book standard.

The following formula will help you estimate your storage needs. If you are using two channels for stereo, double the result.

(sampling rate * bits per sample) / 8 = bytes per second

You face important trade-offs when deciding how to manage digitized sound in your multimedia project. How much sound quality can you sacrifice in order to reduce storage? What compression techniques make sense? Will compressed sound work in your authoring platform? What is good enough but not amateurish? Can you get away with 8 bits at 11.025 kHz for voice mail, product testimonials, and voice-overs and then switch to higher sampling rates for music?

::::::::::::::::::::::::::::::::::::::

With the collaboration of composer Dave Soldier, Komar & Melamid's Most Wanted Painting project (http://www.diacenter.org/km/index.html) was extended into the realm of music. A poll, written by Dave Soldier, was conducted on Dia's Web site (http://www.diacenter.org) in Spring 1996. Approximately 500 visitors took the survey. Dave Soldier and Nina Mankin used the survey results to write music and lyrics for the Most Wanted and Most Unwanted songs.

A note from the composer:

This survey confirms the hypothesis that today's popular music indeed provides an accurate estimate of the wishes of the vox populi. The most favored ensemble, determined from a rating by participants of their favorite instruments in combination, comprises a moderately sized group (three to ten instruments) consisting of guitar, piano, saxophone, bass, drums, violin, cello, synthesizer, with low male and female vocals singing in rock/r&b style. The favorite lyrics narrate a love story, and the favorite listening circumstance is at home. The only feature in lyric subjects that occurs in both most wanted and unwanted categories is "intellectual stimulation." Most participants desire music of moderate duration (approximately 5 minutes), moderate pitch range, moderate tempo, and moderate to loud volume, and display a profound dislike of the alternatives. If the survey provides an accurate analysis of these factors for the population, and assuming that the preference for each factor follows a Gaussian (i.e., bell-curve) distribution, the combination of these qualities, even to the point of sensory overload and stylistic discohesion, will result in a musical work that will be unavoidably and uncontrollably "liked" by 72 plus or minus 12% (standard deviation; Kolmogorov-Smirnov statistic) of listeners. The most unwanted music is over 25 minutes long, veers wildly between loud and quiet sections, between fast and slow tempos, and features timbres of extremely high and low pitch, with each dichotomy presented in abrupt transition. The most unwanted orchestra was determined to be large and features the accordion and bagpipe (which tie at 13% as the most unwanted instrument), banjo, flute, tuba, harp, organ, synthesizer (the only instrument that appears in both the most wanted and most unwanted ensembles). An operatic soprano raps and sings atonal music, advertising jingles, political slogans, and "elevator" music, and a children's choir sings jingles and holiday songs. The most unwanted subjects for lyrics are cowboys and holidays, and the most unwanted listening circumstances are involuntary exposure to commercials and elevator music. Therefore, it can be shown that if there is no covariance—someone who dislikes bagpipes is as likely to hate elevator music as someone who despises the organ, for example—fewer than 200 individuals of the world's total population would enjoy this piece.

Dave Soldier, Composer and Musician, who provides The Most Wanted Song and The Most Unwanted Song on a CD at *http://www.diacenter.org/km/musiccd.html*

Production Tips

A classic physical anthropology law (Leibig's Law of the Minimums) proposes that the evolution of eyesight, locomotor speed, sense of smell, or any other species trait will cease when that trait becomes sufficiently adequate to meet the survival requirements of the competitive environment. If the trait is good enough, the organism expends no more effort improving it. Thus, if consumer-grade electronics and a hand-held microphone are good enough for making your sound, and if you, your client, and your audience are all satisfied with the results, conserve your energy and money and avoid any more expenditure. And keep this Law of Minimums in mind when you make all your trade-off decisions involving other areas of high technology and multimedia, too.

Vaughan's Law of Multimedia Minimums

There is an acceptable minimum level of adequacy that will satisfy the audience, even when that level may not be the best that technology, money, or time and effort can buy.

Audio Recording

Most multimedia developers record their sound material to cassette tapes as the first step in the digitizing process. With tape, you can do many takes of the same sound or voice, listen to all the takes, and pick the best one to digitize. By recording on inexpensive media rather than directly to disk, you avoid filling up your hard disk with throw-away stuff. If your project requires CD-quality digitized sound at 44.1 kHz and 16 bits, you should hire a sound studio. High-fidelity sound recording is a specialized craft, a skill learned in great part by trial and error, much like photography. If you do decide to do it yourself at CD-quality levels, be prepared to invest in an acoustically treated room, high-end amplifiers and recording equipment, and expensive microphones.

As already stated, there are many trade-offs involved in making multimedia. For example, if you are satisfied with 22.05 kHz in your project or are constrained to this rate by storage considerations, any consumer-grade tape recorder of reasonable quality will do fine. This, of course, also applies to conversations recorded from the telephone, where a sampling rate of 11.025 kHz is adequate. Noise reduction circuits and metal tapes are helpful to remove hiss, but at a sampling rate of 22.05 kHz you are only going to be digitizing audio frequencies as high as about 11 kHz, anyway. Both the high and low ends of the audio hearing spectrum are therefore less important to you, and that is OK, because those areas are precisely the add-value focus of very elaborate and expensive consumer equipment.

Video cassette recorders (VCRs) usually have excellent stereo audio circuits, and many good multimedia sounds were first recorded and digitized using the audio tracks of videotape.

Digital audio tape (DAT) systems have now entered the consumer marketplace. They provide a tape-based 44.1 kHz, 16-bit record and playback capability. You may find, however, that DAT is high-fidelity overkill for your needs, because the recordings are too accurate, precisely recording glitches, background noises, microphone pops, and coughs from the next room. A good editor can help reduce the impact of these noises, but at the cost of your time and money.

One day we'll have just one format for multimedia, just like in audio, where we have compact discs, cassettes, vinyl, eight track....

> Tim Carrigan, editor of *Multimedia*, a magazine published in the United Kingdom

Audio Editing

Sound Recorder (Sndrec32.exe) is installed with the Multimedia Programs group in Windows 95 (see Figure 10-11). It is a minimal sound recording and editing tool that provides a few simple effects (echo, reverse, and speed changes) and allows saving only in Microsoft's .WAV format. Even more minimal, but capable of recording sounds, the Macintosh includes an Add... button in the Sound control panel (shown in Figure 10-1).

Excellent waveform editing software is available for both Macintosh and Windows platforms. On the Macintosh, you will need third-party editing software such as SoundEdit 16-2 from Macromedia (which supports Shockwave Streaming Audio and RealAudio for the Internet—see Chapter 15), SoundMaker from Micromat (available through Allegiant Technologies), SoundTools from DigiDesign, or Turtle Tools from Turtle Beach. With editing software you can manipulate your digitized sounds in myriad ways— cutting and pasting, adding special effects, mixing various sounds together, and, if you wish, literally putting words into people's mouths. DeckII from Macromedia offers high-end synchronization, digital editing and mixing, and can drive MIDI sequencers at the same time. Midiscan software from

10

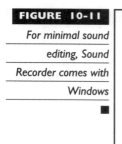

FIGURE 10-11

For minimal sound editing, Sound Recorder comes with Windows

Musitek can be used with a scanner to recognize notation and convert sheet music to multitrack MIDI files (see Figure 10-12). Other software lets you print your MIDI score.

• •

http://www.musitek.com

Scanner software reads sheet music and turns it into MIDI files

Keeping Track of Your Sounds

Be sure your tape deck or recorder has a good counter built into it, so that you can mark and log the locations of various takes and events on the tape and quickly find them later. Get into the habit of jotting down the counter position and tape content whenever you record sounds.

In an elaborate project with many sounds, maintain a good database, keeping a physical track of your original material—just in case you need to revert to it when your disk drive crashes. This database is particularly important because you may need to give your sound files such unhelpful names as SND0094A.WAV or CHAPT1-3.WAV; these names won't contain many cues about the files' actual content, and you will need at hand a more descriptive cross-reference. You don't want to have to load and play all the sound files from SND0080.WAV through SND0097.WAV just to find the one you need.

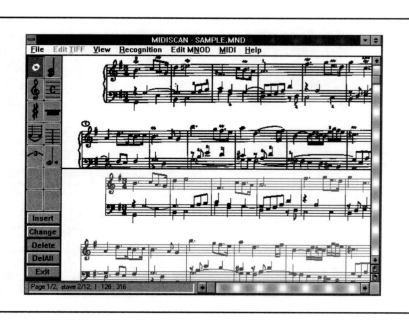

FIGURE 10-12

Midiscan converts sheet music to multitrack MIDI files

See Chapter 16 for suggestions about the management of such multimedia project resources.

Testing and Evaluation

Putting everything together can be tough, but testing and evaluating what you've done can be even tougher—especially if your project involves a complicated live presentation, or if you're shipping a commercial multimedia application.

The most serious challenge is synchronization of sound elements with presentation of visual images on computers that are faster or slower than the machine on which the sound elements were created. Unless you plan ahead, problems will not emerge until you begin testing.

Both digital audio and MIDI are time-based events, but most animation and computer-based video will play only as fast as the CPU can handle it. A 60-second digital audio or MIDI file will play for the same length of time on a slow Macintosh Classic, a fast PowerMac 9500, a slow 386SX, or a fast Pentium. On the other hand, an animation on a Pentium/100 may run five to ten times faster than on a 4896/25. If you time your music to animations running on a slow machine, and then play it back on a faster machine, you may find that the music plays on after the speedier animation sequences are done. Since you can't make a slow machine run faster, the usual solution is to make a fast machine run slower. Chapter 4 discusses the need for determining minimum platform specifications early in the development of any project.

---

t i p   *During editing and authoring, regularly test the sound-and-image synchronization of your project on the slowest platform as well as the fastest. If you are delivering your sound on the Web, test it with different browsers and different connection speeds.*

10

Don't forget to evaluate your sound storage medium. How much RAM does your project need to run effectively? Some authoring and delivery packages will stream sound directly off the hard disk or CD-ROM; others require the sound to be loaded into memory from the hard disk before they play. Sometimes you will need to break a sound or a music file into smaller parts. Some 8-bit audio cards may choke on a 16-bit file. And MIDI files that sound terrific on an expensive General MIDI sound card during development will not have the same quality on a low-end FM-synthesis device at the end user's site.

In the world of professional film and video production, sound is incorporated during postproduction, or a *post* session, after all the film and video footage has been assembled. Just so with multimedia—and don't give it short shrift because of time or budget constraints. The soundtrack can make or break your project!

Copyright Issues

Ownership rights are significant issues for multimedia producers who would love to use a few bars of Madonna's latest hit or a nostalgic background of Bach suites played by Pablo Casals. Producers may rightfully fret about copyrights and permissions. Most developers play it safe by always making their own custom music from scratch in a sound studio, or with synthesizers, or by using sounds that have a clear and paid-for ownership and permission trail. Others simply take a risk and break the law.

---

warning *You are breaking the law if you record and use copyrighted material without first securing the rights from the owner or publisher of the material.*

Over the coming years, as more and more multimedia is produced by more and more developers hungry for sound content, the copyright of sounds and images will become a major issue—not so much about who owns something, but how much of it they own. Because it is so easy to manipulate and edit a sound, just how much of someone's original work do you have to change before it then becomes your own? Copyright issues and methods of securing permission for use (equally relevant for sounds, still images, and motion video) are discussed in more detail in Chapter 19.

A number of software vendors have entered the multimedia marketplace by selling digitized clip sounds with an unlimited-use, royalty-free license. Among them are ProSonus (SoundBytes) and Voyetra (MusiClips). Some of these products include musical clips, and some just include sound effects (doors closing, dogs barking, and water dripping). Other products have a mixture of both. But beware of public domain sources downloaded from online sites that offer "Phaser" and "Beam-Me-Up" clips from such favorites as *Star Trek*, or one-liners from Humphrey Bogart movies; these sounds have likely been used without permission.

We needed some digital sound effects for the Dr. J and Larry Bird basketball game we were making. So we bought some Warriors tickets and took a tape recorder to the Oakland Coliseum and just recorded the sounds while we watched the game. It was a great tax deduction, and we got to go to the game for nothing!

Trip Hawkins, Chairman & CEO, 3DO Company

Multi

[At the beginning of a project, the screen is a blank canvas, ready for you, the multimedia designer, to express your craft.]

visual
connection

media

Many multimedia designers are known to experience
a mild shiver when they pull down the New... menu
and draw their first colors onto a fresh screen.

chapter 11

Images

WHAT you see on a multimedia computer screen at any given time is a composite of elements: text, symbols, photograph-like bitmaps, vector-drawn graphics, three-dimensional renderings, distinctive buttons to click, and windows of motion video. Some parts of this image may even twitch or move so that the screen never seems still and tempts your eye. It may be a very colorful screen with gentle pastel washes of mauve and puce, or it may be brutally primary with splashes of Crayola red and blue and yellow and green. It might be stark black and white, full of sharp angles, or softened with gray-scale blends and anti-aliasing. It may be elegant or, by design, not. The computer screen is where the action is: it contains much more than your message; it is also the viewer's primary connection to all of your project's content.

This chapter will help you understand the visual elements that make up a multimedia screen. Graphic elements can usually be scaled to different sizes, colorized or patterned or made transparent, placed in front of or behind other objects, or be made visible or invisible on command. How you blend these elements, how you choose your colors and fonts, what tricks you use that catch the eye, how adept you are at using your tools—these are the hallmarks of your skill, talent, knowledge, and creativity coalesced into the all-important visual connection to your viewers.

Before You Start to Create

At the beginning of a project, the screen is a blank canvas, ready for you, the multimedia designer, to express your craft. The screen will change again and again during the course of your project as you experiment, as you stretch and reshape elements, draw new objects and throw out old ones, and test various colors and effects—creating the vehicle for your message. Indeed, many multimedia designers are known to experience a mild shiver when they pull down the New... menu and draw their first colors onto a fresh screen. Just so; this screen represents a powerful and seductive avenue for channeling creativity.

---

warning *Multimedia designers are regularly lured into agonizingly steep learning curves, long nights of cerebral problem solving, and the pursuit of performance perfection. If you are fundamentally creative, multimedia may become a calling, not a profession.*

Plan Your Approach

Whether you use templates and ready-made screens provided by your authoring system; whether you use clip art or objects crafted by others; even if you simply clone the look and feel of another project—there will always be a starting point where your page is "clean." But even before reaching this starting point, be sure you have given your project a good deal of thought and planning. Work out your graphic approach either in your head or during creative sessions with your client or colleagues. There are strong arguments against drawing on a fresh screen without such foresight and preparation. See Chapter 16 for advice on organizing a multimedia project, and Chapter 17 for more about the design process.

Organize Your Tools

Most authoring systems provide the tools with which you can create the graphic objects of multimedia (text, buttons, vector-drawn objects, and bitmaps) directly on your screen. If one of these tools is not included, the authoring system usually offers a mechanism for importing the object you need from another application. When you are working with animated objects or motion video, most authoring systems include a feature for activating these elements, such as a programming language or special functions. You'll also usually have a library of special effects—zooms, wipes, and dissolves, for instance. Many multimedia designers do not limit their toolkits to the features of a single authoring platform, but employ a variety of applications and tools to accomplish many specialized tasks; see Chapters 6 and 8 for advice on gathering the tools you need.

Multiple Monitors

When developing multimedia, it is helpful to have more than one monitor, or a single high-resolution monitor with lots of screen *real estate*, hooked up to your computer. In this way, you can display the full-screen working area of your project or presentation and still have space to put your tools and other menus. This is particularly important in an authoring system such as Macromedia Director, where the edits and changes you make in one window are immediately visible in the presentation window—provided the presentation window is not obscured by your editing tool! During development there is a lot of cutting and pasting among windows and among various applications, and with an extra monitor, you can open many windows at once and spread them out.

A few weeks of having to repeatedly bring windows to the front and then hide them again to see the results of your editing will probably convince you to invest in a second or larger monitor. A satisfactory second monitor may even be a simple black-and-white unit; you can use it for commands and menu activity.

Making Still Images

Still images may be small or large, or even full screen. They may be colored, placed at random on the screen, evenly geometric or oddly shaped. Still images may be a single tree on a wintry hillside; stacked boxes of text against a gray, tartan, or Italian marble background; an engineering drawing; a snapshot of your department manager's new BMW. Whatever their form, still images are generated by the computer in two ways: as *bitmaps* (or paint graphics) and as *vector-drawn* (or just plain drawn) graphics.

Bitmaps are used for photo-realistic images and for complex drawings requiring fine detail. Vector-drawn objects are used for lines, boxes, circles, polygons, and other graphic shapes that can be mathematically expressed in angles, coordinates, and distances. A drawn object can be filled with color and patterns, and you can select it as a single object. The appearance of both types of images depends on the display resolution and capabilities of your computer's graphics hardware and monitor. Both types of images are stored in various file formats and can be translated from one application to another or from one computer platform to another. Typically, image files are compressed to save memory and disk space; many image formats already use compression within the file itself—for example, GIF, JPEG, and PNG.

Still images may be the most important element of your multimedia project. If you are designing multimedia by yourself, put yourself in the role of graphic artist and layout designer. Take the time necessary to discover all the tricks you can learn about your drawing software. Competent, computer-literate skills in graphic art and design are vital to the success of your project. Remember—more than anything else, the user's judgment of your work will be most heavily influenced by the work's visual impact.

A few years ago a large corporation asked us and one other multimedia developer to bid on a long-term contract for computer-based training. Though busy with other active projects, we didn't want this possibly lucrative opportunity to slip by, so we spent a few days hastily putting together a demonstration of our technical skills for building nifty databases, designing tricky telecommunications systems, and integrating live video from videodisc into the computer. We even "wire-framed" a bit of a working multimedia database with real data we got from the corporation.

We showed our demo to about a dozen management and training executives, in a fancy boardroom that had a built-in projector and sound system with mixers and light dimmers—a place where we could knock the socks off anybody. But within 30 seconds, the disaster bells started tinkling: most of our presentation was going way over their heads. Afterward, there were one or two vague questions and some thank-you's.

Our competitor's presentation, on the other hand, provided a slick series of finely rendered bitmapped screen images and elegant visuals. It was heavy on pretty menu screens and very light on how-it-is-done technology. We later learned that one of their graphic artists had worked for two solid weeks on the color bitmaps for that demo. In the follow-up phone call, we were told by our potential clients that the competition's "incredible artwork" had won out over our "excellent technology demonstration."

To cover our disappointment, we mumbled something to ourselves about not wanting to work with computer illiterates, anyway—people who could be taken to the cleaners by fresh paint. But we knew we'd missed a hefty piece of contract work because we hadn't invested serious graphic art talent in our demonstration. We decided that's why the real peas in the can are never the same bright green as the ones on the label. So we learned a marketing lesson.

Bitmaps

A *bitmap* is a simple information matrix describing the individual dots that are the smallest elements of resolution on a computer screen or other display or printing device. A one-dimensional matrix is required for monochrome (black and white); greater depth (more bits of information) is required to describe the more than 16 million colors the picture elements may have, as illustrated in Figure 11-1. These picture elements (known as *pels* or, more commonly, *pixels*) can be either on or off, as in the 1-bit bitmap, most often "monochrome" black or white but, depending upon your software, they can be any 2 colors that represent the on and off states. Or they can represent varying shades of color (4-bit, 16 colors; 8-bit, 256 colors; 15-bit, 32,768 colors; 16-bit, 65,536 colors; 24-bit, 16,772,216 colors). Together, the state of all the pixels on a computer screen (in about 1/60 second, which is about how often the screen is redrawn) make up the image seen by the viewer, whether in combinations of black and white or colored pixels in a line of text, a photograph-like picture, or a simple background pattern.

11

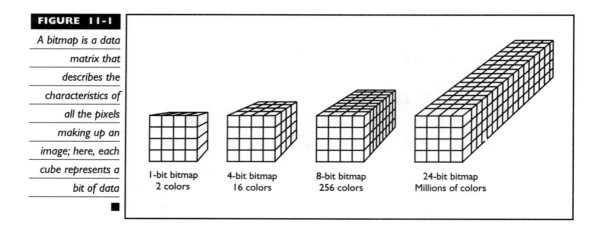

1-bit bitmap
2 colors

4-bit bitmap
16 colors

8-bit bitmap
256 colors

24-bit bitmap
Millions of colors

Is there a colour scheme that will appear coloured or at least solid black for the colour-impaired?

If you're gathering empirical evidence, I have something called red-green colour blindness (it is quite common in males). It doesn't mean that you don't know which traffic light is showing! What it means mainly is that the tone *of red-type colours doesn't seem so different to the tone of greens—the obvious case is a poppy field. I can see the poppies as red OK if I look carefully or they are pointed out to me, but other people see them kind of exploding out of the green...*

For people like me, a vibrant yellow always works. I read somewhere that black on yellow is a reliable "strong" combination. Certainly it is used by one of the motoring organisations in the UK for special diversion notices and the like.

Graham Samuel, Educational Software Developer,
The Living Fossil Co., London

You have three different ways to make a bitmap:

■ Make a bitmap from scratch with a paint or drawing program.

■ Grab a bitmap from an active computer screen with a screen capture program, and then paste it into a paint program or your application.

■ Capture a bitmap from a photo, artwork, or a television image using a scanner or video capture device that digitizes the image.

Clip Art

If you do not want to make your own, you can get bitmaps from suppliers of clip art, and from photograph suppliers who have already digitized the images for you. Clip art is available on CD-ROMs and through on-line services. Many graphics applications are shipped with clip art and useful graphics, or the company will send you a collection when you register the product. A clip art collection may contain a random assortment of images, or it may contain a series of graphics, photographs, sound, and video related to a single topic. For example, Corel, Micrografx, and Fractal Design bundle extensive clip art collections with their image-editing software. Some 3-D modeling programs incorporate libraries of premade 3-D models into the application, allowing you to drag and drop common objects into a scene.

Figure 11-2 shows a page of thumbnails from a commercially available resource called PhotoDisc. Each CD-ROM contains about 400 full-color, high-resolution bitmaps with a license for "unlimited use." But you should note that "unlimited use" often contains caveats: in many cases there is an upper limit to the number of "units" of your own product that you may distribute without paying more, so you need to read the fine print. These fees are usually reasonable, however, and affect only commercial multimedia publishers. In the case of ClipPix from PhotoDisc, for example, 10,000 units is the break point. Figure 11-3 shows portions of text from that license agreement (reproduced here with the permission of PhotoDisc, Inc.).

Once you have a clip art bitmap, you can then manipulate and adjust many of its properties (such as brightness, contrast, color depth, hue, and size). You can also cut and paste among many bitmaps using specialized image-editing or "darkroom" programs. If the clip art image is high resolution (aimed at 300 dpi printers, not 72 dpi monitors), you may discover that you can grab just a tiny portion of the high-res image, say a sheep in the far corner of a farmyard or a car in a parking lot, and it will look great when enlarged to monitor resolution.

Bitmap Software

The abilities and features of paint programs for both the Macintosh and Windows range from simple to complex. The better painting applications are available in versions that run and look the same on both platforms, and the graphics files you make can be saved in many formats, readable across platforms. The Macintosh does not ship with a painting tool, and Windows 95 provides only the rudimentary Paint (see Figure 11-4) and WIN95 Graphics Editor applications, so you will need to acquire this very important software separately—often paint programs come as part of a bundle when you purchase your computer, monitor, or scanner. Most multimedia authoring tools offer bitmap editing features. Director (see Figure 11-5) includes a powerful image editor that provides advanced tools such as "onion-skinning" and image filtering using common plug-ins from Photoshop and other third-party designers.

11

FIGURE 11-2

A page of
thumbnails from
the index of a
PhotoDisc CD-ROM
■

PhotoDisc™   **Volume 2: People and Lifestyles**

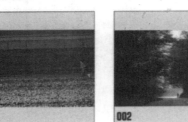

001

002

003

004

005

006

007

008

009

010

011

012

013

014

015

FIGURE 11-3

Text from the

PhotoDisc license

agreement, typical

of usage rights you

receive when you

purchase a clip

art library

■

END USER LICENSE AGREEMENT

THIS IS A LEGAL AGREEMENT BETWEEN YOU AND PHOTODISC. INC. BY OPENING THIS PACKAGE YOU AGREE TO BE BOUND BY THE TERMS OF THIS AGREEMENT. IF YOU DO NOT AGREE, PROMPTLY RETURN THE UNOPENED CD PACKAGE IN THE ORIGINAL CARTON FOR A FULL REFUND.

GRANT OF LICENSE. PhotoDisc grants you the nonexclusive, nonassignable right to install and use the ClipPix images and any derivatives or copies thereof (collectively, the "Images") and the other software on this disc on one computer and with one user at a time. The Images may be copied, modified, and incorporated in materials in accordance with the following provisions:

(1) Personal Use. You may make copies of the Images in digital or printed form for personal or internal company use.

(2) Advertising and Promotions. You may make copies of the Images, in digital or printed form, for use in advertising or promotional materials for you or your clients.

(3) Products for Sale.

- Copies of the Images, in digital (but not printed form), may be incorporated in up to 10,000 individual product copies made by you (your "Products") and may be distributed as part of your Products.

- You may sublicense the right to use the Images in digital form as part of your Products. You may not sublicense the right to copy the Images or to incorporate the Images into other materials or other products.

- You agree not to distribute or market copies of the Images separately in any manner. You agree not to use the Images in any product which is similar to or competitive with this disc.

- Your Products must include the following language in the Product credits or on the Product packaging: "PhotoDisc ClipPix Images ©1994 PhotoDisc, Inc."

Any use of the Images not explicitly granted by this agreement is prohibited. If you wish to use the Images in television programming, cable programming, motion pictures, or wide area networks, you must first obtain additional licensing from PhotoDisc. Pornographic use of the Images is prohibited. Except as specifically permitted above, you may not copy this disc.

11

More sophisticated are elaborately featured bitmap painting and editing programs such as Adobe's Photoshop or Fractal Design's Painter. Painter, for both Macintosh and Windows, provides astoundingly realistic classical art effects, using a complete palette of brushes and digital tools. Painter can work with millions of colors, depending upon your system's video card and monitor hardware (see Figure 11-6 and Color Plate 8).

FIGURE 11-4

*The Windows Paint
accessory provides
rudimentary
bitmap editing*

■

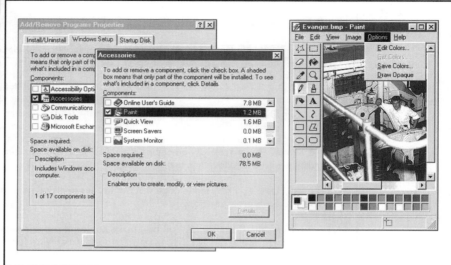

FIGURE 11-5

*Macromedia
Director, like most
serious multimedia
authoring
packages, includes
powerful
image-editing tools*

■

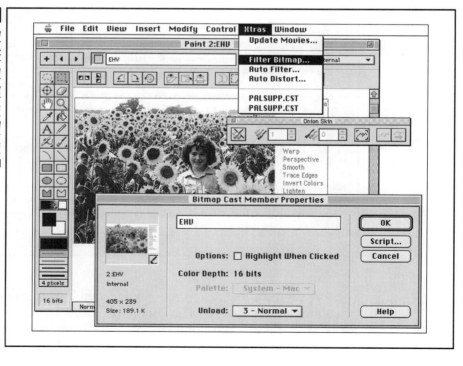

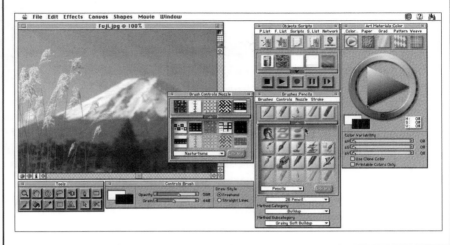

FIGURE 11-6

Some tool palettes

from Painter, an

elaborate painting

program by

Fractal Design

tip *It is virtually impossible to paint a photo-realistic bitmap using a painting program. For photo-realism, use images that are first scanned and then pasted into your paint or image-editing program. Use your paint program for drawing cartoons, text, icons, symbols, buttons, and abstract screens that have a refined "graphic" look.*

Capturing and Editing Images

The image you see on your monitor is a digital bitmap stored in video memory, updated about every 1/60 second or faster, depending upon your monitor's scan rate (see Chapter 5). As you assemble images for your multimedia project, you may often need to capture and store an image directly from your screen. The simplest way to capture what you see on the screen at any given moment is to press the proper keys on your computer keyboard. This causes a conversion from the video bitmap to a bitmap in a format that you can use.

- On the Macintosh, the keystroke combination COMMAND-SHIFT-3 creates a readable PICT2-format file named Picture and places it in your active disk drive's root directory. You can then import this file's image into your multimedia authoring system or paint program.

■ Both the Macintosh and Windows environments have a Clipboard, an area of memory where data such as text and images are temporarily stored when you cut or copy them within an application. In Windows, when you press PRINTSCREEN, a copy of your screen's image goes to the Clipboard. From the Clipboard, you can then paste the captured bitmap into an application (such as Paint, which comes with Windows).

■ Screen capture utilities for Macintosh and Windows go a step further and are indispensable to multimedia artists. With a keystroke, they let you select an area of the screen and save the selection in various formats (see Figure 11-7). With this facility, you can quickly copy and paste small or large 72 dpi images between applications.

The way to get more creative power when manipulating bitmaps is to use an image-editing program. These are the king-of-the-mountain programs that let you not only retouch the blemishes and details of photo images but also do tricks like placing an image of your own face at the helm of a square-rigger or right at the sideline at last year's Super Bowl. Figure 11-8 shows just such a composite image, made from two photographs. It was

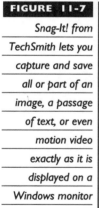

FIGURE 11-7

Snag-It! from TechSmith lets you capture and save all or part of an image, a passage of text, or even motion video exactly as it is displayed on a Windows monitor

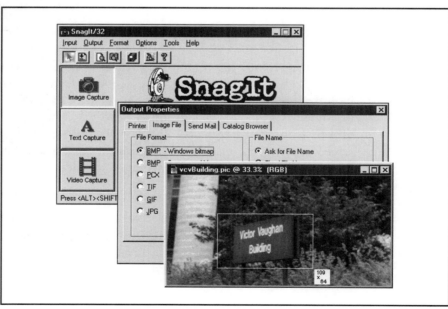

FIGURE 11-8

Image-editing programs let you add and delete elements, as Adobe's Russel Brown showed by adding himself to this famous picture (courtesy of "The NBC Today Show")

■

created by Russel Brown, one of the designers of Adobe's Photoshop, during a nationally broadcast live television show. While you might recognize his name in the credits every time you launch Photoshop, with Photoshop he deftly and seamlessly placed himself between a better-known couple in order to illustrate to the viewing audience the power of image-editing tools and the potential for misuse of this technology in everyday life.

In addition to letting you enhance and make composite images, image-editing tools allow you to alter and distort images. A color photograph of a red rose can be changed into a purple rose, or blue if you prefer. A small child standing next to her older brother can be "stretched" to tower over him.

Morphing is another effect that can be used to manipulate still images or to create interesting and often bizarre animated transformations. *Morphing* allows you to smoothly blend two images so that one image seems to melt into the next, often producing some amusing results. Color Plate 13, created using Morph, a software application by Gryphon, shows an example of a girl morphing into a boy.

Image-editing programs may, indeed, represent the single most significant advance in computer image processing during the late 1980s, bringing truly amazing power to PC desktops. Color Plate 7 illustrates a few of the many special effects for manipulating bitmaps. Such tools are indispensable for excellent multimedia production.

11

---

cross platform   *When you import a color or gray-scale bitmap from the Macintosh to Windows, the colors will seem darker and richer, even though they have precisely the same red, green, and blue (RGB) values. In some cases, this may improve the look of your image, but in other cases you will want to first lighten (increase the brightness and possibly lower the contrast) of the Macintosh bitmap before bringing it into Windows.*

We have to keep saturation in mind all the time when doing our Web pages... viewing the graphics on both Macs and PCs before actually using them. For instance, when doing our Halloween pages, we used a very cool pumpkin background that was beautifully saturated on the Mac side. On Windows, though, it was way too dark, and you couldn't read the overlying text. We had to lighten the GIF on the Mac side a few times before using it cross platform.

Rich Santalesa, Editor, *NetGuide* Magazine

Scanning Images

After pouring through countless clip art collections, you still haven't found the unusual background you want for a screen about gardening. Sometimes when you search for something too hard, you don't realize that it's right in front of your face. Everyday objects can be scanned and manipulated using image-editing tools, such as those described in the previous section, to create unusual, attention-getting effects. For example, to enliven a screen with a gardening motif, scan a mixture of seeds, some fall foliage, or grass-stained garden gloves. Open the scan in an image-editing program and experiment with different filters, the contrast, and various special effects. Be creative, and don't be afraid to try strange combinations—sometimes mistakes yield the most intriguing results.

Another alternative to computer-generated graphics is to create artwork using traditional methods: watercolors, pastels, and even crayons. You can then scan the image, make necessary alterations, and tweak pixels on the computer. Too many designers have fallen into the trap of trying to draw detailed sketches using a mouse or drawing tablet, when a pencil or pen on paper would have produced better results quicker.

Vector Drawing

Most multimedia authoring systems provide for use of vector-drawn objects such as lines, rectangles, ovals, polygons, and text.

- Computer-aided design (CAD) programs have traditionally used vector-drawn object systems for creating the highly complex and geometric renderings needed by architects and engineers (CAD tools are discussed in Chapter 6).

- Graphic artists designing for print media use vector-drawn objects because the same mathematics that put a rectangle on your screen can also place that rectangle (or the fancy Bezier curves of a good line-art illustration) on paper without jaggies. This requires the highest resolution of the printer, using a page description language such as PostScript.

- Programs for 3-D animation also use vector-drawn graphics. For example, the various changes of position, rotation, and shading of light required to spin the extruded corporate logo shown in Figure 11-9 must be calculated mathematically. (Animation is discussed in Chapter 12.)

How Vector Drawing Works

Vector-drawn objects are described and drawn to the computer screen using a fraction of the memory space required to describe and store the same object in bitmap form. A *vector* is a line that is described by the location of its two endpoints. A simple rectangle, for example, might be defined as follows:

RECT 0,0,200,200

Using Cartesian coordinates, your software will draw this rectangle starting at the upper-left corner of your screen, going 200 pixels horizontally to the right, and 200 pixels downward. This rectangle would be a square, as all sides are identical lengths. For this description:

11

RECT 0,0,200,200,RED,BLUE

your software will draw the same square with a red boundary line and fill the square with the color blue. You can, of course, add other parameters to describe a fill pattern or the width of the boundary line.

Vector-Drawn Objects Versus Bitmaps

The concise description of the vector-drawn colored square described in the previous section contains less than 30 bytes of alphanumeric data (even less when the description is tokenized or compressed). On the other hand, the same square as an uncompressed bitmap image, in black and white (which requires the least memory, at 1-bit color depth per pixel) would take 5,000 bytes to describe ($200 \times 200 / 8$). Furthermore, an image made in 256 colors (8-bit color depth per pixel) would require a whopping 40K as a bitmap ($200 \times 200 / 8 \times 8$).

In terms of performance, when you draw many objects on your screen, you may experience a slowdown while you wait for the screen to be refreshed—the size, location, and other properties for each of the objects must be computed. Thus a single image made up of 500 individual line and rectangle objects, for example, may take longer for the computer to process and place on the screen than an image consisting of just a few drawn circle objects. Vector objects are easily scalable without losing resolution or image quality—a large drawn image can be shrunk to the size of a postage stamp, and, while it may not look good on a computer monitor at 72 dpi, it will likely still look good when printed at 300 dpi to a color printer.

tip   *Using a single bitmap for a complicated image may give you faster screen-refresh performance than using a large number of vector-drawn objects to make that same screen.*

Converting Between Bitmaps and Drawn Images

Most drawing programs offer several file formats for saving your work, and, if you wish, you can convert a drawing that consists of several vector-drawn objects into a bitmap when you save the drawing. You can also grab a bitmapped screen image of your drawn objects with a capture program.

Converting bitmaps to drawn objects is more difficult. There are, however, programs and utilities that will compute the bounds of a bitmapped image or the shapes of colors within an image and then derive the polygon object that describes the image. This procedure is called *autotracing*. It is available in some authoring systems that integrate both bitmapped and drawn objects (such as SuperCard), as well as in specialized packages such as Adobe's Streamline.

3-D Drawing and Rendering

Drawing in perspective or in 3-D on a two-dimensional surface takes special skill and talent. Dedicated software is available to help you *render* three-dimensional scenes, complete with directional lighting and special effects, but get ready for another steep learning curve! From making 3-D text with Specular's LogoMotion to creating detailed walk-throughs of 3-D space with Virtus VR (see Figure 11-10), each application will demand study and practice before you are efficient and comfortable with its feature set and power.

The production values of multimedia projects have increased dramatically since the late 1980s, and as the *production bar* has risen, end users' expectations have also ratcheted upward. The multimedia production bar moves like a high jump or pole vault contest—as each new project improves on the last, competitors must jump to meet the new, higher standard. Flat and colorless 2-D screens are no longer sufficient for a successful commercial

FIGURE 11-10

Virtus VR lets you create 3-D virtual environments in which you can "walk" around and even through objects, and you can save them as VRML (Virtual Reality Modeling Language) to put them on the Web

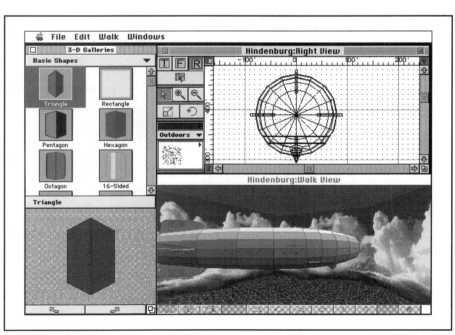

11

multimedia project. 3-D-rendered graphic art and animation has become commonplace, providing more lifelike substance and feel to projects. Luckily, in an arena where only high-powered workstations could supply the raw computing horsepower for effective 3-D designing, inexpensive desktop PCs and excellent software have made 3-D modeling attainable by most multimedia developers.

Today many products—including Ray Dream Designer, Caligari True Space 2, Specular Infini-D, form*Z, and Macromedia's Extreme 3-D—are touted as essential tools for illustration, animation, and multimedia production.

Creating objects in three dimensions on a computer screen can be difficult for designers used to drawing squares, circles, and other x (width) and y (height) geometries on a two-dimensional screen. Be prepared for late nights and steep learning curves as you become familiar with nurbs, deformations, mesh generations, and skinning:

Form*Z is a state-of-the-art 3-D solid and surface modeler with drafting and rendering, Boolean operations, 3-D form editing and sculpting, terrain modeling, curved splines, and meshes including NURBS, 3-D text, object rounding, symbol instances and libraries, helixes, deformations, metaformz, image-based mesh generation and displacements, skinning, numerous file format translators, and more. RenderZone adds photo-realistic rendering, and RadioZity provides the most accurate simulation of light effects.

Marketing literature from auto*des*sys, Inc. (www.formz.com)

For 3-D, the depth (z dimension) of cubes and spheres must be calculated and displayed so the perspective of the rendered object seems correct to the eye. As illustrated in Figure 11-11, most 3-D software packages provide adjustable views so you can see your work from the top, bottom, or sides.

A great deal of information is needed to display a 3-D *scene*. Scenes consist of *objects* that in turn contain many small elements such as blocks, cylinders, spheres, or cones (described using mathematical constructs or formulas). The more elements contained in an object, the more complicated its structure will be and, usually, the finer its resolution and smoothness.

Objects and elements in 3-D space carry with them *properties* such as shape, color, texture, shading, and location. A scene contains many different objects. Imagine a scene with a table, chairs, and a background. Zoom into one of the objects—the chair, for example, in Figure 11-12. It has eleven objects made up of various blocks and rectangles. Objects are created by *modeling* them using a 3-D application.

To model an object that you want to place into your scene, you must start with a *shape*. You can create a shape from scratch, or you can import a

FIGURE 11-11

*Macromedia's
Extreme 3D provides
x, y, and z axes
and adjustable
perspective views*

■

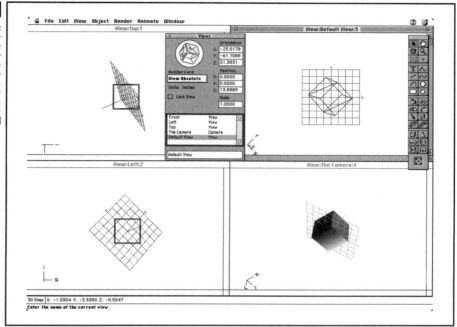

premade shape from a library of shapes, typically blocks, cylinders, spheres, and cones. In most 3-D applications, you can create any 2-D shape with a drawing tool or place the outline of a letter, then *extrude* or *lathe* it into the third dimension along the z axis (see Figure 11-13). When you extrude a plane surface, it extends its shape some distance, either *perpendicular* to the shape's outline or along a defined path. When you lathe a shape, a profile of the shape is *rotated* around a defined axis (you can set the direction) to create the 3-D object. Other methods for creating 3-D objects differ among the various software packages.

Once you have created a 3-D object, you can apply textures and colors to it to make it seem more realistic—rough and coarse or shiny and smooth. You can also apply a color or pattern or even a bitmapped picture to texture your object. Thus you can build a table, apply an oak finish, then stain it purple or blue or iridescent yellow. You can add coffee cup rings and spilled cheese dip with appropriate coloring and texturing.

To model a scene, you place all of your objects into 3-D space. Some complex scenes may contain hundreds (if not thousands) of elements. In modeling your scene, you will also set up one or more lights that will create diffuse or sharp shade and shadows on your objects and will also reflect or *flare* where the light is most intense. Then you will add a background and

11

set a camera view, the location and angle from which you will view the final *rendered* scene.

Shading can usually be applied in several ways. As illustrated in Figure 11-14, *flat shading* (b) is the fastest for the computer to render and is most often used in *preview* mode. *Gouraud shading* (a), *Phong shading* (d), and *ray tracing* (c) take longer to render but provide photo-realistic images.

When you have completed the modeling of your scene or an object in it, you then must *render* it for final output. Rendering is when the computer finally uses intricate algorithms to apply the effects you have specified on the objects you have created. Figure 11-15 shows a background, an object, and the rendered composite.

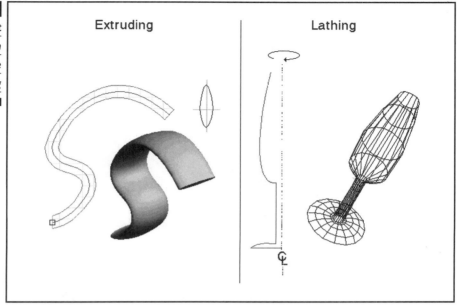

FIGURE 11-13

A free-form object created by extrusion and a wine flute created by lathing

Extruding

Lathing

FIGURE 11-14

A scene rendered with four different methods of shading

a

b

c

d

11

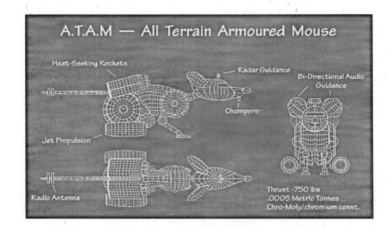

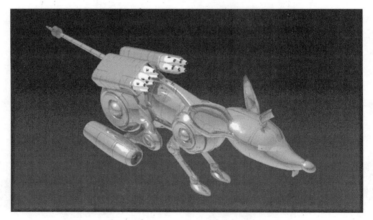

Rendering an image requires great computing muscle and often takes many hours for a single image—you will feel the strength (or weakness) of your hardware. Indeed, some multimedia and animation companies dedicate certain computers solely for rendering.

::::::::::::::::::::::::::::::::::

Sun Goes Hollywood
117 SPARCstations render *Toy Story*, the first feature-length computer-animated film

With Toy Story, *the company began an odyssey into territory owned by Hollywood.*

"There are two ways to look at the film: one is that it is the culmination of 20 years of research that have brought us to this point," said Pixar founder and chief technical officer Ed Catmull. "The other is that this is a whole new way of making feature animated films, and with this technology we are at the start of a long period of improved productivity and quality."

Toy Story is also something of a coup for Sun Microsystems. The movie's final image rendering was accomplished on a "farm" of 87 dual-processor and 30 quad-processor 100 MHz SPARCstation 20s—representing more computing power than 300 Cray 1's.

"There is more computer power applied to this film than [to] any film in history," Catmull said.

Even with that, rendering the film's 110,000 frames required the equivalent of 46 days of continuous processing; put another way, rendering each frame took one to three hours of SPARC processor time. "We could use 1,000 times more power, and we know exactly how we'd use it—we're limited by the budget, not our appetite," Catmull said.

"It's not like someone who is doing a spreadsheet and wants two or three times more power for faster turnaround but isn't going to do anything fundamentally different."

The farm itself is essentially a wall with 117 SPARCstations configured as headless servers, each with 192 to 384 megabytes of RAM (each processor has an average of 96 megabytes of RAM) and three to five gigabytes of local disk storage. The local disks hold a copy of Solaris, some proprietary job control software, and Pixar's RenderMan.

"There has to be a huge swap space, and space to download models," said David Ching, Pixar's manager of computer operations.

::::::::::::::::::::::::::::::::::

From a story by Jeff Ubois, "Sun Goes Hollywood," Sunworld Online (http://www.sun.com/sunworldonline), November, 1995. Reprinted with permission of Sunworld Online.

11

note *Farms of many computers hooked together may also be called "clusters of workstations," or COWs. There is occasionally humorous contention regarding proper nomenclature: it seems that developers who live and work in cities tend to prefer the notion of computer farms; developers in rural communities already familiar with farms prefer to call these beasts COWs.*

Color

Color is a vital component of multimedia. This section explains where color comes from and how colors are displayed on a computer monitor. Management of color is both a subjective and a technical exercise. Picking the right colors and combinations of colors for your project can involve many tries until you feel the result is right. But the technical description of a color may be expressed in known physical values (humans, for example, perceive colors with wavelengths ranging from 400 to 600 nanometers on the electromagnetic spectrum), and there are several methods and models to describe color space using mathematics and values.

Understanding Natural Light and Color

Light comes from an atom when an electron passes from a higher to a lower energy level; each atom produces uniquely specific colors. This explanation of light, known as the *quantum theory,* was developed by physicist Max Planck in the late 19th century. Niels Bohr, another physicist, later showed that an excited atom that has absorbed energy and whose electrons have moved into higher orbits will throw off that energy in the form of *quanta,* or *photons,* when it reverts to a stable state. This is where light comes from.

Color is the frequency of a light wave within the narrow band of the electromagnetic spectrum to which the human eye responds. The letters of the mnemonic ROY G. BIV, learned by many of us to remember the colors of the rainbow, are the ascending frequencies of the visible light spectrum: red, orange, yellow, green, blue, indigo, and violet. Light that is infrared, or below the frequency of red light and not perceivable by the human eye, can be created and viewed by electronic diodes and sensors, and it is used for TV and VCR remote controls and for night goggles used in the military. Infrared light is radiated heat. Ultraviolet light, on the other hand, is beyond the higher end of the visible spectrum and can be damaging to humans.

The color white is a noisy mixture of all the color frequencies in the visible spectrum. Sunlight and fluorescent tubes produce white light; tungsten lamp filaments produce light with a yellowish cast; sodium vapor lamps, typically used for low-cost outdoor street lighting, produce an orange light characteristic of the sodium atom. These are the most common sources of light in the everyday (or every night) world. The light these sources produce typically reaches your eye as a reflection of that light into the lens of your eye.

The cornea of the eye acts as a lens to focus light rays onto the retina. The light rays stimulate many thousands of specialized nerves called *rods* and *cones* that cover the surface of the retina. Receptors in the cones are sensitive to red, green, and blue light, and all the nerves together transmit the pattern of color information to the brain. The eye can differentiate among millions of colors, or *hues,* consisting of combinations of red, green, and blue.

As color information is sent to the brain, other parts of the mind massage the data en route to its point of cognitive recognition. Human response to color is complicated by cultural and experiential filters that cause otherwise straightforward color frequencies to carry pleasant, unpleasant, soothing, depressing, and many other special meanings. In Western cultures, for example, red is the color of anger and danger; in Eastern cultures, red is the color of happiness. Red is the traditional color for Chinese restaurant motifs, to make them attractive and happy places; Western restaurants are often decorated in quieter pastels and earth tones. White, not black, is the color of funerals in Chinese culture.

Green, blue, yellow, orange, purple, pink, brown, black, gray, and white are the ten most common color-describing words used in all human languages and cultures. Komar and Melamid's interesting Internet study (http://www.diacenter.org/km/index.html) has determined that the favorite color in the world is blue.

Computerized Color

Because the eye's receptors are sensitive to red, green, and blue light, by adjusting combinations of these three *additive primary colors,* the eye and brain will interpolate the combinations of colors in between. This is the psychology, not the physics of color: what you perceive as orange on a computer monitor is a combination of two frequencies of green and red light, not the actual spectral frequency you see when you look at that namesake fruit, an orange, in sunlight. All these factors make computerized color pretty tricky to manage.

The reflected light that reaches your eye from a printed page is made up of tiny halftone dots of a few primary colors (printers use the *subtractive primary colors,* cyan, magenta, and yellow, with black). In contrast, the screen of a computer monitor is, like the sun, a source of light. On the back of the glass face of a monitor are thousands of phosphorescing chemical color dots (red, green, and blue), which are bombarded by electrons that paint the screen at very high speeds. These dots are each about .30 mm or less in diameter (the *dot pitch*) and are positioned very carefully and very close together.

The red, green, and blue dots light up when hit by the electron beam, and the eye sees the combination of red, green, and blue (RGB) light and interpolates it. When one of the primary colors is subtracted from this RGB mix, the subtractive primary color is perceived, as follows:

RGB Combination	Perceived Color
Red only	Red
Green only	Green
Blue only	Blue
Red and green (blue subtracted)	Yellow
Red and blue (green subtracted)	Magenta
Green and blue (red subtracted)	Cyan
Red, green, and blue	White
None	Black

Various color models are illustrated in color in Color Plates 2 and 3.

Monitors and Color

Most multimedia today is presented on color monitors that display a matrix of 640 pixels across and 480 pixels down (640×480); each pixel may be one of 256 colors. With fewer colors, there is not enough range to make good photo-realistic images, although gray-scale pictures with 16 shades of gray often come out well. With more colors, your computer must work much harder to display the image on the screen, and performance takes a serious hit unless you boost it with faster, expensive processors and added memory devices.

---

w a r n i n g   *Sometimes the term "video card" is used synonymously with "graphics adapter," which is the hardware that makes the monitor work. Do not confuse "video card" with "video capture card" or "video display card," which are the terms used for video (television) editing and display.*

The 640×480, 256-color (8-bit) setup is called VGA (for Video Graphics Array), and it is the minimum design configuration for most Windows and

Macintosh multimedia applications. If you wish to reach the widest audience with your multimedia work, you must design for this installed base.

Computer Color Models

The color of a pixel on your computer monitor is typically expressed as an amount of red, green, and blue. It takes more computer memory and processing speed to digitally manage and display the greater combinations of red, green, and blue values that make more shades of color visible to the eye.

Models or methodologies used to specify colors in computer terms are RGB, HSB, HSL, CMYK, CIE, and others. Using the RGB (red, green, blue) model, you specify a color by setting the amount of red, green, and blue, in the range 0 to 65535. Color Plate 2 illustrates the RGB color cube, where the three dimensions represent the values of the three color channels that specify a color.

Red	Green	Blue	Color
65535	65535	65535	White
65535	65535	0	Yellow
65535	0	65535	Magenta
0	65535	65535	Cyan
65535	0	0	Red
0	65535	0	Green
0	0	65535	Blue
0	0	0	Black

In the HSB (hue, saturation, brightness) and HSL (hue, saturation, lightness) models, you specify hue or color as an angle from 0 to 360 degrees on a color wheel, and saturation, brightness, and lightness as percentages. Lightness or brightness is the percentage of black or white that is mixed with a color. A lightness of 100 percent will yield a white color; 0 percent is black; the pure color has a 50 percent lightness. Saturation is the intensity of the color. At 100 percent saturation, the color is pure; at 0 percent saturation, the color is white, black, or gray, as follows:

Color	Degrees
Red	0°
Yellow	60°

Color	Degrees
Green	120°
Cyan	180°
Blue	240°
Magenta	300°

The CMYK color model is less applicable to multimedia production. It is used primarily in the printing trade where cyan, magenta, yellow, and black are used to print process color separations.

Other color models include CIE, YIQ, YUV, and YCC. CIE describes color value in terms of frequency, saturation, and illuminance (blue/yellow or red/green, which in turn corresponds to the color receptors in the cones of the eye). CIE more closely resembles how human beings perceive color, but certain devices such as scanners are unable to replicate the process.

YIQ and YUV were developed for broadcast TV (composite NTSC, as explained in Chapter 13). They are based on luminance and chrominance expressed as the amplitude of a wave and the phase of the wave relative to some reference. Detail is carried by luminance (black and white), so reduction in color does not result in the loss of image definition detail. This analog process can be translated to a number value so that the computer can use a palette or CLUT (color lookup table) to assign a pixel a color.

The Photo YCC model has been developed by Kodak to provide a definition that enables consistent representation of digital color images from negatives, slides, and other high-quality input. YCC is used for PhotoCD images.

Color Palettes

Palettes are mathematical tables that define the color of a pixel displayed on the screen. On the Macintosh, these tables are called *color lookup tables* or CLUTs. In Windows, the term *palette* is used. The most common palettes are 1, 4, 8, 16, and 24 bits deep:

Color Depth	Colors Available
1-bit	Black and white (or any two colors)
4-bit	16 colors
8-bit	256 colors (good enough for color images)
16-bit	Thousands of colors (excellent for color images)
24-bit	More than 16 million colors (totally photo-realistic)

For 256-color, 8-bit VGA systems, your computer uses a color lookup table or palette to determine which 256 colors out of the millions possible are available to you at any one time. Color Plate 1 shows the default Macintosh system palette as well as other combinations of 256 and 16 colors. The default colors were statistically selected by Apple and Microsoft engineers (working independently) to be the colors and shades that are most "popular" in photographic images; the two palettes are, of course, different.

To generate a palette which is best for representing a particular image, we support Heckbert's median cut algorithm. This algorithm first builds a three-dimensional table (a histogram cube) indicating how popular any given color in the RGB cube is in the image being converted. It then proceeds to subdivide this histogram cube (by dividing boxes in half) until it has created as many boxes as there are palette entries. The decision as to where to divide a box is based on the distribution of colors within the box. This algorithm attempts to create boxes which have approximately equal popularity in the image. Palette entries are then assigned to represent each box. There are other methods of generating a palette from an image, but Heckbert's algorithm is generally regarded as the best trade-off between speed and quality.

Allan Hessenflow of HandMade Software, makers of Image
Alchemy, describing how an 8-bit palette is made

Paint programs provide a palette tool for displaying available colors. Most color pickers and selectors (see examples shown in Color Plate 3) also provide a mechanism for specifying a palette color numerically when precision is required. Palette display and color picking tools, however, are not uniform among applications or across platforms.

In 24-bit color systems, your graphics adapter works with three channels of 256 discrete shades of each color (red, green, and blue) represented as the three axes of a cube. This allows a total of 16,777,216 colors (256×256×256). Like the 44.1 kHz sampled-sound standard for CD music on compact discs that is discussed in Chapter 10, the color range offered by 24-bit systems covers what the human eye can sense. Even though millions of colors can be painted on a computer screen in 24-bit mode, only 307,200 (640×480) actual pixels are available at any one time on typical Macintosh and Windows display monitors. This is, however, more than sufficient for excellent gradients and photo-realism. Sixteen-bit provides a total of 32,768 different colors (32×32×32) that are quite realistic and smooth.

11

About Palette Flashing

When you work with the 256 colors of an 8-bit palette, only one combination of any 256 colors can be displayed on your monitor at any given moment. If you change the colors in the current palette by remapping, there will be an annoying flash of strange colors in your image while the computer remakes its color lookup table and the old colors change to the new. This *palette flashing* is a serious practical problem for multimedia designers. For example, it occurs when you show a series of images (an animation), each with its own optimal palette; when the new image replaces the old one, a flash occurs.

All techniques for handling the palette-flashing problem involve design solutions:

- The simplest solution is to map all images in your project to a single, shared palette. The disadvantage here is that you will trade the best 256 colors that show a single image for an "average" of 256 colors shared among all images. Applications such as Equilibrium's DeBabelizer specialize in creating "super palettes."

- A less simple but more effective technique is to fade each image to white or black before showing the next image. Black and white are usually present in all palettes.

Most image-editing, painting, and authoring applications let you remap, optimize, and customize palettes. When you input an image with a flat-bed color scanner or a video frame-grabber, the resulting image file will likely be three 8-bit channels of color information. Your images will be highly detailed, showing rich and subtle color variations, wood grain, and various lighting conditions. If you dither this image to 8 bits, you must weigh the compromises.

And here are some color techniques to avoid when the destination of your animation is a videotape:

- Avoid using a pattern or mosaic.
- Avoid thin horizontal lines.
- Avoid extremely bright or intense colors that may flare up on a television screen; stick to pastels and earth colors.
- Avoid some reds that may turn brown on television.

Dithering

If you start out with a scanned image that contains millions of colors, it must be dithered to 256 colors. *Dithering* is a process whereby the color value of each pixel is changed to the closest matching color value in the target palette, using a mathematical algorithm. Often the adjacent pixels are also examined, and patterns of different colors are created in the more limited palette to best represent the original colors. Thus any given pixel might not be mapped to its closest palette entry, but instead to the average over some area of the image; this average will be closer to the correct color than a substitute color would be. Depending upon the algorithm used, dithering can render a very good approximation of the original. Color Plate 6 compares the same scanned image dithered from millions of colors to 256 colors, 16 colors, 16 grays, and black and white.

---

tip   *To improve performance on the Web, a common trick is to make two files: a very compact black-and-white dithered image and the full-color image. Use Netscape's <lowsrc> attribute for the <img> graphic tag so the black-and-white picture displays fast. Then later, Netscape draws the full-color graphic over the black-and-white one.*

Dithering concepts are important to understand when you are working with bitmaps that are derived from RGB information or are based upon different palettes or color lookup tables. The palette for the image of a rose, for example, may contain mostly shades of red with a number of greens thrown in for the stem and leaves. The image of your pretty Delft vase, into which you want to electronically place the rose, may be mostly blues and grays. Your software will use a dithering algorithm to find the 256 color shades that best represent both images, generating a new palette in the process.

11

Multimedia is just another way to transform ambiguity. There were so many ambiguous colors in this scan, I decided to make them unambiguous. How do you like the purple?

Lars Hidde, explaining why he dithered a perfectly fine 8-bit image into a 16-color default palette

Dithering software is usually built into image-editing programs and is also available in many multimedia authoring systems as part of the application's palette management suite of tools.

---

tip *Instead of trying to display a photo-realistic image using 16 colors, or if you are not satisfied with the colors of your image, consider dithering your photo to a gray-scale image. It will show extraordinary detail.*

---

warning *It is very difficult to create outstanding graphics with just 16 colors. Using various two-color dithers will certainly improve your range of perceived colors, but you will need to double your graphics budget—optimizing the look of drawn and painted objects at this color depth is painstaking and time consuming.*

Image File Formats

As mentioned earlier in this chapter, there are many file formats used to store bitmaps and drawings. Developers of paint and draw applications continually create native file formats that allow their programs to load and save files more quickly or more efficiently. Most of these applications, however, offer a Save As option that lets you write files in other common formats. And third-party translators are now widely available, for files generated on the same platform as well as for going cross platform between Macintosh and PC/Windows (and others).

If you are using a specialized application to make bitmaps or drawings, make sure your multimedia authoring package can import the image files you produce, and that your application can export such a file. You need a common format.

First Person

I needed to get about 40 bitmap files from the Macintosh to the Sun SPARCstation. "Piece of cake," I said. "Give me a few minutes." The network hadn't gone down in three days, and we were connected at Ethernet speeds. Well, the files had been saved in native Photoshop format on the Macintosh. So I launched Photoshop, opened each file, and then saved it in PICT format. The translator program I wanted to use to convert Macintosh PICT files to Sun raster files was an MS-DOS application, so I renamed all the Macintosh files to fit the DOS eight-plus-three-character file name convention. Then I cranked up the 486, launched the translator, and batch-processed all of the files into .RAS files using the network. The 40 new files were now on the Macintosh, mixed in with the original PICTs. I collected the needed raster files into a single folder on the Macintosh and then sent the whole thing over to the Sun.

A few minutes? The process kept three chairs warm for about two hours.

Macintosh Formats

On the Macintosh, just about every image application can import or export PICT files. PICT is a complicated but versatile format developed by Apple as a common format that is always available to Macintosh users. In a PICT file, both bitmaps and vector-drawn objects can live side by side, and programs such as SuperCard or Canvas make use of this feature, providing editors for both drawn and bitmapped graphics. Many drawing programs for the Macintosh, such as Illustrator or Freehand, will allow you to import a bitmap but offer no facility for editing it. Multimedia authoring programs that can import PICT images may not utilize the drawn objects that are part of the file, but will usually convert them to bitmaps for you.

Windows Formats

Windows uses device-independent bitmaps (DIBs) as its common image file format, usually written as .BMP files. DIBs can stand alone, or they can be buried within a Resource Interchange File Format (RIFF) file. A RIFF is actually the preferred file type for all multimedia development in Windows, because this format was designed to contain many types of files, including bitmaps, MIDI scores, and formatted text. In Windows, there is no "standard" provision for managing drawn objects in a common format, as is provided by Macintosh PICT files.

The bitmap formats used most often by Windows developers are DIB, BMP, PCX, and TIFF. A BMP file is a Windows bitmap file. PCX files were originally developed for use in Z-Soft MS-DOS paint packages; these files can be opened and saved by almost all MS-DOS paint software and desktop publishing software. TIFF, or Tagged Interchange File Format, was designed to be a universal bitmapped image format and is also used extensively in desktop publishing packages. Often, applications use a proprietary file format to store their images. Adobe creates a .PSD file for Photoshop and an .AI file for Illustrator; Corel creates a .CDR file; Micrografx Designer and Picture Publisher applications use .DSF and .PPF files. If you import your artwork into other programs, such as multimedia authoring systems, be sure you save your bitmaps in a format that can be imported by that application.

The following list contains image file formats you might find in the Windows environment:

Format	Extension
Microsoft Windows DIB	BMP, DIB, and RLE
Microsoft RLE DIB	DIB
Microsoft Palette	PAL

Format	Extension
Microsoft RIFF DIB	RDI
Computer Graphics Metafile	CGM
Micrografx Designer/Draw	DRW
AutoCAD Format 2-D	DXF
Encapsulated PostScript	EPS
CompuServe GIF	GIF
HP Graphic Language	HGL
JPEG	JPG
PC Paintbrush	PCX
Apple Macintosh PICT	PIC or PCT
Lotus 1-2-3 Graphics	PIC
AutoCAD Import	PLT
Truevision TGA	TGA
TIFF	TIF
Windows Metafile	WMF
DrawPerfect	WPG

Cross-Platform Formats

For handling drawn objects across many platforms, there are two common formats: DXF and IGS. DXF was developed by AutoDesk as an ASCII-based drawing interchange file for AutoCAD, but the format is used today by many computer-aided design applications. IGS (or IGES, for Initial Graphics Exchange Standard) was developed by an industry committee as a broader standard for transferring CAD drawings. These formats are also used in 3-D rendering and animation programs. Applications such as Equilibrium Software's deBabelizer for the Macintosh (see Figure 6-9 in Chapter 6) and Handmade Software's Image Alchemy for the PC provide specialized image format translators.

JPEG and GIF images are the most common bitmap formats used on the Web and may be considered cross platform, as all browsers will display them. These formats are discussed in detail in Chapter 18.

• •

http://www.w3.org/pub/WWW/Graphics/
http://www.itsi.disa.mil/ismc/

More information about image file formats and standards

Multi

[
Animation is possible because of
a biological phenomenon known
as persistence of vision
]

Animation is a button actually moving across the screen...

dynamic action

media

12

Animation

- a spinning globe of our earth;
- a car driving along a line-art highway;
- a bug crawling out from under a stack of disks,
- with a screaming voice from the speaker telling you to "Shoot it, now!"

Animation adds visual impact to your multimedia project. Many multimedia applications for both Macintosh and Windows provide animation tools, but you should first understand the principles of how the eye interprets the changes it sees as motion.

The Power of Motion

You can animate your whole project, or you can animate here and there, accenting and adding spice. For a brief product demonstration with little user interaction, it might make sense to design the entire project as a movie and keep the presentation always in motion. For speaker support, you can animate bulleted text or fly it in, or you can use charts with quantities that grow or dwindle; then, give the speaker control of these eye-catchers. In a parts-assembly training manual, you might show components exploding into an expanded view.

Visual effects such as wipes, fades, zooms, and dissolves are available in most authoring packages, and some of these can be used for primitive animation. For example, you can slide images onto the screen with a wipe, or you can make an object implode with an iris/close effect. Figure 12-1 shows the many transition effects available in Macromedia Director and in Adobe Premiere.

But animation is more than wipes, fades, and zooms. Animation is an object actually moving across or *into* or *out of* the screen; a spinning globe of our earth; a car driving along a line-art highway; a bug crawling out from under a stack of disks, with a screaming voice from the speaker telling you to "Shoot it, now!" Until QuickTime and AVI motion video became more commonplace, animations were the primary source of dynamic action in multimedia presentations.

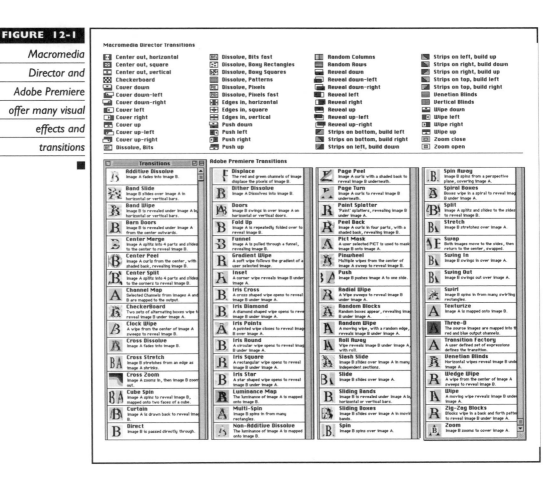

FIGURE 12-1

Macromedia Director and Adobe Premiere offer many visual effects and transitions

Tools for designing animated multimedia presentations are discussed in detail in Chapters 6 and 8. Creating and displaying animations for World Wide Web pages is discussed in Chapter 15.

Principles of Animation

Animation is possible because of a biological phenomenon known as persistence of vision. An object seen by the human eye remains mapped on the eye's retina for a brief time after viewing. This makes it possible for a series of images that are changed very slightly and very rapidly, one after the other, to seemingly blend together into a visual illusion of movement. In other words, if you just change slightly the location or shape of an object rapidly enough, the eye will perceive the changes as motion. The following shows a

12

few cells or frames of a rotating logo. When the images are progressively and rapidly changed, the arrow of the compass is perceived to be spinning.

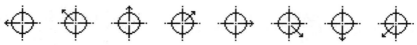

Television video builds 30 entire frames or pictures every second; the speed with which each frame is replaced by the next one makes the images appear to blend smoothly into movement. Movies on film are typically shot at a shutter rate of 24 frames per second, but using projection tricks (the projector's shutter flashes light through each image twice), the flicker rate is increased to 48 times per second, and the human eye thus sees a motion picture. Quickly changing the viewed image is the principle of an animatic, a flip-book, or a zoetrope. To make an object travel across the screen while it changes its shape, just change the shape and also move or *translate* it a few pixels for each frame. Then, when you play the frames back at a faster speed, the changes blend together and you have motion and animation. It's the same magic as when the hand is quicker than the eye, and you don't see the pea moving in the blur of the gypsy's cups.

Animation Techniques

Today, computers have taken a great deal of handwork out of the animation and rendering process, and commercial films such as *Jurassic Park, Beauty and the Beast,* and *Toy Story* have utilized the power of computers (see Chapter 11 for an account of the "computer wall" of 117 Sun SPARCstations used to render the animated feature *Toy Story*).

When you create an animation, organize its execution into a series of logical steps. First, gather up in your mind all the activities you wish to provide in the animation; if it is complicated, you may wish to create a written script with a list of activities and required objects. Choose the animation tool best suited for the job. Then build and tweak your sequences; experiment with lighting effects. Allow plenty of time for this phase when you are experimenting and testing. Finally, post-process your animation, doing any special renderings and adding sound effects.

Cel Animation

The animation techniques made famous by Disney use a series of progressively different graphics on each frame of movie film (which plays at 24 frames per second). A minute of animation may thus require as many as 1,440 separate frames. The term *cel* derives from the clear celluloid sheets that were used for drawing each frame, which have been replaced today by acetate or plastic. Cels of famous animated cartoons have become sought-after, suitable-for-framing collector's items.

Cel animation artwork begins with *keyframes* (the first and last frame of an action). For example, when an animated figure of a man walks across the screen, he balances the weight of his entire body on one foot and then the other in a series of falls and recoveries, with the opposite foot and leg catching up to support the body. Thus the first keyframe to portray a single step might be the man pitching his body weight forward off the left foot and leg, while his center of gravity shifts forward; the feet are close together and he appears to be falling. The last keyframe might be the right foot and leg catching the body's fall, with the center of gravity now centered between the outstretched stride, and the left and right feet positioned far apart.

The series of frames in between the keyframes are drawn in a process called tweening. *Tweening* an action requires calculating the number of frames between keyframes and the path the action takes, and then actually sketching onto a cel with pencil the series of progressively different outlines. As tweening progresses, the action sequence is checked by flipping through the frames. The penciled frames are assembled and then actually filmed as a pencil test to check smoothness, continuity, and timing.

When the pencil frames are satisfactory, they are permanently inked, and acrylic colors are painted on. In the hands of a master, cel paint applied to the back of acetate can be simply flat and perfectly even or it can produce beautiful and subtle effects, with feathered edges or smudges.

The cels for each frame of our example of a walking man—which may consist of a text title, a background, a left arm, a right arm, legs, shoes, a body, and facial features—are carefully registered and stacked. It is this composite that becomes the final photographed frame in an animated movie.

Computer Animation

Computer animation programs typically employ the same logic and procedural concepts as cel animation, using layer, keyframe, and tweening techniques, and even borrowing from the vocabulary of classic animators. On the computer, paint is most often filled or drawn with tools using features such as gradients and anti-aliasing. The word *inks,* in computer animation terminology, usually means special methods for computing RGB pixel values, providing edge detection, and layering so that images can blend or otherwise mix their colors to produce special transparencies, inversions, and effects.

You can usually set your own frame rates on the computer, but the rate at which changes are computed and screens are refreshed will depend on the speed and power of your display platform and hardware. Although your

12

animations will probably never push the limits of your monitor's scan rate (about 60 to 70 frames a second), animation does put raw computing horsepower to task. If you cannot compute all your changes and display them as a new frame on your monitor within, say, 1/15 second, then the animation may appear jerky and slow.

---

tip *The smaller the object, the faster it can move. Bouncing a 10-pixel-diameter tennis ball on your screen provides far snappier motion than bouncing a 150-pixel-diameter beach ball.*

KINEMATICS Kinematics is the study of the movement and motion of structures that have joints, such as a walking man. Animating a walking step is tricky: you need to calculate the position, rotation, velocity, and acceleration of all the joints and articulated parts involved—knees bend, hips flex, shoulders swing, and the head bobs. Fractal Design's Poser, a 3-D modeling program, provides preassembled adjustable human models (male, female, infant, teenager, and superhero) in many poses, such as "walking" or "thinking." As Figure 12-2 shows, an appendage can be adjusted or a pose quickly configured simply by dragging or rotating the appropriate body part. And surface textures can then be applied to create muscle-bound hulks or smooth chrome androids. Inverse kinematics is the process in which you link objects such as hands to arms and define their relationships and limits (for example, elbows cannot bend backwards), then drag these parts around and let the computer calculate the result.

FIGURE 12-2

Fractal Design's Poser understands human motion and inverse kinematics: move an arm, and the shoulders follow

MORPHING Morphing is a popular (if not overused) effect in which one image transforms into another. Morphing applications and other modeling tools that offer this effect can transition not only between still images but often between moving images as well. Some products that offer morphing features are Avid's Elastic Reality, Black Belt's WinImages, Gryphon Software's Morph, Human Software's Squizz, ImageWare's MorphWizard, MetaTools' Digital Morph, North Coast's PhotoMorph, RomeBlack's RomeBlack, Strata's Visual FX, Ulead's MorphStudio, Valis Group's Flo and MetaFlo, and Villa Crespo's MetaMorf. Color Plate 13 illustrates part of a morph where 16 kindergarten children are dissolved one into the other in a continuous compelling motion video.

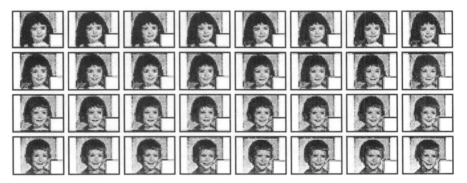

The morphed images shown here were built at a rate of eight frames per second, with each transition taking a total of four seconds (32 separate images for each transition), and the number of key points was held to a minimum to shorten rendering time. Setting key points (see Figure 12-3) is crucial for smooth transition between two images. The point you set in the start image will move to the corresponding point in the end image—this is important for things like eyes and noses, which you want to end up in about the same place (even if they look different) after the transition. The more key points, the smoother the morph.

Animation File Formats

Some file formats are designed specifically to contain animations, and they can be ported among applications and platforms with the proper translators. Those formats include Director (dir), AnimatorPro (fli using 320×200 pixel images and flc), 3D Studio Max (max), SuperCard and Director (pics), Windows Audio Video Interleaved Format (avi), Macintosh Time-Based Data Format (quicktime, mov), Motion Video (mpeg or mpg), CompuServe (gif), Shockwave (dcr). Because file size is a critical factor when downloading animations to play on World Wide Web pages, file compression is an

Matching key
points in the start
and end image
guide the morphing
transition

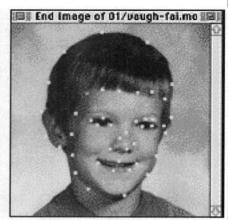

essential part of preparing animation files for the Web. A Director movie file (dir), for example, must be preprocessed and compressed into a proprietary Shockwave animation file (dcr) for the Web. Compression for Director movies is as much as 75 percent or more with this tool, turning 100K files into 25K files and significantly speeding up download/display times on the Internet.

http://www.macromedia.com
http://www.3dsite.com/3dsite/)
http://www2.cinenet.net/GWEB/
http://www.idsonline.com/business/3dfoley/home.html
http://www.prism.uvsq.fr/public/wos/multimedia/
http://www.idsonline.com/business/3dfoley/home.html
http://www-ci.u-aizu.ac.jp/VisualComputer/
http://www.univ-rennes1.fr/ASTRO/fra/xanim.html
http://www.north.net/alchemy/gifcon.html
news:comp.graphics.animation
news:comp.graphics.apps.alias
news:comp.graphics.apps.lightwave
news:comp.graphics.apps.photoshop
news:comp.graphics.apps.softimage
news:comp.graphics.apps.wavefront
news:comp.graphics.misc
news:comp.graphics.packages.3dstudio
news:comp.graphics.raytracing

....

news:comp.graphics.rendering.misc
news:comp.graphics.rendering.raytracing
news:comp.graphics.rendering.renderman
news:comp.graphics.visualization

Information about animation is available on the Web and from many newsgroups on the Internet

Making Animations That Work

Animation catches the eye and makes things noticeable. But, like sound, animation quickly becomes trite if it is improperly applied. Unless your project has a backbone of movielike animated imagery, use animation carefully and sparingly to achieve the greatest impact. Your screens will otherwise become busy and "noisy."

Multimedia authoring systems typically provide tools to simplify creating animations within that authoring system. And they often have a mechanism for playing the special animation files created by dedicated animation software. Today, the most widely used tool for creating multimedia animations for Macintosh and Windows environments is Macromedia's Director (see Chapter 8).

The following sections provide examples to demonstrate that computer-generated animations actually consist of many bits and pieces carefully orchestrated to appear as one image, in motion—just like the many layers in classical cel animation.

A Rolling Ball

Billiard-ball spheres can be made quickly using Photoshop and Kai's Power Tools' Spheroid Designer (see Figure 12-4), a set of graphic manipulation plug-ins. First, create a new, blank image file that is 100×100 pixels, and fill it with a sphere:

12

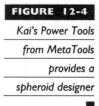

FIGURE 12-4

*Kai's Power Tools
from MetaTools
provides a
spheroid designer* ∎

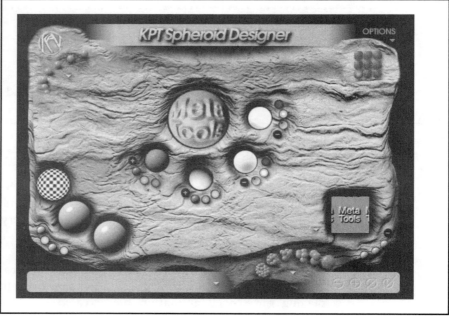

Create a new layer in Photoshop, and place some white text on this layer at the center of the image:

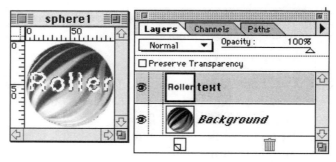

Sphererize the text using Photoshop's distortion plug-in, and save the result:

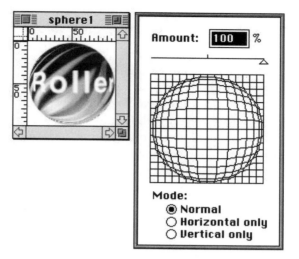

To animate the sphere by rolling it across the screen, you first need to make a number of rotated images of the sphere. Rotate the image in 45-degree increments to create a total of eight images, rotating a full circle of 360 degrees. When displayed sequentially at the same location, the sphere spins:

For a realistic rolling effect, the circumference (calculated at pi times 100, or about 314 pixels) is divided by 8 (yielding about 40 pixels). As each image is successively displayed, the ball is moved 40 pixels along a line. Being where the rubber meets the road, this math applies when you roll any round object in a straight line perpendicular to your line of sight.

A Bouncing Ball

With the simplest tools, you can make a bouncing ball to animate your Web site using GIF89a (animating with GIF89a files is discussed in Chapter 15). Like the rolling ball, you simply need to flash a ball on the computer screen rapidly and in a different place each time to make it bounce up and down. And like the rolling ball, where you should compute the circumference of the ball and divide by the number of images to determine how far it rolls each time it flashes, there are some commonsense computations to consider with a bouncing ball, too. In the formula, *s* equals distance, *g* equals gravity, and *t* equals time:

$$s = \tfrac{1}{2}gt^2$$

Gravity makes your bouncing ball accelerate on its downward course and decelerate on its upward course (when it moves slower and slower until it actually stops and then accelerates downward again). As Galileo discovered while dropping feathers and rocks from the leaning tower of Pisa, a beach ball and a golf ball accelerate downward at the same rate until they hit the ground. But the real world of Italy is full of air, so the feather falls gently while the rock pounds dirt. It is in this real world that you should compose your animations, tempering them always with commonsense physics to give them the ring of truth.

Unless your animation requires precision, ignore the hard numbers you learned in high school (like 32 feet per second per second), and simply figure that your ball will uniformly accelerate and decelerate up and down the pixels of your screen by the squares: 1, 4, 9, 16, 25, 36, 49, 64, 81, 100 are the squares of 1, 2, 3, 4, 5, 6, 7, 8, 9, and 10. This is illustrated in Figure 12-5. In the case of a perpetual-motion bouncing ball (even better than silly putty), it goes up the same way it comes down, forever, and this makes the job easy, because the up and down movements are symmetrical. You can use the same images for downward motion as you use for upward—as in frames 11 through 18 in Figure 12-5.

Open a graphics program and paint a ball about 15 pixels in diameter (if you have an odd-number diameter, there is a middle pixel that can be your center alignment point). If you wish to be fancy, make the ball with a 3-D graphics tool that will shade it as a sphere. Then duplicate the ball, placing each copy of it in a vertical line at the ten locations 1, 4, 9, 16, 25, 36, 49, 64, 81, 100. The goal is to create a separate image file for each location of the ball, like the pages of a flip-book. With Photoshop, you can create a single file with ten layers to contain each ball at its proper location, and you

FIGURE 12-5

To make a bouncing ball seem natural, don't forget the effects of gravity. If you loop the 18 images shown here, the ball will bounce forever

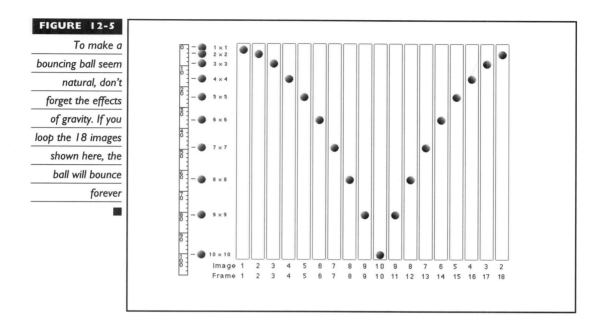

can add an eleventh background layer, too. Then save each layer showing against the background as a separate file (use numbers in your file names like BALL1.GIF, BALL2.GIF, etc., to keep them organized):

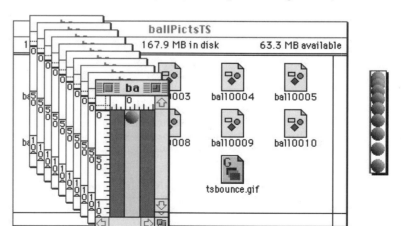

This is a construction process also easily managed with Director, where you can place the same cast member (the ball) where you wish on the Director stage. Use the scores's extended view, because the precise vertical location of your object is reported along the bottom line:

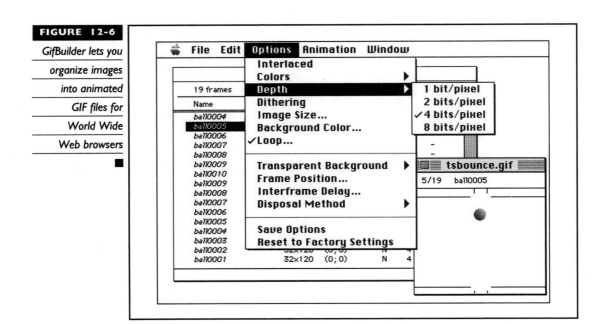

You can also add a background and other art elements, and when you are done, you can export each frame as a graphics file using Director's export function. You will probably also wish to set the size of Director's stage to a small area just sufficient for your animation, say 32×120 pixels. The smaller the better if users will be downloading this animated GIF file into their World Wide Web browsers.

To turn your collection of images into a GIF89a animation, you need an application like GifBuilder (for Macintosh; see Figure 12-6) or Gif Construction Set (for Windows). These tools organize the sequence of images to be shown, set timing and transparency, and (most importantly) let you save the final GIF file in the proper format. See Chapter 15 for more details about animated GIF files and where to use them.

Creating an Animated Scene

The animation example presented here became a small piece of the rollout presentation to developers and the press of Microsoft's Multimedia Extensions for Windows. The event is described in the "First Person" anecdote that follows.

FIGURE 12-6

GifBuilder lets you organize images into animated GIF files for World Wide Web browsers

A creative committee organized a brief storyboard of a gorilla chasing a man. From a CD-ROM containing many unlimited-licensed images, a photograph was chosen of Manhattan's Central Park where a bridge crossed a small river and high-rise apartments lined the horizon. The chase scene would occur across the bridge. To produce frames of the running man, an actor was videotaped running in place against an ultimatte blue background in a studio; a few frames of this were grabbed with a video capture board, and the blue background was removed from each image. The gorilla was difficult to find, so a toy model dinosaur about 25 centimeters tall was used; again, a few frames were captured and the background made transparent. That was all that was required for image resources.

As illustrated in Figure 12-7A, the background was carefully cut in half along the edge of the bridge, so the bridge railing could be placed in front of the runners. The running man was organized in a series of six frames that could be repeated many times across the screen to provide the pumping motions of running. The same was done for the dinosaur, to give him a lumbering, bulky look as he chased the little man across the bridge (see Figure 12-7B). The result, in Figure 12-7C, was simple and quickly achieved.

First Person

The animation storyboard called for a photo-realistic monster chasing a running man through a city park amid screams of terror. The man was already in Director, running in great strides across an arched footbridge in a woodsy scene with high-rises in the background; he even looked over his shoulder a few times in panic. We were scouting around for an effective Godzilla when a friend dropped by with a motorized, 12-inch Tyrannosaurus Rex from Toys 'R' Us. It was perfect—opening a toothy, gaping mouth every few steps as it lumbered along on C batteries.

I took the dinosaur and a video camera home to the delight and fascination of my three-year-old daughter, who helped rig a white sheet in front of the living room fireplace and a cardboard-box runway where Mr. TRex could strut his stuff before the camera. A couple of lamps gave him a sweaty sheen. We ran about five minutes of VHS tape as my daughter happily retrieved Mr. TRex each time he nosed off the "cliff" at the end of the stage.

Playing the tape on a VCR with a five-head, single-frame advance feature, I grabbed about every fourth frame with an old ColorSpace digitizing board on the Macintosh and imported the resulting PICT files into Director as cast members. They needed a little cleanup and scaling, but the fellow looked really convincing when he was finally scored to run across the bridge. Next day, I mixed a bunch of sounds—singing birds, running footsteps, screams, roars, sirens, and gunshots—and it was done. We exported it from the Macintosh to Windows as an MMM file.

A few weeks later, in November 1990, Mr. TRex helped introduce Bill Gates to a crowd of 600 at the opening of the first Microsoft Multimedia Developers' Conference.

12

FIGURE 12-7

The upper portion of the photo (A) was placed behind the runners (B) and the lower portion in front of them, to make them appear to run behind the bridge railing (C) ∎

A

B

C

Multi

Carefully planned, well-executed video clips can make a dramatic difference in a multimedia project.

Digital video is the most **engaging** of multimedia venues

compelling

media

pow!

chapter

13

Video

powerful

it is a very **powerful** tool to bring computer users closer to the real world.

S
INCE the first silent movie flickered to life, people have been fascinated with "motion" pictures. To this day, motion video is the element of multimedia that can draw gasps from a crowd at a trade show or firmly hold a student's interest in a computer-based learning project. Digital video is the most engaging of multimedia venues, and it is a powerful tool for bringing computer users closer to the real world. It also is an effective method for delivering multimedia to an audience raised on television. With video elements in your project, you can effectively present your messages and reinforce your story, and viewers tend to retain more of what they see. But take care! Video that is not thought out or well produced can degrade your presentation.

Full-motion video on personal computers changes everything. It is like turning a ten-speed bicycle into a Harley-Davidson.

David Bunnell, Editor-in-Chief, *NewMedia* Magazine

Standards and formats for digital text, imagery, and sound are well established and familiar. But video is the most recent addition to the elements of multimedia. And it is still being refined as transport, storage, compression, and display technologies take shape in laboratories and in the marketplace. Working with multimedia video today can be like a Mojave Desert camping trip: you may pitch your tent on comfortable high ground and find that overnight the shifting sands have buried both your approach and your investment. Firm ground tends to shift rapidly in the 100 mph back draft of the many silicon engineers, computer scientists, and startup company salespeople driving in the fast lane of video overlay boards, compression schemes, RAID hard disk towers, and interleaving software.

Of all the multimedia elements, video places the highest performance demand on your computer and its memory. Consider that the still high-quality color image on a computer screen could require as much as a megabyte of memory. Multiply this by 30, the number of times per second that the picture is replaced to provide the appearance of motion, and you would need 30 megabytes of memory per second to play your video—or 1.8 gigabytes of memory per minute, or 108 gigabytes per hour. Just moving all this picture data from computer memory to the screen at that rate would challenge the processing capability of a supercomputer. These massive memory storage demands make the Library of Congress look like a magazine rack at your local grocery store. Some of the hottest and most arcane multimedia technologies and research efforts today deal with compressing this digital video image data into manageable streams of information.

If you control the delivery platform for your project, you can get the highest video performance by specifying special hardware and software enhancements. A video compression board will allow you to work with full-screen, full-motion video. A sophisticated audio board will allow you to use CD-quality audio. You can install a super-fast RAID (Redundant Array of Independent Disks) system that will support high-speed data transfer rates. You can include instructions in your authoring system that will spool video into RAM for rapid playback.

Using Video

Carefully planned, well-executed video clips can make a dramatic difference in a multimedia project. A clip of John F. Kennedy proclaiming, "Ich bin ein Berliner" in video and sound is more compelling than a scrolling text field containing that same speech. Before deciding whether to add video to your project, however, it is essential to have an understanding of the medium, its limitations, and its costs. This chapter provides a basic foundation to help you understand how video works, the different formats and standards for recording and playing video, and the differences between computer and television video. The equipment needed to shoot and edit video, as well as tips for adding video to your project, are also covered.

Since multimedia gives you the ability to present information in a variety of ways, let the content drive the selection of media for each chunk of information to be presented. Use traditional text and graphics where appropriate; add animation when "still life" won't get your message across; add audio when further explanation is required; resort to video only when all other methods pale by comparison.

13

David A. Ludwig, Interactive Learning Designs

Obtaining Video Clips

If your project will include video, consider whether you should shoot new footage or acquire preexisting content for your video clips. There are many sources for film and video clips: a friend's home movies may suffice, or you can go to a "stock" footage house or a television station or movie studio. But acquiring footage that you do not own outright can be a nightmare—it is expensive, and licensing rights and permissions may be difficult, if not impossible, to obtain. Each second of video could cost $50 to $100 or more to license. Even a "public domain clip" from the National Archives will cost a minimum of $125 to copy the footage, and the turnaround time can take up to six weeks.

On some projects, you will have no choice but to pay the price for required footage. If it is absolutely essential that your project include a clip of Elvis Presley crooning "You Ain't Nothing but a Hound Dog," and an Elvis impersonator just won't do, you will have to negotiate for rights to use the real thing. If your budget can't cover the cost of licensing a particular video clip, you may want to consider using other alternatives: locating a less expensive archival video source, using a series of still images rather than video, or shooting your own video. If you shoot your own video for a project, make sure you have releases from all persons who appear or speak and permission to use the audio effects and music you weave into it. Licensing, permissions, and legal issues are discussed more fully in Chapter 19.

Before you head out to the field with your camcorder in hand, it is important to understand at least the basics of video recording and editing, as well as the constraints of using video in a multimedia project. The remainder of this chapter will help you to understand how video works and will provide practical guidelines for shooting your own videos.

How Video Works

When light reflected from an object passes through a video camera lens, that light is converted into an electronic signal by a special sensor called a charge-coupled device, or CCD. Top-quality broadcast cameras may have as many as three CCDs to improve the resolution of the camera. The signal from the camera contains three channels of color information (red, green, and blue) and synchronization pulses (sync). If each channel of color information is transmitted as a separate signal, the signals are called RGB, which is the preferred method for higher-quality and professional video work. The video signal can also be split into two separate chroma channels and a brightness channel, to make component video. If the signals are mixed together and carried on a single cable, it is a composite of the three color channels and the sync signal; this system yields less-precise color definition, which cannot be manipulated or color corrected as much as an RGB signal.

The video signal is delivered to the Video In connector of a VCR, where it is recorded on magnetic videotape. One or two channels of sound may also be recorded on the tape. The video signal is written to tape by a spinning recording head that changes the local magnetic properties of the tape's surface in a series of long diagonal stripes. Because the head follows a helical path, this is called helical scan recording. As illustrated in Figure 13-1, each stripe represents information for one field of a video frame. A single video frame is made up of two fields that are interlaced.

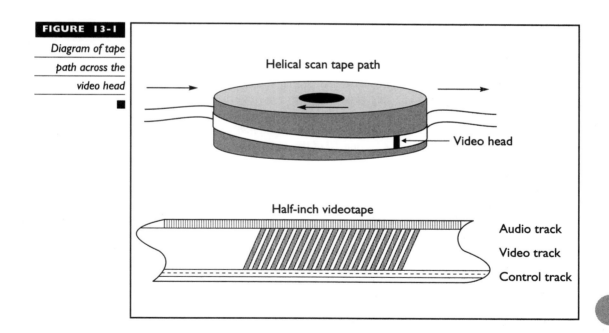

FIGURE 13-1

Diagram of tape path across the video head

Helical scan tape path

Video head

Half-inch videotape

Audio track

Video track

Control track

First Person

Surf Alligators live within the cusps of breaking technology waves. They can be snuffed with good knowledge, tools, and a network of colleagues willing to answer arcane questions. Catching these alligators requires the patience of Costa Rican beach children who cast unbaited three-barbed hooks into the incoming waves to yank out their surprised and luckless silver prey.

My 19-inch RGB monitor, a Hitachi re-branded by both SuperMac and Silicon Graphics, has BNC inputs for red, green, and blue and requires that horizontal sync be superimposed on the green channel. This is supported by SuperMacs and other NuBus video cards at 8-bit color depth. I wanted the Quadra 840AV's internal video support for 19-inch monitors at 16-bits, claimed in Apple's literature. But no way would my monitor work, and it took four days of calling around to discover why. Sorry, no sync on green from that Quadra, they said. Throw the monitor away. Get one with more BNC inputs.

Apple's User Assistance Center (usually busy and not open at 1:00 a.m.) was of no help. My arcane questions were not in the annoying hierarchy of voice message help, and it took two days to get hold of a real person to tell me the answer wasn't in her data bank. I felt like trolling with those Costa Rican fish hooks across the many rows of phone-answering cubicles at the Assistance Center, and yanking real hard.

Real information was finally forthcoming when I contacted two guys on Apple's Quadra hardware team through AOL and AppleLink. They had docs that explained all and included the peculiar sensing codes (pins 4, 7, and 10 of the 15-pin monitor connector) used by the Quadra's built-in video to automatically adjust to most monitors. I felt 100 percent better when I knew the WHY of it, even though I had to buy a new monitor.

Every time you upgrade your computer hardware, and occasionally when you upgrade your software, you are likely to attract surf alligators. These perils aren't like the steep learning curves where with effort you can incrementally improve your skill; they are brutally mechanical and test you in other ways: either you know it or you don't. If you don't know it, it won't work. Period.

From "Alligators," a monthly column written by Tay Vaughan for Morph's Outpost, October, 1993
Author's Note: By 1998, small and inexpensive cable adapters were widely available with lots of little dip switches to set the TTL signals Apple uses to declare monitor size and frequency, and for mixing sync onto the green channel.

Audio is recorded on a separate straight-line track at the top of the videotape, although with some recording systems (notably for 3/4-inch tape and for 1/2-inch tape with high-fidelity audio) sound is recorded helically between the video tracks. At the bottom of the tape is a control track containing the pulses used to regulate speed. Tracking is fine adjustment of the tape so that the tracks are properly aligned as the tape moves across the playback head.

A video cassette recorder can also add the video and sound signals to a subcarrier and modulate them into a radio frequency in the FM broadcast band. This is the NTSC, PAL, or SECAM signal available at the Antenna

Out connector of a VCR (these signal standards are explained in the next section). Usually you can choose between Channel 3 or Channel 4 frequencies, and the resulting signal or picture can be viewed on a television. Many television sets provide a separate composite signal connector to avoid the unnecessary step of modulating and demodulating the signal into the broadcast frequency bands.

Colored phosphors on the screen glow red, green, or blue when they are energized by the electron beam. Because the intensity of the beam varies as it moves across the screen, some colors glow brighter than others. Finely tuned magnets around the picture tube aim the electrons precisely onto the phosphor screen while the intensity of the beam is varied according to the video signal. All of these electronic activities work in concert to yield a television picture.

Broadcast Video Standards

Three broadcast and video standards and recording formats are commonly in use around the world: NTSC, PAL, and SECAM. Planned for international implementation during the first decade of the new millenium is a new standard called HDTV (high-definition television). Because these standards and formats are not easily interchangeable, it is important to know where your multimedia project will be used. A video cassette recorded in the United States will not play on a television set in any European country, even though the recording method and style of the cassette is "VHS." Likewise, tapes recorded in European PAL or SECAM formats will not play back on an NTSC video cassette recorder. Each system is based on a different standard that defines the way information is encoded to produce the electronic signal that ultimately creates a television picture. Multiformat VCRs can play back all three standards but typically cannot dub from one standard to another; dubbing between standards still requires high-end, specialized equipment.

NTSC

The United States, Japan, and many other countries use a system for broadcasting and displaying video that is based upon the specifications set forth by the 1952 National Television Standards Committee. These standards define a method for encoding information into the electronic signal that ultimately creates a television picture. As specified by the NTSC standard, a single frame of video is made up of 525 horizontal scan lines drawn onto the inside face of a phosphor-coated picture tube every 1/30th of a second by a fast-moving electron beam. The drawing occurs so fast that your eye perceives the image as stable. The electron beam actually makes two passes as it draws a single video frame, first laying down all the odd-numbered lines, then all the even-numbered lines. Each of these passes (which happen at a rate of 60 per second, or 60 Hz) paints a field. The process of building a single frame from two fields is called *interlacing*, a technique that helps to prevent flicker on television screens. Remember that computer monitors use *progressive-scan* technology and draw the lines of an entire frame in a single pass, without interlacing them.

Sometimes we define "NTSC" as "Never The Same Color."

Richard Santalesa, R&D Technologies

PAL

The Phase Alternate Line (PAL) system is used in the United Kingdom, Europe, Australia, and South Africa. PAL is an integrated method of adding color to a black-and-white television signal that paints 625 lines at a frame rate of 25 frames per second. Like NTSC, the even and odd lines are interlaced, each field taking 1/50th of a second to draw (50 Hz).

SECAM

The Sequential Color and Memory (SECAM) system is used in France, Russia, and a few other countries. Although SECAM is a 625-line, 50 Hz system, it differs greatly from both the NTSC and the PAL color systems in its basic technology and broadcast method. Often, however, TV sets sold in Europe utilize dual components and can handle both PAL and SECAM systems.

HDTV

High Definition Television (HDTV) is scheduled to be the next step in television technology. At this point in the development of this standard, it provides high resolution in a 16:9 aspect ratio (see Figure 13-2). This aspect ratio allows the viewing of Cinemascope and Panavision movies. There is contention between the broadcast and computer industries about whether to use interlacing or progressive-scan technologies. The broadcast industry has promulgated an ultra-high-resolution, 1920×1080 interlaced format to become the cornerstone of a new generation of high-end entertainment centers, but the computer industry would like to settle on a 1280×720 progressive-scan system for HDTV. While the 1920×1080 format provides more pixels than the 1280×720 standard, the refresh rates are quite different. The higher-resolution interlaced format delivers only half the picture every 1/60th of a second, and because of the interlacing, on highly detailed images there is a great deal of screen flicker at 30 Hz. The computer people argue that the picture quality at 1280×720 is superior and steady. These issues will be resolved by the Advanced Television Systems Committee (ATSC, http://www.atsc.org), which was formed to establish voluntary technical standards for advanced television systems in the United States. Broadcast HDTV signals are scheduled to arrive in selected markets in the United States during the fall of 1998.

---

warning   *Today's multimedia monitors typically use a screen pixel ratio of 4:3 (640x480), but the new HDTV standard specifies a ratio of 16:9 (1280x720), much wider than tall (see Figure 13-2). There is no easy way to stretch and shrink existing graphics material to fit this new aspect ratio, so new multimedia design and interface principles will need to be developed for HDTV presentations.*

Integrating Computers and Television

There is some confusion of terms when discussing video in computer and television contexts. Bear in mind that current television video is based on

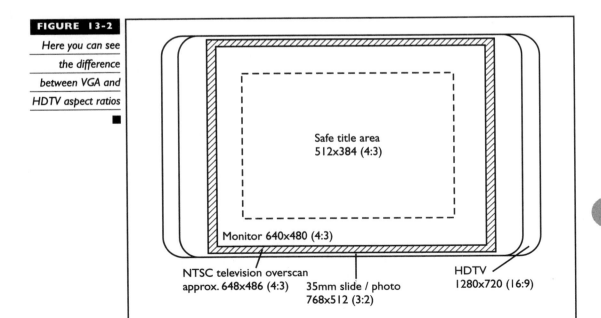

FIGURE 13-2

Here you can see the difference between VGA and HDTV aspect ratios

Safe title area
512x384 (4:3)

Monitor 640x480 (4:3)

NTSC television overscan
approx. 648x486 (4:3)

35mm slide / photo
768x512 (3:2)

HDTV
1280x720 (16:9)

13

analog technology and fixed international standards for the broadcast and display of images. Computer video is based on digital technology and other, more extensible standards for displaying images. In the early 2000s these two technologies—television and computer-based video—will merge, with the introduction of DVD and HDTV.

The First Step: Video Overlay Systems

The video/computer marriage began when computers were used simply to control analog video images from tape decks and videodisc players displayed on a television. A common computer-based training (CBT) configuration is still a dual-monitor workstation, where one monitor shows computer-managed training material and a television displays supporting video from a source that is controlled by the computer (see Figure 13-3). Trainees using these systems move their heads in a rhythmic tennis-match tempo set by the application's design metronome. As you might imagine, there was early pressure from CBT developers and vendors alike to integrate both the digital and analog images onto a single monitor.

To display analog video (television) images on a computer monitor, the video signal must first be converted from analog to digital form. A special video digitizing overlay board or hardware on the motherboard must be installed in your computer to take the video signal and convert it to digital information. The analog video signal (converted to digital information) and the computer's own digital graphics are mixed, yielding either a full screen of motion video or a window of video cut into the computer's normal display (see Figure 13-4). Video overlay boards offer real advantages over today's fully digital systems: the video is of excellent quality and can be full screen, full motion, and full color. On the other hand, the added cost of these boards and the videodisc players or tape decks required can double the price of your system.

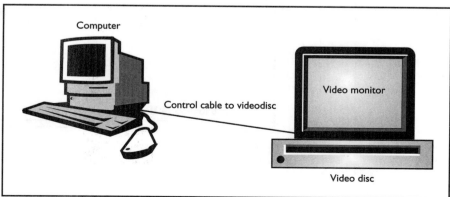

FIGURE 13-3

Videodisc players can be controlled by a computer

Computer

Control cable to videodisc

Video monitor

Video disc

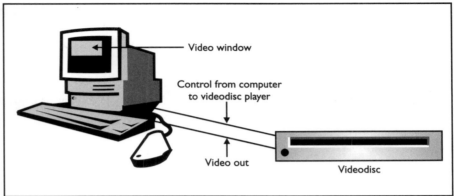

Video window

Control from computer to videodisc player

Video out

Videodisc

Some video overlay boards simply let you display video images on your computer screen, usually with several choices of window size. Better and more expensive boards offer visual effects such as freezing, fades, spins, mirrors, and chroma keys. Chroma keys allow you to choose a color or range of colors that become transparent, allowing the video image to be seen "through" the computer image. A newscast's weatherman is shot against a blue background that is made invisible when merged with the electronically generated image of the weather map. Some boards can capture a single 1/30-second frame and save it as a digitized still image, and some also provide control of stereo audio.

Commands such as play, forward, reverse, stop, rewind, and pause are sent over a serial cable connected between the computer and the videodisc player or tape deck. Videodisc players with serial communication ports (these are not the consumer variety) are most commonly used to supply the video image because these players provide "random access" to all the frames on the videodisc, allowing programmers to select with their software a video sequence to play at a given time and in a specific way. For example, a typical CAV (Constant Angular Velocity) format videodisc may contain as many as 54,000 individual frames of analog video. With the combination of video board special effects and the programmer's control of the videodisc player, multimedia designers have terrific power to mix eye-grabbing motion into their computer productions. Videodiscs can also be used to store many thousands of video-quality still images, and the computer can be programmed to display each image on demand using these same visual effects.

13

Video Capture Boards

Video overlay boards can often capture or digitize video frames as well as play them back from analog video sources, and they are commonly used for making QuickTime, MPEG, and AVI movies (see Chapter 7). Many video boards also incorporate audio input and sound management so that the audio portion of a video clip can be digitally interleaved and synced with the images during digitizing.

---

tip *Always import video and sound at the highest resolution available. You can reduce the resolution later according to your needs.*

Some video overlay boards offer hardware compression. On even the fastest PCs or Macintoshes, some frames will be lost or dropped during digitizing because the computer is overwhelmed by the demands of managing the video data as they come in. To relieve the processing bottleneck, some boards use specialized chips to speed up the digitizing process and can successfully digitize full-screen, full-motion video at 60 fields (or 30 frames) per second. Some video overlay boards also support output of NTSC video so that you can record what you see on the computer monitor to videotape.

---

tip *If your hardware is struggling to keep up with the digitizing process, shut down all unnecessary programs and network connections. This may make all the difference you need.*

Differences Between Computer and Television Video

Although most computer screens have the same 4:3 aspect ratio as a television screen, a typical computer screen scans only 480 horizontal lines from top to bottom, not the 525 or 625 lines of NTSC or PAL and SECAM television. Also, a computer monitor scans each line progressively, with no interlacing; the scan is full frame at a rate of typically 66.67 Hz or higher, compared to 60 Hz for a television frame that is only half the interlaced picture.

Overscan and the Safe Title Area

As illustrated in Figure 13-2, it is common practice in the television industry to broadcast an image larger than will fit on a standard TV screen so that the "edge" of the image seen by a viewer is always bounded by the TV's physical frame or bezel. This is called overscan. In contrast, computer monitors display a smaller image on the TV's picture tube (underscan). Consequently, when a digitized video image is displayed on an RGB screen, there is a border around the image; and when a computer screen is converted to video, the outer edges of the image will not fit on a TV screen. Only about 360 of the 480 lines of the computer screen will be visible.

tip   *Avoid using the outer 15 percent of the screen when producing computer-generated graphics and titles for use in television video. The safe title area, where your image will not be affected by overscanning, even in the worst conditions, is illustrated in Figure 13-2.*

Video Color

Color reproduction and display are different between televisions and computer monitors. Because computers use RGB component video (that is, they split colors into red, green, and blue signals), their colors are purer and more accurate than those seen on a television monitor. Consequently, colors used in a graphic image created for computer video may display differently when that image is transformed into NTSC television video.

Indeed, NTSC television uses a limited color palette and restricted luminance (brightness) levels and black levels (the richness of the blacks). Some colors generated by your computer that display fine on an RGB monitor may be "illegal" for display on an NTSC television. These colors are particularly apparent in shades of red and cause bleeding or noisy shimmering when displayed on a television. Most commercial broadcast facilities and TV studios will refuse to run video programs that include illegal colors. Filters to convert illegal colors to legal colors are available in image editing and processing applications such as Photoshop, ColorSense, and JAG II.

First Person

Captain's Log: We received some excellent design tips from Bernice T. Glenn:

As intermedia applications continue to proliferate, producers and designers need to know how to float between print and color pigment, digital color and RGB as viewed on a monitor, and analog color as viewed on a television screen. Color formulas for multimedia, especially when it is interactive, depend heavily on human factors.

Contrast—the degree of tonal difference between one color and another—is often more important when working with color on a computer screen. A combination of pure yellow with pure violet, or blue and orange, for example, will vibrate when viewed in RGB. On video, disturbing flickers, extraneous colors, and other artifacts usually appear on the borders between pure complementary colors. On top of that, colors that look great on your computer monitor may not even show up when transferred to video.

Important elements can be emphasized by using fully saturated colors against a neutral background, whose color may complement as a grayed-down tint of the color.

When readability is important, contrast in color saturation and value between the type and its background really works, using almost any color combination.

Red or green may need to be avoided as cue colors [for menu buttons and icons] because 8 percent of the population is color blind to some extent and cannot see reds or greens in their true color value.

From "Ask the Captain," a monthly column written by Tay Vaughan for **NewMedia** Magazine, January 1994.

13

When producing a multimedia project, you should consider whether it will be played back on an RGB monitor and/or on a conventional television set. If your work is destined, for example, for a set-top player such as SEGA Saturn, Sony PlayStation, Nintendo, or CD-I, choose your colors to meet the NTSC color specifications.

There are many variables in providing perfect colors on a television. End users can control hue and balance (an adjustment not available on most RGB monitors), and it is likely that few viewers of your project will have perfectly calibrated television sets. So you are fighting an uphill battle from the beginning.

It helps to do color corrections and editing on your computer, then view the corrected image on a real television screen, not just the RGB monitor. For this, you need a signal converter card or hardware on the motherboard that can provide NTSC output; video overlay cards often offer this feature.

---

tip   *A useful trick is to grab a standard broadcast color test bar using a video frame grabber, then save it as a PICT or TIFF image. When viewing the bar in Photoshop, for example, you can check the levels of each color by viewing red, green, and blue one at a time. The gradient of grays in the color bar should be smooth and even for each color channel.*

Interlacing Effects

In television, the electron beam actually makes two passes on the screen as it draws a single video frame, first laying down all the odd-numbered lines, then all the even-numbered lines—they are interlaced. On an RGB monitor, lines are painted one-pixel thick and are not interlaced. Single-pixel lines displayed on an RGB monitor look fine; on a television, these thin lines flicker brightly because they only appear in every other field. To prevent this flicker, make sure your lines are greater than two pixels thick and that you avoid typefaces that are very thin or have elaborate serifs. If you are capturing images from a video signal, you can filter them through a de-interlacing filter provided by image editing applications such as Photoshop or JAG II. With typefaces, interlacing flicker can often be avoided by anti-aliasing the type to slightly blur the edges of the characters. The term "interlacing" has a different meaning on the Web, where it describes the progressive display of lines of pixels as image data are downloaded, giving the impression that the image is coming from blurry into focus as increasingly more data arrive (see Chapter 15).

Working with Text and Titles

Titles for video productions can be created with an analog character generator, but your computer can do this digitally using video and image editing software. Here are some suggestions for creating good titles:

- Fonts for titles should be plain, sans serif, and bold enough to be easily read.

- When you are laying text onto a dark background, use white or a light color for the text.

- Use a drop shadow to help separate the text from the background image.

- Never use black or colored text on a white background.

- Do not kern your letters too tightly.

- If you use underlining or drawn graphics, always make your lines at least two pixels wide. If you use a one-pixel-wide line (or a width measured in an odd number of pixels), the line will flicker when transferred to video due to interlacing.

- Use parallel lines, boxes, and tight concentric circles sparingly. When you use them, draw them large and with thick lines.

- Avoid colors that are too hot.

- Neighboring colors should be markedly different in intensity. For example, use a light blue and a dark red, but not a medium blue and a medium red.

- Keep your graphics and titles within the safe area of the screen. Remember that televisions overscan computer output (see the earlier section, "Differences Between Computer and Television Video").

- Bring titles on slowly, keep them on screen for a sufficient interval, and then fade them out.

- Avoid making busy title screens; use more pages instead.

Shooting and Editing Video

To add full-screen, full-motion video to your multimedia project, you will need to invest in specialized hardware and software or purchase the services

13

of a professional video production studio. In many cases, a professional studio will also provide editing tools and post-production capabilities that you cannot duplicate with your Macintosh or PC.

Expensive professional video equipment and services may not yield proportionately greater benefits than if you used consumer-grade equipment. As with audio equipment (see Chapter 10), you need to make balancing decisions using Vaughan's Law of Multimedia Minimums. Most likely, your goal is to expend resources without diminishing returns—to produce multimedia that is adequate and does its job, but doesn't break your bank. If you can, experiment with various combinations of video recording and playback devices hooked to your video digitizing hardware, and test the results using your multimedia authoring platform. You can do a great deal of satisfactory work with consumer-grade video cameras and recording equipment if you understand the limitations of the technology.

Software tools for editing and working with digital video on the Macintosh and PC are described in detail in Chapter 7.

Video Tips

Listed below are some tips for shooting video for your multimedia project.

Shooting Platform

Never underestimate the value of a steady shooting platform. A classic symbol of amateur home movies is shaky camera work. Using a tripod or even placing the camera on a stable platform, such as a rolled-up sweater on the hood of a car, can improve a shot. With a little care, and careful adjustment of the lockdown screws, a sturdy conventional tripod can do wonders. If you must shoot hand-held, try to use a camera with an electronic image stabilization feature for static shots—a "steady-cam" balancing attachment—or use camera moves and a moving subject to mask your lack of steadiness.

Lighting

Perhaps the greatest difference between professional camcorders and consumer camcorders is their ability to perform at low light levels. With proper lighting, however, it may be difficult for uninitiated viewers to differentiate between shots taken with an expensive Betacam SP camcorder and a Hi-8 camcorder. Using a simple floodlight kit, or even just being sure that daylight illuminates the room, can improve your image.

Onboard battery lights for camcorders can be useful, but only in conditions where the light acts as a "fill light" to illuminate the details of a subject's face. As in photography, good lighting techniques separate amateurs from professionals in video shoots.

Illustrated in Figure 13-5 is a screen from The Lighting Lab (a project available on the installer CD-ROM of Adobe's Premiere). The standard lighting arrangement of a studio is displayed with fill, key, rim, and background lights. Changing any of these lights can make a dramatic difference in the shot. This Macromedia Director project uses a QuickTime movie containing several hundred single-frame images of the model as she is lighted by every permutation of lamp and intensity; clicking a light switch instantly shows the effect of that combination. If you are not convinced that lighting is critical to the success of a photo or video shoot, it will become immediately clear with this exercise!

Chroma Key or Blue Screen

A useful tool easily implemented in most digital video editing applications is "blue screen," "Ultimatte," or "chroma key" editing. When Captain

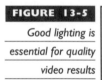

FIGURE 13-5

Good lighting is essential for quality video results

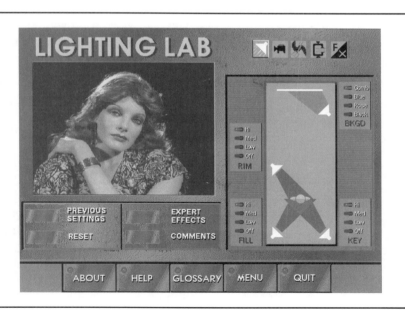

13

Picard of *Star Trek* fame walks on the surface of the moon, it is likely that he is actually walking on a studio set in front of a screen or wall painted blue. Actually placing Picard on the moon was, no doubt, beyond the budget of the shoot, but it could be "faked" using blue screen techniques. After shooting the video of Picard's walk against a blue background and shooting another video consisting of the desired background moonscape, the two videos were mixed together: wherever there was blue in the Picard shot, it was replaced by the background image, frame by frame.

Blue screen is a popular technique for making multimedia titles because expensive sets are not required. Incredible backgrounds can be generated using 3-D modeling and graphic software, and one or more actors, vehicles, or other objects can be neatly layered onto that background. Applications such as VideoShop and Premiere provide this capability on Macintoshes and PCs.

When you are shooting blue screen, be sure that the lighting of the screen is absolutely even; fluctuations in intensity will make this "key" appear choppy or broken. Shooting in daylight, letting the sun illuminate the screen, will mitigate this problem. Also be careful about "color spill." If your actors stand too close to the screen, the colored light reflecting off it will spill onto them, and parts of their body will key out. While adjustments in most applications can compensate for this, the adjustments are limited. Beware of fine detail, such as hair or smoke, that wisps over the screen; this does not key well.

Figure 13-6 shows frames taken from a video of an actor shot against blue screen on a commercial stage. The video was digitized, the blue background was removed from each frame, and the actor himself was turned into a photo-realistic animation that walked, jumped, pointed, and ran from a dinosaur.

Composition

The general rules for shooting quality video for broadcast use apply to multimedia.

Shooting video for playback from CD-ROM in a small computer window, it is best to avoid wide panoramic shots. The effect of sweeping panoramas is lost in small windows. Use close-ups and medium shots, head-and-shoulders or even tighter. Depending upon the compression algorithm used (see the section on video compression later in the chapter), consider also the amount of motion in the shot: the more a scene changes from frame to frame, the more "delta" information needs to be transferred from the computer's memory to the screen, and the slower the playback speed will be. Keep the camera still instead of panning and zooming; let the subject add the motion to your shot, walking, turning, talking.

FIGURE 13-6

FIGURE 13-6

This walking,

jumping, and

pointing actor was

videotaped against

a blue screen

■

Taking Care of Your Tapes

warning   *Your original videotapes are irreplaceable, so always make a backup copy of these tapes before you begin editing—tapes can break, be erased, or be eaten up by machinery.*

- Always fast-forward new tapes to the end and then rewind them, a technique known as "packing," to make sure that tape tension is even from beginning to end. Unequal tape tension can cause timing and editing problems.

- Black-stripe your tape by running it through the recorder once with the lens cap on and without audio input. Only black and a uniform control track is recorded. Later, during editing, blank spots in your video program will be a quiet black instead of snowy noise.

- Before you begin editing, always remove the break-off tab on the back of your original video cassettes, to avoid accidental erasure or overwriting.

- Editing videotape requires a lot of shuttling backward and forward, and this can deform the tape. For best results, do not reuse 8 mm video cassettes.

13

Recording Formats

S-VHS Video

In S-VHS video, color and luminance information are kept on two separate tracks. The result is a definite improvement in picture quality. This standard is also used in Hi-8. Although basically oriented toward consumers, this format is gaining rapid acceptance among lower-end broadcasters. Still, if your ultimate goal is to have your project accepted by broadcast stations, this would not be the best choice.

Component (YUV)

In the early 1980s, Sony began to experiment with a new portable professional video format based on Betamax. Called Betacam, it required speeding up the tape considerably (a 2-hour tape was used up in 20 minutes) and laying the signal on the tape in three channels, one for red, one for blue, and one for luminance information. The resulting format (called "component") produced images that had none of the problems of traditional composite video such as color shift and bleed and crawling edges on graphics. This has evolved into Betacam SP, which features four channels of audio and is superior to 1-inch and even the D-2 digital format in some cases. Though Panasonic has developed their own standard based on a similar technology, called "MII," Betacam SP has become the industry standard for professional video field recording. This format may soon be eclipsed by a new digital version called "Digital Betacam." Featuring four channels of CD-quality audio, its video quality is almost equal to D-1 digital.

Betacam SP is without a doubt *the* choice for the broadcast industry. No format is so widely used and praised. Looking at a typical jerky, one-quarter screen QuickTime movie in a multimedia title, you may think shooting on Betacam SP would be overkill. But you should start thinking to the next wave, when full screen/full motion becomes a reality and the difference between S-VHS or Hi-8 and Betacam becomes apparent.

Component Digital

Around the same time Sony was developing Betacam, they also began research into digital video, where the signal was converted to digital information before it was recorded as bits and bytes. The advantages were many, including better color and image resolution and an ability to make almost unlimited copies without loss of quality. The result of this research was D-1, or "Component Digital." Using a 19 mm (3/4-inch) tape, and recording the signal in a digital version of the component technology developed for Betacam, it quickly proved itself as the format of choice for graphics. Although it is the oldest of digital video formats, D-1 is the standard by which all others are compared. It has most recently spawned DCT (from Ampex), D-5 (from Panasonic), and Digital Betacam (from Sony).

D-1 is at the pinnacle of NTSC video and is the mastering standard of choice among high-end editing facilities. However, this quality comes with an extremely high price tag (a Quantel Henry editing system costs over $900,000 and can only work with 15 minutes of video). The result is that this format really only fits super-high-end broadcast projects and not your standard multimedia title.

Composite Digital

Although D-1 was a vastly superior recording format, its steep price scared away broadcasters; recording decks, for example, cost $110,000 or more. To reduce hardware costs, other less expensive formats were developed to record an NTSC composite signal in digital form: D-2 and D-3 (from Panasonic).

Though surpassed in quality by D-1, composite digital may be the most common digital standard for broadcast and editing facilities. Again, this format is more expensive to work with than is justified for multimedia.

Video Hardware Resolutions

Video horizontal resolution is the number of lines of detail a camera is able to reproduce; this aspect is not to be confused with the vertical scan lines on a TV set. The lens used and the number, size, and quality of the CCDs determine this resolution. Poor resolution and image quality when using consumer-grade equipment is usually the result of an inferior lens, cheaper circuit design, and shoddy video record heads.

The following table provides typical resolutions offered by various video recording hardware systems:

Video Type	Resolution
8 mm	230
VHS	240
3/4-SP	330
S-VHS	400
Hi-8	400
Beta-SP	550
MII	550
Broadcast-quality	1000

13

Consumer-Grade Equipment

Consumer-grade video equipment is designed for mass production and low manufacturing cost. In general, it is easier to use than industrial-grade or broadcast-quality equipment but is not built to suffer wear and tear. The tape transport mechanisms are both fragile and imprecise. VCRs that incorporate special circuits to enhance sharpness provide a superior perceived picture image than do regular VCRs (some less-expensive VCRs do not have these circuits). Both Beta- and VHS-type recorders are available with high-fidelity (hi-fi) sound with a dynamic range of up to 90 dB. Hi-fi sound is recorded diagonally on the tape between the video scans (but lower on the tape), so video and audio are recorded at the same time.

The High-Band 8 mm (known as Hi-8) and Super VHS (known as S-VHS) formats split the composite video signal into other components to provide a higher-quality signal. Two additional channels are added, one containing luminance or brightness information (Y channel), and one containing chroma or color intensity information (C channel). Cameras and camcorders working in the Hi-8 and S-VHS formats use a four-pin DIN or S connector and produce pictures that are far superior to those of regular VHS and 8 mm systems, especially when viewed on a television or monitor designed for these formats.

Most S-VHS and 3/4-inch industrial equipment have built-in noise reduction circuitry to overcome the poor audio quality inherent in consumer-grade VHS decks. The regular 8 mm tape decks, however, employ a recording method similar to that used for digital audio tape (DAT). Audio is digitized and recorded on a track separate from the video signal, providing a dynamic range of about 88 dB.

Hi-8 is the most widely accepted tape format used for industrial and corporate video communications. One reason for this is the wide availability of Sony's Video System Control Architecture (VISCA), a platform-independent command language that lets you control up to seven video peripherals from a personal computer. With VISCA-compatible hardware, any 8 mm or VHS consumer deck or camcorder can be controlled through the computer's serial port. Working with video-capture and movie-making digitizer boards, video can be imported into a project, assembled and stored, and later printed to videotape. VISCA includes the V-Box, a computer/video interface for controlling playback and recording devices, and the V-Deck, a computer-controllable Hi-8 VCR. For video images that will be scaled to smaller windows than full screen, standard VHS format recording will work fine. Super VHS is better yet, and Hi-8 is probably the best you can do with consumer-grade equipment.

---

tip   *When you shop for a new camcorder, exercise and test several camera/recorder combinations, then view the result on a good video monitor (not a television). You will see a difference.*

Making Tape Copies

If you ever plan to copy the tape you make during a production shoot to another tape (say, for a promotion or demo), use at least Super VHS. This will prevent your copies from bleeding colors and being disappointingly fuzzy due to signal loss. Better yet, use Hi-8, which will allow unlimited VHS copies to be made without degradation. If you plan to do video editing on tape (not on the computer), Hi-8 is the consumer-grade option of choice.

Successful copying of video (dubbing) depends upon the format of the tape recording and the quality of equipment used. Copying from Hi-8 to VHS, for example, produces excellent results. Copying from Beta-SP to Super VHS gets good results as long as the Y/C connections are maintained. Dubbing from 1-inch tape to other formats works well, copy after copy.

When copying from VHS to VHS, color smear and loss of image resolution are very noticeable. The bandwidth of the VHS signal is limited, and during dubbing much information is lost—even in a first generation dub from a Beta-SP edited master to a VHS submaster. A second generation dub (from a VHS master to a first copy) is proportionately worse. Yet another copy of the copy (a third generation) produces a tape that is practically unrecognizable.

Always dub in SP mode, never in LP or SLP, because the faster the video heads write on the tape, the better the recorded image will be. Always use the highest-quality tape to prevent clogging the video heads with loose magnetic particles.

Video Window Size

When you digitize a video image and shrink it to, say, half- or quarter-size, you will notice improvement in the perceived sharpness. This also happens when you switch from watching television on a 19-inch screen to watching a 12-inch screen. The image becomes crisper because the scan lines are physically much tighter. So VHS will work fine in these circumstances. Super VHS and Hi-8 will provide better full-screen images, but your digitizing video board must be able to utilize this resolution; in digitizing the video signal, the board dithers the image on the fly.

13

Editing with Consumer VCRs

Using two consumer-grade VCRs for editing will cause glitches, picture noise, and rolling, because the VCRs will not be in sync. You may also experience considerable loss in quality when dubbing, and possibly an audio lag. With consumer-grade decks, it is impossible to accurately preroll a tape prior to editing a scene.

To solve this problem, you have to use the tape counter on both the playback deck and the record deck, to reverse both tapes a given distance and then start them playing at exactly the same time. When they are both at speed and have reached the appropriate counter number for your edit, depress the Record button on the recording machine (or release it from Pause mode). If your edit comes in too late, you will have to reverse both machines and try again; if you cut into the scene too soon, you will have to repeat the entire edit of the previous shot and then try again. This can be tedious and time consuming—even if your decks have flying erase heads to avoid edit glitches—and the results may be disappointing.

To make fancy transitions, cross-fades, and wipes between scenes, you need two source players feeding into a switcher, all of which are in sync. This is called A/B roll editing. For this you need a time base corrector (TBC) for each VCR. This device corrects timing errors present in all VCRs and replaces the sync with one generated by the TBC.

Two terms are often heard at editing facilities: off-line editing and on-line editing. In off-line editing, you spend most of your time making a rough cut—a quick assemblage of everything you decide to use. Then you make an edit decision list (EDL) of all the scenes on your rough cut, the name of the original cassette where the scene is located, and the times of your edit in-points and out-points, using time codes. You take this list and your original footage to an on-line post-production facility that has expensive equipment to auto assemble your tape according to the EDL, inserting transitions, wipes, graphics, titles, audio, and music segments as required. The result is an edited master.

Editing with two VCRs is less common today in multimedia production than editing with digital editing software designed specifically for use on Macintoshes and PCs, such as Premiere, After Effects, or VideoFusion. In either case, an edit decision list is useful.

Digital Video

The next evolution toward fully integrating motion video computers eliminates the analog television form of video from the multimedia delivery platform. If a video clip can first be converted from analog to digital, then stored as data on a hard disk, CD-ROM, or other mass-storage device, that clip can be played back on the computer's monitor without overlay boards, videodisc players, or second monitors. This playback is accomplished using software architectures such as QuickTime or Video for Windows (replaced by Microsoft's newer Active Movie for Windows), which are explained in Chapters 5 and 7.

As a multimedia producer or developer, you will need to convert your video source material from its common analog form (videotape) to a digital form manageable by the end user's computer system. So an understanding of analog video and some special hardware must remain in your multimedia toolbox.

Analog to digital conversion of video can often be accomplished using the video overlay hardware described above, but to repetitively digitize a full-screen color video image every 1/30 second and store it to disk or RAM severely taxes both Macintosh and PC processing capabilities—special hardware, compression software, and massive amounts of digital storage space are required. And repetitively reading from disk and displaying to the monitor the full-screen color images of motion video, at a rate of one frame every 1/30 second, taxes the computational and display power of both the Macintosh and the PC.

The final evolutionary step to fully digital video will not occur until the acquisition and recording of video becomes entirely a digital procedure and analog videotape is removed from the process.

Video Compression

To digitize and store a 10-second clip of full-motion video in your computer requires transfer of an enormous amount of data in a very short amount of time. Reproducing just one frame of digital video component video at 24-bits requires almost 1MB of computer data; 30 seconds of video will fill a gigabyte hard disk. Full-size, full-motion video requires that the computer deliver data at about 30MB per second—this is simply more than Macintoshes and PCs can handle. Typical hard disk drives transfer data at only about 1MB per second, and quad-speed CD-ROM players at a paltry 600K per second. This overwhelming technological bottleneck is currently being overcome by digital video compression schemes or *codecs* (coders/decoders). A codec is the algorithm used to compress a video for delivery and then decode it in real-time for fast playback. Real-time video compression algorithms such as MPEG, P*64, DVI/Indeo, JPEG, Cinepak, ClearVideo, RealVideo, and VDOwave are now available to compress digital video information at rates that range from 50:1 to 200:1. JPEG, MPEG, and P*64 compression schemes use Discrete Cosine Transform (DCT), an encoding

13

algorithm that quantifies the human eye's ability to detect color and image distortion. All of these codecs employ lossy compression algorithms.

. . . .

http://www.CodecCentral.com

Where detailed information about video codecs can be found

In addition to compressing video data, *streaming* technologies are being implemented to provide reasonable quality low-bandwidth video on the Web. By starting playback of a video as soon as enough data have transferred to the user's computer to sustain this playback, users do not have to wait for an often very large file to download. Microsoft, RealNetworks, VXtreme, VDOnet, Xing, Precept, Cubic, Motorola, Vivo, Vosaic, and Oracle are actively pursuing the commercialization of streaming technology on the Web. RealNetworks (http://www.real.com) claims that by 1998 more than 28 million copies of its RealPlayer software had been downloaded electronically and more than 100,000 hours per week of live audio and video content were being broadcast over the Web using their RealAudio and RealVideo technology, and more than 150,000 Web pages were using RealNetworks' streaming software. Tools such as Terran Interactive's Media Cleaner Pro (http://www.terran-int.com—see Figure 13-7) allow you to customize the movie and audio compression chores and optimize your media for either CD-ROM or Web delivery.

QuickTime, Apple's software-based architecture for seamlessly integrating sound, animation, text, and video (data that change over time), is often thought of as a compression standard, but it is really much more than that. See Chapter 6 for a detailed discussion about QuickTime.

MPEG

The MPEG standard has been developed by the Moving Picture Experts Group (http://drogo.cselt.stet.it/mpeg/), a working group convened by the International Standards Organization (ISO) and the International Electrotechnical Commission (IEC) to create standards for digital representation of moving pictures and associated audio and other data. MPEG1 and MPEG2 are the current standards. Using MPEG1, you can deliver 1.2 Mbps (megabits per second) of video and 250 Kbps (kilobits per second) of two-channel stereo audio using CD-ROM technology. MPEG2, a completely different system from MPEG1, requires higher data rates (3 to 15 Mbps) but delivers higher image resolution, picture quality, interlaced video formats, multi-resolution scalability, and multichannel audio features.

FIGURE 13-7

Media Cleaner Pro from Terran Interactive is a powerful post-production tool for optimizing motion video and audio compression and delivery

MPEG may become the method of choice for encoding motion images because it has become widely accepted for both Internet and DVD-Video (see Chapters 5 and 15). For MPEG1, hardware playback will become common on motherboards and video cards. Software decompression algorithms for MPEG1, while slower than hardware solutions, are incorporated in QuickTime, and Microsoft has licensed a driver from MediaMatics for use with Windows 95. MPEG2 requires dedicated hardware for playback but looks better than a television screen. Players are widely available for playback of MPEG video on the Web.

MPEG-4 is in development and will provide a new content-based method for assimilating multimedia elements. It will also offer not only indexing, hyperlinking, querying, browsing, uploading, downloading, and deleting functions but also "hybrid natural and synthetic data coding," which will enable harmonious integration of natural and synthetic audiovisual objects. With MPEG-4, multiple views and multiple soundtracks of a scene, as well as stereoscopic and 3-D views, will be available, making virtual reality workable.

MPEG-7, on the standards horizon, goes a step further by integrating information about the image, sound, or motion video elements being used in a composition—information carried already in the MPEG-4 standard—with *how* these elements are being used. MPEG-7, for example, may include classes for facial expressions, personality characteristics, or any number of content-related variables.

13

....

http://www.mpeg.org

All about MPEG

::

:::::::::::::::::::::::::::

MPEG-4 video aims at providing standardized core technologies allowing efficient storage, transmission, and manipulation of video data in multimedia environments. This is a challenging task given the broad spectrum of requirements and applications in multimedia. In order to achieve this broad goal rather than a solution for a narrow set of applications, functionalities common to clusters of applications are under the scope of consideration. Therefore, video activities in MPEG-4 aim at providing solutions in the form of tools and algorithms enabling functionalities such as efficient compression, object scalability, spatial and temporal scalability, error resilience. The standardized MPEG-4 video will provide a toolbox containing tools and algorithms bringing solutions to the above mentioned functionalities and more.

:::::::::::::::::::::::::::::::::

From Document ISO/IEC JTC1/SC29/WG11 N1410
(Description of MPEG-4)

DVI/Indeo

DVI (also known as "Indeo") is a proprietary, programmable compression/decompression technology based on the Intel i750 chip set. This hardware consists of two VLSI (Very Large Scale Integrated) chips to separate the image processing and display functions.

Two levels of compression and decompression are provided by DVI: Production Level Video (PLV) and Real Time Video (RTV). PLV is a proprietary asymmetrical compression technique for encoding full-motion color video; it requires that compression be performed by Intel at its facilities or at licensed encoding facilities set up by Intel. RTV provides image quality comparable to frame-rate (motion) JPEG and uses a symmetrical, variable-rate compression. PLV and RTV both use variable compression rates.

DVI's algorithms can compress video images at ratios between 80:1 and 160:1. DVI will play back video in full-frame size and in full color at 30 frames per second, whereas JPEG provides only an acceptable image in a small picture window on the computer screen. When tied in with a mainframe computer, DVI playback approaches the quality of broadcast video.

Other Compression Methods

P*64 (pronounced "pee star sixty-four") is a video telephone conferencing standard for compressing audio and motion video images, from the

International Telegraph and Telephone Consultative Committee (CCITT). P*64 complies with CCITT's recommendation H.261 and incorporates multiplexing, demultiplexing, framing of data, transmission protocol and bandwidth congruence, and call setup and teardown. Encoder products from telephone service providers such as AT&T and Northern Telecom use P*64 to deliver wide-spectrum telecommunication capabilities incorporating high-speed and very high throughput data transmission over both copper and fiber-optic digital telephone networks.

P*64 encodes real-time motion video and audio for transmission over copper or fiber-optic telephone lines at 30 frames per second, at a bandwidth between 40 Kbps and 4 Mbps.

Other compression systems are being developed by companies including Kodak, Sony, Storm Technology, Iterated Systems, Zing, and C-Cube Micro-systems, and rapid progress is being made in this field.

Optimizing Video Files for CD-ROM

CD-ROMs provide an excellent distribution medium for computer-based video: they are inexpensive to mass produce, and they can store great quantities of information. CD-ROM players offer slow data transfer rates (see Chapter 20), but adequate video transfer can be achieved by taking care to properly prepare your digital video files. QuickTime and AVI video file formats are discussed in Chapter 6, and the multimedia authoring systems for integrating these digital video files into your project are discussed in Chapter 8. Without great care, these digital files may display poorly in low-bandwidth/high-compression environments.

- Limit the amount of synchronization required between the video and audio. With Microsoft's AVI files, the audio and video data are already interleaved, so this is not a necessity, but with QuickTime files, you should "flatten" your movie. *Flattening* means you interleave the audio and video segments together.

- Use regularly spaced key frames, 10 to 15 frames apart, and temporal compression can correct for seek time delays. *Seek time* is how long it takes the CD-ROM player to locate specific data on the CD-ROM disc. Even fast 24× drives must spin up, causing some delay (and occasionally substantial noise).

- The size of the video window and the frame rate you specify dramatically affect performance. In QuickTime, 20 frames per second played in a 160×120-pixel window is equivalent to playing 10 frames per second in a 320×240 window. The more data that

13

have to be decompressed and transferred from the CD-ROM to the screen, the slower the playback.

■ Although interleaving CD-quality audio into your video production will theoretically yield the highest-quality sound, the volume of data required may be too great to transfer from the CD-ROM in real-time. Try a lower sampling rate and sample size to reduce the quantity of audio data.

■ The software compression algorithm you specify will make a dramatic difference in performance. The Cinepack algorithm, available within both AVI and QuickTime, is optimized for CD-ROM playback. But take care: it can take many hours of computation to compress just a few minutes of digital video.

■ Use Norton Speed Disk from Symantec to defragment your files before burning the master.

■ If you are working with QuickTime, consider using a specialized application such as Media Cleaner Pro to automatically optimize your digital video file for playback from CD-ROM.

Multi

> During the coming years, most multimedia experiences on the Internet will occur on the World Wide Web.

Predictions claim that more than 35 million

experience

media

part

5

Multimedia and the Internet

American households will be connected to the Internet by the year 2000.

network

Multi

Inside the event horizon of the
amazing World Wide Web
explosion are many uncertainties
and unsolved challenges.

Predictions claim that more than 35 million

connections

media

How the Internet Works

American households will be connected to the Internet by the year 2000.

network

T H E material covered in this chapter is designed to give you an overview of the Internet while describing particular features that may be useful to you as a developer of multimedia for the World Wide Web. This chapter does *not* provide details about technology for connecting and using the Internet, about setting up servers and hosts, about installing and using applications, or what to do when you are warned of the following:

 This program posts news to thousands of machines throughout the civilized world. Please be sure you know what you are doing.

Embarrassing yourself on the stage of the civilized world can be avoided by easy education—visit your local bookstore, where, along with the work you are now reading, you may discover as many as a hundred helpful volumes about all the simple and arcane aspects of the Internet. Buy one or two of these and dig in.

If you are already connected to the Internet, much of the documentation you may require can be found by surfing the Net itself. Use a search service such as those listed below. Look particularly for documents called FAQs (Frequently Asked Questions), because they contain answers.

http://www.yahoo.com
http://www.lycos.com
http://www.infoseek.com
http://www.webcrawler.com
http://www.excite.com
http://www.mckinley.com
http://www.savvy.cs.colostate.edu:2000
http://www.easypage.com/all4one
http://www.altavista.digital.com

Some search engines on the World Wide Web

History

The Internet began as a research network funded by the Advanced Research Projects Agency (ARPA) of the U.S. Defense Department, when the first node of the ARPANET was installed at the University of California at Los Angeles in September 1969.

By the mid-1970s, the ARPANET "internetwork" embraced more than 30 universities, military sites, and government contractors, and its user base expanded to include the larger computer science research community. By 1983, the network still consisted of but several hundred computers on only a few local area networks.

In 1985, the National Science Foundation (NSF) arranged with ARPA to support a collaboration of supercomputing centers and computer science researchers across the ARPANET. The NSF also funded a program for improving the backbone of the ARPANET, increasing its bandwidth from 56 Kbps to T-1 and then T-3 (see "Connections" a little later in the chapter) and branching out with links to international sites in Europe and the Far East.

In 1989, responsibility and management for the ARPANET was officially passed from military interests to the academically oriented NSF, and research organizations and universities (professors and students alike) became increasingly heavy users of this ever-growing "Internet." Much of the Internet's etiquette and rules for behavior (such as for sending e-mail and posting to newsgroups) was established during this time.

More and more private companies and organizations linked up to the Internet; by the mid-1990s, the Internet included connections to more than 60 countries and more than 2 million host computers with more than 15 million users worldwide. Commercial and business use of the Internet was not permitted until 1992, but businesses have since become its driving force. Predictions claim that more than 35 million American households will be connected to the Internet by the year 2000. Table 14-1 shows the explosive growth of the Internet from 1981 to 1998 measured by the number of hosts with IP addresses that connect to the Internet.

---

note   *The wizards at Network Wizards claim it is not possible to determine the exact size of the Internet, where hosts are located, or how many users there are. A single network number could span many countries, and a single domain may have hosts on multiple network numbers. A host used to be a single machine on the Net. However, the definition of a host has changed in recent years due to virtual hosting, where a single machine acts like multiple systems (and has multiple domain names and IP addresses).*

14

Date	Host Count	Domains	Date	Host Count	Domains
August 1981	213		January 1992	727,000	
May 1982	235		April 1992	890,000	
August 1983	562		July 1992	992,000	
October 1984	1,024		October 1992	1,136,000	
October 1985	1,961		January 1993	1,313,000	21,000
February 1986	2,308		April 1993	1,486,000	
November 1986	5,089		July 1993	1,776,000	26,000
December 1987	28,174		October 1993	2,056,000	
July 1988	33,000		January 1994	2,217,000	30,000
October 1988	56,000		July 1994	3,212,000	46,000
January 1989	80,000		October 1994	3,864,000	
July 1989	130,000		January 1995	4,852,000	71,000
October 1989	159,000		July 1995	6,642,000	120,000
October 1990	313,000		January 1996	9,472,000	240,000
January 1991	376,000		July 1996	12,881,000	488,000
July 1991	535,000		January 1997	16,146,000	828,000
October 1991	617,000		July 1997	19,540,000	1,301,000
			January 1998	29,670,000	

TABLE 14-1   *Explosion of the Internet, 1981 to 1998 (Source: Network Wizards at http://www.nw.com)* ∎

In 1998, Cyber Dialogue (http://www.cyberdialogue.com) reported the results of its American Internet User Survey: More than 41.5 million adults in the United States were actively using the Internet; 58 percent were male; 42 percent were female. Eighty-five percent of adults online used the Web and 75 percent used e-mail, and 51 percent used the Web on a daily basis. A NUA Internet Survey (http://www.nua.ie/surveys/how_many_online/index.html) estimates that a total of 101 million people were online world-wide at the beginning of 1998, with that number rising to 133 million by the end of the year 2000!

First Person

When I was a kid, I took it for granted that you could see a million stars in the summer sky, and it wasn't until much later that I discovered the truth: only a paltry few thousand stars are actually visible to the naked eye from Earth. While "millions" is a perfect number for a ten-year-old's perception of an infinite universe, the term needs definition. For example, what does "133 million users on the Internet in the year 2000" really mean? The following exercise might help: Start counting to a million, incrementing by one every second: (One) (Two) (Three).... In a minute, you will have counted to 60; in an hour, to 3,600. In 277.77 hours, you will reach a million—that's 11.57 24-hour days of nonstop counting, no pizza, no beer. You could try for the Guinness Book of Records, but you won't stay awake long enough!

Internetworking

In its simplest form, a *network* is a cluster of computers, with one computer acting as a server to provide network services such as file transfer, e-mail, and document printing to the client computers of that network. Using gateways and routers, a local area network (LAN) can be connected to other LANs to form a wide area network (WAN). These LANs and WANs can also be connected to the Internet through a server that provides both the necessary software for the Internet and the physical data connection (usually a high-bandwidth telephone line). Individual computers not permanently part of a network (a home computer or a laptop) can dial up to one of these Internet servers and, with proper identification and onboard client software, obtain an IP address on the Internet (see "IP Addresses and Data Packets" later in the chapter).

Internet Addresses

Let's say you get into a taxi at the train station in Trento, Italy, explain in English or Spanish or German or French that you wish to go to the Mozzi Hotel, and half an hour later you are let out of the car in a suburban wood—you have an address problem. You will quickly discover, as you return to the city in the back of a bricklayer's lorry to report your missing luggage, that you also have a serious language problem.

If you know how addresses work and understand the syntax of the Internet, you will likely not get lost and will save much time and expense during your adventures. You will also be able to employ shortcuts and work-arounds.

14

Top-Level Domains

When the original ARPANET protocols for communicating among computers were remade into the current scheme of TCP/IP (Transmission Control Protocol/Internet Protocol) in 1983, the Domain Name System (DNS) was developed to rationally assign names and addresses to computers linked to the Internet. *Top-level domains* were established as categories to accommodate all users of the Internet:

Com	Commercial entities
Edu	Four-year degree-granting colleges and universities (schools and two-year colleges register in the country domain)
Gov	U.S. federal government agencies (state and local agencies register in the country domain)
Int	Organizations established by international treaties and international databases
Mil	U.S. military
Net	Computers belonging to network providers
Org	Miscellaneous and nongovernment organizations
Two-letter country codes	Per the ISO 3166 List of Countries

In 1997, the International Ad Hoc Committee (http://www.isoc .org/whatsnew/itlds.html), made up of government, business, and academic Internet experts, agreed to create 7 new top-level domain names and set up 28 name registration organizations to administer the names worldwide. The following year, the U.S. Department of Commerce (http://www.ntia .doc.gov) proposed setting up a nonprofit organization in the United States to manage a similar scheme to increase available top-level domain names (without the .rec and .info names). Expect some or all of these names to be in use by the year 2000:

Web	Entities emphasizing activities related to the WWW
Arts	Entities emphasizing cultural and entertainment activities
Shop	Entities and businesses offering goods to purchase
Firm	Online companies and businesses
Nom	Personal sites
Rec	Entities emphasizing recreation/entertainment activities
Info	Entities providing information services

Companies such as Microsoft, Apple, and IBM have *second-level domain* addresses that read microsoft.com, apple.com, and ibm.com—they are commercial (com) operations. Government (gov) agencies such as the Federal Bureau of Investigation, the Internal Revenue Service (a branch of the United States Treasury Department), and the White House have addresses that read fbi.gov, irs.ustreas.gov (a *third-level* address), and whitehouse.gov.

Concerns about "rights" and "ownership" of domains are inappropriate. It is appropriate to be concerned about "responsibilities" and "service" to the community.

> J. Postel, from the Network Working Group RFC 1591, March 1994

Many second-level domains contain huge numbers of computers and user accounts representing local, regional, and even international branches as well as various internal business and management functions. So the Internet addressing scheme provides for subdomains that can contain more subdomains. Like a finely carved Russian matryoshka doll, at the epicenter of a cluster of domains live individual workstations.

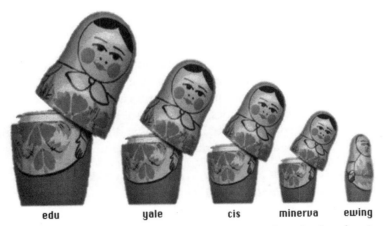

edu   yale   cis   minerva   ewing

Within the education (edu) domain containing hundreds of universities and colleges, for example, is a second-level domain for Yale University called yale. At that university are many schools and departments (medicine, engineering, law, business, computer science, etc.), and each of these entities in turn has departments and possibly subdepartments and many users. These departments operate one or even several servers to manage traffic to and from the many computers in their group and to the outside world. At Yale, the server for the Computing and Information Systems Department is named

14

cis. It manages about 11,000 departmental accounts—so many accounts that a cluster of subsidiary servers was installed to deal efficiently with the demand. These subsidiary servers are named minerva, morpheus, and mercury. Thus, minerva lives in the cis domain, which lives in the yale domain, which lives in the edu domain. Real people's computers are networked to minerva. Other real people are connected to the morpheus and mercury servers. The computer belonging to the Director of the Science and Engineering Computing Facility, Martin Ewing, is named **martin.ewing@minerva.cis.yale.edu**. To make things easy (exactly what computers are for), the mail system database at Yale maintains a master list of all its people. So as far as the outside world is concerned, the director's e-mail address can be simply **martin.ewing@yale.edu**; the database knows he is really connected to minerva. In e-mail headers, you may see the complete destination address listed as well as names of computers through which your mail may have been routed.

The levels of a domain name are separated by a period (spoken as "dot"); individual computers belonging to people are said to be "at" a domain (written with the @ sign). There are never any blank spaces in an Internet address, and while addresses on the Internet are normally case insensitive, conventional use dictates using all lowercase: the Internet will find **tay@timestream.com**, **TAY@TIMESTREAM.COM**, and **Tay@Timestream .Com** to be at the same address.

Maintenance and management of domain names (not including the country coded domains—see the next section) is the job of InterNIC. Originally a loose organization funded by the NSF to keep the domains organized, the InterNIC has contracted this service to a private company, Network Solutions, that charges an annual fee for registering and maintaining domain names on the Internet of $100 for two years. At the InterNIC site, you can apply for your own domain, check if a domain name is taken, and find out to whom a domain name is registered.

••

http://www.internic.net
ftp://rs.internic.net/rfc/rfc1591.txt

For more information about domain names and registration, check out the InterNIC site

The US Domain and Country Codes

The two-letter US domain is based on political boundaries and is used by federal, state, and local government agencies, community colleges, high schools, technical/vocational schools, private schools, elementary schools, libraries, fire and police departments, and regular citizens. Any computer in the United States can be in the US domain. Some fictitious examples might be

Statue_Liberty.NPS.Interior.FED.US	Federal agency
Senate.FED.US	U.S. Senate
Senate.STATE.PA.US	Pennsylvania state senate
Assembly.STATE.UT.US	Utah state assembly
dmv.state.ca.us	California Department of Motor Vehicles
Oakland.DMV.STATE.CA.US	Local office of DMV
Police.CI.Miami.FL.US	City department
fire.ci.weston.ma.us	City department
Sheriff.CO.Alameda.CA.US	County department
ccsf.cc.ca.us	Public community college
Lincoln-High.EH-Parish.K12.LA.US	Public school
GDA.PVT.K12.MA.US	Private school
Chevron.Richmond.CA.US	Business
LeFigaro.Portland.OR.US	Restaurant
Paddys.Boston.MA.US	Bar

* *

ftp://rs.internic.net/rfc/rfc1480.txt

The Internet RFC 1480 describes the hierarchical rules for addresses in the US domain

Two-letter country codes, based on the International Standards Organization (ISO) document ISO-3166, are used in the addresses of all computers located outside the United States. Each country has an administrator who is responsible for organizing the naming hierarchy within that country's domain. Some countries use categories similar to com, edu, and org. Others base their naming hierarchies on political boundaries, as in the US country code.

schmidt@cage.rug.ac.be	Professor at University of Gent, Belgium
smythe@fiqus.unl.edu.ar	Student at L.C.S.A, Argentina
smith@iskratel.si	Commercial account, Slovenia
smithe@idsc.gov.eg	Student at Cairo University, Egypt
smithy@udcf.gla.ac.uk	Researcher at University of Glasgow, Scotland
tsmith@library.usyd	.edu.au Scholar at University of Sydney, Australia

14

· ·

ftp://venera.isi.edu/in-notes/iana/assignments/country-codes
List of two-letter country codes

IP Addresses and Data Packets

When a stream of data is sent over the Internet by your computer, it is first broken down into packets by the Transmission Control Protocol. Each packet includes the address of the receiving computer, a sequence number ("this is packet #5"), error correction information, and a small piece of your data. After a packet is created by TCP, the Internet Protocol then takes over and sends the packet to its destination along a route that may include many other computers acting as forwarders. TCP/IP is two key Internet protocols working in concert.

The 32-bit address included in a data packet, the *IP address*, is the "real" Internet address. It is made up of four numbers separated by periods, for example, 140.174.162.10. Some of these numbers are assigned by Internet authorities, and some may be dynamically assigned by an Internet Service Provider (ISP) when a computer logs on from a dial-up account. There are domain name servers throughout the Internet whose sole job is to quickly look up domain name addresses in large distributed databases, convert them into IP addresses, and return them to you for insertion into your data packets. Every time you connect to **http://netscape.com** or send mail to **president@whitehouse.gov**, the domain name server is consulted and the destination address is converted to numbers.

---

tip *IP addresses and domain names can be used interchangeably. Thus, **allegiant.com** is the same Internet address as **204.212.150.2**. If you have trouble connecting to **http//:allegiant.com**, try **http//:204.212.150.2**. There are occasional problems with the Internet's DNS servers, and with the IP address, you may get connected immediately. With a Ping utility, or using the "whois" function in Unix, or by visiting InterNIC's site at **http://www.internic.org**, you can discover a domain's IP address.*

Connections

If your computer is connected to an existing network at an office or school, it is possible you are already connected to the Internet. Check with your system administrator about procedures for connecting to Internet services such as the World Wide Web; necessary browser software may already be installed on your machine. If you are an individual working from home, you will need a dial-up account to your office network or to an Internet Service Provider or an online service. You will also need a modem (see Chapter 5), an available telephone line, and software.

If you are connecting to the Internet through an online service such as America Online (AOL), CompuServe, Microsoft Network (MSN), or Prodigy (see Figure 14-1), you will need special software provided by that service. AOL provides WWW, FTP, and Gopher features (see "Internet Services" later in the chapter). CompuServe also provides ready access to the Internet. MSN software is built into Windows 95 and can be installed during Windows 95 setup.

- -

http://www.aol.com
http://www.compuserve.com
http://www.msn.com
http://www.prodigy.com
http://www.mediaone.com

Information about online services

For connecting to the Internet through an ISP, software typically consists of the PPP (Point-to-Point Protocol) application for dialing up and TCP/IP software for properly sending and receiving data once you are connected.

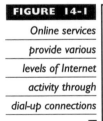

FIGURE 14-1

Online services

provide various

levels of Internet

activity through

dial-up connections

ISPs usually provide one or more POPs (Points of Presence), which is a local telephone number for connecting to the ISP's server. Figure 14-2 shows the PPP control panel for Macintosh; Figure 14-3 the Network Control Panel for Windows 95. Getting connected to the Internet can be a bit daunting, as there are many options to configure. Most ISPs offer detailed instructions and kits to make this job easy.

The Bandwidth Bottleneck

Bandwidth is how much data, expressed in bits per second, you can send from one computer to another in a given amount of time. The faster your transmissions (or the greater the bandwidth of your connection), the less time you will spend waiting for text, images, sounds, and animated illustrations to upload or download from computer to computer, and the more satisfaction you will have with your Internet experience. Table 14-2 lists the bandwidth of some common data transfer methods.

The bottleneck at a typical user's low-bandwidth modem connection is the most serious impediment to sending multimedia across the Internet. At low bandwidth, a page of text (3,000 bytes) can take less than a second to send, but an uncompressed 640×480, 8-bit/256-color image (about 300,000 bytes) can take a few minutes; an uncompressed 640×480, 24-bit/16 million-color image (about 900,000 bytes) can take many minutes to send.

Find bad Web sites 8× faster. Hit the Veeblefester's home page with an analog modem, and it could be days before you get out. But hit it with BitSURFER Pro ISDN modem and you'll be out long before the first of their 26 vacation pictures starts to appear.

From an advertising campaign by Motorola, April 1996

FIGURE 14-2

PPP is used to connect to an Internet Service Provider

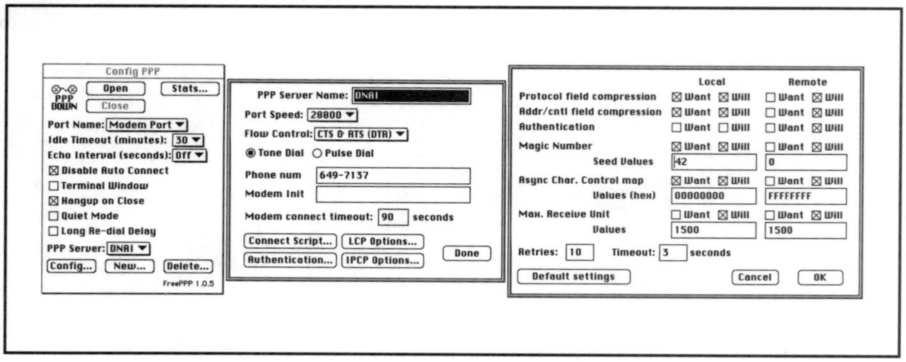

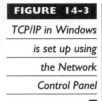

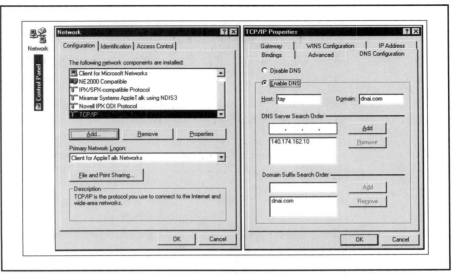

To work within the constraints of this challenging bottleneck (until the bottleneck is cleared by the introduction of inexpensive higher-speed cable modems and telephone connections—see Chapter 5), multimedia developers on the Internet have but a few options:

■ Compress data as tightly as possible before transmitting.

■ Require users to download data only once, then store the data in a local hard disk cache (this is automatically managed by most WWW browsers).

■ Design each multimedia element to be efficiently compact—don't use a greater color depth than is absolutely necessary.

■ Design alternate low-bandwidth and high-bandwidth navigation paths to accommodate all users.

■ Implement streaming methods that allow data to be transferred and displayed incrementally (without waiting for the complete dataset to arrive).

14

Name	Bandwidth (in bits per second) Without Compression	Comment
14.4K Modem	14,400 bps	Analog modulator/demodulator technology
28.8K Modem	28,800 bps	Maximum analog modem speed for copper wires
56K	56,000 bps	Leased line
ISDN	56,000 bps to 128,000 bps	Integrated Services Digital Network basic services (128,000 bps if no voice mixed in)
CableModem	300,000 bps upload; 1,500,000 bps download	Even though copper coaxial TV cable can be used in a bi-directional fashion, it was originally designed to carry limited signals in one direction.
LocalTalk	230,400 bps	Apple networking hardware and protocol, outdated
T-1	1,544,000 bps	Equal to 24 56 Kbps leased lines
E-1	2,000,000 bps	European equivalent of a T-1 connection
DSL	1,500,000 to 9,000,000 bps	Digital Subscriber Line service available in various technologies (HDSL, SDSL, ADSL, VDSL, and RDSL) with differing data rates, operating distances, and ratios between downstream and upstream speeds.
EtherNet	10,000,000 bps	Networking hardware and protocol
T-3	45,000,000 bps	Typical backbone speed of major Internet Service Providers in the U.S. (1996)
Frame Relay	56,000 to 45,000,000 bps	Service offered by long-distance phone companies
Fast SCSI III	80,000,000 bps	Data transfer rate for Fast SCSI III or Ultra SCSI
Fast Ethernet	100,000,000 bps	Networking hardware and protocol
OC-3	155,000,000 bps	Upgrade for Internet Service Providers in the U.S. (1997)
OC-48	2,400,000,000 bps (2.4 gigabits per second)	Typical speed for intercity fiber-optic lines (called SONET or Synchronous Optical Network)
ATM	In steps, from 45,000,000 to 145,000,000 to 2,400,000,000 bps	Asynchronous Transfer Mode—protocol for sending and receiving voice and other data (53-byte cells, each with 5-byte headers and 48-byte content; cell headers waste about 10 percent of available bandwidth). The cell sign was a compromise between U.S. and European members of the standards committee, one group wanting 48, the other group, more. The 53-byte compromise was based on the size needed for video without too much packet delay.

TABLE 14-2 *Bandwidth of Some Typical Internet Connections* ■

FTP.ARL.MIL Bandwidth Information

This site is connected to the National Science Foundation Network (NSFNET) backbone at both Fix-East in Washington, D.C., and Fix-West in San Francisco by a pair of T-3 (45Mbit/sec, or 5.6MB/sec) communications lines. The line to Fix-East is a single hop, while the line to Fix-West passes first through Corps of Engineers (Vicksburg, Mississippi), New Mexico, and San Diego.

Regrettably, the full bandwidth of the T-3 line is not available for FTP and Web transfers, as there is a 10Mbit/sec Ethernet between the T-3 line and the host FTP.ARL.MIL. So you have to suffer with about 8Mbit/sec (1MB/sec) actual speed for now. Moving 1MB of data over the T-3 link takes about 1 second, if your end is up to it.

Naturally, no single file transfer ever gets the full bandwidth of these communications lines, as they are a shared resource. This information should help you make a lower-bound estimate on how much time large file transfers might take.

sys-admin@ftp.arl.mil, May 1996

Internet Services

To many users, the Internet means the World Wide Web. But the World Wide Web is only the latest and most popular of services available today on the Internet. E-mail; file transfer; discussion groups and newsgroups; real-time chatting by text, voice, and video; and the ability to log into remote computers are common as well. Internet services include the following:

Service	Purpose
http	For posting and reading documents (from the Hypertext Transfer Protocol used by the World Wide Web)
Pop	For receiving electronic mail (from Post Office Protocol)
ftp	For transferring files between computers; can be anonymous or password-protected (from File Transfer Protocol)
Gopher	For menus of material available on the Internet
Usenet	For participating in discussion groups (from USErs NETwork)
Telnet	For logging on and working from remote computers
Irc	For real-time text messaging (from Internet Relay Chat)
Smtp	For sending mail (from Simple Mail Transport Protocol)
Mud	For real-time game playing (from Multiuser Dimension)

Each Internet service is implemented on an Internet server by dedicated software known as a *daemon* (actually, daemons only exist on Unix systems—on other systems, such as Windows NT, the services may run as regular applications or background processes). Daemons are agent programs that run in the background, waiting to act on requests from the outside. In the case of the Internet, daemons support protocols such as the Hypertext Transport Protocol (HTTP) for the World Wide Web, the Post Office Protocol (POP) for e-mail, or the File Transfer Protocol (FTP) for exchanging files. You have probably noticed that the first few letters of a URL (Uniform Resource Locator)—for example, **http://www.timestream.com/index .html**—notify a server which daemon to bring into play to satisfy a request. In many cases, the daemon for the World Wide Web, mail, news, and FTP may run on completely different servers, each isolated by a security fire wall from other servers on a network.

MIME-Types

To work with multimedia on the Internet, you must work within the requirements of the appropriate protocol, using documents and formats that are recognizable. A voice attachment to an e-mail message, for example, must be identified by the Post Office daemon for what it is, then be transmitted with the correct coding to the receiving computer. The receiver must have the proper software (and hardware) for decoding the information and playing it back. Most browsers allow you to define additional MIME-types and map "helper apps" to the type for decoding and playing. For example, with Netscape Navigator you can define Adobe's Acrobat files (.PDF) as a MIME-type and select the Acrobat Reader as the player application.

To identify the nature of the data transmitted and, by inference, the purpose of those data, the Internet uses a standard list of file name extensions called MIME-types (for Multipurpose Internet Mail Extensions). These are not just used by the mail daemon but, by convention, by other Internet daemons, including the World Wide Web's HTTP daemon. Table 14-3 shows a list of common MIME-types and their uses (note that many come from the Unix world, where the Internet was born).

• •

http://www.oac.uci.edu/indiv/ehood/MIME/MIME.html
http://www.cis.ohio-state.edu:82/rfc/rfc822.html
http://www.cis.ohio-state.edu:82/rfc/rfc1341.html
ftp://ftp.ncd.com/pub/usenet/comp.mail.mime/

More information about MIME-types

Extension	Type	Use
Ai	Application/postscript	PostScript program
Aif	Audio/x-aiff	Audio
Aifc	Audio/x-aiff	Audio
AIFF	Audio/x-aiff	Audio
Aiff	Audio/x-aiff	Audio
Au	Audio/basic	ULAW audio data
Avi	Video/x-msvideo	Microsoft video
Bin	Application/octet-stream	Binary executable
Cpio	Application/x-cpio	Unix CPIO archive
Csh	Application/x-csh	C shell program
Dcr	Application/director	Shockwave animation
Dvi	Application/x-dvi	TeX DVI data
Eps	Application/postscript	PostScript program
Exe	Application/octet-stream	Binary executable
Fif	Application/fractals	Fractal image format
Gif	Image/gif	CompuServe image format
Gtar	Application/x-gtar	GNU tape archive
Gz	Encoding/x-gzip	GNU zip compressed data
Hqx	Application/mac-binhex40	Macintosh BinHex archive
Htm	Text/html	Hypertext Markup Language
Html	Text/html	Hypertext Markup Language
Ief	Image/ief	Image
Jpe	Image/jpeg	JPEG image
Jpeg	Image/jpeg	JPEG image
Jpg	Image/jpeg	JPEG image
Latex	Application/x-latex	LaTeX document
Man	Application/x-troff-man	Unix manual page
Me	Application/x-troff-me	TROFF document
Mov	Video/quicktime	QuickTime video
Movie	Video/x-sgi-movie	SGI video
Mpe	Video/mpeg	MPEG video

TABLE 14-3   *Common MIME-Types Used on the Internet* ■

14

Extension	Type	Use
Mpeg	Video/mpeg	MPEG video
Mpg	Video/mpeg	MPEG video
Ms	Application/x-troff-ms	TROFF document
Pbm	Image/x-portable-bitmap	PBM image
Pgm	Image/x-portable-graymap	PGM image
pnm	Image/x-portable-anymap	PBM image
Ppm	Image/x-portable-pixmap	PPM image
Ps	Application/postscript	PostScript program
Qt	Video/quicktime	QuickTime video
Ra	Audio/x-pn-realaudio	RealAudio sound
Ram	Audio/x-pn-realaudio	RealAudio sound
Ras	Image/x-cmu-raster	CMU raster image
Rgb	Image/x-rgb	RGB image
Roff	Application/x-troff	TROFF document
Rtf	Application/rtf	Rich Text Format
Sh	Application/x-sh	Bourne shell program
Shar	Application/x-shar	Unix shell archive
Sit	Application/x-stuffit	Macintosh archive
Snd	Audio/basic	ULAW audio data
T	Application/x-troff	TROFF document
Tar	Application/x-tar	Unix tape archive
Tcl	Application/x-tcl	TCL program
Tex	Application/x-tex	TeX document
Texi	Application/x-texinfo	GNU TeXinfo document
Texinfo	Application/x-texinfo	GNU TeXinfo document
Text	Text/plain	Plain text
Tif	Image/tiff	TIFF image
Tiff	Image/tiff	TIFF image
Tr	Application/x-troff	TROFF document
Txt	Text/plain	Plain text
Vox	Audio	VoxWare

TABLE 14-3   *Common MIME-Types Used on the Internet*   (continued) ∎

Extension	Type	Use
Wav	Audio/x-wav	WAV audio
Xbm	Image/x-xbitmap	X bitmap
Xpm	Image/x-xpixmap	X pixmap
Xwd	Image/x-xwindowdump	X Window dump image
Z	Encoding/x-compress	Compressed data
Zip	Application/x-zip-compressed	Zip compressed data

TABLE 14-3   *Common MIME-Types Used on the Internet*   (continued) ■

Multimedia elements are typically saved and transmitted on the Internet in the appropriate MIME-type format and are named with the proper extension for that type. For example, Shockwave animation files end in .dcr; image files end in .jpg, .jpeg, or .gif; sound files end in .au, .wav, .aif, or another conforming format; QuickTime movies end in .qt.

warning   *Because some MIME-types for multimedia data are new or experimental, not all servers may recognize them. If you have problems with a multimedia file, check with your Internet Service Provider to be sure your server can serve "experimental" MIME-types such as Shockwave. Some ISPs, if they provide insufficient bandwidth in their connection to the Internet, will not support high-bandwidth sound-streaming MIME-types such as RealAudio.*

The World Wide Web

The World Wide Web (WWW or W3, http://www.w3.org) started in 1989 at the European Particle Physics Laboratory (CERN) as a "distributed collaborative hypermedia information system." It was designed by Tim Berners-Lee as a protocol for linking a multiplicity of documents located on computers anywhere within the Internet. This new Hypertext Transfer Protocol (HTTP) provided rules for a simple transaction between two computers on the Internet consisting of (1) establishing a connection, (2) requesting that a document be sent, (3) sending the document, and (4) closing the connection. It also required a simple document format called Hypertext Markup Language (HTML) for presenting structured text mixed with inline images.

14

An HTML document could contain hyperlinks or anchors (see Chapter 9) that referred to other similar documents. With browser software, users could then click on designated areas of hot text in one document and jump to another, which itself might have more hot text pointing to yet other documents. Users could surf from document to document across the Web, with HTML as the underlying buoyant framework.

First Person

Each year, in the middle of summer, one of my colleagues has a birthday party at the beach. Her friends, a great many of them well-known San Francisco Bay Area multimedia developers and pundits, assemble picnic chests, volleyballs, children, suntan lotion, dogs, and watermelons to gather for an afternoon around a circle of hot and smoky charcoal grills.

During the party of 1994, they carried on about their latest multimedia ventures while turning chicken breasts, salmon, and barbecue meat; the buzz was about getting CD-ROM titles and products into the retail sales channel.

But shadows fell on the CD-ROM marketplace later that year, and the channels grew muddy and expensive—many multimedia developers were badly hurt in the Christmas shake-out.

When those same good developers gathered at the grills in the summer of 1995, the undertow of conversation was about HTML and migration to the growing World Wide Web. This was a new challenge, a new gold rush, and that channel needed *multimedia!*

Multimedia on the Web

During the coming years, most multimedia experiences on the Internet will occur on the World Wide Web, programmed within the constraints of HTML, then stretched by the enhanced capabilities provided by Java, JavaScript, special plug-ins, and players to enable browsers to exceed their limits. To design and make effective multimedia for this environment, developers need to understand not only how to create and edit the elements of multimedia, but how to deliver it for HTML browsers and plug-in/player vehicles. Well-crafted, professionally rendered sites on the Web include text, images, audio, and animation presented in a user-friendly interface that balances the bandwidth deficit against user patience. HTML, the plug-in tools, and players are discussed in Chapter 15. Techniques, tricks, and presentation styles for delivering multimedia on the Web are discussed in Chapter 20.

Commercial online services and the WWW will play a major role in sustaining niche markets open to numerous companies with business models that borrow elements from recorded music and book publishing. The need for CD-ROM distribution channels then becomes questionable, as the Broadband Web may become all that a multimedia entrepreneur will need to market and distribute products successfully.

Fred Greguras and Sandy Wong, Law Firm of Fenwick & West

Inside the event horizon of the amazing World Wide Web explosion are many uncertainties and unsolved challenges. The bandwidth deficit will certainly be met with technology solutions that will be effectively marketed into homes and businesses. But the pressure of more and more users entering the Web will create a terrific need for high-quality, compelling content; multimedia developers and entrepreneurs will fill this creative void. To deal with perhaps the greatest uncertainty, the nonprofit CommerceNet consortium has been formed of more than 130 electronics, computer, financial service, and information service companies. Their work is to accelerate even further the use of the Internet for business applications and, more importantly, to figure out how to earn money there.

http://www.americanexpress.com
http://www.visa.com
http://www.mastercard.com
http://www.fv.com
http://www.digicash.com
http://www.cybercash.com

Where the money is

Multi

Web site and page developers need
creative tools; surfers need browsers
and the plug-ins and players to
make them work.

By 1996, more than 75 percent—

connections

media

chapter

15

Tools for the
World Wide Web

— of all Web site hits were being made by Netscape's Navigator.

T HIS chapter presents an organized overview of the many Internet tools you may wish to acquire for your multimedia toolbox as you learn to make the World Wide Web stand up and dance. URLs and other pointers are included here to lead you to information about how to obtain, install, and use these applications and utilities. Some are demonstrated and applied in the design examples of Chapter 18.

Plug-ins and commercial tools aimed at the Web are entering the marketplace at a furious pace, each competing for visibility and developer/user mind share in an increasingly noisy venue. In the few years since the birth of the first line-driven HTTP daemon in Switzerland, millions of Web surfers have become hungry for "cool" enhancements to entertaining sites. Web site and page developers need creative tools to feed the surfers; surfers need browsers and the plug-ins and players to make these cool multimedia enhancements work.

The explosion of tools and user demand for performance is stressing the orderly development of the core HTML standard. Unable to evolve fast enough to satisfy the demand for features (there are committees, international meetings, rational debates, comment periods, and votes in the standards process), the HTML language is constantly being extended de facto by commercial interests (mainly Netscape and Microsoft), who regularly release new versions of Web browsers containing *tags* (HTML commands) and features not yet formally approved. By the time (measured in weeks!) millions of users have become dependent upon the features of new browser versions, the more carefully considered official specification has no choice but to incorporate them. By the time features are "official," of course—after more meetings, votes, and understated demonstrations of power—still newer browser versions have been released with yet newer, unofficial features.

What keeps this cycle from being chaotic are the natural selection forces of the marketplace: developers strive toward a successful product that works better and satisfies more users without mutating so far from the core standard that there are no sales and the company collapses. Developers also complain about the contention between Netscape and Microsoft because

15

they must program work-arounds that compensate for the differences between these two benchmark browsers, and they must test the performance of their site on both.

Netscape's Navigator and Microsoft's Internet Explorer contain many unofficial features and extensions to official HTML. Each provides a method for third-party developers to "plug in" special tools that take over certain computational and display activities. Navigator and Explorer also support the Java and JavaScript language by which programmers can create *applets* to extend and customize a browser's basic HTML capabilities, especially into the multimedia realm. Thus, while browsers provide the orchestrated foundation of HTML, third-party players and even nonprogrammers can create their own cadenzas to enhance browser performance or perform special tasks. It is often through the plug-ins and applets described in this chapter that multimedia reaches end users. Many of these tools are available as freeware and shareware, while others, particularly servers, are available as expensive engines—most any tool can be downloaded from the Internet in a trial version. Try it. If you like it or use it, buy it.

The explosion of the Internet—Internet usage doubled every 100 days during 1998—has caused many software developers to redirect their creative efforts toward providing solutions on the World Wide Web. This is the new frontier. No developer wishes to be left behind.

April 1998—I'm writing to inform you of a difficult decision we've made here at Intuit.... This fall, we will not be releasing a new version of Quicken for Macintosh as we have in years past. Instead of developing another desktop release for Macintosh, we've decided to assign our Macintosh development resources to the important task of implementing expanded personal finance capabilities on the Web, providing significant new benefits on Quicken.com to all our valued Intuit customers....

May 5, 1998—Apple Computer Inc. and Intuit, Inc. today announced that Intuit has recommitted to support and develop its Quicken product for Macintosh, after being disclosed on Apple's upcoming consumer products and strategies. Apple and Intuit will work together to promote Intuit's current version, Quicken 98, and Intuit will proceed to develop a new version of Quicken for Macintosh, to be available in 1999.

Announcement and Press Release from Intuit Inc.

eb Servers

As you learned in Chapter 14, the workings of the Web involve communication between two computers: a server and a client. The server delivers a file when a client asks for it. Because the playback or display performance of your multimedia content—particularly when it is a streaming MIME-type such as RealAudio or Shockwave or a QuickTime video—depends upon the speed and capabilities of the computer and software serving it (as well as the bandwidth and load factors of the Internet), you should know some basics.

A growing number of software vendors provide Web servers of varying strength and capacity and for a variety of platforms, all of which meet the requirements of the Hypertext Transfer Protocol discussed in Chapter 14. A server is technically not the hardware but the software—you should invest in server software that will stand up to your intended use and be supported by the vendor. Most vendors will also recommend hardware configurations. This combination of software and hardware is critical to your success and happiness if you wish to optimize response time (less than a second), your connections per second (as many as possible), and your throughput (plenty of room before your Internet connection is overwhelmed by traveling packets).

---

warning   *If you do not develop growth predictions based upon sound business practices and install adequate server performance, you may discover that those 6,000 hits you received in the hour after you and your brother held up the bedsheet boasting your company's URL during the Super Bowl are being served at 87 bytes per second or refused. At least be sure your choice of server provides a sensible migration path for growth; people don't usually come back to an unsatisfying experience.*

Web Browsers

Your computer's performance is as important as the bandwidth of your connection to the Web. Web browsers are applications that run on a user's personal computer (on the client side on the Internet) to provide the interactive graphical interface for searching, finding, and viewing text documents, sounds, animations, and other multimedia resources on the Web. In 1996, as many as 50 browsers competed for market share, each boasting special or unique features, performance, and cost. Rich Santalesa, editor of *NetGuide* magazine, predicted even then that "the browser wars are over—it's a battle between Microsoft and Netscape, and everyone else is going to dry up and blow away." Indeed, by 1998, only two serious competitors remained: Netscape and Microsoft.

Despite the legal and financial seriousness of this competition, manifest in very real congressional hearings and complicated multimillion-dollar antimonopoly lawsuits, some of those involved kept their sense of humor. Back in October 1997, late in the night after the gala announcement and rollout of Microsoft's new Explorer 4.0 in San Francisco, a group of Microsoft engineers drove 30 miles south to Netscape's headquarters and placed a truck-sized Explorer logo (the world-circling "e") on the front lawn of the competitor's headquarters, accented with a helium balloon saying "We Love You" and a greeting card with the message, "It's just not fair. Good people shouldn't have to feel bad. Best wishes, the IE team." By midmorning, Netscape's own engineers had crowned the Explorer logo with a giant dinosaur (their company mascot, named Mozilla) and nailed up a cardboard sign declaring, "Netscape 72, Microsoft 18," (the companies' market share at that time).

The majority of visitors to your Web site will be using Netscape's Navigator or Microsoft's Internet Explorer. In designing a Web site, then, you should be certain that your documents and plug-ins work and look good using those browsers. Other browsers, such as the one supported by America Online (AOL), may or may not support the features you have written into your HTML pages. By 1998, AOL had merged with CompuServe and claimed to have 12 million subscribers, more than a million of them in Europe. That's a lot of real people, if only a small percentage of the total number of Internet users; remember, it takes about 277 hours just to count to a million, one per second!

Web Page Makers and Site Builders

To deliver multimedia on the Web today, you should know some HTML—you must place the proper tags and references into your documents to launch and control your multimedia. Examples of launching multimedia plug-ins and enablers are found in Chapter 18. Many HTML editors and Web page-making applications offer to shortcut your HTML learning curves and working effort. If you use one of these editors, let it ease your work effort, but do not shy away from learning the syntax and tags of the HTML language.

HTML documents are simple ASCII text files saved to disk without any formatting at all—no bolding, underlining, special fonts, margins or tabs. Professional Web page developers often use only a word processor like

BBEdit (see Figure 15-1) rather than a souped-up drag-and-drop HTML editor, and they insert text and tags into their documents manually or with personalized shortcut keys and helper scripts. HTML currently includes about 50 tags, and once you understand their properties and uses, coding or *marking up* a document and saving it to your Web site can be a straight-forward process.

HTML translators are built into many word processing programs, so you can export a word-processed document with its text styles and layout converted to HTML tags for headers, bolding, underlining, indenting, and so on. Some are more powerful than others. These work well for simple text documents but tend to choke on powerful HTML features such as tables, forms, frames, and other extensions offered by Navigator, Explorer, or other browsers. Dedicated editors are usually WYSIWYG (What You See Is What You Get) word processors, and they provide more power and more features specifically geared to exploiting HTML.

FIGURE 15-1

BBEdit is a professional programmer's text editor with dedicated features for Web page development

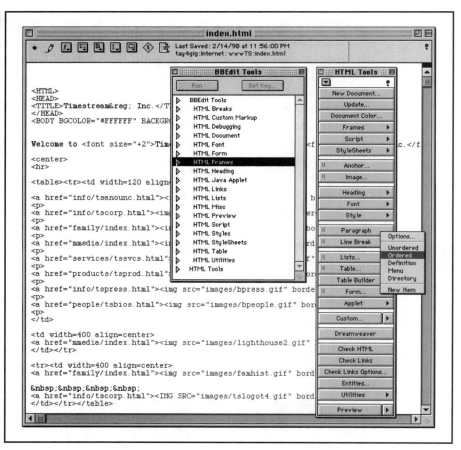

When I was 16, my grandmother loaned me $500 so I could buy my first car. It was a lovely, previously owned, British racing green 1950 MG-TD, happiest doing about 45 miles per hour on tree-lined summer roads in New England. When you hinged up the hood sideways, everything inside was simple and well defined; there was plenty of room to tweak the twin SU carburetors, adjust the distributor, and replace simple parts like the electric fuel pump. I even took the tiny 4-cylinder engine entirely out and replaced the shell bearings on the crankshaft. A decade later, with

my previously owned 1960 Ford pickup, it was the same—replacing the radiator or changing the starter motor was a piece of cake, and there was plenty of room to work on the engine. But then automobiles got complicated. It started with elaborate emission control systems, then electronic ignitions, then air conditioning, and finally, computers. Opening the hood of a car today, most of us can only stare dumbly at the myriad hoses and wires and color-coded containers for special fluids; and it's so compact a fit, you can't slip a screwdriver between the engine and the fire wall. When the "check engine" light comes

on, an expert needs to "pull" the computer codes with a special, expensive reader to see what's wrong.

Writing HTML for the Web today is still simple. But unless you are an expert, by 2002 you will be staring dumbly at the complex source code created by a new generation of high-powered special Web tools that will deliver mind-boggling multimedia pages built—no muss, no fuss—with simple drag and drop. But like my car today, which is happiest at 70 miles per hour and could cruise at twice that, you won't be doing much under the hood.

Among the many tools in this emerging marketplace, FrontPage from Microsoft links to Microsoft Office and provides not only WYSIWYG support for many of the latest HTML formatting extensions but also extensive Web site management support through its FrontPage Explorer application. Pagemaker from Adobe saves pages as HTML documents and as Acrobat .PDF files. HoTMetaL Pro from SoftQuad imports and converts files created in Word, WordPerfect, Ami PRO, and other word processors; it has a point-and-click interface for inserting valid HTML tags and elements and provides an enhanced URL editor to manage references and calls to other documents and files. Terry Morse's Myrmidon is a page builder for Macintosh that creates an HTML page from most any document by "printing" it to analyze the content and converting it to HTML. HTML Transit from InfoAccess also converts and reformats word processor documents into full-color, hypertext-linked Web pages. Internet Creator from Forman Interactive allows novice users to create business-oriented Web sites with no programming knowledge. The Netscape Navigator editor offers a one-click interface for inserting images, Live Objects, Java applets, JavaScript scripts, and frames, and it supports inline plug-ins such as Acrobat, Shockwave, RealAudio, WebFX, and others, so multimedia can be incorporated in your

HTML document. Adobe's Page Mill is a WYSIWYG editor that lets you create and edit text pages, import images, and link to other documents; Site Mill will manage the site. PowerMedia from RAD Technologies is an authoring and delivery tool specializing in large-scale marketing, training, customer service, sales, and educational on-line systems for the World Wide Web; a viewing-only version of PowerMedia allows users to "play back" PowerMedia content from the Web. QuickSite from DeltaPoint is a site creation and management tool with Wizards to walk you through, step-by-step; it has a graphical interface and uses a database architecture to organize, lay out, and update your Web site. From Asymetrix, Web 3D is a template-based page editor that builds graphically rich Web pages; it includes a full-bore 3-D modeling tool. NetObjects Fusion, shown in Figure 15-2, offers premade templates to establish the look of your site, and drag-and-drop page building with overall site management.

Managing and maintaining a Web site is a serious undertaking when the site contains many thousands of text documents, images, and other resources. Software and expert system tools for automated Web page development, document management, and site activity analysis are being developed and will be widely available by the year 2000. Combined with page builders and multimedia editors, these applications will become the ubiquitous "word processors" of the new information age, essential to every home and office with outreach to the Web, and able to integrate and present all the elements of multimedia.

Plug-ins and Delivery Vehicles

Plug-ins add the power of multimedia to Web browsers by allowing users to view and interact with new types of documents and images. *Helper applications* or *players* also provide multimedia power by displaying or running files downloaded from the Internet by your browser, but helpers are not seamlessly integrated into the operation of the browser itself. When an unfamiliar embedded MIME-type is called from an HTML document (sounds, movies, unusual text or image files), most browsers will automatically launch a helper application (if it is specified in the browser's preferences) to view or run it, but this helper starts up and runs on your computer separately from the browser.

Many plug-ins are designed to perform special tasks not available without the plug-in installed. If you land on a Web page containing embedded compressed images, for example, and the proper plug-in to decompress those

15

FIGURE 15-2

NetObjects Fusion offers ready-made graphical templates, page layout tools, and site management facilities to maintain consistency throughout complex sites with many documents ∎

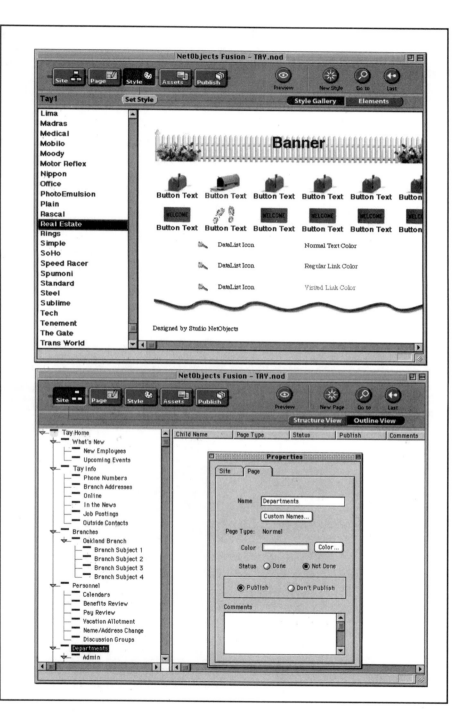

images is not installed, you will not see the images. In their place may be a "broken" plug-in icon:

Designers work around this problem by including in their pages hyperlinks to the site where the missing plug-in may be found. Users must then go there, download and install the required plug-in, then restart their browser. This is all a bit cumbersome. Until the marketplace determines which plug-ins will become de facto standards for the Web, however, developers have no alternative.

Because downloading and installing plug-ins is perceived as a hassle for the end user, many tool developers use the Java capability built into today's Web browsers. With applications such as Astound's WebMotion or Geo-Interactive's Emblaze Creator (see Figure 15-3) to build the page, animations appear whether viewed by Navigator, Explorer, or any other Java-enabled Web browser running in Windows, Macintosh, or Unix.

FIGURE 15-3

Emblaze Creator creates pages and Web sites to be viewed with Java-enabled browsers

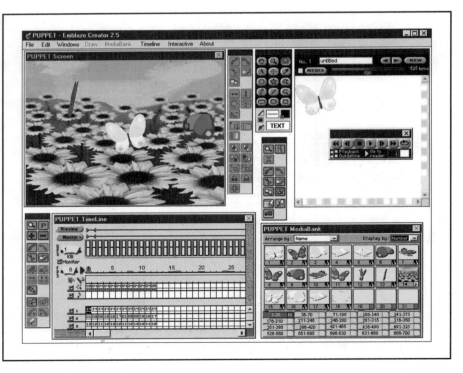

To offer a plug-in's functionality to visitors at your own Web site, many plug-ins require the addition of MIME-type information to a special setup file on your server (for example, in a file called mime.types on a Netscape Commerce Server; .bhtaccess on best.com's servers; ServerRoot/conf/mime.types on NCSA HTTPD servers; server_root/config on CERN HTTPD servers; or MacHTTP.config on Mac HTTP servers). If you do not control or operate your own server, you should let your service provider know what MIME-types you need to have supported. Setting up servers for some of the multimedia plug-ins is not a trivial task, and many Internet Service Providers will not support high-bandwidth data streams for fear of overwhelming their Internet connection by serving your streaming voice or video to the world. Indeed, while a plug-in or a player may be free and readily available to anyone who wishes it, the software to actually build, compress, manipulate, and serve the special data (such as for compressed images, compressed audio, streaming video, animations, and VRML worlds) may be expensive and difficult to use.

The following sections provide a survey of multimedia plug-ins that work with Navigator and Explorer, but not necessarily on both Windows and Macintosh platforms. To get a plug-in, access the Web site of the plug-in's vendor (see the following table) and download the version suited to your platform and browser. Most plug-ins are free or have a free trial period. Install the downloaded plug-in into a special folder where the browser can find it when it starts up. Then, when your browser comes across a file of a MIME-type supported by your plug-in, it transfers operations to the plug-in, and you're off, doing what that plug-in was designed to do! Here are some useful plug-ins and players:

Name	Company	For More Information
Acrobat Reader	Adobe	http://www.adobe.com
ActivePresenter	Software Publishing Corporation	http://www.spco.com
Chemscape Chime	MDL Information Systems	http://www.mdli.com
ClearFusion	Iterated Systems	http://www.iterated.com
CMX Viewer	Corel	http://www.corel.com
Crescendo	Live Update	http://www.liveupdate.com
docActive	NCompass Labs	http://www.ncompasslabs.com
EchoSpeech	EchoSpeech Corporation	http://www.echospeech.com
4U2C	Summus	http://www.summus.com
InterCAP InLine	InterCAP Graphics	http://www.intercap.com
Koan	SSEYO	http://www.sseyo.com

Name	Company	For More Information
Lightning Strike	InfinetOp	http://www.infinop.com
Live3D	Netscape	http://home.netscape.com
Look@Me	Netopia	http://www.netopia.com
MacZilla	Knowledge Engineering	http://maczilla.com
mBed	Mbed Software	http://www.mbed.com
PreVU	InterVU	http://www.intervu.com
QuickTime VR	Apple	http://www.apple.com
QuickVector	Micrografx	http://www.micrografx.com
RapidTransit	Fastman	http://fastman.com
RealPlayer	Progressive Networks	http://www.realaudio.com
Shockwave	Macromedia	http://www.macromedia.com
Sizzler	Totally Hip	http://www.totallyhip.com
StreamWorks	Xing Technology	http://www.xingtech.com
Superscape 3-D	Superscape	http://www.superscape.com
Talker	MVP Solutions	http://www.mvpsolutions.com
ToolVox	VoxWare	http://www.voxware.com
TrueSpeech	DSP Group	http://www.dspg.com
VDOLive	VDOnet	http://www.vdolive.com
Vdraft	Softsource	http://www.softsource.com
ViewDirector	TMS	http://www.tmsinc.com
VREALM	Ligos	http://www.ligos.com
Whip!	Autodesk	http://www.autodesk.com
Wirl	Platinum	http://www.platinum.com
Word Viewer	Inso Corporation	http://www.inso.com

Text and Documents

Text and document plug-ins get you past the display limitations of HTML and Web browsers, where fonts are unchangeable and page layout is primitive. In file formats provided by Adobe Acrobat, for example, special fonts and graphic images are embedded as data into the file and travel with it, so what you see when you view that file is precisely what the document's maker intended.

Acrobat Reader

 With Acrobat Reader from Adobe you can view, navigate, annotate, and print platform-independent Portable Document Format (PDF) Acrobat files within your browser's window, one page at a time. Acrobat offers a new method for optimizing .PDF files for the Internet and a method for progressive display: text first, then images, then embedded fonts. Embedded fonts appear first as substitution fonts until the embedded font outline is fully retrieved, then the characters are "blitted" onto the screen.

Word Viewer

Inso's Word Viewer plug-in lets you view any Microsoft Word 6.0 or 7.0 document from inside your browser, with its original formatting intact. Word Viewer uses the application/MSWord MIME-type, so the server must be set up properly. The Word Viewer plug-in will not handle older Word for Windows 2.0 documents. Word documents that are embedded in HTML documents will print as blank space when the containing HTML file is printed.

Images

Most browsers will read only bitmapped JPEG and GIF image files. Vector files (see Chapter 11) are a mathematical description of the lines, curves, fills, and patterns needed to draw a picture, and while they typically do not provide the rich detail found in bitmaps, they are smaller and can be scaled without image degradation. Plug-ins to enable viewing vector formats are useful, particularly when some provide high-octane compression schemes to dramatically shrink file size and shorten the time spent downloading and displaying them. File size and compression sound a recurring theme on the Internet, where data-rich images, movies, and sounds may take many seconds, minutes, or even longer to reach the end user.

Vaughan's Bandwidth Rule

$$\frac{Bandwidth}{File\ Size} = Satisfaction$$

Satisfaction with the Internet is a function of connection speed and the size of the data elements accessed.

Vector graphics are also *device independent*—the image is always displayed at the correct size and with the maximum number of colors supported by the computer. Unlike bitmapped files, a single vector file can be downloaded, cached, and then displayed multiple times at different scaled sizes on the same or a different Web page.

Chemscape Chime

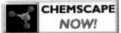

Chemscape Chime from MDL Information Systems can display 2-D and 3-D structures embedded within an HTML page or table. It is primarily used for chemical information management systems in the pharmaceutical, agrochemical, and chemical industries. Used in tables, you can display multiple chemical structures on a single HTML page, and structures within the plug-in are "live"—they can be rotated in real-time in wireframe, backbone, sticks, spacefill, ball and stick, ribbons, strands, and cartoon formats. The plug-in supports multipart XYZ files, so HTML authors can animate molecular transformations and rotate the structures without user intervention.

Chemscape Chime supports some rather esoteric file formats: MDL Molfile, Brookhaven Protein Databank (PDB), Minnesota Supercomputer Center's (MSC) XMol XYZ, Gaussian Input, IEMBL Nucleotide Format, RasMol Script File, Mopac Input File, and Chemical Structure Markup Language Files. If your 3-D animation tool does not export to these, you will need MDL Information Systems' ISISTM/Draw application (freeware to schools and homes) to create your files.

CMX Viewer

The CMX viewer lets you display Corel's open standard vector format CMX files with your browser (image/x-cmx MIME-type). Because they are in vector format (see Chapter 11 for more about the difference between bitmapped, or raster, formats and vector, or drawn, formats), CMX files are usually much smaller than GIF and JPEG files containing similar imagery. And unlike transparent GIF89a formats, where color masking is required to create transparent backgrounds, the background of CMX files is automatically transparent. Corel's base of more than 2.5 million users worldwide can use CMX images at their Web sites without converting them first to bitmaps. The massive clip art libraries available from Corel are also ready for the Internet with CMX Viewer.

As with other plug-ins, to place a CMX file into an HTML document, you use the EMBED tag. You can also scale the size and change the alignment of your CMX image using standard HTML syntax, for example: <embed src="http://www.timestream.com/images/tay.cmx" width=200 height=100>.

Vdraft DWG/DXF

Vdraft from SoftSource is a vector file format viewer for displaying and manipulating DWG and DXF format (AutoCAD) drawings on the Web. It offers single-download navigational capabilities and scalable graphics for zooming and panning. The sister SVF (Simple Vector Format) plug-in also provides navigation via HTML hyperlinks. The DWG/DXF plug-in is useful for on-line distribution of architectural and engineering drawings and vector images that have been exported using AutoCAD's open DXF format.

The SVF plug-in, also available from SoftSource, displays drawings in the SVF format. It not only includes the viewer features of the DWG/DXF plug-in but also lets you include URLs for linking to other documents.

FreeHand Shockwave

FreeHand Shockwave from Macromedia is a plug-in to display and manipulate images created in FreeHand. Using the URL Manager Xtra while working in the FreeHand application, you can drag and drop URL links into objects in your image so that when the plug-in displays the image in your browser's window, hot spots on the image become clickable and lead to other URLs. Shockwave for FreeHand can read the standard FreeHand file format: add the extension .fh8 to the file name of the FreeHand document. But it is recommended that you compress your document into a smaller .fhc file. To serve a FreeHand file in an HTML document, the embed tag is, for example: <embed SRC="tayfree.fhc" width=500 height=400>.

The plug-in offers hotlinks, zooming, and panning. If you wish fonts other than Times and Courier to work, you should use the Text to Paths option within FreeHand to convert your local fonts to path outlines before using Afterburner. To serve these files, the files require the MIME-type image/x-FreeHand and file extensions .fh4, .fh5, and .fhc.

InterCAP InLine

InterCAP Graphics Systems provides a viewer for the CGM (Computer Graphics Metafile) vector graphic files used internationally for 2-D vector and raster graphics. InterCAP is actually a subsidiary of Intergraph, which develops serious graphics support software for large clients such as the Department of Defense, Northrop/Grumman, Boeing-Bell-Allison, and

Lockheed Martin. The InterCAP InLine plug-in supports viewing, zooming, dynamic panning, magnification, and animation of CGM files within your browser.

Lightning Strike

Wavelet-based compression reduces the size of a bitmapped image file 10 to 100 times greater than the compression of a GIF file and offers far greater image quality than JPEG. Lightning Strike from InfinetOp is an optimized wavelet image codec that plugs into your browser. The viewer plug-in is free, and beta versions of plug-ins for Photoshop are available to generate wavelet-compressed files. For intranet service, where there are many users in a controlled environment, dramatic speeding up of downloads across the network can be an important benefit.

QuickVector

Micrografx QuickVector 3 works as an ActiveX control for the Microsoft Internet Explorer 3.0 browser and as a plug-in to the Netscape Navigator 3.0 Web browser. Once you have installed Micrografx QuickVector, either browser can display the vector-based objects in Micrografx Designer drawings.

The Micrografx QuickVector plug-in lets Web developers use Designer to create and display vector graphics instead of raster graphics on the Web. Besides the numerous advantages vector graphics have over the traditional raster graphics used in most Web pages, Micrografx QuickVector makes these Designer files interactive within Web pages.In addition, Micrografx QuickVector 3 lets Web developers display WMF and EMF graphics on the Web.

QuickSilver from Micrografx lets users place, view, and click on object graphics made with the ABC Graphics Suite. More than just a vector graphics viewer, this plug-in senses clicks on the vector-drawn objects that make up the image, and it can link to new pages, update the browser status line, or actually edit the appearance of objects in the drawing. For example, you could create a "rollover" effect for any of the objects in an image—when the cursor rolls over the object (an OnMouseEnter event), you could display a warning or words of cheer in the browser status line. Or you could associate a URL with an object in the drawing to do document linking without knowing HTML.

ViewDirector

The free ViewDirector image plug-in from TMS allows users to view, zoom, and enhance images stored in industry-standard formats, including TIFF G3 and G4, CALS Type 1, JPEG, PCX/DCX, and BMP. ViewDirector also offers image manipulation for scale-to-gray for better reading quality, color pixel smoothing, and printing. A fee-based professional version includes additional features such as user-defined zooming, magnifiers, rotation, copy to Clipboard, three scale-to-gray levels, and multipage image (TIFF, DCX) support.

4U2C

The 4U2C plug-in from Summus, like Lightning Strike, decompresses and displays wavelet images embedded into HTML pages with tags such as <embed src="tayimage.wi" width=256 height=200>. The 4U2C plug-in can scale images to fit a size defined by the width and height parameters of the EMBED tag, and the images can be displayed progressively by setting an optional progressive parameter equal to true and specifying the number of bytes (the buffer size) to receive between displays: <embed src="tayimage.wi" width=256 height=200 progressive=true bufsize=1024>.

Whip!

Whip! from Autodesk is a free plug-in for viewing DWF (Drawing Web Format) files, a new 2-D vector file format introduced by Autodesk to let users download design data efficiently over the Internet. Whip! offers high-speed pan and zoom and support for embedded URLs for linking. The DWF format provides for both secure and open data: an associated Auto-CAD drawing file (DWG) can be embedded within a DWF file, allowing drag and drop of the source data file into an AutoCAD session. The DWF file format is an "open" standard like DXF, but until other CAD vendors support it, you will need AutoCAD (Release 13) to create the DWF files. Autodesk estimates that there are about 1 billion DWG files in use today.

Sound

Sound over the Web is managed in a few different ways. Digitized sound files in various common formats such as .WAV, .AIF, or .AU may be sent to your computer and then played, either as they are being received (streaming playback) or once they are fully downloaded (using a player). MIDI files may also be received and played; as discussed in Chapter 10, these files are more compact, but they depend upon your computer's MIDI setup for quality. Speech files can be specially encoded into a token language and sent at great speed to another computer to be untokenized and played back in a choice of voices. Sound elements may also be embedded into projects made with Director, Authorware, Astound, SuperCard, WebShow, or other applications. And sounds may be embedded into QuickTime, AVI, and MPEG movie files. Some sounds can be multicast (using the multicast IP protocols for the Internet—see RFC 1112), so multiple users can simultaneously listen to the same data streams without duplication of data across the Internet. Web-based telephones also transmit data packets containing sound information.

Crescendo

Live Update's Crescendo plug-in lets you play streaming MIDI music from Web pages. On the Macintosh, QuickTime 2.1 must be installed. A control panel offers play, stop/pause, fast forward, and rewind buttons as well as an LED display to show time elapsed in the MIDI file you are playing. With Crescendo PLUS, the music starts playing as soon as the data begins coming in. To serve up Crescendo in your own pages, using HTML, simply embed the MIDI file as the source and declare a height of 49 and a width of 196: <EMBED SRC="midifilename.mid" WIDTH=196 HEIGHT=49>. The control panel can be adjusted so the color matches your page.

EchoSpeech

The EchoSpeech plug-in is a decoder for playing back voice files made with EchoSpeech's proprietary 18.5:1 compression algorithm. These 16-bit speech files sampled at 11025 Hz can be played in real-time across the Internet using 14400 Kbps modems without loss of fidelity. The coder software is available for a fee, and you can serve these files using EMBED tags in your documents: <EMBED SRC=taytest.es WIDTH=150 HEIGHT=60>. You will need to add the MIME-types audio/echospeech (.es) or audio/echospeech-list (.esl).

Koan

Specially formulated and randomly changing ambient music generated by computer is called *Koan* music, a term made up by its inventor, Tim Cole, in 1994, from the word for a Zen puzzle or mystery that has no rational solution. This is "generative music." The Koan plug-in from SSEYO plays back Koan music files that can be smaller than 1K yet play music for up to eight hours. The Koan file provides basic parameters, but the music itself is created by your PC in real-time using 150 specially designed variable controls. Curiously, you never hear the same music twice, even from the same Koan file.

You can create a Koan piece using SSEYO's Koan Pro and embed the files into your Web documents: <EMBED SRC="taysound/koantest.skp" ALIGN=RIGHT Height=32 width=32 AUTOSTART=true>. You will need to add the proper MIME-type to your server's list. This plug-in also plays back MIDI music files.

RapidTransit

RapidTransit from Fastman decompresses and plays 16-bit, 44.1 kHz, CD-quality sound files compressed at rates of 20:1 or better. For example, a 36-second excerpt from Bach's Brandenburg Concerto No. 5, originally sampled at 16 bits, 44.1 kHz, produced an uncompressed file size of 3.21MB; RapidTransit compressed the file to 57K at a ratio of 56:1. These files use an extension of .lcc and are of the MIME-type audio/fastman.

RealPlayer

RealPlayer from Progressive Networks provides live real-time receiving of streaming audio and video over the Internet. The plug-in version of the player allows you to embed player controls directly into your Web pages, but unless you specifically include the player controls in your page, the player will be launched as a helper application when it encounters the MIME-type audio/x-pn-realaudio with extensions .ra or .ram. More than half a million players were downloaded by users during the first months of its availability in 1995, and a growing number of Web sites offer RealAudio and RealVideo content. An encoder is available from Progressive Networks to convert 8-bit and 16-bit audio files into RealAudio format files. If you intend to serve RealAudio from your own pages, you must configure your Web server to recognize the MIME-types; otherwise, when a user clicks on a link, he or she will see unrecognizable text instead of receiving audio.

StreamWorks

Xing Technology's StreamWorks plug-in uses multicast IP protocols to decode and play broadcast MPEG video streams scaled to very low bit rates. *Multicasting* means that many clients can receive the same data at the same time. Offering full-motion video and audio at ISDN speeds for PCs connected to the Internet by modem, StreamWorks' CGI programs at the server "thin" down the data stream, allowing one to two frames per second of video (with FM radio-quality audio) on a 28.8 modem, or about a frame every one to two seconds (and AM radio-quality audio) on a 14.4 modem where audio uses 8 Kbps and video 4 Kbps of a 12 Kbps stream.

Talker

Talker from MVP Solutions uses Apple's PlainTalk Speech Synthesis technology to decode text files into speech on the Macintosh. The voice generated by Talker can sound like robots, whispers, singing, and even laughter. Apple's Text-to-Speech software *must* be installed on your Macintosh. To make text speak from your own pages, you first create a text document containing the text you wish to be spoken and name it with the extension .talk. Then embed a reference to this file into your HTML document with a tag like <EMBED SRC="tayspeech.talk" WIDTH=10 HEIGHT=10>. To serve Talker files on your own Web pages, however, your server must support the MIME-type text/x-speech and associated file extensions .spc and .talk.

ToolVox

The ToolVox plug-in from VoxWare plays 50:1 compressed voice clips, where 15 seconds can be squeezed into 4.5K. These voice clips are actually proprietary MetaVoice files containing a template of the user's vocal characteristics or *spectral shape* and a record of the user's vocal articulation and frequency. Because these files are a representation of speech and not a recording of the speech itself, you can then manipulate every element of the human voice, including resonance, pitch, timbre, timing, and character, without distortion and without requiring large amounts of bandwidth, storage space, or processing. You can speed up or slow down playback by up to a factor of two (without changing the pitch or character of the original voice) or shift a bass voice into soprano (without distorting vocal character).

ToolVox has two components: the ToolVox plug-in, to listen to sound files when you access Web sites that include VOX files, and the ToolVox encoder, to downsample your recorded files (to 8 kHz at 2400 bps) and compress them into VOX files. With the plug-in installed, speech begins playing within a few seconds of the start of downloading. To serve VOX files, you must enable the MIME-type audio/x-toolvox.

TrueSpeech

TrueSpeech from DSP Group is a streaming audio plug-in that decompresses speech files at rates ranging from 15:1 to about 35:1 (depending upon quality) and offers Internet communications at 9600 bps or better. The TrueSpeech technology has been licensed by Microsoft, Intel, AT&T, Creative Labs, U.S. Robotics, and Cirrus Logic and is an established speech coder for the H.324 videoconferencing standard. VDOnet licensed TrueSpeech to enable real-time on-demand Internet audio and video broadcasts, and Net-Speak (makers of the WebPhone Internet telephone) and Telescape also licensed TrueSpeech for Internet use. An encoder is available from DSP Group, but to serve these .tsp files, you must set your server's MIME-type to application/dsptype.

Animation, Video, and Presentation

The most data-intense multimedia elements to travel the Internet are video streams containing both images and synchronized sound, commonly packaged as Apple's QuickTime, Microsoft's Video for Windows (AVI), and as MPEG files (see Chapters 6 and 13 for more details about these formats). Also data rich are the files for proprietary formats such as Director, Authorware, Astound, SuperCard, WebShow, and other presentation applications. In all cases, the trade-offs between bandwidth and quality are constantly in your face when designing, developing, and delivering animations or motion video for the Web.

mBed

The mBed plug-in lets you display streaming graphics, animation, and sound in the form of "mbedlets," built by mBED Interactor; mbedlets also respond to user actions such as mouse clicks and keystrokes. An mbedlet consists of *players*, which are interacting sprites, visual effects, paths, and scores. An .mbd file is a simple text file containing a list of players and their data; the .mbd file resides on the Web server along with the HTML page in which the mbedlet is to run. The mBed engine is also available as an ActiveX control and a Java applet.

ActivePresenter

The ActivePresenter plug-in from Software Publishing lets you view presentations made with ActivePresenter or PowerPoint. ActivePresenter

contains a gallery of 22 layouts, 14 designs, and 18 colors. It comes with ActiveChart, for adding a wide variety of tables and charts, and Publish Wizard, for moving an ActivePresenter or PowerPoint document onto the World Wide Web.

ClearFusion

 ClearFusion, the Netscape plug-in formerly known as CoolFusion from Iterated Systems, streams Video for Windows (.avi) files on Windows 95/NT platforms. With the plug-in, users can control the video (stop, start, pause), loop the clip, and abort downloading after the first few frames (good for very large files that are not interesting). You should keep about 10MB of free hard drive space for caching downloaded AVI files.

MacZilla

 Knowledge Engineering's MacZilla is a Macintosh plug-in that lets you watch movies (QuickTime, AVI, and MPEG) and listen to AU, WAV, MIDI, AIFF, and MP2 music clips. Indirectly meeting the multimedia bandwidth challenge of the Web, MacZilla lets you play games while lengthy files are downloading. The MPEG and AVI modules will stream data.

PreVU

 PreVU is a plug-in from InterVU for streaming MPEG video. PreVU shows the image of the first frame of a video prior to downloading or streaming it. When the file has been downloaded, it is cached on the local hard disk, and PreVU allows these cached files to be played back at greatly improved performance. With interruptible transmission, you can quit downloading the file if you decide you do not want to continue.

QuickTime

The Apple QuickTime plug-in lets you view QuickTime and QuickTime VR scenes. See Chapter 6 for more about QuickTime. After installing, be sure the video/quicktime MIME-type is set to the application QTVR Player. Also be sure you have installed QuickTime 2.1 on your computer.

Shockwave

The Shockwave plug-ins from Macromedia come in three flavors: for Director and Flash files, for Authorware files, and for FreeHand image files (see FreeHand Shockwave in the "Images" section earlier in the chapter).

SHOCKWAVE FOR DIRECTOR, FLASH, AND AUTHORWARE The Shockwave for Director, Flash, and Authorware plug-ins let users interact with presentations made with these authoring tools (see Chapter 8) within your browser's window. Animation, clickable buttons, links to URLs, digital video movies, sound, and more complicated Lingo programming can be integrated into your Web presentation with Shockwave. You must first create a Director movie or a Flash or Authorware project using Director version 4.0 or later (for Macintosh or Windows). Then you must postprocess your project to compress it by about 60 percent and optimize it for the World Wide Web. The "shocked" file is then embedded in your HTML document: <EMBED height=120 width=320 SRC="http://www.timestream.com/tayshock.dcr">. To serve "shocked" Director files, your server requires the MIME-type application/x-director with extensions .dcr, .dir, and .dxr to be enabled. To serve "shocked" Authorware files, you need to add the MIME-types application/x-authorware-map (.aam), application/x-authorware-seg (.aas), and application/x-authorware-bin (aab).

The Internet is quickly evolving from a static, text-based medium to an interactive broadcasting network complete with multimedia content. With Shockwave technology, we can instantly publish our multimedia productions to a global audience. We can easily update and exchange Director movies to keep Web sites dynamic, and this keeps people coming back to those sites.

Lee Swearingen, partner, DXM Productions

Sizzler

Totally Hip's Sizzler plug-in allows users to play streaming real-time interactive animation and multimedia files created using Totally Hip's Object Scenario application, which converts QuickTime movies and non-frame-differenced PICS files into a highly compressed interactive animation file with the extension .sprite or .spr. To serve sprite files, you need to enable the MIME-type application/x-sprite and extensions sprite and spr. Then you embed the file into your calling HTML document, setting its size: <EMBED

SRC="taysizzle.sprite" WIDTH=100 HEIGHT=100>. The WIDTH and HEIGHT attributes must be present.

VDOLive

VDOLive is a streaming video plug-in from VDOnet that plays real-time video applications from any browser at dial-up to T1 speeds without special hardware requirements. The speed of the connection determines frame delivery rate: for example, with a 28.8 Kbps modem, VDOLive runs at 10 to 15 frames per second; with a 14.4 Kbps PPP connection, it runs at about 1 frame each one to three seconds. This scalable technology requires installation of the VDOLive Internet Video Server, which provides for capture, compression, and storage of video and audio; the server can be configured to deliver over 100 simultaneous video streams. A less expensive "personal" server is also available to deliver two simultaneous video streams of two-minute video clips. VDOLive plays directly from the network and does not cache files to the local disk.

Beyond HTML

When an ingot of pure silicon is "pulled" from a furnace, the process begins with a *seed crystal*, around which the ingot forms. HTML is the seed crystal that is shaping and forming the nature of multimedia on the World Wide Web as it extrudes itself onto the Internet's data highway. Within the latticework of HTML servers and browsers, new tags such as <EMBED> and <INSERT> enable text, sound, images, animations, and motion video across the Web. Hooks for powerful platform-independent Java applets and JavaScripts (see Chapter 18) are built into most browsers, so you can design local interaction and activities without a lot of communication between client and server-based CGI (Common Gateway Interface) programming. CGI is a standard for interfacing external applications with information servers, such as HTTP or Web servers, and CGI programs can be written in C/C++, Fortran, PERL, TCL, a Unix shell, Visual Basic, or even AppleScript, as long as the language is supported by the server platform.

Many software tool companies are developing applications and design environments to work with Java. Aimtech's Cruiser uses a WYSIWYG page layout environment for visually specifying "live" objects (such as animation, graphics, and audio) with drag-and-drop actions. Noware's Java from Down Under provides a Wizard-like Activator and plug-in applets to produce code that can be dropped into a Web page. Symantec's Java Development Kit,

15

Café, provides Java developers with class and project management capabilities within a graphical development environment and also uses software, aptly code-named Caffeine, to add Java development capabilities to the Symantec Project Manager (SPM). HyperWire from Autodesk lets you create 2-D and 3-D animations as Java applets, without writing any code. Microsoft offers ActiveX—small, fast, full-featured components for the Internet and the intranet based on OLE Controls. Mbed Software's mbedlets provide programmed multimedia effects for Web pages, working with a point-and-click interface for collecting and placing multimedia content within Web pages.

· ·

http://www.freqgrafx.com/411/jsfaq.html
http://home.netscape.com/comprod/products/navigator/
    version_2.0/script/index.html
http://home.netscape.com/eng/mozilla/3.0/handbook/javascript/index.html
http://home.netscape.com/eng/mozilla/Gold/handbook/javascript/index.html
http://java.sun.com
http://www.aimtech.com
http://www.infoweb.com.au/noware
http://www.symantec.com
http://www.mbed.com
http://www.ktx.com

More about JavaScript and Java tools

Conferencing and collaboration software with strong multimedia components is becoming available on the Internet. BeingThere, for example, is an Internet video phone with chat, file transfer, whiteboarding, and live window sharing. CU-SeeMe from White Pine is a popular desktop video conferencing system for real-time person-to-person or group conferencing on the Internet that offers many features typical of conferencing software:

■ Multiplatform compatibility for Windows, Windows 95, Macintosh, and Power Macintosh

■ Ability to view up to eight participant windows; unlimited number for audio and talk window

■ Message alert box for incoming connections (caller ID)

■ Whiteboard for collaboration during conferences; supports multiple users

■ Mosaic browser support for direct launch of CU-SeeMe from Web page

■ Selectable audio compression algorithms with 100 ms and 50 ms sampling settings:

— 2.4K and 8.5K audio codecs to support 14.4K and 28.8K modem connections

—16K and 32K codecs for higher bandwidth connections

■ Color support for 24-bit true color and 4-bit gray-scale

■ Ability to save, add, and edit participant addresses and Reflector sites (Phone Book)

■ Video compression at standard and high-resolution settings

■ Password, caller ID, and other conference and inbound call security

Netscape's LiveMedia (CoolTalk and CoolView) is a standards-based framework for real-time audio and video in network-based communications and collaborative multimedia applications supported by industry developers, including Progressive Networks, Adobe Systems, Digital Equipment, Macromedia, NetSpeak, OnLive!, Precept, Silicon Graphics, VDOnet, VocalTec, and Xing. The Look@Me plug-in (based on Timbuktu) lets you view another Look@Me user's screen anywhere in the world in real-time, so you can view a remote computer screen and edit documents, collaborate on presentations, review graphics, and provide real-time training and support. Connectix's VideoPhone (including a digital camera) lets you videoconference in or between offices with a shared whiteboard. WebBoard from O'Reilly & Associates is an advanced multithreaded conferencing system for on-line conferencing to any Windows Web server that fully supports the Windows-CGI interface. Web Crossing from Lundeen & Associates lets you set up a discussion group on a Web site. And for just plain telephoning over the Internet, Voxware's TeleVox lets users make real-time Internet-based "phone calls" to other TeleVox users anywhere in the world, for the price of a local Internet connection.

VRML

VRML (Virtual Reality Modeling Language) is not an extension to HTML, but is an independent environment specifically designed to handle

15

high-performance 3-D *worlds* containing 3-D text and images, textures, animations, morphs, multiple viewpoints, collision detection, gravity, sounds, and all the arcade elements associated with full-bore action. VRML Web features allow users to

- Visualize database information in real-time
- See true 3-D graphics derived from complex spreadsheet data
- Walk through virtual product showrooms with other on-line shoppers
- Participate in multiplayer virtual reality games
- Interact within multimedia chat rooms
- Study photorealistic 3-D geographies
- Collaborate on product designs

Netscape supports Live3D, a high-performance 3-D VRML platform that lets you fly through VRML worlds on the Web and run interactive, multiuser VRML applications written in Java. The V•Realm, WebFX, and WIRL plug-ins can browse full-motion worlds where users can fully interact with surroundings. Black Sun Interactive produces a VRML product line that includes CyberGate, a browser for 3-D information visualization and multiuser interaction; CyberHub, a VR server to support operation, administration, and usage tracking of virtual worlds; and CyberKit, a VR authoring tool for creating virtual worlds. Caligari's Fountain and Virtus' Walkthrough Pro have fly modes, which let you soar through your world.

Live3D In an attempt to provide rational standards in this rapidly developing area, in 1996 some 56 companies agreed to support an "official" implementation of VRML 2.0, called Moving Worlds. This is a platform-independent specification for dynamic 3-D environments that conforms to open standards and leverages Java and JavaScript. But wide implementation of VRML across the Web is currently constrained both by limited bandwidth and by the heavy processing requirements that tax even the most powerful desktop computers—even when the data arrive quickly from the Internet, it may still take many minutes to render a world's rich texture-mapped images and animations.

First Person

When I received a press release from Alternate Realities Corporation, a small startup company spun out of a large research effort in North Carolina, I was intrigued. ARC's president, David Bennett, claimed "We are redefining Virtual Reality!" He went on to describe "*a new generation virtual environment that is a 3-D, immersive, full-color, interactive system enclosed in a 16-foot dome or sphere that* can be either portable (inflatable or interlocking) or permanent. The system includes a 360-degree projection system with a 180-degree field of view. Imagine a 16-foot helmet that fits over 15 people at the same time and is nonrestrictive! Larger units (in the 24-foot and up range) are in the early development stage."

I knew I had to have one for my experiments with VRML! The five-meter model, which fits in a 20×20-foot trade-show booth space, was available for $280,000, and the seven-meter model, perfect for my backyard, was only slightly more: $340,000.

Multi

[
*Plan for the whole process,
beginning with your first ideas
and ending with completion and
delivery of a finished product.*
]

You must develop an organized outline

experience

media

part

6

Assembling and Delivering a Project

and a plan that is rational in terms of what skills, time, budget, tools, and resources are at hand.

[
Before you begin a multimedia
project, you must first develop
a sense of its scope and content.
]

You must develop an organized outline

experience

media

chapter

16

Planning and Costing

and a plan that is rational in terms of what skills, time, budget, tools, and resources are at hand.

B E F O R E you begin a multimedia project, you must first develop a sense of its scope and content, letting the project take shape in your head as you think through the various methods available to get your message across to your viewers. Then you must develop an organized outline and a plan that is rational in terms of what skills, time, budget, tools, and resources are at hand. Proper project planning is as important as planning the layout and content. Your plans should be in place before you start to render graphics, sounds, and other components, and you should refer to them throughout the project's execution.

Project Planning

Planning for multimedia projects is like slicing a watermelon at the family picnic: The big picture of your idea is divided into production phases, and these are divided again into smaller and more manageable tasks and items. The resultant pieces are then spread out over a given amount of time to be dealt with one-by-one.

Tasks are the building blocks of project management. Some tasks are prerequisites, and must be completed before others begin, so planning ahead is important. Allocate an estimated amount of time to each task, and place each one along a calendar-based timeline. This is your project plan.

---

tip   *The end of each phase is a natural place to set a milestone—that is, a time to deliver work-in-progress, to invoice based upon real work done, to assess or test progress, and/or to solicit and receive constructive feedback. Depending upon the complexity of the project, you may wish to place these milestones at the end of each task as well.*

It is, of course, easiest to plan a project using the experience you have accumulated in similar past projects. Over time, you can maintain and improve your multimedia planning format like a batch of sourdough starter. Just keep adding a little rye and water every time you do a project, and the starter for your next job gets a bit more potent as your estimates become tempered by experience.

Plan for the entire process, beginning with your first ideas and ending with completion and delivery of a finished product. Think in the overview. The step-wise process of making multimedia is illustrated in Figure 16-1. Use this chart to help you get your arms around a new Web site or CD-ROM production! Note the feedback loops for revisions based upon testing and experiment. Note also the constant presence of an "evaluation committee" (who could be simply a project manager) to oversee the whole.

First Person

When I was nine, my father told me about China. He brought the big spinning globe into the kitchen and used a fork to point out where we were and where China was. He explained that if we dug a hole deep enough in the backyard, eventually we would come out in someplace called "Peking." After school the next day, I began, unannounced, trenching a pit into the rocky soil of our New England backyard: the first layer was tough sod, then there was some topsoil and loam, and then a thick stratum of moist pea gravel. I was knee-deep into the next layer—hard-packed clay—when my father discovered the work site at the end of his day. He was pleased I had missed the septic tank by several feet and sternly suggested that more study would be required before I dug any further.

This was my first lesson in project planning, not to mention my first experience with project abandonment. Be sure you analyze the requirements of your multimedia project before you go to the toolshed.

The Process of Making Multimedia

Usually something will click in your mind or in the mind of a client that says, "Hey, wouldn't it be neat if we could...." Your visions of sound and music, flashy images, and perhaps some video will solve a business need, provide an attention-grabbing product demo, or yield a slick front end to an otherwise drab computer database. You might want to spark a little interest or a laugh in an otherwise dull meeting, build an interactive photo album for Christmas greetings to your family, or post your company's annual report in a new set of pages on the Web.

Idea Analysis

The important thing to keep in mind when you are toying with an idea is balance. As you think through your idea, you must continually weigh your purpose or goal against the feasibility and cost of production and delivery.

FIGURE 16-1

The process of

making multimedia

■

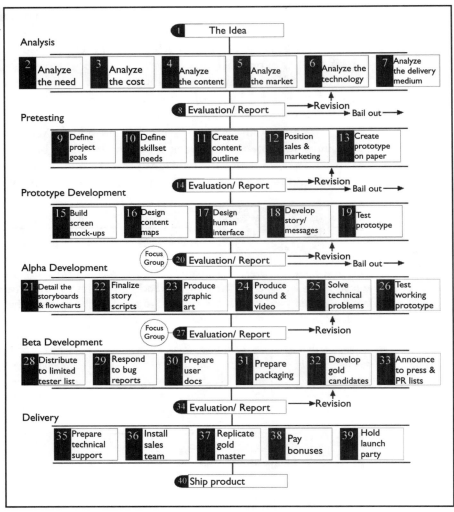

We locked eight people in a room with pizza and out popped a design....

Mike Duffy, Chief Technical Officer, Software Toolworks,
describing how the design for the "20th Century Almanac"
was developed

Use note paper and scratch pads as you flesh out your idea, or use a
note-taking or outlining program on your computer. Start with broad brush
strokes, then think through each constituent multimedia element. Ulti-

mately, you will generate a plan of action that will become your road map for production. Who needs this project? Is it worthwhile? Do you have the materials at hand to build it? Do you have the skills to build it? Your idea will be in balance if you have considered and weighed the proper elements:

- What is the essence of what you want to do? What is your purpose and message?

- How can you organize your project?

- What multimedia elements (text, sounds, and visuals) will best deliver your message?

- Do you already have content material with which you can leverage your project, such as videotape, music, documents, photographs, logos, advertisements, marketing packages, and other artwork?

- Is your idea derived from an existing theme that can be enhanced with multimedia, or will you create something totally new?

- What hardware is available for development of your project? Is it enough?

- How much storage space do you have? How much do you need?

- What hardware will be available to your end users?

- What multimedia software is available to you?

- What are your capabilities and skills with both the software and the hardware?

- Can you do it alone? Who can help you?

- How much time do you have?

- How much money do you have?

- How will you distribute the final project?

You can maintain balance between purpose and feasibility by dynamically adding and subtracting multimedia elements as you stretch and shape your idea. You can start small and build from minimum capabilities toward a satisfactory result in an additive way. Or you can shoot the moon with a heavy list of features and desired multimedia results, then discard items one-by-one because they are just not possible. Both additive and subtractive processes can work in concert. In the end, this process will yield very useful cost estimates and a production road map.

Consider the following scenario: You have a videotape with four head-and-shoulders testimonials that will be perfect for illustrating your message. So add motion video to your list. You will need to purchase a video digitizing board and digitizing software, so add those items and their cost to your list as well. But you want to make your product available at a Web site, which means people without high-speed connections will wait minutes for the video to play. Subtract motion video, but add tiny framed still images of the four talking heads (captured with your new video equipment) using short, one-sentence voice-overs of the speakers (recorded from the videotape). Subtract one of the four testimonials because you discover that particular executive is no longer with the firm. Add animation instead. Subtract. Add. Subtract. In this manner, you will flesh out your idea, adding and subtracting elements within the constraints of the hardware, software, and your budget of cost and expertise.

The time you spend defining your project in this way—reality-testing it against technology and your abilities—might be your most valuable investment, even before you boot up a computer. At any point, you can decide to go forward or bail out.

---

tip *Treat your multimedia idea like a business venture. As you visualize in your mind's eye what you want to accomplish, balance the project's profit potential against the investment of effort and resources required to make it happen.*

Pretesting

If you decide that your idea has merit, take it to the next step. Define your project goals in greater detail and spell out what it will take in terms of skills, content, and money to meet these goals. If you envision a commercial product, sketch out how you will sell it. Work up a prototype of the project on paper, with an explanation of how it will work. All of these steps help you organize your idea and test it against the real world.

Prototype Development

When you have decided that a project is worth doing, you should develop a working prototype. This is the point at which you begin serious work at the computer, building screen mock-ups and a human interface of menus and button clicks. Your messages and story lines will take shape as you explore ways of presenting them. For the prototype, sometimes called a proof-of-concept or feasibility study, you might select only a small portion of a large project and get that part working as it would in the final product. Indeed, after trying many different approaches in the course of prototying, you may end up with several different approaches or candidates. Test your prototype along several fronts: technology (will it work on your proposed delivery platform(s)?), cost (can you do this project within budget constraints?), market (can you sell it or will it be properly used, if it is an in-house project?), and human interface (is it intuitive and easy to use?). At this point you may wish to arrange a focus group, where you watch potential end users play with your prototype and analyze their reactions. The purpose of any prototype is to test the initial implementation of your idea and improve on it based upon test results. So you should never feel commited or bound to any one option, and you should be ready and willing to change things!

Alpha Development

As you go forward, you should continually define the tasks ahead—like navigating a supertanker, you should be aware of the reefs and passages that will appear along your course and be prepared. With a prototype in hand and a commitment to proceed, the investment of effort will increase and, at the same time, become more focused. More people may become involved as you begin to flesh out the project as a whole.

Beta Development

By the time your idea reaches the beta stage of development, you will have committed serious time, energy, and money, and it is likely too late to bail out. You have gone past the point of no return and should see it through. But by now you have a project that is looking great! Most of the features are working, and you are distributing it to a wider arena of testers. In fact, you are on the downhill slope, now, and your concern should be simply successfully steering the project to its well-defined goal.

Delivery

By the time you reach the delivery stage, you are "going gold." Your worries slide toward the marketplace. How will your project be received by its intended audience? And you must also deal with a great many practical details, such as who will answer the support hotline, or whether to co-locate a server or trust the current ISP to handle the predicted increased volume of hits. The Alpha, Beta, and final Gold stages of project delivery for CD-ROM and the Web are discussed in Chapter 20.

Hardware

Hardware is the most common limiting factor for realizing a multimedia idea: no sound board, then no sound effects; no synthesizer, then no MIDI composed by you on-site; no high-resolution color display, then no pretty pictures; no modem or network, then no Internet.

Begin by listing the hardware capabilities of the end user's computer platform (not necessarily the platform on which you will develop the project). If the capabilities are not enough, then examine the cost of enhancing that delivery platform and balance those results against your purpose and resources.

Available Skills and Software

You should also list the skills and software capabilities available to you. This list is not as limiting as the hardware list because you can always budget for new and more powerful software and for the learning curve (or consultant fees) required to make use of it. Indeed, the software is usually necessary only for development of the project, not its playback or delivery, and should not be a cost or learning burden passed on to end users.

The Paper Napkin

The very early idea processing and preliminary planning sketched on the working-lunch paper napkin shown in Figure 16-2 evolved into a complex multimedia project of many months duration.

First, the idea was discussed, refined, and cultivated as a preliminary project plan. Then work began with the building of a prototype, shown as the A-B portion of the napkin notes, which quite literally answered the question "How do we get from A to B with this idea?" The prototype was then carefully examined in terms of projected work effort and the technology required to implement a full-blown version of the prototype. Based upon experience, a more complete plan and cost estimate for full implementation was then developed, and the project was launched in earnest. Figure 16-3 shows a screen from the final product.

FIGURE 16-2

The ideas on this luncheon napkin evolved into an animated guided tour for Lotus's Multimedia 1-2-3 ■

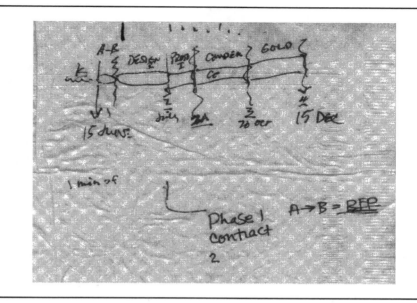

FIGURE 16-3

A screen from the guided tour for Lotus 1-2-3 for Windows with Multimedia SmartHelp, which is shipped on CD-ROM ■

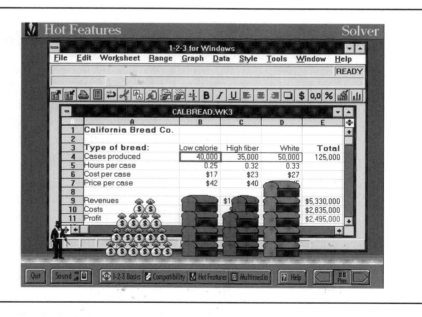

First Person

Last time I took the red-eye home, the fat guy behind me was pretty ill, sneezing and hawking incessantly over my headrest on the full, hot plane. My glasses blurred with misty droplets, and I wiped the fog away with the damp cocktail napkin under my Coke. That trip cost me four days sick in bed, and I promised I would never fly night coach again to make a meeting, no matter how important.

Then I broke my promise and, after a sleepless night on the plane, found myself sitting in the muggy summer air on the bank of the Charles River, having lunch with Rob Lippincott and his multimedia team from Lotus. I pretended to be alert, but residual white noise from the plane ride beat in my ears, and my dry eyes wouldn't focus in the umbrella sunlight. Rob made intelligent notes with a ballpoint pen on a paper napkin while my own input to the creative

process was reduced to grunts and short sentences. The smartest thing I did, though, was slip the paper napkin with its notes into my briefcase as we left the table. After some sleep, I was able to retrieve the napkin and craft those luncheon thoughts into the backbone of a rational project proposal and action plan. We launched the venture, and about ten months later it went gold, shipping with Lotus's new Multimedia 1-2-3 product.

Idea Management Software

Software such as Inspiration (see Figure 16-4), MacProject, Microsoft Project, Designer's Edge (see Figure 16-5), Screenplay System's Movie Magic Screenwriter and Dramatica Pro, outlining programs such as MORE, and spreadsheets such as Lotus 1-2-3 or Excel can be useful for arranging your ideas and the many tasks, work items, employee resources, and costs required of your multimedia project. Project management tools provide the added benefit of built-in analysis to help you stay within your schedule and budget during the rendering of the project itself.

---

warning *Budget your time if you are new to project management software. It may be difficult to learn and to use effectively.*

Project management software typically provides Critical Path Method (CPM) scheduling functions to calculate the total duration of a project based upon each identified task, earmarking tasks that are critical and that, if lengthened, will result in a delay in project completion. Program Evaluation Review Technique (PERT) charts provide graphic representations of task relationships, showing what tasks must be completed before others can commence. Gantt charts depict all the tasks along a time line.

16

Inspiration allows you to organize ideas in interrelated structures ∎

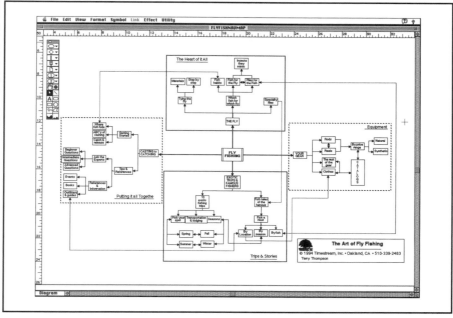

Designer's Edge, an integrated pre-authoring idea management tool from Allen Communications, generates helpful documents for instructional designers. ∎

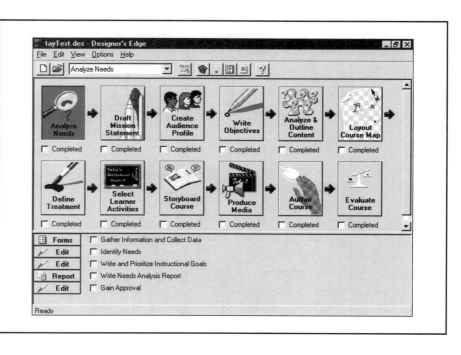

Building a Team

Multimedia is an emerging technology requiring a set of skills so broad that multimedia itself remains poorly defined. Players in this technology come from all corners of the computer and art worlds as well as from a variety of other disciplines, so if you need to assemble a team, you need to know what people and skills it takes to make multimedia. (Refer to Chapter 3 for a description of the various skills and talents needed and how others have built successful teams.) Building a matrix chart of required skills is often helpful to describe the makeup of your team. Figure 16-6 shows a skill matrix developed when four medium-sized multimedia development companies came together to bid on a single, large CD-ROM project. If you are building a complex Web site, substitute Java/Perl programmer, HTML programmer, and Server Specialist into the proper row.

FIGURE 16-6

A matrix of available skills can assist you in planning for your project

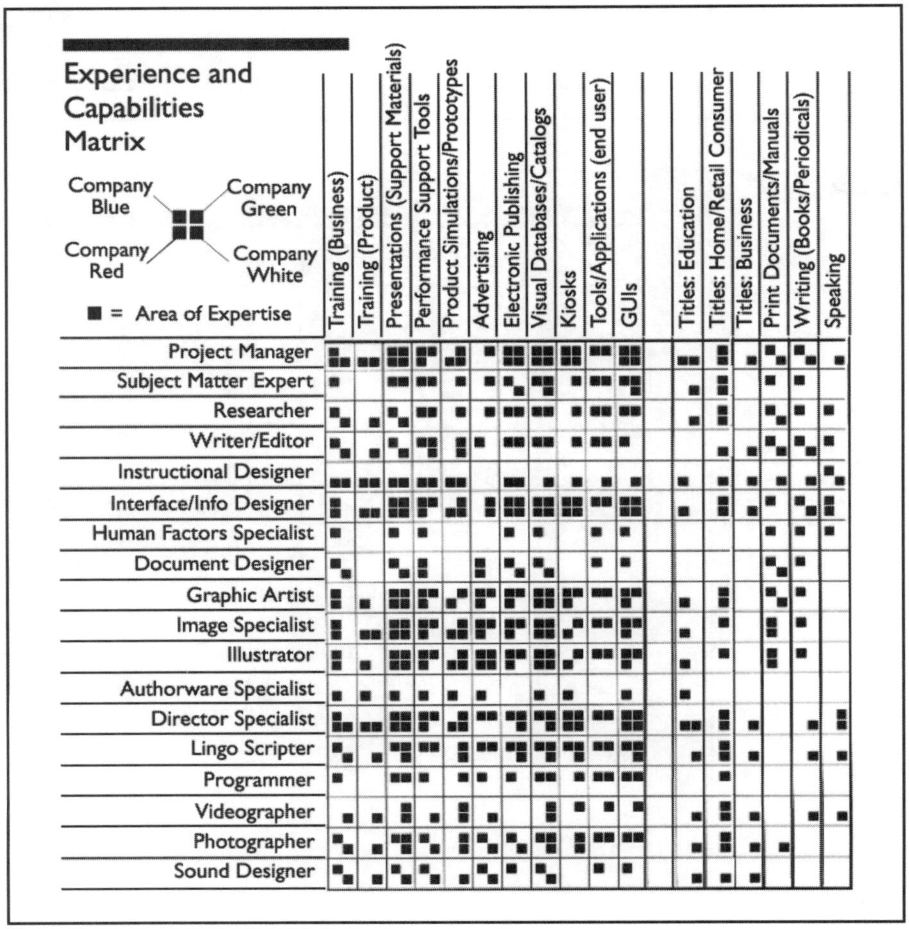

Experience and Capabilities Matrix

Company Blue · Company Green
Company Red · Company White

■ = Area of Expertise

Column headings:
- Training (Business)
- Training (Product)
- Presentations (Support Materials)
- Performance Support Tools
- Product Simulations/Prototypes
- Advertising
- Electronic Publishing
- Visual Databases/Catalogs
- Kiosks
- Tools/Applications (end user)
- GUIs
- Titles: Education
- Titles: Home/Retail Consumer
- Titles: Business
- Print Documents/Manuals
- Writing (Books/Periodicals)
- Speaking

Row labels:
- Project Manager
- Subject Matter Expert
- Researcher
- Writer/Editor
- Instructional Designer
- Interface/Info Designer
- Human Factors Specialist
- Document Designer
- Graphic Artist
- Image Specialist
- Illustrator
- Authorware Specialist
- Director Specialist
- Lingo Scripter
- Programmer
- Videographer
- Photographer
- Sound Designer

In a business where success and failure often depends upon our ability to monitor and anticipate emerging technology, job recruiters see multimedia as very challenging. Not only does the fledgling multimedia industry incorporate some of the hottest computer technology tools, it draws on talent that comes from outside the traditional boundaries of data processing and MIS recruitment. The ill-defined but very technical skills needed for multimedia provide us, the industry recruiters, an exceptional opportunity for creativity. Our clients, too, need to be open minded and flexible about the talent and skills required of multimedia developers.

Heinz Bartesch, Director of Sales and Marketing,
The Search Firm (San Francisco)

Staying at the leading edge is important. If you remain knowledgeable about what's new and expected, you will be more valuable to your own endeavors, your team, and to your employer or prospective clients. But be prepared for steep learning curves and difficult challenges in keeping your own skills and those of your employees current and in demand. And don't neglect team morale as hours grow long, deadlines slip, and tempers flare.

---

tip   *If you are looking for multimedia talent, try placing a Help Wanted ad in one of the special-interest group forums on CompuServe, America Online, or a local or national bulletin board such as that operated by the Boston Computer Society (BCS) or the Berkeley Macintosh User Group (BMUG). Job seekers will also find these forums valuable.*

* *

http//:www.careerpath.com/
http://www.occ.com/occ/
http://sun.cc.westga.edu/~coop/
news://comp.multimedia

Help Wanted ads are appearing on the World Wide Web

Pilot Projects and Prototyping

When organizing your multimedia project, it may be advisable to incorporate a proof-of-concept or pilot project phase. During this phase you can test ideas, mock up interfaces, exercise the hardware platform, and develop a sense about where the alligators live. These alligators are typically found in the swampy edges of your own expertise, in the dark recesses of software platforms that almost-but-not-quite perform as advertised, and in your misjudgment of the effort required for various tasks. The alligators will appear unexpectedly behind you and nip at your knees, unless you explore the terrain a little before you start out.

Persuade the client to spend a small amount of money and effort up front to let you build a skeletal version of the project, including some artwork, interactive navigation, and performance checks. Indeed, there may be some very specific technology issues that need thorough examination and proof before you can provide a realistic estimate of the work and cost required. The focused experience of this proof will allow both you and the client to assess the project's goals and the means to achieve them.

Build in your experimental pilot as the first phase of your project. At the pilot's conclusion, prepare a milestone report and a functional demo. You will be paid for the work so far, and the client will get real demonstration material that can be shown to bosses and managers. If your demo is good, it will be a very persuasive argument within the client's management hierarchy for completing the full-scale project. Figure 16-7 is excerpted from trial calculations that were the result of a prototype five-language PhotoCD project. In the prototyping, office staff read the voice-over script as a "scratch track," like using a stand-in for the real thing; later, professional talent was used in the recording studio. As a result of building a prototype, accurate estimates of required storage space on the disc were possible.

As part of your delivery at the end of the pilot phase, reassess your estimate of the tasks required and the cost. Prepare a written report and analysis of budgets and anticipated additional costs. This is also the proper time to develop a revised and detailed project plan for the client. It allows the client some flexibility and provides a reality check for you. At this point you can also finalize your budget and payment schedule for the continuation of the project, as well as ink a contract and determine overrun procedures.

Difficulties may arise if your client is disappointed in the quantity of material delivered or is otherwise not satisfied with your work. If you have kept good accounts of the time and effort spent during prototyping, you may be able to smooth the rough waters. Remember that developing multimedia is a "trying" experience—try this, try that, then try this again a bit differently—and soaks up a lot of hours. Listen carefully to the client's reaction to your prototype; many problems might be quickly fixed, and all constructive comments can certainly be woven into the next phase of development.

FIGURE 16-7

Trial calculations

are possible after

prototyping

■

Calculation Sheet

PhotoCD Project

Allocation of Disc Space

Note 1: The following trial calculations are based upon the file sizes yielded by an early voice rendering of the Project's English script.

Note 2: File sizes for base resolution images of 640×480 and 768×512 pixel dimensions are estimated at 768K each.

Note 3: File sizes for full imagePacs may range from 3.7MB to 4.5MB, depending upon image complexity and compression rates. The conservative figure of 4.5MB per imagePac is used in these estimates.

Note 4: More accurate real estate estimates will be available following finalization of the script and recording of the English version narration.

Note 5: Firm count of base resolution images and their pixel dimensions will be calculated upon script freeze.

SUMMARY: There is adequate room on the disc for both sound and images if each language recording is limited to no more than 9 minutes.

Scratch Track File (English)	Duration	Scratch Track File (English)	Duration
SNDE01A	18.369	SNDE12A	14.314
SNDE01B	9.180	SNDE13A	14.193
SNDE01C	9.295	SNDE14A	7.487
SNDE02A	17.609	SNDE15A	16.172
SNDE03A	17.932	SNDE16A	19.450
SNDE04A	11.156	SNDE17A	5.830
SNDE05A	18.035	SNDE18A	21.443
SNDE06A	8.050	SNDE19A	12.295
SNDE07A	12.790	Total	306.800 Seconds
SNDE08A	16.218		5.113 Minutes
SNDE09A	27.468	plus Intro Fanfare	30.0 Seconds
SNDE10A	5.658	(Shared by all languages)	
SNDE11A	23.856		

16

Not every prototype segues naturally into a full-blown project. Sometimes a project is shut down at this milestone due to reality shock: the client chokes on cost-to-completion estimates. Sometimes it's the reorg alligator: new managers with new agendas axe the project. Sometimes the client just plain doesn't like your work. Then sometimes a project simply disappears like a dream forgotten by mid-morning.

We were invited to prepare the prototype for a large and intricate intranet site behind a corporate fire wall—potentially a two-year involvement. We proposed a first phase, an analysis and definition of the company's structure and information gathering and dissemination needs so we could lock down major content areas and the navigation design. We wanted to know how many buttons to put on the main menu and what they would say, before we spent long hours creating the bitmaps and animated .GIFs of a neat interface. "No, no," they said,

"our guys have put that together already."

So we negotiated for creation of artwork and HTML page styles that would provide a consistent "look and feel" through the site. We set a fixed price and provided a list of deliverables: (1) Graphic style and GIF/JPEG elements for main home and sub pages; (2) A complete site structure and map with navigationally functional "under construction" pages based on the organizational charts they would provide; and (3) Working "demo" pages for two of the company's departments.

Then came our first team meeting, and it soon became clear they needed hand-holding while their own MIS people transitioned from other tasks and got up to speed in their new jobs as in-house intranet team and webmasters. None had coded a page of HTML, although some had used editors and builders to get pages working. The database guy was stopped dead by an undefined Java error when accessing his massive SQL database. The server guy was still getting set up. The HTML guy was learning

his authoring tools. There was neither a graphic artist nor a handy pool of company graphic art from which our own contribution might spring. OK, we thought, so they're on the learning curve. We can start from scratch. We took the group leader aside and quietly suggested that she consider bringing on a full-time graphics person to support her team.

During the next weeks, we developed a classy look and feel and theme. After a couple of feedback/change loops, they loved it. We worked up the more detailed bits and pieces of our deliverable and tightened up the organization of their proposed navigation map. By prototype deadline, we had spent all the hours we had estimated for the job, and they had the site up and working in test mode. We had gotten their motor running.

Last we saw of the SQL database programmer, on the afternoon we picked up our milestone check, he was removing shrinkwrap from a new copy of Photoshop, and the HTML guy was deep into NetObjects Fusion. We never heard from them again.

Task Planning

There may be many tasks in your multimedia project. Here is a brief checklist of action items for which you should plan ahead as you think through your project:

- ☐ Design Instructional Framework
- ☐ Hold Creative Idea Session(s)
- ☐ Determine Delivery Platform
- ☐ Determine Authoring Platform
- ☐ Assay Available Content
- ☐ Draw Navigation Map
- ☐ Create Storyboards
- ☐ Design Interface
- ☐ Design Information Containers
- ☐ Research/Gather Content
- ☐ Assemble Team
- ☐ Build Prototype
- ☐ Conduct User Test
- ☐ Revise Design
- ☐ Create Graphics
- ☐ Create Animations
- ☐ Produce Audio
- ☐ Produce Video
- ☐ Digitize Audio and Video
- ☐ Take Still Photographs
- ☐ Program and Author
- ☐ Test Functionality
- ☐ Fix Bugs
- ☐ Conduct Beta Test
- ☐ Create Golden Master
- ☐ Replicate
- ☐ Prepare Package
- ☐ Deliver or Install at Web Site
- ☐ Award Bonuses
- ☐ Throw Party

16

FIGURE 16-8

Portion of a spreadsheet used to schedule manpower and project costs

	SALARY	1	2	3	4	5	6	7	8	9	10
PROJECT CALC SHEET		MARCH				APRIL				MAY	
C. 5 5 $112,000		1	2	3	4	5	6	7	8	9	10
1 CONTEN ORIGINATION FEE											
DIRECTOR	40	0.1	0.1	0.1	0.1	0.1	0.1	0.1	0.1	0.1	0.1
cost		0.22	0.22	0.22	0.22	0.22	0.22	0.22	0.22	0.22	0.22
EDITOR	20					1	1				
cost		0.00	0.00	0.00	0.00	1.12	1.12	0.00	0.00	0.00	0.00
WRITER A	40	1	1	1	1	1					
cost		2.24	2.24	2.24	2.24	2.24	0.00	0.00	0.00	0.00	0.00
RESEARCHER	16										
cost		0.00	0.00	0.00	0.00	0.00	0.00	0.00	0.00	0.00	0.00
subtotal number personnel		1.1	1.1	1.1	1.1	2.1	1.1	1.1	0.1	0.1	0.1
cost		2.46	2.46	2.46	2.46	3.58	1.34	0.22	0.22	0.22	0.22
2 ART											
DIRECTOR	35	1	1	1	1	1	1	1	1	1	1
cost		1.40	1.40	1.40	1.40	1.40	1.40	1.40	1.40	1.40	1.40
ART 1	18								1	1	1
cost		0.00	0.00	0.00	0.00	0.00	0.00	0.00	1.01	1.01	1.01
ART2	13										
cost		0.00	0.00	0.00	0.00	0.00	0.00	0.00	0.00	0.00	0.00
subtotal number personnel		1	1	1	1	1	1	1	2	2	2
cost		1.40	1.40	1.40	1.40	1.40	1.40	1.40	2.41	2.41	2.41
3 TECHNICAL											
DIRECTOR	35								1	1	1
cost		0.00	0.00	0.00	0.00	0.00	0.00	0.00	1.40	1.40	1.40

Scheduling

When you have worked up a plan that encompasses the phases, tasks, and work items you feel will be required to complete your project, you need to lay out these elements along a timeline. To do this, you must estimate the total time required for each task and then allocate this time among the number of persons who will be asynchronously working on the project (see, for example, Figure 16-8). Again, the notion of balance is important: if you can distribute the required hours to perform a task among several workers, completion should take proportionally less time.

warning   *Assigning twice as many people to work on a task may not cut the time for its completion precisely in half. Consider the administrative and management overhead of communication, networking, and necessary staff meetings required when additional staff is added.*

Scheduling can be difficult for multimedia projects because so much of the making of multimedia is artistic trial and error. A recorded sound will need to be edited and perhaps altered many times. Animations need to be run again and again and adjusted so that they are smooth and properly placed. A QuickTime or MPEG movie may require many hours of editing and tweaking before it works in sync with other screen activities.

Scheduling multimedia projects is also difficult because the technology of computer hardware and software is in constant flux, and upgrades while your project is under way may drive you to new installations and concomitant learning curves. The general rule of thumb when working with computers and new technology under a deadline is that everything will take longer to do than you think it will.

In scheduling for a project that is to be rendered for a client, remember that the client will need to approve or sign off on your work at various stages. This approval process takes time, and it may also require revision of your submitted work. These client feedback loops depend upon factors beyond your control and can wreak havoc with your schedule.

tip *When you negotiate with your client, limit the number of revisions allowed (each revision costs time and money) before you rename the revisions as change orders and bill extra.*

First Person

M any times we have heard about the Feedback Alligator. Its mottled skin boasts an Escher-like pattern of lines and marks, showing apparently clear definition along the head and neck, but converging to a brown muddled wash at the tail. When the tail wags this alligator, all hell breaks loose, and multimedia contracts can be severely strained or lost altogether.

Feedback Alligators can appear when you throw a client into the mix of creative people... when necessary-for-client-satisfaction approval cycles can turn your project into an anorexic nightmare of continuing rework, change, and consequently diminished profit. These alligators typically slink out from the damps after you have locked down a contract and scope of work, when the creative guys are already being well paid to ply their craft.

For client protection, multimedia creative artists should be hired with a cap on budget and time. They should be highly skilled, efficient, and have a clear understanding of what a project's goals are, and they should be allowed to accomplish these goals with as much freedom as possible. But good multimedia artists should come close to the mark the first time.

They don't always. For example, you agree to compose background theme music to play whenever your client's logo shows on the screen. You master a sample cassette tape and pass it to the client. She doesn't quite like the sound but is not sure why. You go back to the MIDI sequencer and try again. The client still isn't sure that's it. Again, you make up a tape and pass it to her for review. No, maybe it needs a little more Sgt. Pepper... this is our logo, remember?

The process of client feedback can go on and on forever in a resonance of desire-to-please and creative uncertainty unless you have developed rules for limiting these cycles. While your client might always be right, you will still go broke working unlimited changes on a fixed budget.

So do two things to ward off the Feedback Alligator. First, make it clear up front (in your contract) that there will be only a certain number of review cycles before the client must pay for changes. Second, invite the client to the workstation or studio where the creative work is done. For sound, tickle the keyboard until the client says, "That's it!" Make 'em sign off on it. For artwork and animations, let the client spend an afternoon riding shotgun over the artist's shoulder, participating in color and design choices. Get the client involved.

If your client contact isn't empowered to make decisions but simply carries your work up to the bosses for "management approval," you are facing the unpleasant Son of Feedback Alligator. Demand a client contact who has budget and design authority.

Estimating

In production and manufacturing industries, it is a relatively simple matter to estimate costs and effort. To make chocolate chip cookies, for example, you need ingredients, such as flour and sugar, and equipment, such as mixers, ovens, and packaging machines. Once the process is running smoothly, you can turn out hundreds of cookies, each tasting the same and each made of the same stuff. You then control your costs by fine-tuning known expenses, negotiating deals on flour and sugar in quantity, installing more efficient ovens, and hiring personnel at a more competitive wage. In contrast, making multimedia is not a repetitive manufacturing process. Rather, it is by its very nature a continuous research and development effort characterized by creative trial and error—a "trying" experience, as described above. Each new project is somewhat different from the last, and each may require application of many different tools and solutions. Philosophers will counsel you that experience is something you get only after you need it!

In the area of professional services, let's consider some typical costs in the advertising community. Production of a storyboard for a 30-second commercial spot costs about $50,000. Post-production editing time in a professional video studio runs upwards of $500 per hour. An hour of professional acting talent costs $350 or more at union scale. The emerging multimedia industry, on the other hand, does not have a track record long enough to have produced "going rates" for its services. A self-guided tour distributed with a software product, for example, may cost $15,000 for one client and $150,000 for another, depending upon the tour's length and polish. A short original musical clip may cost $50 or $500, based on the talent used and the nature of the music. A graphical menu screen might take 2 or 20 hours to develop, depending on its complexity and the graphic art talent applied. Without available going rates for segments of work or entire projects, you must estimate the costs of your multimedia project by analyzing the tasks that it comprises and the people who build it.

The first time you accomplish a multimedia task, it will demand great effort as you learn the software and hardware tools and the techniques required. The second time you do a similar task, you will already know where the tools are and how they work, and the task will require less effort. On the third take, you should be quite proficient.

tip *To recoup learning-curve costs when you first perform a task, you must factor extra time into your budget; later you can increase your billing rate to reflect your improved skill level.*

Be sure you include the hidden costs of administration and management. It takes time to speak with clients on the telephone, to write progress reports, and to mail invoices. In addition, there may be many people in your workforce who represent specialized skills, for example, a graphic artist, musician, instructional designer, and writer. In this case, you'll need to include a little extra buffer of time and expense in your estimate to pay for these artists' participation in project meetings and creative sessions.

As a general rule, there are three elements that can vary in project estimates: time, money, and people. As illustrated below, if you decrease any one of these elements, you'll generally need to increase one or both of the others. For example, if you have very little time to do a project (an aggressive schedule), it will cost more money in overtime and premium sweat, and it may take more people. If you have a good number of people, the project should take less time. By increasing the money spent, you can actually decrease the number of people required by purchasing efficient (but costly) experts; this may also reduce the time required.

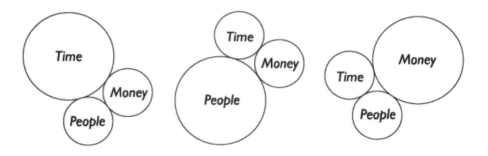

Do your best to estimate the amount of time it will take to perform each task in your plan. Multiply this estimate by your hourly billing rate. Sum the total costs for each task, and you now have an estimate of the project's total time and cost. Though this simple formula is easy, what is not so easy is diligently remaining within the budgeted time and money for each task. For this, you need good tracking and management oversight.

Billing Rates

Your billing rate should be set according to your cost of doing business plus a reasonable profit margin. Typical billing rates for multimedia production companies and Web designers range from $60 to $150 an hour, depending upon the work being done and the person doing it. If consultants or specialists are employed on a project, the billing rate can go much higher. You can establish a rate that is the same for all tasks, or you can specify different rates according to the person assigned to a task.

Everyone who contributes to a project should have two rates associated with their work: the employee's cost to the employer (including salary and benefits), and the employee's rate billed to the customer. The employee's cost, of course, is not included in your estimate, but you need to know this as part of your estimate—because your profit margin is the difference between the rate you charge the client and the cost to your company, less a proportion of overhead expenses (rental or leasing of space, utilities, phones, shared secretarial and administrative services, and so forth). If your profit margin is negative, you should reconsider both your project plan and your long-term business plan.

Multimedia production companies and Web site builders with high billing rates claim their skillset and experience allow them to accomplish more work in a given amount of time, expertly, thus saving money, time, and enhancing the finished quality and reliability of a project. This is particularly the case with larger-scale, complex projects. Smaller and leaner companies that offer lower billing rates may claim to be more streamlined, hungry, and willing to perform extra services. Lower rates do not necessarily mean lower-quality work, but rather imply that the company either supports less overhead or is satisfied with a reduced profit margin. The business of making multimedia is a "low entry barrier" enterprise because all you need to get started is some (relatively) inexpensive computer hardware and software, not a 70,000 square foot factory or expensive tooling. You can make multimedia in a living room, basement, or garage. As more and more multimedia producers and Web developers enter this marketplace, the competition is increasing and the free hand of supply and demand is driving prices (down).

Purchasers of multimedia services must, however, thoroughly examine the qualifications of a prospective contracting person or company to ensure that the work required can be accomplished on time and within budget. There is no more difficult business situation than a half-completed job and an exhausted budget.

16

We were asked by a large institution to complete a project that had fallen on the floor. It was really worse than that—the project had actually slipped through the cracks in that floor. The single known copy of the work—representing about $30,000 in paid billings—had been copied to 19 high-density floppy disks and stored in a file cabinet. Here, they were discovered by the secretarial pool and formatted, to be used for WordPerfect documents. The secretaries remembered the whole thing because the stored backups contained protected files, so the disks were unusually difficult to erase! Luckily, bits and pieces of the project were unearthed on the hard disk of a computer that had been disconnected and stored in the basement. We were able to reconstruct much of the artwork, but not the interactive links.

As we studied the leavings of the embarrassed progenitors, we discovered a trail of mistakes and errors. It became clear that the institution made a bad decision in hiring a well-qualified engineering firm at great expense (standard billing rates) to construct a difficult multimedia presentation. CAD/CAM drawings and finite element analysis were the forte of these engineers—not animated icons and colorful bitmaps with sound tracks.

Furthermore, the engineering firm erred in selecting software that performed on the target hardware platform at about the speed of snails chasing a dog. Money had been spent, the product didn't work, and everyone involved was in gray limbo, slinking around, looking for a solution.

We determinedly pulled together the bits and pieces we could find, designed a snappy navigational structure we were proud of, and quickly fixed the big problem for a small fee (based upon our own standard billing rate). The institution, of course, was delighted and became a client of long standing.

Contractors and consultants can bring specialized skills such as graphic art, C and Java programming, database expertise, music composition, and video to your project. If you use these experts, be sure your billing rate is higher than theirs. Or, if you have a task the client has capped with a not-to-exceed cost, be sure your arrangement with the contractor is also capped. Contractors place no burden on your overhead and administration other than a few cups of coffee, and they should generate a generous profit margin for you during the course of your project. Be sure that contractors perform the majority of their work off-site, using their own equipment; otherwise, federal tax regulators may reclassify these freelancers as employees and require you to pay employee benefits. In 1998, in *Vizcaino v. Microsoft,* the U.S. Supreme Court required the Microsoft Corporation to pay employee benefits to hundreds of workers that the court determined were regular employees rather than independent contractors. There are about 20 factors, according to the IRS, in making a determination whether a worker is an employee or an independent contractor for tax purposes, and companies may be liable for all employment benefits, including (as Microsoft discovered) stock option and stock sharing plans, if the work arrangement is not carefully constructed.

Example Cost Sheets

Figure 16-9 contains groups of expense categories for producing multimedia. If you use these in your own work, be sure to temper your guesses with experience; if you are new to multimedia production, get some qualified advice during this planning stage.

First Person

I was downbound from Puget Sound to San Francisco, and the weather was up, with seas running heavy and winds gusting to 80 knots in our face. The Master and the First Mate were on the bridge, the old man sitting curled up in his upholstered highchair on the darkened starboard wing, the First pacing on the rubber mat behind the helmsman. The Third Mate was on watch, leaning over the radar screen and making fluorescent notes with a grease pencil. As I was a guest with no duties, I mostly hung out in the chart room while white water broke over the bows and the shuddering propeller came out of the sea; wind screamed in the vents on the roof of the bridge. There wasn't much conversation that night, but the Master slowed us to 5 knots, concerned about the containers lashed to the forward deck.

When the young Third Mate came into the chart room, I asked, "Where are we?" and he took a sharp pencil, made a fine point on the chart, and drew a tiny circle around the point; he smiled, proud to have good radar bearings. The First Mate came in about a half hour later, and, when I asked the same question, he circled an area about the size of a walnut. As the Master left the bridge for his cabin, I asked him, too, where we were. He took his thumb and rubbed it on the chart in a rough oval about the diameter of his fist, saying, "Somewhere in here," and grinned at me as the ship heaved suddenly and we grabbed for the handholds.

The more experience these professionals had, the larger the circle they drew, and the less they relied upon pinpoint navigation. You should be prudent when costing a multimedia production; precision estimating can wreck your project.

FIGURE 16-9

There are many costs associated with producing multimedia

■

PROJECT DEVELOPMENT COSTS

Salaries
Client Meetings
Acquisition of Content
Communications
Travel
Research
Proposal & Contract Prep
Overhead

PRODUCTION COSTS

Management
  Salaries
  Communications
  Travel
  Consumables
Content Gathering
  Salaries
  Research Services
  Licenses
Graphics Production
  Salaries
  Hardware/Software
  Fees for Content Use
  Animation
  Consumables
Audio Production
  Salaries
  Hardware/Software
  Studio Fees
  Licenses
  Consumables

Data Storage
Talent Fees
Video Production
  Salaries
  Hardware/Software
  Equipment Rental
  Talent Fees
  Location Fees
  Studio Fees
  Digital Capture & Editing
  Consumables
Authoring
  Salaries
  Hardware/Software
  Consumables

TESTING COSTS

Salaries
Focus Groups
Editing
Beta Program

DISTRIBUTION COSTS

Salaries
Documentation
Packaging
Manufacturing
Marketing
Advertising
Shipping

RFPs and Bid Proposals

Often potential clients don't have a clue about how to make multimedia, but they have a vision or a mandate. You field a telephone call, a voice describes a need or a want, and you explain how you (and your company) can satisfy that need. Much of the talk may be instructional as you teach the client about the benefits and pitfalls of multimedia in all its forms. You seldom will glean enough information during this initial discussion to accurately estimate time or cost, so be prepared to answer these queries in vague terms while you present your available skillsets and capabilities in the most favorable light. If the client is serious and your instruction well received, in short time you may be able to guide this client into good choices and reasonable decisions, working together to conceive and design an excellent product. Discussions will soon turn into design meetings. Somewhere along the way, you will sign a contract.

Occasionally you may encounter a more formal Request for Proposal (RFP). These are typically detailed documents from large corporations who are "outsourcing" their multimedia development work. Figure 16-10 is an example of such a document that provides background information, scope of work, and information about the bidding process. Still, you should note that there is little "hard" information in this document; most bid proposals require contact with the client to fill in details prior to bidding.

A multimedia bid proposal will be passed through several levels of a company so that managers and directors can evaluate the project's quality and its price. The higher a bid proposal goes in the management hierarchy, the less chance it has of being read in detail. For this reason, you always want to provide an executive summary or overview as the first page of your proposal, briefly describing the project's goals, how the goals will be achieved, and the cost.

In the body of the proposal, include a section dealing with creative issues, and describe your method for conveying the client's message or meeting the graphic and interactive goals of the project. Also incorporate a discussion of technical issues, in which you clearly define the target hardware platform. If necessary, identify the members of your staff who will work on the project, and list their roles and qualifications.

The backbone of the proposal is the estimate and project plan that you have created up to this point. It describes the scope of the work. If the project is complicated, prepare a brief synopsis of both the plan and the timetable; include this in the overview. If there are many phases, you can present each phase as a separate section of the proposal.

Cost estimates for each phase or deliverable milestone, as well as payment schedules, should follow the description of the work. If this section is lengthy, it should also include a summary.

---

tip *Make the proposal look good—it should be attractive and easy to read. You might also wish to provide an unbound copy so that it can be easily photocopied. Include separate, relevant literature about your company and qualifications. A list of clients and brief descriptions of projects you have successfully completed are also useful for demonstrating your capabilities.*

<table>
<tr><td>

FIGURE 16-10

Some Requests for

Proposals provide

great detail

■

</td><td>

<h2 style="text-align:center">Smythe Industries
Request for Proposal</h2>

Summary: The objective is to produce a family of materials that will develop a unique personality and visual image for the Smythe Campus in Vancouver, British Columbia, home of multiple Smythe subsidiaries and divisions.

As background, Smythe Industries was launched in 1995 following the acquisition of Wilson Aluminum Foundries, Ltd. (Canada) and Fenwick Rolling Mills, Inc. (U.S.A.) and is based in Vancouver. The site is also the headquarters for Global Aluminum Research, a research and development subsidiary. In addition, there are discussions concerning the establishment of a special alloy research institute at the Vancouver campus.

Each of the entities has unique personality traits, management structures, and business cultures which will need to be recognized and incorporated into the design process.

Audience and Message
Potential Employees - "employer of choice"
Business Development - "partner of choice"
  Metals Companies
  Academic Institutions
Government/Community officials - "good neighbor/citizen"
Smythe Employees - "credible/proud"
Scientific/Engineering Organizations - "credible research/scientifically advanced"

Tone and Manner
Innovative, scientifically advanced, sophisticated, credible
Colorful: jewel colors/crisp/high contrast
Energetic, modern, innovative, cutting edge
Geometric lines and shapes (vs. free form)
A human element: photography, illustration, etc.
Personable, warm, intellectually inviting

<h2 style="text-align:center">Electronic Communications RFP</h2>

Multimedia Presentation Capabilities
Summary: The objective is to create a set of tools that will deliver key messages while positioning Smythe Vancouver as an innovative user of technology for communication. There will be two components to this project: a presentation format and a library of images. We would like to develop a library, including still imagery, audio, and QuickTime movies, that can be contained on a set of CDs. Note: all images should be created with the goal of repurposing across different mediums and projects.

The key purpose is to make core messages and the corporate personality come alive by utilizing sound and motion. These multimedia assets will be used for recruiting purposes at career centers, job fairs, and in-house for visiting recruits. They will also serve as presentation support material at scientific and engineering forums. Smythe will work with the multimedia design firm to create and identify existing television clips, video, and other material that can serve to reinforce key messages.

</td></tr>
</table>

FIGURE 16-10

Some Requests for

Proposals provide

great detail

(continued)

■

External Web Site
Summary: As the most visible element of Smythe's Vancouver identity, the Web site will set the stage for positioning the company in the research community as an employer of choice and a key player in esoteric alloy and metallurgical research. The Web site will provide easy navigation for users to reach the areas of greatest interest to them, e.g., a particular business division, academic papers, employment opportunities, etc.

The multimedia design firm will also be expected to create a library of images that can be utilized to update the site periodically. The design firm should also be prepared to provide input on ways to easily update and cost-effectively maintain the site. In addition, the Web site should be created so that audio and live imagery can be incorporated and downloaded easily by users who have the appropriate equipment.

Internal Web Site
Summary: The internal Web site is the primary medium for employee communication. It will be a usable, interesting tool for internal users and serve to reinforce corporate messages and the campus culture. Since the Web site represents and includes different business entities on campus, this internal site will also introduce employees to activities in which other business units and groups are involved.

The site will need to be designed with a template format so that it can be easily updated.

Production Elements for all Electronic Communications
Icons: Develop an illustrative style for a family of icons shared across the CD-ROM, internal Web site, and external Web site.

Interface Design: Develop an interface design that provides design parameters and a personality for the internal Web site and external Web site. (Note: Internal and external Web sites should carry a similar look and feel; however, it must be easy to distinguish between the two.)

Visual Image: Produce a library of visual images. This will require the additional production of video clips and sound clips.

Photography: A photo shoot schedule and plan will be developed with Smythe to most effectively maximize time and resources in shooting photos which can be used in print, in the Web sites, and in multimedia materials.

RFP Process
Quotations: Itemize quotes, e.g. project management, copy writing, editing, design, photography, illustrations, etc. Also provide three references.

Note: Smythe will write the HTML directives in-house and will also be posting to a server that is maintained in-house.

All quotes should be submitted to:
Suzanne Petruski
Project Manager
Smythe Industries
65 Silver Foil
Vancouver, BC, CANADA

Finally, include a list of your terms. Contract terms may become a legally binding document, so have your terms reviewed by legal counsel. An example is shown in Figure 16-11. Terms should include the following:

- A description of your billing rates and invoicing policy.

- Your policy for billing out-of-pocket expenses for travel, telephone, courier services, and so forth.

- Your policy regarding third-party licensing fees for run-time modules and special drivers (the client pays).

- Specific statements of who owns what upon completion of the project. You may wish to retain the rights to show parts of the work for your own promotional purposes and to reuse in other projects segments of code and algorithms that you develop.

- An assurance to the client that you will not disclose proprietary information.

- Your right to display your credits appropriately within the work.

- Your unlimited right to work for other clients.

- A disclaimer for liability and damages arising out of the work.

It is a significant task to write a project proposal that creatively sells a multimedia concept, accurately estimates the scope of work, and provides realistic budget costs. The proposal often becomes a melting pot—you develop the elements of your idea during early conversations with a potential client and add in the results of discussions on technique and approach with graphic artists and instructional designers. You blend what the client wants done with what you can actually do, given the client's budgetary constraints, and when the cauldron of compromise cools, your proposal is the result.

The Cover and Package

You have many options for designing the look and feel of your proposal. And though one is often warned to avoid judging a book by its cover, the reality is that it takes about two seconds for executives to assess the quality of the document they are holding. Sometimes, they decide before even touching it. Size up the people who will read your proposal and ferret out their expectations; tailor your proposal to these expectancies.

FIGURE 16-11

Sample contract

terms adapted from

language developed

by the HyperMedia

Group, Inc. (do not

use without

appropriate legal

counsel)

■

Sample Terms:
We will undertake this assignment on a time-and-expenses basis at our current hourly rate of $___ per hour for __job title__, $___ per hour for __job title__, $___ per hour for __job title__ , plus applicable taxes and reimbursement of authorized out-of-pocket expenses. Reasonable travel, express, freight, courier and telecommunication expenses incurred in relation to the project, will be considered pre-authorized. [Client] will be responsible for all licensing fees of third-party products incorporated (with [Client]'s knowledge and approval) into the final product. We will invoice [Client] either upon [Client]'s acceptance of the specified deliverables for each work phase specified above, or monthly, whichever is more often. [Client]'s authorization, either written or verbal, to commence a work phase will constitute acceptance of the previous phase's deliverables. Invoices are due and payable upon presentation. To commence work, we require a retainer in the amount of $_____, which will be deducted from the final invoice for the project.

Upon our receipt of final payment, [Client] shall own all rights, except those noted below, to the completed work delivered under this agreement, including graphics, written text, and program code. [Client] may at [Client]'s sole discretion copyright the work in [Client]'s name or assign rights to a third party. Ownership of material provided by third parties and incorporated in our work with [Client]'s knowledge and approval shall be as provided in any license or sale agreement governing said materials. We reserve the right to use in any of our future work for ourselves or any client all techniques, structures, designs and individual modules of program code we develop that are applicable to requirements outside those specified above. Further, our performance of this work for [Client] shall in no way limit us regarding assignments we may accept from any other clients now or at any time in the future.

We shall be allowed to show [Client]'s finished work, or any elements of it, to existing and prospective clients for demonstration purposes. If such demonstration showings would reveal information [Client] has identified to us as proprietary or confidential, we shall be allowed to create a special version for demonstrations which omits or disguises such information and/or [Client]'s identity as the client. We shall also be allowed to include a production credit display, e.g. "Produced by [Our Name]" or equivalent copy, on the closing screen or other mutually agreeable position in the finished work. Following [Client]'s acceptance of this proposal we shall also be allowed to identify [Client] as a client in our marketing communications materials.

In the event it is necessary in the course of this assignment for us to view or work with information of [Client]'s that [Client] identify to us as proprietary and confidential (possibly including customer lists, supplier data, financial figures and the like), we agree not to disclose it except to our principals, associates and contractors having confidentiality agreements with us.

We make no warranty regarding this work, or its fitness for a particular purpose, once [Client] accepts it following any testing procedures of [Client]'s choice. In any event, our liability for any damages arising out of this work, expressly including consequential damages, shall not exceed the total amount of fees paid for this work.

If your client judges from the cover of your proposal that the document inside is amateurish rather than professional, you are already fighting an uphill battle. There are two strategies for avoiding this negative first impression:

1. Develop your own special style for a proposal cover and package, including custom fonts, cover art and graphics, illustrations and figures, unique section and paragraph styles, and a clean binding. Do your proposal first class.

2. Make the entire package plain and simple, yet businesslike. The "plain" part of the approach means not fussing with too many fonts and type styles. This austerity may be particularly successful for proposals to government agencies, where 10-point Courier Elite or 12-point Pica may be not just a de facto standard, but a required document format. For the "simple" part of the approach, a stapled sheaf of papers is adequate. Don't try to dress up your plain presentation with Pee-Chee folders or cheap plastic covers; keep it lean and mean.

16

Table of Contents

Busy executives want to anticipate a document and grasp its content in very short order. A table of contents or index is a straightforward way to present the elements of your proposal in condensed overview. In some situations, you may also wish to include an Executive Summary—a prelude containing no more than a few paragraphs of pithy description and budget totals. The summary should be on the cover page or immediately following.

Needs Analysis and Description

In many proposals, it is useful to describe in some detail the reason the project is being put forward. This Needs Analysis and Description is particularly common in proposals that must move through a company's executive hierarchy in search of approval and funding.

Target Audience

All multimedia proposals should include a section that describes the target audience and target platform. When the end user's multimedia capabilities have a broad and uncertain range, it is very important to describe the hardware and software delivery platform you intend to provide. For instance, if your project requires a compact disc player but the end user platform has none, you will need to adjust your multimedia strategy by revising the design or by requiring the end user to acquire a player. Some clients will clearly control the delivery platform, so you may not need to provide detail regarding system components.

Creative Strategy

A Creative Strategy section—a description of the look and feel of the project itself—can be important to your proposal, especially if the executives reviewing your proposal were not present for creative sessions or did not participate in preliminary discussions. If you have a library of completed projects that are similar to your proposed effort, it is helpful to include them with your proposal, pointing the client to techniques and presentation methods that may be relevant. If you have designed a prototype, describe it here, or create a separate heading and include graphics and diagrams.

Project Implementation

A proposal must describe the way a project will be organized and scheduled. Your estimate of costs and expenses will be based upon this description. The Project Implementation section of your proposal may contain a detailed calendar, PERT and Gantt charts, and lists of specific tasks with associated completion dates and work hours. This information may be general or very detailed, depending upon the demands of the client. The Project Implementation section is not just about how much work there is, but how the work will be managed and performed. You may not need to specify time estimates in work hours, but rather in the amount of calendar time required to complete each phase.

Budget

The budget relates directly to the scope of work you have laid out in the Project Implementation section. Distill your itemized costs from the Project Implementation description and consolidate the minute tasks of each project phase into categories of activity meaningful to the client.

Multi

[Feedback loops and good communication between the design and production effort are critical to the success of a project.]

strengths and limitations

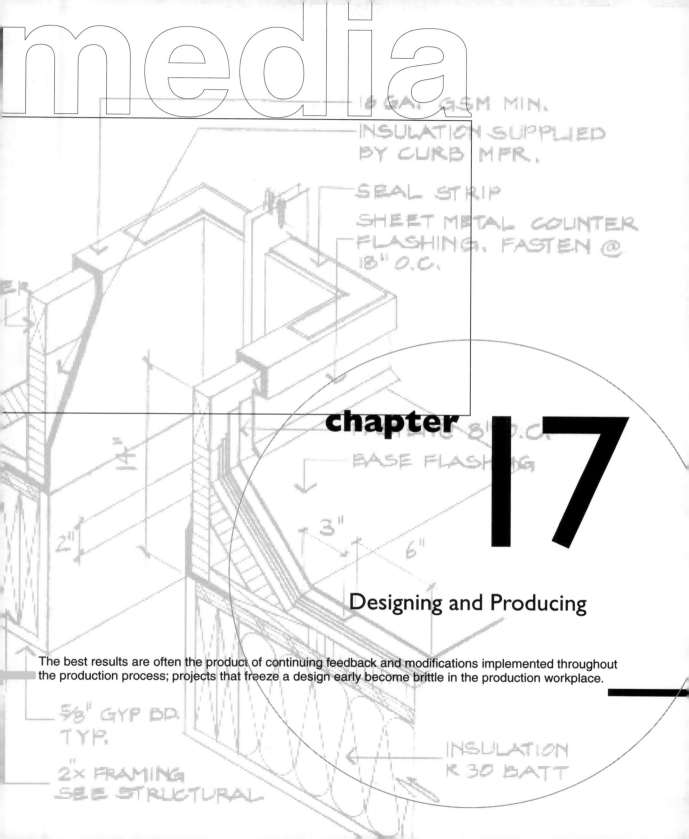

media

6 GA. GSM MIN.

INSULATION SUPPLIED
BY CURB MFR.

SEAL STRIP

SHEET METAL COUNTER
FLASHING, FASTEN @
18" O.C.

chapter 17

BASE FLASHING

3"   6"

Designing and Producing

The best results are often the product of continuing feedback and modifications implemented throughout the production process; projects that freeze a design early become brittle in the production workplace.

5/8" GYP BD.
TYP.

2" FRAMING
SEE STRUCTURAL

INSULATION
R 30 BATT

D E S I G N I N G and building multimedia projects go hand-in-hand. Indeed, design input to a project is never over until the product is actually frozen and shipped. The best products are often the result of continuing feedback and modifications implemented throughout the production process; projects that freeze a design too early become brittle in the production workplace, losing the chances for incremental improvement. But there is a danger: too much feedback and too many changes can kill a project, draining it of time and money. Always balance proposed changes against their cost to avoid the "creeping features" syndrome.

Just as the architect of a high-rise office tower must understand how to utilize the materials with which he or she works (lest the construction collapse on trusting clients), designers of multimedia projects must also understand the strengths and limitations of the elements that will go into their project. It makes no sense, for example, to design the audio elements of a multimedia project in memory-consuming 16-bit, 44.1 kHz stereo sound when the delivery CD-ROM will not have sufficient room for it; or to produce lengthy full-screen QuickTime movies to play at 30 frames per second over the Internet when end users connect with 28.8 Kbps modems; or to design 24-bit color graphics for elementary schools when that environment supports 8-bit graphics. Architects don't design inner-city parking garages with 14-foot ceilings and wide turning radii for 18-wheel big rigs, and they don't build them using wood or mud laid on a swampy foundation.

Designers must work closely with producers to ensure that their ideas can be properly realized, and producers need to confirm the results of their work with the designers. "These colors seem to work better—what do you think?" "It plays faster now, but I had to change the animation sequence...." "Doing the index with highlighted lines slows it down—can we eliminate this feature?" Feedback loops and good communication between the design and production effort are critical to the success of a project.

The idea processing (described in Chapter 16) of your multimedia project will have resulted in a detailed and balanced plan of action, a production schedule, and a timetable. Now it's time for implementation!

Designing

The design part of your project is where your knowledge and skill with computers, your talent in graphic arts, video, and music, and your ability to conceptualize logical pathways through information are all focused to create the real thing. Design is thinking, choosing, making, and doing. It is shaping, smoothing, reworking, polishing, testing, and editing. When you design your project, your ideas and concepts are moved one step closer to reality. Competence in the design phase is what separates amateurs from professionals in the making of multimedia.

---

tip *Never begin a multimedia project without first outlining its structure and content.*

Depending on the scope of your project and the size and style of your team, you can take two approaches to creating an original interactive multimedia design. You can spend great effort on the *storyboards,* or graphic outlines, describing the project in exact detail—using words and sketches for each and every screen image, sound, and navigational choice, right down to specific colors and shades, text content, attributes and fonts, button shapes, styles, responses, and voice inflections. This approach is particularly well suited for teams that can build prototypes quickly and then rapidly convert them into finished goods. Or you can use less-detailed storyboards as a rough schematic guide, exerting less design sweat up front and more effort actually rendering the product at a workstation.

Both approaches require the same thorough knowledge of the tools and capabilities of multimedia, and both demand a storyboard or a project outline. The first approach is often favored by clients who wish to tightly control the production process and labor costs. The second approach gets you more quickly into the nitty-gritty, hands-on tasks, but you may ultimately have to give back that time because more iterations and editing will be required to smooth the work in progress.

Designing the Structure

A multimedia project is no more than an arrangement of text, graphic, sound, and video elements (or *objects*). The way you compose these elements into interactive experiences is shaped by your purpose and messages.

How you organize your material for a project will have just as great an impact on the viewer as the content itself. With the explosive growth of the World Wide Web and proliferation of millions and millions of multimedia-capable HTML documents that can be linked to millions of other similar documents in the cyberspace of the Web, your designs and inventions may actually contribute to the new media revolution: other creators may discover your work and build upon your ideas and methods.

Navigation

Mapping the structure of your project is a task that should be started early in the planning phase, because navigation maps outline the connections or links among various areas of your content and help you organize your content and messages. A *navigation map* (or *site map*) provides you with a table of contents as well as a chart of the logical flow of the interactive interface. As a more detailed design document, it may show your multimedia objects and describe what happens when the user interacts.

Just as eight story plots might account for 99 percent of all literature ever written (boy meets girl, protagonist versus antagonist, etc.), a few basic structures for multimedia projects will cover most cases: linear, hierarchical, nonlinear, and composite. Figure 17-1 illustrates the four fundamental organizing structures used in multimedia projects, often in combination:

- *Linear:* Users navigate sequentially, from one frame or bite of information to another.

- *Hierarchical:* Users navigate along the branches of a tree structure that is shaped by the natural logic of the content.

- *Nonlinear:* Users navigate freely through the content of the project, unbound by predetermined routes.

FIGURE 17-1

The four primary

navigational

structures used in

multimedia

■

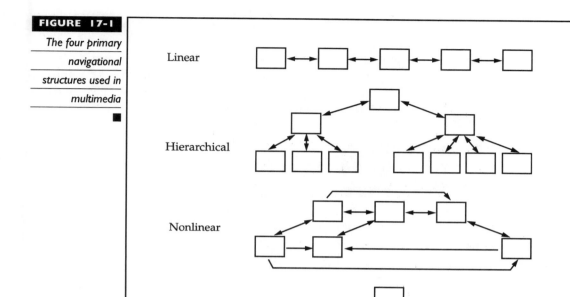

Linear

Hierarchical

Nonlinear

Composite

■ *Composite:* Users may navigate freely (nonlinearly), but are occasionally constrained to linear presentations of movies or critical information and/or to data that are most logically organized in a hierarchy.

The method you provide to your viewers for navigating from one place to another in your project is part of the user interface. The success of the user interface depends not only upon its general design and graphic art implementations but also upon myriad engineering details—such as the position of interactive buttons or hot spots relative to the user's current activity, whether these buttons "light up," and whether you use standard Macintosh or Windows pull-down menus. A good user interface is critical to the overall success of your project.

First Person

With regard to the creation of interactive fiction, what kinds of software engineering strategies would you recommend for creating stories that maintain a strong sense of cumulative action (otherwise known as plot) while still offering the audience a high frequency of interaction? In other words, how do you constrain the combinatoric explosion of the narrative pathways, while still maintaining the Aristotelian sense of a unity of plot?

—Patrick Dillon, Atlanta, GA

One and one-half T-shirts to Patrick Dillon! Would have been two for your invocation of a famous Greek philosopher, but then I couldn't find "combinatoric" in Webster's. Aristotle himself would have been pleased by the harmonious balance of your reward: you have asked a really good question.

As multimedia and the power of computers begin to change our approach to literature and storytelling, new engineering strategies do need to be implemented.

When fiction becomes nonlinear, and users can choose among alternative plot lines, the permutations can become staggering. To an author, this means each new plot pathway chosen by user interaction requires its own development, and one story may actually become several hundred or more. To constrain this fearsome explosion of narrative pathways, yet retain a high frequency of interaction, try designing your fiction around a single core plot that provides the cumulative action, and use arrays of returning branches for detail and illustration. In this way you can entirely avoid the permutations of alternative universes and still offer the adventure of interactive exploration.

Dear Tay: I just read your answer to Patrick Dillon's question about interactive fiction in your column for March 1993. My response is difficult to contain: "Aaarrrrgggghhhh!!!! You Ignorant Slut!" OK, perhaps I am overreacting, but you are refusing to let go of linearity. Why ever do you want to

"constrain the combinatoric explosion of narrative pathways"? Good Lord, that's what makes the gametree bushy. This is exactly the kind of work that's well-suited for a computer to perform—grinding out three billion story variations!

—Chris Crawford, San Jose, CA

Chris, I've been called a lot of things over the years (like Fay and Ray), and it's with a smile that I add your gift to my collection. Playing Jane Curtin to your Dan Aykroyd, I'll be happy to counter your counterpoint.

Your challenge represents a serious subject for multimedia designers today. I agree that interactive stories with too few branches are disappointingly flat and shallow. When a plot is broadly nonlinear, however, the permutations of events and possible outcomes become staggering, and the story as a whole becomes difficult to visualize and manage. Producing such work is also an intellectual challenge and costly in time and effort.

A truly open-ended "hypermedia" navigation system for consumer consumption risks

First Person *continued*

death by shock caused by open arterial branches and loss of story pressure, where plot lines become too diffuse and users founder in trivia. Most users may, indeed, prefer a structured, organized, and well-defined story environment.

The argument for simplicity is voiced by Steven Levy, the author of Hackers and Artificial Life, who says, "There's really something to be said for documents with a beginning, middle, and end."

The shape of this new literature made possible by multimedia computers and wide-bandwidth cable and telephone delivery systems is being born in the working designs of developers. The final test for successful multimedia design is the marketplace, where consumers will decide.

Your interesting "algorithms for interpersonal behavior, personality models, artificial personality, languages of expression, and facial displays"

represent, perhaps, a successful marriage of this computer power with literature containing malleable plots and seemingly endless variations. Indeed, your forthcoming epic game, Le Morte D'Arthur, will surely break new ground and quite possibly prove your point. Can't wait to get a copy!

From correspondence in "Ask the Captain," a monthly column by Tay Vaughan in NewMedia magazine (March and July 1993).

Many navigation maps are essentially nonlinear. In these navigational systems, viewers are always free to jump to an index, a glossary, various menus, Help or About... sections, or even to a rendering of the map itself. It is often important to give viewers the sense that free choice is available; this empowers them within the context of the subject matter. Nonetheless, you should still provide consistent clues regarding importance, emphasis, and direction by varying typeface size and look, colorizing, indenting, or using special icons.

The architectural drawings for your multimedia project are the storyboards and navigation maps. The storyboards are married to the navigation maps during the design process.

Because all forms of information—including text, numbers, photos, video, and sound—can exist in a common digital format, they can be used simultaneously as people browse through an information stream, just as people use their various senses simultaneously to perceive the real world.

Bill Gates, Chairman, Microsoft Corporation

A simple navigation map is illustrated in Figure 17-2, where the subject matter of a small project is organized schematically. The items in boxes are not only descriptions of content but also active buttons that can take users directly to that content. At any place in the project, users can call up this screen and then navigate directly to their chosen subject.

A storyboard for this same project is organized sequentially, screen by screen, and each screen is sketched out with design notes and specifications before rendering. At the left of Figure 17-3 is part of the storyboard for this project; at the right are corresponding finished screens.

Multimedia provides great power for jumping about within your project's content. And though it is important to give users a sense of free choice, too much freedom can be disconcerting, and viewers may get lost. Try to keep your messages and content organized along a steady stream of the major subjects, letting users branch outward to explore details. Always provide a secure anchor, with buttons that lead to expected places, and build a familiar landscape to which users may return at any time.

Really good software products should be simple, hot, and deep. People need to get into your software in about 20 seconds and get immediate positive feedback and reward; then they are smiling and having a good time and they want to go further. Hot means that you've got to be fully cooking the machine, with all its graphics and sound capabilities, conveying something dynamic and exciting that competes with what people are used to seeing in a movie or on TV. In terms of deep, it's kind of like the ocean where there are people of all ages: some kids will just wade out in a foot of surf, other guys with scuba gear go way out and way deep. Make it possible for me to go as deep as I want, but don't force it on me. Just let the depth of your product unfold to me in a very natural way.

Trip Hawkins, Chairman & CEO, 3DO Company

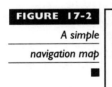

FIGURE 17-2

A simple navigation map

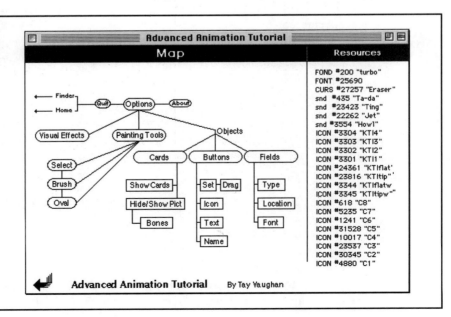

Your content may not always be an assembly of discrete subjects as illustrated in Figure 17-2. If your material deals with a chronology of events occurring over time, for example, you may wish to design the structure as a linear sequence of events and then send users along that sequence, allowing them to jump directly to specific dates or time frames if desired (see Figure 17-4).

17

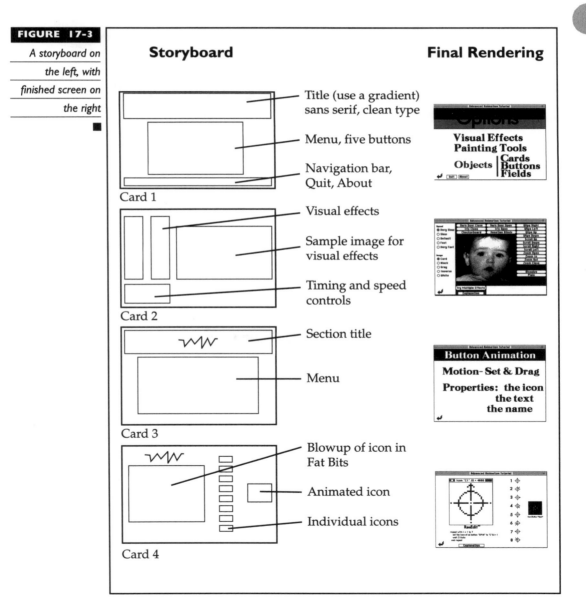

FIGURE 17-3

A storyboard on the left, with finished screen on the right

FIGURE 17-4

A chronological navigation map with active buttons

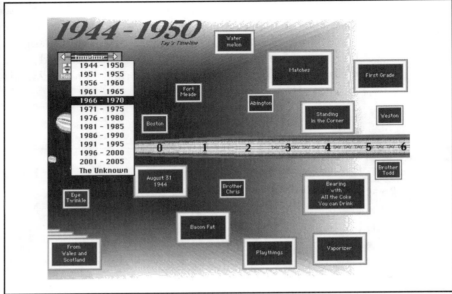

Even within a linear, time-based structure, you may still wish to sort events into categories regardless of when they occur. There is no reason you can't do this and offer more than one method of navigating through your content. Figure 17-5, for instance, illustrates a navigation map that accesses the same events from the time-line form of Figure 17-4, but arranged here instead into meaningful groups of events.

Hot Spots and Buttons

Most multimedia authoring systems allow you to make any part of the screen, or any object, into a button or "hot spot." When users click a button at that location, something happens—this makes multimedia not just interactive, but also exciting. Your navigation design must provide buttons that make sense, so their actions will be intuitively understood by means of their icon or graphic representation or via text cues. Do not force your viewers to learn many new or special icons; keep the learning curve to a minimum. It's also important to include buttons that perform basic housekeeping tasks, such as quitting the project at any given point, or canceling an activity.

FIGURE 17-5

A navigation map based on events that are active buttons

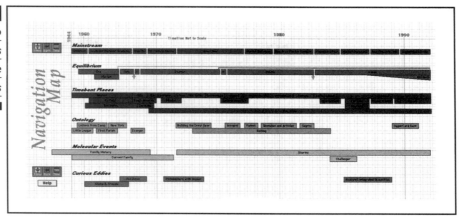

First Person

One day I launched an application named Disk Formatter on my Macintosh, just to see what it was about. Suddenly I was in a pretty scary user-interface predicament (Figure 17-6 is what I saw). I could tell from its name that the software erased and formatted hard disks and cartridges: my mounted hard disks were listed on the screen by SCSI number, and I was being prompted to select one of them. I looked over at the CPU and was pleased that the disk drive access light wasn't ticking away at sector-length intervals. I

didn't know what the software was doing because I hadn't read the manual; I did know, however, what I wanted to do—back out and quit. Too much at stake to be fooling around here!

Well, there was no Cancel button and no Quit button, and OK was too risky with the radio button for my 200MB internal hard disk turned on. Did OK mean "OK, start formatting," or did it mean "OK, thanks for selecting that drive, now on to further options"? As a dialog box, the Disk Formatter application limited my choices to its own, and I didn't like any of

them. I figured I would do an emergency power-down by pulling the plug on the CPU, and then I could restart. But before employing that ultimate solution for sticky-cursors, I tried ⌘-Q. This is the conventional Macintosh keyboard method to quit an application, and it worked. The screen went away.

I was pretty unhappy about the application's design, though, because there was no clear route to back out of the formatting activity, and OK implies going forward in most user interactions.

There are three general categories of buttons: text, graphic, and icon. Text buttons and their fonts and styles are described in Chapter 10. Graphic buttons can contain graphic images or even parts of images—for example, a map of the world where each country is color-coded, and a mouse click on a country yields further information. Icons are graphic objects designed specifically to be meaningful buttons and are usually small (although size is,

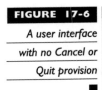

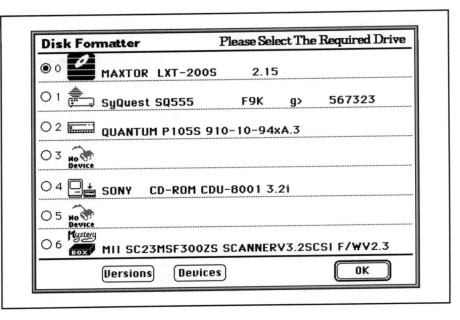

in theory, not a determining factor). Icons are fundamental graphic objects
symbolic of an activity or concept. Figure 17-7 shows samples of clip art
icon buttons available to users of ToolBook, and Figure 17-8 shows a few

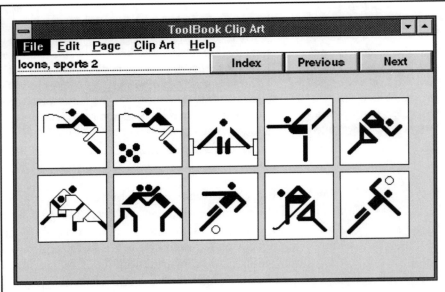

FIGURE 17-8

WebTools from StatMedia and Artbeats offers thousands of buttons and other design elements optimized for Web page construction ∎

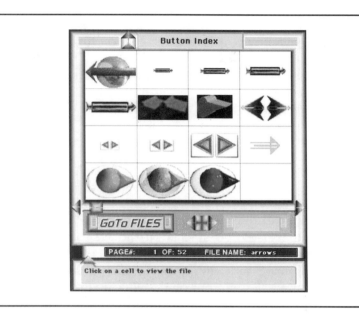

of the hundreds of buttons supplied with the Artbeats WebTools CD-ROM. Most authoring systems provide a tool for creating text buttons of various styles (radio buttons, check boxes, push buttons, animated buttons, and spin buttons), as well as graphic and icon buttons.

tip *Designing a good navigation system and creating original buttons appropriate for your project are not trivial artistic tasks. Be sure you budget sufficient time in your design process for many trials, so you'll be able to get your buttons looking and acting just right.*

cross platform *Windows does not manage icon resources in the same manner as Macintosh. Each Windows multimedia authoring tool allows for the construction and use of graphic buttons in its own way. If you are bringing Macintosh icons into a Windows tool, export them from the Macintosh as bitmaps, import them into your Windows authoring tool, and create appropriate mouse-clicking activities for highlighting and other effects.*

Highlighting a button or object is the most common method of distinguishing it as the object of interest when single-clicking. When a button is double-clicked, it should be highlighted before the intended activity occurs, to let the user know that the button was, indeed, clicked. Highlighting is usually accomplished by reversing the object's colors: changing black to white or vice versa, or otherwise altering its colors. Drop shadows placed slightly below and to the right of a button can give it a 3-D look and, depending upon how you arrange the highlighting, can make a button appear out (not pressed) or in (pressed). In Windows, when the Help button is pressed (clicked or selected), the perimeter shading is changed, and the text is offset to the right, as illustrated here:

HTML documents do not directly support interactive buttons that follow the rules of good interface design—by highlighting or otherwise confirming a mouse-down action. But you *can* make plain and animated buttons for your HTML documents on the Web using plug-ins and scripts such as Shockwave and Java. A simple JavaScript in an HTML document can replace one image with another on mouseOver (see Chapter 18 for the code snippet). The simplest buttons on the Web are the text anchors that link a document to other documents—usually a browser application colors this anchor text differently and underlines it so it stands out from the body text (although default colors are a user-defined preference, you can override these preferences in your own code).

Other common buttons found on the Web consist of small JPEG or GIF graphic images that are themselves anchors. Larger images may be sectioned into "hot" areas with associated links; these are called *image maps*. In most World Wide Web browsers, you know you have clicked on a button only after the cursor changes while the browser seeks another document to load. Ways to make interesting buttons and interactive graphical interfaces on the World Wide Web are described more fully in Chapter 18.

Designers will build screens where there are tiny little things going on all over it at different places, and everything has momentous significance. And then the user is supposed to be able to find these momentous things. So people just glaze over. If you want them to hit a button, put a big button right in the middle of the screen.

Trip Hawkins, Chairman & CEO, 3DO Company

Icons

On the Macintosh, icons have a special meaning; they constitute a suite of image resources that can be linked to the Finder and used to identify an application or project. ResEdit, the resource editing tool from Apple, allows you to create and edit System icons. They are small (16×16 pixels) or large (32x32 pixels), may be colored, and may have a text label attached, as shown by some of the icons used by Microsoft Word98:

17

---

tip   *For a quick and simple way to change a Macintosh icon, highlight any file's icon by clicking on it once, open the Get Info... dialog (Command-I), click once on the icon shown at the top left of the Get Info panel to highlight it, and paste any 32×32-pixel bitmap from the Clipboard. The old icon is replaced with the new. You can also copy an icon to the Clipboard from the Get Info panel (Command-C). With this trick, you can customize the look of your desktop.*

Icons can be embedded within a Macintosh application or project (in the resource fork) for use as buttons, but these icons are limited in size to 32×32 pixels. To make larger icon buttons, you can group several into a single object and program the whole element to respond when any element is clicked. This is a useful trick in HyperCard and SuperCard, for example, where changing the icon resource of a button using HyperTalk or SuperTalk scripts will provide very fast graphical changes suitable for animation (much faster than going to another card in the HyperCard stack). When rapidly changed, but kept in the same position, these icons create the effect of a spinning arrow:

In Windows 95, you can change the icon used to represent an application or other file. Select My Computer, then click on the following menus: View | Options... | File Types | New Type... | Change Icon.... You will then see the icons currently available in the system's SHELL32.DLL (see Figure 17-9). If you are building a multimedia project in Windows, you can create custom icons and store them as .ICO files. Visual Basic, for example, ships with a library of more than 450 icons ready to use in the following categories: arrows and pointers, communication, computers, drag and drop, elements, flags, industry and transportation, mail, miscellaneous, office, traffic signs,

FIGURE 17-9

In Windows 95,

many icons are

installed with

the system

■

and writing. These icons are quite useful simply as clip art, but they are either small (32×32 pixels) or smaller (16×16 pixels). These smaller icons are primarily used as mouse pointers or cursors.

Icons (and .ICO files that contain icons) are created using an icon editor such as IconDraw (available in the Microsoft Resource Kit) or another editor utility. Many icon editing utilities can also be found on electronic bulletin boards (BBSs). Icons in Windows, however, relate to the Windows operating system and to Program Manager (as do Finder icons on the Macintosh), and these icons are typically not available for use within an authoring tool.

Designing the User Interface

The user interface of your multimedia product is a blend of its graphic elements and its navigation system. If your messages and content are disorganized and difficult to find, or if users become disoriented or bored, your project may fail. Poor graphics can cause boredom. Poor navigation aids can make viewers feel lost and unconnected to the content; or, worse, viewers may sail right off the edge and just give up and quit the program.

Novice/Expert Modes

Be aware that there are two types of end users: those who are computer literate and those who are not. Creating a user interface that will satisfy both types has been a design dilemma since the invention of computers. The simplest solution for handling varied levels of user expertise is to provide a *modal interface*—one where the viewer can simply click a Novice/Expert button and change the approach of the whole interface, to be either more or less detailed or complex. Modal interfaces are common on bulletin boards, for example, allowing novices to read menus and select desired activities, while experts can altogether eliminate the time-consuming download and display of menus and simply type an activity code directly into an executable command line. Both novices and experts alike may quickly learn to click the mouse and skip the annoying ragtime piece you chose for background music.

Unfortunately, in multimedia projects, modal interfaces are not a good answer. It's best to avoid designing modal interfaces because they tend to confuse the user. Typically, only a minority of users are expert, and so the majority are caught in between and frustrated. The solution is to build your multimedia project to contain plenty of navigational power, providing access to content and tasks for users at all levels, as well as a Help system to provide some hand holding and reassurance. Present all this power in easy-to-understand structures and concepts, and use clear textual cues. Above all, keep the interface simple! Even experts will balk at a complex screen full of tiny buttons and arcane switches, and will appreciate having neat and clean doorways into your project's content.

17

Two readers didn't notice the screen had changed in different circumstances. This happened when the button they clicked on took them to a visually similar screen, and there was no visual effect as the screens changed. One reader was looking at the details of a hostel and clicked on the left-hand Next arrow. He arrived at a screen with details about another hostel, but did not notice he was looking at a different screen. He tried the right-hand Next arrow as well, and the screen changed back to the one he had been viewing initially, but again he did not notice the change and concluded the Next buttons did nothing. A visual effect or animation here would have provided a cue to make the screen changes more noticeable.

Lynda Hardman of the Scottish HCI Centre, after focus group testing the "Glasgow Online" hypertext system

GUIs

The Macintosh and Windows graphical user interfaces (GUI, pronounced "gooey") are successful partly because their basic point-and-click style is simple, consistent, and quickly mastered. Both these GUIs offer built-in Help systems, and both provide standard patterns of activity that produce standard expected results. The following actions, for example, are consistently performed by similar keystrokes when running most programs on the Macintosh or in Windows.

Action	Macintosh Keystroke	Windows Keystroke
New file	⌘-N	ALT-F-N or CTRL-N
Open file	⌘-O	ALT-F-O or CTRL-O
Save file	⌘-S	ALT-F-S or CTRL-S
Quit	⌘-Q	ALT-F-X or CTRL-Q
Undo	⌘-Z	ALT-E-U or CTRL-Z
Cut	⌘-X	ALT-E-T or CTRL-X
Copy	⌘-C	ALT-E-C or CTRL-C
Paste	⌘-V	ALT-E-P or CTRL-V

For your multimedia interface to be successful, you, too, must be consistent in designing both the look and the behavior of your human interface. Multimedia authoring systems provide you with the tools to design and implement your own graphical user interface from scratch. Be prudent with all that flexibility, however. Unless your content and messages are bizarre or require special treatment, it's best to stick with accepted conventions for button design and grouping, visual and audio feedback, and navigation structure.

Vaughan's General Rule for Interface Design

The best user interface demands the least learning effort.

Stick with real-world metaphors that will be understood by the widest selection of potential users. For example, consider using the well-known trash can for deleting files, a hand cursor for dragging objects, and a clock or an hourglass for pauses. If your material is time-oriented, develop metaphors for past, present, and future. If it is topic-oriented, choose metaphors related to the topics themselves. If it is polar (the pros and cons of an issue, for example), choose relevant contrasting images.

tip *Most multimedia authoring systems include tutorials and instructions for creating and using buttons and navigation aids. Typically, they also supply templates or examples of attractive backgrounds and distinctive buttons that serve as an excellent starting place. In a large project, you might want to use a different metaphor as the backbone of each major section, to provide a helpful cue for users to orient themselves within your content. For the Travel section, for example, you could use icons that are sailing ships with various riggings; for the Finance section, buttons that are coins of different denominations; and for the buttons of the International Business section, you could use colorful flags from various countries.*

Users like to be in control, so avoid hidden commands and unusual keystroke/mouse click combinations. Design your interface with the goal that no instruction manual or special training will be required to move through your project. Users do not like to have to remember keywords or special codes, so always make the full range of options easily available as interactive buttons or menu items. And finally, users do make mistakes, so allow them a chance to escape from inadvertent or dangerous predicaments ("Do you really want to delete? Delete/Escape"). Keep your interface simple and friendly.

17

Throw out your tried and true training or software development methodologies, and pretend that you're Spielberg or Lucas: think of what the viewer sees and hears and how the viewer interacts with the system you deliver. Create an "experience" for the viewer.

David A. Ludwig, Interactive Learning Designs

Graphical Approaches

Designing excellent computer screens requires a special set of fine art skills, and not every programmer or graduate in fine arts may be suited to creating computer graphics. Like programmers who must keep up with current operating systems and languages, computer graphic artists must also stay informed about the rapidly changing canvas of new features, techniques, applications, and creative tools.

Computer graphics is more left- and right-brained—and not so spontaneous as doing it by hand. The ramp time is tedious; I am used to instant gratification with my fine artwork.

Cornelia Atchley, a fine artist creating multimedia art with computers, Washington, D.C.

The artist must make broad design choices: cartoon stick figures for a children's game, rendered illustrations for a medical reference, scanned bitmaps for a travel tour of Europe. The graphic artwork must be appropriate not only for the subject matter, but for the user as well. Once the approach is decided, then the artist has to put real pixels onto a computer screen and do the work. A multimedia graphic artist must always play the role of the end user during the design and rendering process, choosing colors that look good, specifying text fonts that "speak," and designing buttons that are clearly marked for what they do.

THINGS THAT WORK   Here are some graphical approaches that get good results:

- Neatly executed contrasts: big/small, heavy/light, bright/dark, thin/thick, cheap/dear (see Figure 17-10)

- Simple and clean screens with lots of white space (see Figure 17-11)

- Eye-grabbers such as Drop caps, or a single brightly colored object alone on a gray-scale screen

- Shadows and drop shadows in various shades

- Gradients

- Reversed graphics to emphasize important text or images

- Shaded objects and text in 2-D and 3-D

THINGS TO AVOID   Here are some mistakes you will want to avoid in creating computer graphics:

- Clashes of color

- Busy screens (too much stuff)

FIGURE 17-11

Use plenty of white space ("noninformation areas") in your screens

- Trite humor in oft-repeated animations
- Clanging bells or squeaks when a button is clicked
- Frilly pattern borders
- Cute one-liners from famous movies
- Requiring more than two button clicks to quit
- Too many numbers (limit charts to about 25 numbers; if you can, just show totals)
- Too many words (don't crowd them; split your information into bite-sized chunks)
- Too many substantive elements presented too quickly

Most graphic artists will tell you that design is an "intuitive thing," but they will be hard pressed to describe the rules they follow in their everyday work. They know when colors are not "working" and will change them again and again until they're right, but they usually won't be able to explain why the colors work or don't work. A project with a good navigation design, though it may have been developed with good planning and storyboarding, is indeed more often the result of many hours of crafty finagling with buttons and editors.

A Multimedia Design Case History

This section presents an example of the design process for a simple multimedia project about the construction and launch of a 31-foot ocean-going sailboat. This project was initially crafted in SuperCard, but it was later ported to Director so that it could be played on both Mac and Windows platforms (see Chapter 9).

Storyboarding a Project

The source material (all that was available) practically sorted itself into logical groups: a pile of old photographs, a magazine article and newspaper clippings, engineering drawings, official documents, and some cassettes with recorded sounds. The first storyboard was a simple hierarchical structure with branches to each subject area, as shown in Figure 17-12.

Putting It Together

The most eye-catching photograph was chosen as a background for the main menu, and, as shown in Figure 17-13, the main menu was planned to contain clearly labeled buttons navigating to linear presentations of each topic area. From every screen in the project, users would be able to return to the main menu. Where sound bites were appropriate, sounds would be

---

FIGURE 17-12

The first storyboard

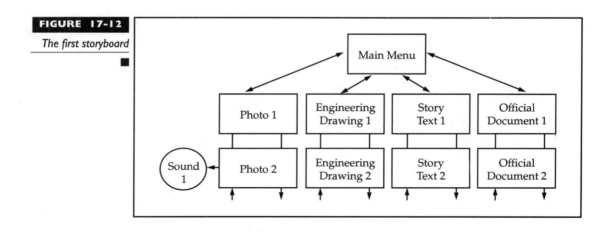

FIGURE 17-13

Main menu screen

with relevant artwork

as background

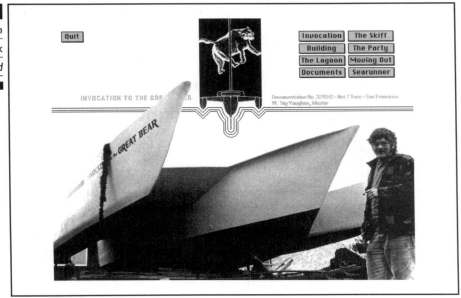

played by buttons to be clicked on screens. And a Quit button was necessary, also on the main menu, so that users would never be more than two button clicks from exiting the project (back to the main menu, and then quit).

The 50 or so 4×5 photographs were old color prints that offered poor contrast and faded colors (due to a saltwater dunking in a storm off the Central American coastline). Digitized on a flat-bed scanner in gray-scale, however, they worked fine, and an image manipulation program was available to improve contrast. All the prints were scanned, cropped to the same dimension, optimized, and stored as bitmapped objects within SuperCard. While at the scanner, merchant marine licenses and documents were also digitized, and the magazine article was scanned using OCR software to bring it into ASCII format. The story text was placed into a SuperCard text field.

After all the content was on cards in the computer (see Chapter 8 for more about SuperCard cards), and work on the navigation system was under way, several issues emerged. First, it is terrifically boring to read a 3,000-word story by scrolling a long text field. Second, the photos were too small to be placed alone on a single card. So it made sense to combine the story line with the images, even though they were not directly related; the story about launching the boat would progress from beginning to end as the boat was slowly built in the pictures. The storyboard changed to that shown in Figure 17-14.

FIGURE 17-14

FIGURE 17-14

The second

storyboard

■

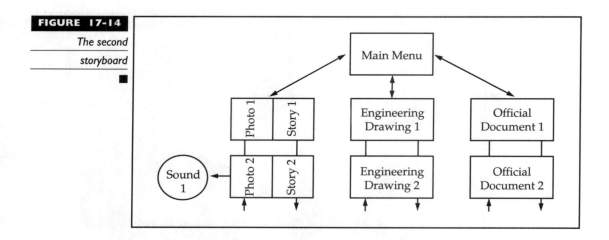

The photo-essay-and-story combination worked out to about 20 screens. The photos were placed, and the text was cut and pasted to fit (see Figure 17-15). After reworking the basic navigation pattern for this new model, it became clear that users might want to scan rapidly through the photographs to watch the boat being built, ignoring the text of the story. So a special

FIGURE 17-15

Snapshots are

combined with text

to form a 28-screen

story line

■

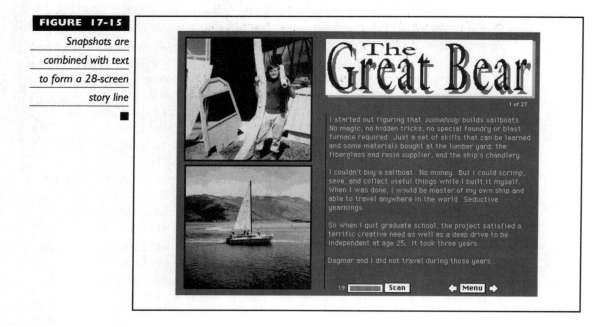

button was programmed to scan through the images until the mouse was clicked; here is the program:

```
on mouseUp
  repeat                              (Begin endless loop)
    set cursor to busy               (Cursor prompt for busy)
    if the mouse is down then        (Test for mouse click)
      exit to superCard              (Escape from loop)
    end if                           (End of test)
    put the number of this cd into cN (Get num of current cd)
    if cN = 28 then                  (If last, start again)
      visual barn door open          (Use visual effect)
      go to cd 2                     (Start again with card 2)
    else                             (If not last card then)
      visual barn door open          (Use visual effect)
      go next                        (Go next card in series)
    end if                           (End of test)
  end repeat                         (End of loop)
end mouseUp                          (End of handler)
```

Images that did not fit into the photo essay about building the boat—for instance, the launching party with its roast pig; the long haul to the beach by trailer; and setting the mooring—were withdrawn from the pile of construction photographs, but because they were interesting, they were attached as separate branches accessible by button from the main menu. This was the third time the navigation changed, proving that you can continue to hang elements on a menu until the menu screen is too busy (and then you use submenus), or until you run out of material, as shown in Figure 17-16.

Next, the sound bites were recorded, digitized, and added to the project. Figure 17-17, the screen where the sounds were to play, shows the special button installed to play sound bites. It's simply a picture of a loudspeaker with this simple programming:

```
on mouseUp
  playSound "Great Bear"
end mouseUp
```

The documents for the project included engineering drawings, highway permits, and licenses. The highway permit, for example, was 8.5×11 inches (portrait), but after some experimentation, once it was scaled to 480 pixels in height, it was (barely) readable and acceptable for this project. The licenses and drawings were in landscape orientation and fit more easily on the 640×480-pixel screen (see Figure 17-18).

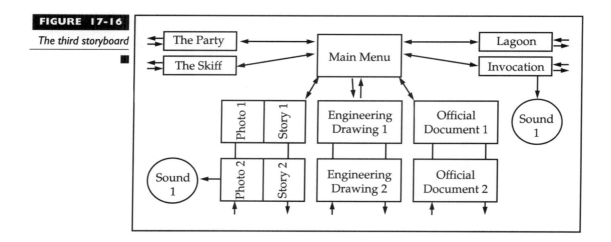

FIGURE 17-16

The third storyboard

Reworking

The buttons on the main menu were the wrong color, so they were changed a few times until the color worked. Helvetica title text wasn't fancy enough, so it was reworked and a drop shadow was laid in. A special slider button was built to allow the construction sequence to go immediately to

FIGURE 17-17

Sound is played

when the

loudspeaker icon

is clicked

FIGURE 17-18

Larger fonts of some scanned documents can be read at 72 dpi resolution, and engineering drawings in landscape orientation can be resized to fit

■

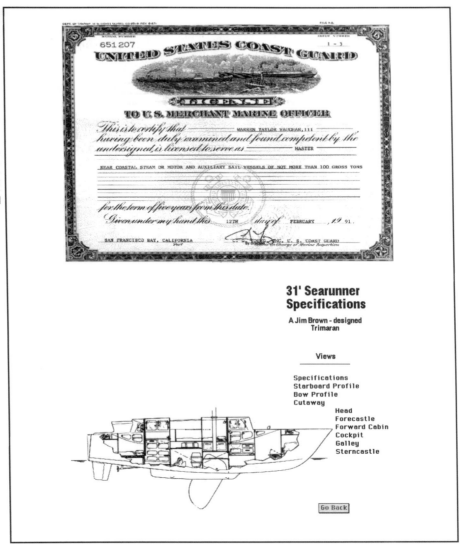

any of the pictures in the sequence. The backgrounds were tweaked a little, and the order of images changed somewhat. A small red car was animated to drive along the edge of the lagoon.

The project described above was simple and straightforward. With the exception of designing a few custom buttons for autoscanning through some of the images and designing the animations, the entire project was a progression of screens of information, with links activated by clicking buttons.

Producing

By the time you reach the development phases of your multimedia project and you start building (see Figure 16-1), you should already have taken care to prepare your plan and to get organized. The project plan (see Chapter 16) now becomes your step-by-step instruction manual for building the product. For many multimedia developers, following this plan and actually doing the construction work—being down in the trenches of hands-on creation and production—is the fun part of any project.

Developing multimedia can be like taking a joy ride in a washer/dryer. When it's all over you feel like you've been washed, rinsed, spun, and tumble-dried.

Kevin McCarthy, Director of Business Development,
Medius IV

Production is the phase when your multimedia project is actually rendered. During this phase you will contend with important and continuing organizing tasks. There will be times in a complex project when graphics files seem to disappear from the server, when you forget to send or cannot produce milestone progress reports, when your voice talent gets lost on the way to the recording studio, or when your hard disk crashes. So it's important to start out on the right foot, with good organization, and to maintain detailed management oversight during the entire construction process. This rule applies to projects large and small, projects for yourself or for a client, and projects with 1 or 20 people on staff. Above all, provide a good time-accounting system for everyone working on the project. At the end of the week, it's hard to remember how much time you spent on tasks done on Monday.

tip *If your project is to be built by more than one person, establish a management structure in advance that includes specific milestones and production expectations for each contributor.*

Starting Up

Before you begin your multimedia project, it's important to check your development hardware and software and review your organizational and administrative setup, even if it is you working alone. This is a serious last-minute task. It prevents you from finding yourself halfway through the project with nowhere to put your graphics files and digitized movie segments when you're out of disk space, or stuck with an incompatible version of a critical software tool, or with a network that bogs down and quits every two days. Such incidents can take many days or weeks to resolve, so try to head off as many potential problems as you can before you begin.

- Desk and mind clear of obstructions?
- Fastest CPU and RAM you can afford?
- Time-accounting and management system in place?
- Biggest (or most) monitors you can afford?
- Sufficient disk storage space for all work files?
- System for regular backup of critical files?
- Conventions or protocols for naming your working files and managing source documents?
- Latest version of your primary authoring software?
- Latest versions of software tools and accessories?
- Communication pathways open with client?
- Breathing room for administrative tasks?
- Financial arrangements secure (retainer in the bank)?
- Expertise lined up for all stages of the project?
- Kick-off meeting completed?

17

First Person

At 18, I used to hang around with people who drove fast cars, and once volunteered to help an acquaintance prepare his Ferrari Berlinetta for a race at Watkins Glen. My job was to set the valves while my friend went over the suspension, brakes, and later, the carburetor. The car boasted 12 cylinders and 24 valves, and adjusting the clearance between tappet and rocker arm seemed to me akin to a jeweler's fine work. It required special wrenches and feeler gauges and an uncommon touch to rotate the high-compression engine so the cam was precisely at its highest point for each valve. I was blown away by the sheer quantity of moving parts under the Ferrari's long and shiny valve covers—my own fast car had only four cylinders and eight simple valves. It took me about seven exhausting hours (including double-checking) to get it right. As the sun came up, though, the engine sounded great!

Tuning up and preparing, I learned, is as important to the race as the race itself. My friend, however, learned a much tougher lesson: he spun out and rolled his Ferrari at the hairpin turn in the seventh lap. He crawled unhurt from the twisted wreckage, but all he was able to salvage was the engine.

Making multimedia for clients is a special case. Be sure that the organization of your project incorporates a system for good communication between you and the client as well as among the people actually building the project. Many projects have turned out unhappily because of communication breakdowns.

Client Approval Cycles

Provide good management oversight to avoid endless feedback loops—in this situation the client is somehow never quite happy, and you are forced to tweak and edit many times. Manage production so that your client is continually informed and formally approves artwork and other elements as you build them. Develop a scheme that specifies the number and duration of client approval cycles, and then provide a mechanism for change orders. For change orders, remember that the client should pay extra.

First Person

We made up two sample musical tracks to play in the background and sent them off by overnight courier to the client. Four days later, the client phoned to say that both were good, but couldn't we make it sound a little more like Windham Hill. So we redid the music and sent two more samples. Five days later, the client said the samples were great, but the boss wanted something with a Sergeant Pepper feel. So we sent a fifth creation, this time with a note that they would have to either settle on one of the five styles submitted, supply the music themselves, or pay us more money to keep up the creative composition work. They chose the music the boss liked, but we wound up more than two weeks behind schedule and had spent significantly more money and effort on this task than originally budgeted.

Several months later, in the next job requiring original music composition, we specified a maximum of two review/feedback cycles and added a clause for cost overrun beyond that. The first sound we submitted to this new client was approved, and we stayed ahead of schedule and budget.

Data Storage Media and Transportation

It's important that the client be able to easily review your work. Remember that both you and the distant site need to have matching data transfer systems and media, or you need to provide a Web or FTP site for your project. Organize your system before you begin work, as it may take some time for both you and the client to agree on an appropriate system and on the method of transportation. For storage media, you can use floppy disks, external hard disks, SyQuest removable cartridges, Bernoulli disks, Zip, Jaz, optical disks, or DAT backup tapes.

Because multimedia files are large, your means of transporting the project to distant clients is particularly important. Typically, both you and the client will have access to the Internet. If not, the most cost- and time-effective method for transporting your files is by an overnight courier service (Federal Express, DHL, Airborne Express, or U.S. Postal Service Express Mail). Material completed in time for an afternoon pickup will usually be at the client's site by the next morning. Sending an overnight letter-size package (with floppies or cartridges inside) costs from $10 to $16.

If you use the Internet to deliver your multimedia to the client, be sure that you set up rules and conventions for naming files placed at an FTP site, and use codes in the subject headers of your e-mail to describe the content of the message. After a project has been under way for a while, there will be many files and many communications—keywords and clues will make life easier. This is another place where planning ahead pays off!

Tracking

Organize a method for tracking the receipt of material that you will incorporate into your multimedia project. Even in small projects, you will be dealing with many digital bits and pieces.

Develop a file-naming convention specific to your project's structure. Store the files in directories or folders with logical names. If you are working across platforms, develop a file identification system that uses the DOS file-naming convention of eight characters plus a three-character extension. Use this convention on files for the Macintosh as well as the PC; otherwise, files transferred from the Macintosh to the PC will receive default names with strange characters and extensions that are difficult to remember. You may also need to set up a database with file names as eight-character codes matched to lengthier descriptive names, so you know what the codes mean.

---

warning   *Even if you are working in Windows 95, avoid using use long file names—they may not map effectively to either DOS, Windows 3.1, or Macintosh systems.*

Version control of your files (that is, tracking editing changes) is critically important, too, especially in large projects. If more than one person is working on a group of files, be sure that you always know what version is the latest and who has the current version. If storage space allows, archive all file iterations, in case you change your mind about something and need to go back to a prior rendering.

Copyrights

Macromedia Director, ToolBook, SuperCard, HyperCard, and other commonly used authoring platforms may allow access to the software programming code or script that drives a particular project. The source code of HTML pages on the Web may also be easily viewed.

In such an open-code environment, are you prepared to let others see your programming work? Is your code neat and commented? Perhaps your mother cautioned you to wear clean underclothing in case you were suddenly on a table among strangers in a hospital emergency room—well, apply this rule to your code. You can insert a copyright statement in your project that clearly (and legally) designates the code as your intellectual property (see Figure 17-19), but the code, tricks, and programming techniques remain accessible for study, learning, and tweaking by others.

Hazards and Annoyances

Even experienced producers and developers commonly run into at least some light chop and turbulence during the course of a project's development. The experts, however, never crash when their vehicle shudders or loses some altitude. You can expect the going to get rough at any number of stages—from trying to design the perfect interface, to endless testing, to problems with client sign-off or payment. Expect problems beyond your control and be prepared to accept them and solve them.

FIGURE 17-19

Typical copyright statement embedded as comments at the top of an HTML page

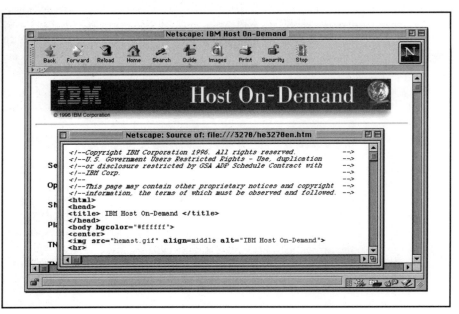

Small annoyances, too, can become serious distractions that are counter-productive. The production stage is a time of great creativity, dynamic intercourse among all contributors, and, above all, hard work. Be prepared to deal with some common irritants, for example:

- Creative co-workers who don't take (or give) criticism well
- Clients who cannot or are not authorized to make decisions
- More than two all-nighters in a row
- Too many custom-coded routines
- Instant coffee and microwaved corn dogs
- Too many meetings; off-site meetings
- Missed deadlines

17

If your project is a team effort, then it is critical that everyone works well together—or can at least tolerate one another's differences—especially when the going gets tough. Pay attention to the mental health of all personnel involved in your project, and be aware of the dynamics of the group and whether people are being adversely affected by individual personalities. If problems arise, deal with them before they become hazardous; the mix of special creative talents required for multimedia can be volatile.

First Person

In 1975, I was hired to deliver a 41-foot cruising sailboat from Fort Lauderdale to the British Virgin Islands for the charter trade. In three days I assembled a crew of strangers, provisioned the boat, and checked all the equipment. Then we took off across the Gulf Stream and into the Bermuda Triangle.

After two days it was clear that the cook was a bad apple. It wasn't just that she couldn't cook—she whined about everything: the stove wouldn't light, the boat heeled too much, her socks were wet, her sleeping bag tore on a cleat, her hair was tangled, she couldn't get her favorite radio station (now a few hundred miles astern). It was unending.

The whining began to envelop her in a smog-colored, onionlike layering, each new complaint accreting to the last one, like growing coral. By the fifth day, her unpleasant aura saturated the entire main cabin; the rest of us sought sanctuary in the cockpit or the small aft cabin. Efforts were made to solve this bizarre situation, but by then, nobody could get near her (or wanted to).

When we pulled into tiny Caicos Island for water and fresh stores, I paid her off and arranged for a room at the quaint waterfront hotel, where she could wait three days for the weekly airplane back to Florida. Everyone felt badly about her disappointment and how it all turned out—for about an hour. The rest of the voyage was jubilant.

Multi

> By 1995, the Web had become a
> full-bore information highway of
> words and pictures with tens of
> millions of users cruising along it.

Theoretically, the Web can support —

connections

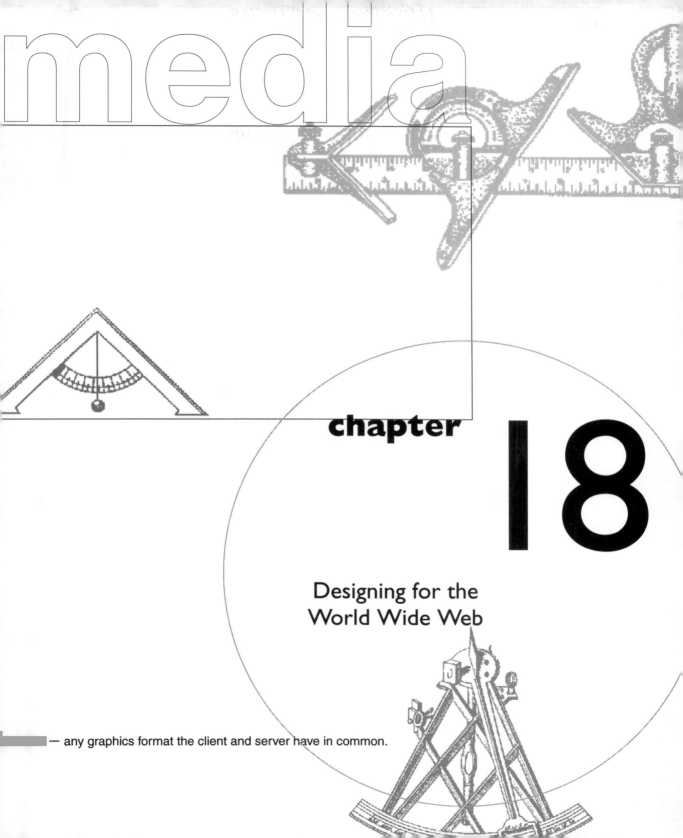

media

chapter

18

Designing for the World Wide Web

— any graphics format the client and server have in common.

L AUNCHED in 1989, the World Wide Web was not originally designed with multimedia in mind, but rather as a simple method for delivering text documents formatted in HTML, with occasional inline graphic illustrations and figures. By 1995, because it was operational, essentially free, and *good enough* to support traffic (see Vaughan's Law of Multimedia Minimums in Chapter 10), the Web had become a full-bore information highway of words and pictures with tens of millions of users cruising along it.

The Doppler backdraft of passing travelers has exposed the gristle of an overwhelming number of disappointing audio and visual experiences on the Web: "This is my home page; here is a list of my favorite places; this is me with my dog..." To fill this vacuum of content and presentation, inventive multimedia solutions and enhancements now compete for mind share, stretching the capabilities of HTML, Web browsers, PCs, and the very fabric of the Internet to bring multimedia power to this environment. You can experience the strong energies of this multimedia rush and the strong forces of market dynamics and entrepreneurial spirit when you visit any of the plug-in developers' Web sites listed in Chapter 15. Plain text and pictures are no longer enough for this highway!

Working on the Web

This chapter investigates and illustrates some methods for developing and presenting the basic elements of multimedia within the constraints of HTML and the World Wide Web. This chapter is not intended to substitute for a more complete library of HTML, Web design, and Internet texts, but to present basic examples that will get you started. In 1998, there were more than 1,700 published books with the word "Internet" in their title!

The Workspace

Make your Web pages look good on a 640×480-pixel VGA monitor showing 256 colors (8-bit graphics). Your working space on this monitor is actually about 600 pixels wide by 300 tall, because browsers include controls and slider bars (see Figure 18-1). This is where you must place the eye-catchers that will be first loaded and viewed by visitors without scrolling.

Nibbling

The principle you must always keep in mind when designing and making multimedia elements for the Web should be called "nibbling." At a serious metal-working supply store you can buy a power tool called a nibbler; it wantonly devours the edges of sheet metal in an ear-damaging staccato of rapid tiny bites. You must apply this tool to the elegant bitmapped logo you created in Photoshop to trim it from 24- to 8- to 4-bit color depth and resize it from 96 pixels square to 64 pixels square. Nibble the audio clip of your client's theme song from 44.1 kHz to 11 kHz, and see if it's acceptable at 8-bit sample size. Text as HTML is cheap: nibble your page design and throw away the pretty shadowed GIF graphic headers and image maps—re-create your text in HTML headers or emphasized text, and try coloring it. Put on

18

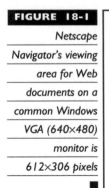

FIGURE 18-1

Netscape Navigator's viewing area for Web documents on a common Windows VGA (640×480) monitor is 612×306 pixels

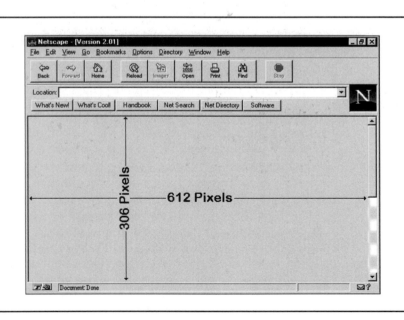

your protective ear muffs—this compromising work is painful—and start nibbling while constantly seeking a balance between quality and the patience of a user who is downloading your material at 14.4 or 28.8 Kbps. Every choice you make should be tempered by bandwidth worry.

warning *For every image referenced in an HTML document, a separate Internet HTTP connection must be made between your computer and that image's server before the image itself is downloaded, so using many tiny images (such as graphic images as bullets) may not be efficient.*

HTML and Multimedia

You should have a basic understanding of HTML before you begin developing multimedia for the Web. HTML-coded documents, which are the fundamental vehicles for all types of information delivered on the World Wide Web, are explained in Chapters 14 and 15.

HTML provides tags for inserting media into HTML documents: the <IMG> tag for inline images; the <INSERT> tag for multimedia objects, including audio, video, and programming tools such as Java applets, Microsoft's Component Object Model (COM) objects, OLE Controls, and OLE; the <EMBED> tag for compound document embedding; and Sun's <APP> and <APPLET> tags for code. The <INSERT> tag and some optional attributes to play a QuickTime movie in HTML 3.0 might look something like,

```
<insert data=lizzie.mov type="application/quicktime">
<param name=loop value=infinite>
<img src=soccer.jpeg alt="The Soccer Match">
</insert>
```

where the browser would play the QuickTime movie named "lizzie" if it supported the .mov format and that MIME-type, and it would loop and play forever. If not supported, the browser would show a substituted JPEG image. Using the <IMG> element here provides backward compatibility with older browsers; if the browser has trouble with the JPEG image, it would display an alternate text label, in this case, "The Soccer Match."

The <EMBED> tag first used by Netscape to enable the many multimedia plug-ins described in Chapter 15 and used in the examples in this chapter may soon be superseded by the more capable <INSERT> tag.

tip *If you develop multimedia for the Internet, budget time and effort for keeping current in this rapidly changing environment—staying at the leading edge takes effort. It will be some years before multimedia delivery tools and techniques for the Web stabilize.*

Text for the Web

Viewers of your Web site may not be displaying the same "preferred" font that you used to design your page because user preferences in the browser may alter the way text in your document looks and flows. Figure 18-2 shows the same Netscape page with font preferences set to Helvetica (on the left) and Impact (on the right). To make the best of this uncertainty, many developers design their documents in Times Roman for the proportional font and Courier as the monospaced font. These fonts readily move across platforms and are the default fonts users typically see if they do not set their own preferences. Although you can specify a font using the <FONT> tag, browsers can only attempt to find a substitute when that font is not installed on the end user's computer.

Great efforts are being made to define standard methods for displaying typefaces on the Web, but neither of the two rival camps, TrueDoc (from Bitstream) and OpenType (supported by Adobe, Microsoft, Agfa, and others), seem able to get their technology properly implemented and launched. The font problem will eventually be solved in one of two ways, or in a combination of both: either many more fonts will become readily and

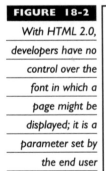

FIGURE 18-2

With HTML 2.0, developers have no control over the font in which a page might be displayed; it is a parameter set by the end user

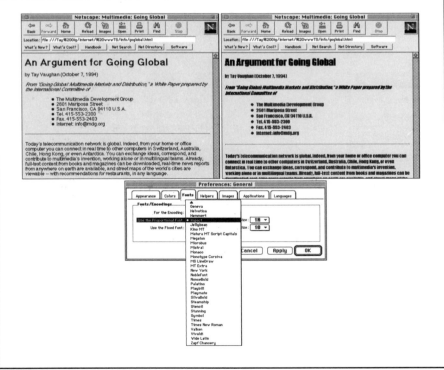

cheaply available and will be commonly installed by end users, or a method of embedding a font's character shapes into an HTML document will allow fonts to "ship" with the document. Both OpenType and TrueDoc embed font information in the HTML document, a more reassuring method for developers, but legal issues surround font foundry copyrights. Using an OpenDoc component called WEFT (Web Embedding Font Tool), Microsoft already offers font-embedding capabilities.

If you are looking for some flexibility in font management at your Web site, you can try using cascading style sheets (CSS), available in dynamic HTML (DHTML), for setting text styles across the pages of your Web site.

As with projects built for CD-ROM using a multimedia authoring tool, if you wish to absolutely control the look of text on your Web page, you must use a graphic bitmap rather than text in your HTML document. Embedding graphics into HTML documents is explained later in the chapter.

As you can see in Figure 18-3, you can tag text to be displayed as headers, bolded, italicized, underlined, and in lists, but the viewer's browser determines how these styles are displayed, and, again, you have little control over its final look. Unofficial extensions to Netscape Navigator include tags by which you can control (somewhat) the attributes of displayed text: the COLOR attribute <FONT COLOR="#0080FF"> will set the color of specific characters of text, and the SIZE attribute <FONT SIZE="+2"> increases or decreases the size of the text displayed. You can also set the background color of individual cells in a table by using the BGCOLOR

FIGURE 18-3

Web browsers currently offer few methods for making pretty text in an HTML document

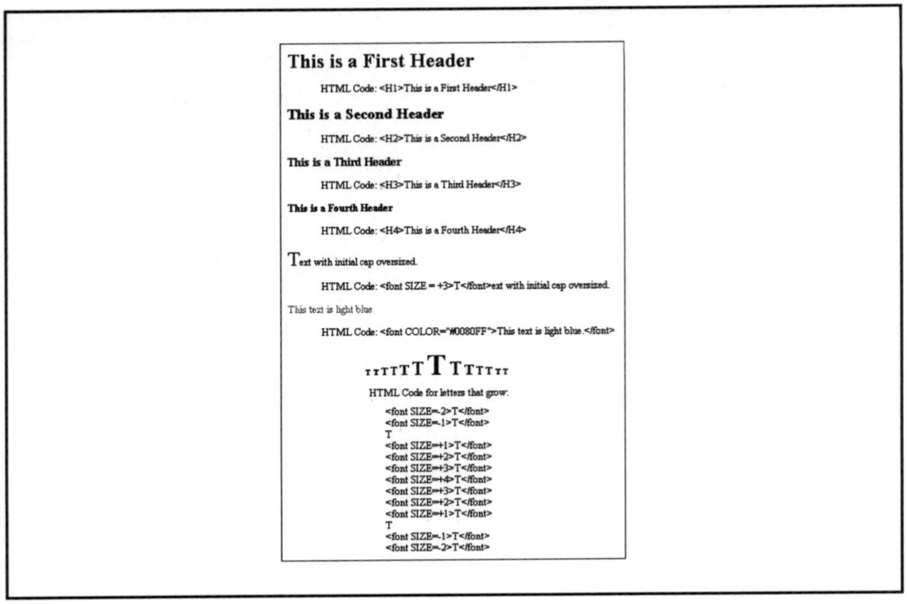

This is a First Header
HTML Code: <H1>This is a First Header</H1>

This is a Second Header
HTML Code: <H2>This is a Second Header</H2>

This is a Third Header
HTML Code: <H3>This is a Third Header</H3>

This is a Fourth Header
HTML Code: <H4>This is a Fourth Header</H4>

Text with initial cap oversized.
HTML Code: <font SIZE=+3>T</font>ext with initial cap oversized.

This text is light blue.
HTML Code: <font COLOR="#0080FF">This text is light blue.</font>

ᴛᴛᴛᴛT**T**Tᴛᴛᴛᴛ

HTML Code for letters that grow:
<font SIZE=-2>T</font>
<font SIZE=-1>T</font>
T
<font SIZE=+1>T</font>
<font SIZE=+2>T</font>
<font SIZE=+3>T</font>
<font SIZE=+4>T</font>
<font SIZE=+3>T</font>
<font SIZE=+2>T</font>
<font SIZE=+1>T</font>
T
<font SIZE=-1>T</font>
<font SIZE=-2>T</font>

attribute in the cell's data tag <TD BGCOLOR="#0080FF">. This is useful to highlight text information in complicated visual presentations.

Making Columns of Text

The most powerful feature of HTML may be found in the <TABLE> tag. Study this tag and its attributes! Using a table, here is how to organize your text into two columns so it displays more like a newspaper or a magazine (see Figure 18-4):

```
<HTML>
<HEAD>
<TITLE>The Explosion</TITLE>
</HEAD>
<BODY>
<CENTER>
<H2>The Explosion</H2>
</CENTER>
<TABLE BORDER=0 CELLSPACING=20>
<TR VALIGN=TOP>
<TD WIDTH=40%>
... text for Column 1 goes here ...
</TD>
<TD WIDTH=40%>
... text for Column 2 goes here ...
</TD>
</TR>
</TABLE>
<HR>
</BODY>
</HTML>
```

Flowing Text Around Images

As you can see in Figure 18-5, it is possible (and easy) to "flow" text around an image using the ALIGN attribute of the <IMG> tag. This is a quick and simple method for mixing text and images in a pleasing layout. Add a <BR CLEAR=left> tag at the end of your text paragraph so that, if there is not enough text to fill the entire vertical height of the image, your next paragraph will begin on a new line, left justified, below the image. To add space around your image so it doesn't butt right up against the text, use the HSPACE and VSPACE attributes of the <IMG> tag.

18

```
<HTML>
<HEAD>
<TITLE>Sailing</TITLE>
</HEAD>
<BODY>
<IMG SRC = "gbsky.gif" ALIGN=left HSPACE=15 VSPACE=5>
<H2>Departure</H2>
... text goes here ...
<BR CLEAR=left>
<hr>
</BODY>
</HTML>
```

The following HTML code sets up a more complicated screen with flowing text (see Figure 18-6, available at http://www.hkkk.fi/mmedia/itp96/). It also includes a background image, a portrait image around which the text flows, and an image map that is used for navigation (background images and image maps are described later in this chapter). This document also contains the foreign language special character ä, which is called out in the document using HTML's special escape sequence for special characters, in this case, "&aumlaut;". Escape characters begin with an

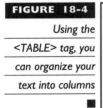

FIGURE 18-4

Using the <TABLE> tag, you can organize your text into columns

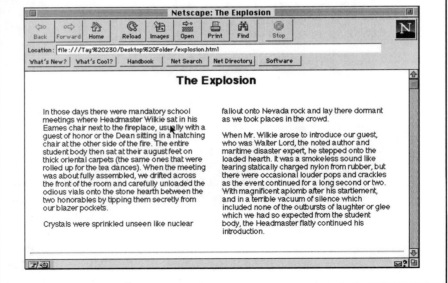

FIGURE 18-5

You can flow text around an image by using the ALIGN attribute of the <IMG> tag

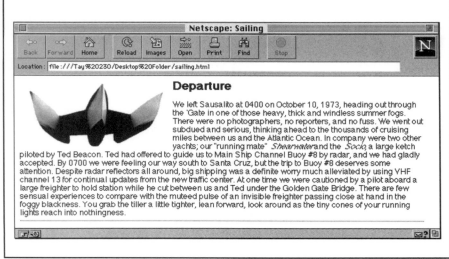

FIGURE 18-6

Images and text can be mixed in an HTML document. Note the use of escape sequences for special characters and the image map for navigation

ampersand and end with a semicolon. Also, note the use of a <FONT size="6"> tag to make paragraphs begin with initial caps. A MIDI file is embedded in this page to provide background music.

```
<html>
<head>
<title>Annan lapsuus</title>
</head>
<body background=misc/annataus.gif>
<img src="misc/trans150.gif" width=20 align=left>
<img src="03/i03b.gif" hspace=10 width=264 height=342 align=left>
<h1>Annan lapsuus</h1>
<pre><i><b>
<font size="6">M</font>in&aumlaut; sain oman huoneen.
Sen sein&aumlaut;t on maalattu vihreiksi. Ja yhdelle
sein&aumlaut;lle on maalattu maisema. Mutta
joelle ei maalattu joutsenia, koska
min&aumlaut; en halunnut. Niihin voi kyll&aumlaut;sty&aumlaut;
niin helposti.

<font size="6">I</font>si on tehnyt minulle kirjahyllyn.
Min&aumlaut; j&aumlaut;rjest&aumlaut;n siihen kaikki tavarat.
Kiiltokuva-albumit ja kirjan. Sen
nimi on "Tiina saa suukon". Vaikka
on minulla muitakin kirjoja, mutta
en min&aumlaut; en&aumlaut;&aumlaut; sellaisia lastenkirjoja
lue.

"T&aumlaut;st&aumlaut; l&aumlaut;htien minun huoneeni on
aina hyv&aumlaut;ss&aumlaut; j&aumlaut;rjestyksess&aumlaut;", sanoin
isille.

<img src="misc/komp4a5a.gif" align= left border="0" usemap="#thispagemap">
</pre>
</i></b>

<map name="thispagemap">
<area shape=circle coords="48,48,12" href ="fhelp.htm">
<area shape=polygon coords="50,50,0,0,100,0" href = "fnavmap.htm">
<area shape=polygon coords="50,50,0,100,100,100" href = "f03.htm">
```

```
</map>

<EMBED SRC="03/pianobg.mid" width=0 height=2 autostart=true>
</body>
</html>
```

Images for the Web

Theoretically, the Web can support any graphics format the client and server have in common. Practically, even though Web standards do not specify a graphics format you must use, browsers typically recognize two image formats, GIF and JPEG, without resorting to special plug-ins. Both formats use built-in compression algorithms to reduce file size (graphic image formats are described in detail in Chapter 11). For other graphics formats, such as CGM, CMX, DXF, and fractal- and wavelet-compressed images, special proprietary creation software and browser plug-ins may be required (see Chapter 15).

GIF and PNG Images

GIF images (discussed in greater detail in Chapter 11) are limited to 8-bits of color depth (256 colors). This is a commercial image format developed by CompuServe Information Services, an on-line company once owned by Unisys and presently folded into America Online. In late 1994, Unisys announced a patent fee charge to all software developers who use the GIF format. In an angry industrywide response, a new "open" format called PNG (for Portable Network Graphics Specification, not requiring fees) was developed to replace GIF. Stay tuned to see if it catches on.

First Person

A few years ago I caught an anecdote from someone who had heard about a quick Web survey: how does the world pronounce .GIF? The results turned out about 50/50 on the hard/soft question, she claimed. Then I spent considerable time using that word (softly) in Europe before realizing everybody was being smirkingly polite about my outlandish pronunciation. In the San Francisco Bay Area, a world center for multimedia development, GIF has the soft "g" of "ginger," "gin," and "gibberish." In New York, where little is soft, and in Europe, .GIF has a more cutting, hard pronunciation, as in "giggling," "gingham," "girdled," "guilty," or "girls." The real question is whether the written word requires a prepended dot.

Color Plate 12 shows images saved in various formats and then displayed from the Web (at http://www.timestream.com/mmedia/graphics/depthtst.html) using Netscape Navigator on Windows and Macintosh platforms set at 16-bit (thousands of colors) and 8-bit (256 colors) color depths. Note that these photos saved in JPEG format seem to work best in all conditions, even dithered to 8-bits on both Windows and Macintosh. The difference between high- and low-quality JPEG compression is hardly noticeable, and the file size savings are great! Also note that dithering to Photoshop's adaptive palette, which optimizes and includes in the 256-color palette as many of the actual colors that are found in that image as possible, is not always displayed well by Navigator or Explorer.

JPEG Images

JPEG images may contain 24-bits of color depth (millions of colors). JPEG uses a powerful but *lossy* compression method that produces files as much as ten times more compressed than GIF.

Use JPEG for photo-realistic images containing many colors, and avoid using it for images already forced into a 256-color palette or for line drawings or 1-bit black-and-white images. GIF compresses drawings and cartoons that have only a few colors in them much better than JPEG, which may introduce visible defects—sharp edges and lines that blur, especially with small-size text. Test the amount of compression acceptable for your JPEG image; stay inside the "threshold of visible error."

---

warning *Do not edit and re-edit files that are in JPEG format. Every time you open a JPEG image and edit it, then recompress and save it as compressed JPEG, the image degrades. After a few editing/saving cycles, you will be very disappointed. Edit and archive your images in a lossless graphic format, then convert to JPEG (if you need to).*

---

tip *If you download JPEG files from the Internet by FTP using Fetch, be sure to add ".jpg" and ".jpeg" to Fetch's list of binary file types (in the Customize/Suffix Mapping... menu). Otherwise Fetch will retrieve JPEG files in text mode and corrupt the data.*

The JPEG (Joint Photographic Experts Group) compression scheme compresses about 20:1 before visible image degradation occurs. To compress an image with JPEG, the image is divided into 8×8 pixel blocks, and the resulting 64 pixels (called a *search range*) are mathematically described relative to the characteristic of the pixel in the upper-left corner. The binary description of this relationship requires far less than 64 pixels, so more information can be transmitted in less time. JPEG compresses slowly—about one to three seconds for a 1MB image depending upon computer speed—but JPEG can compress images as much as 75:1, with loss.

The images in Figure 18-7 are 24-bit (millions of colors), 72 dpi PICT files shown at 3× magnification (so you can see the pixels). The image on the left is uncompressed. The image on the right was compressed in Photoshop using the "JPEG - low quality" setting. The uncompressed file is 60K in size, the compressed file 16K in size. While the compressed image is about one-quarter the size of the uncompressed image, there is a penalty, and it is "lossy."

ftp://rtfm.mit.edu/pub/usenet/news-answers/jpeg-faq
http://melmac.corp.harris.com/transparent_images.html
http://legendre.ucsd.edu/Research/Fisher/fractal.html
ftp://ftp.uu.net/graphics/jpeg
http://www.isi.edu:80/in-notes/iana/assignments/media-types/image/cgm
http://www.boutell.com/boutell/png/
ftp://ftp.std.com:/ftp/vendors/mmedia/lview/lviewpro.zip
ftp://ftp.coast.net:/SimTel/win3/graphics/winjp276.zip
ftp://ftp.coast.net:/SimTel/win3/graphics/psp311.zip
ftp://mac.archive.umich.edu:/mac/graphics/graphicsutil/gifconverter2.37.cpt.hqx
ftp://sumex-aim.stanford.edu:/info-mac/gst/grf/progressify-10.hqx
http://www.timestream.com/mmedia/graphics/depthtst.html

Details and converters for commonly used graphics formats

FIGURE 18-7

Compression schemes save disk space but can degrade an image

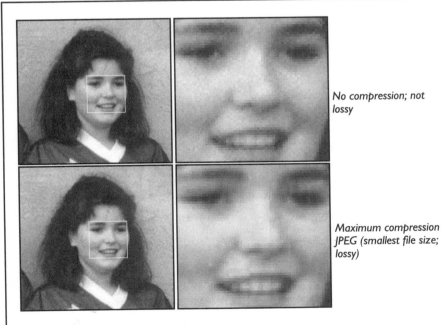

No compression; not lossy

Maximum compression JPEG (smallest file size; lossy)

Using Photoshop

Here are suggestions for using Photoshop to edit and save an image for use on the World Wide Web. If you use a different image editing application, follow the same logic and use the commands appropriate for that application. Always work in native Photoshop format using .PSD files—these images are typically in RGB mode and use the maximum color depth. They are larger, but they contain more information that can be usefully processed when resizing and dithering, and you will get better final results; they also contain layers, a very useful application feature. Use images at 72 pixels per inch resolution. When you convert a 24-bit RGB image to an 8-bit image (change its *mode*), you lose huge amounts of color information that cannot be retrieved—the fine data are gone forever. So do all of your image manipulation (such as resizing, sharpening, and hue adjustments) in RGB mode, and save this source image in RGB mode as a .PSD file (not a lossy compression, like JPEG) so you can make changes later.

When you are satisfied with your image and ready to save it as a GIF or JPEG file, archive it as described above, so if you make any mistakes while converting modes or saving, you will still have the original, complete with any layers you might have used. To be very safe, duplicate the original file and open the copy before saving to other formats.

Saving as JPEG Files

To save your image as a JPEG file, you do not need to change Photoshop's mode from RGB, but if you are using layers, you will need to "flatten" the image, merging all layers into a single bitmap. Once an image is flattened and you have edited or saved it, its layers cannot be remade without a great deal of difficult cutting and pasting, so again, archive your original file! Photoshop will automatically ask if you wish to flatten when you select JPEG from the Save As... menu. You must name your file with the extension .jpg or .jpeg if you will use it on the Web. Then click on Save, and choose Maximum, High, Medium, or Low-quality compression in the dialog box that appears. Color Plate 12 shows images saved in High- and Low-quality settings; you may wish to examine your saved file to see how it looks. Your file is ready for the Web.

Saving as GIF Files

To save a GIF file using Photoshop, you must first set the mode of your image to "Indexed Color," converting it to the best 8-bit palette (256 colors) that will represent the image and be displayed well by Web browsers. Note that the option of saving a Photoshop 24-bit RGB file in GIF format will not be available in Windows, and it will be grayed out on the Macintosh menu until you have converted your image to 8-bit mode: GIF is only for 8-bit images. Only one palette can be active at a time on an 8-bit monitor.

---

tip   *Use GIF files for line art and images that have large areas of the same color. Use JPEG for photo-realistic images.*

PALETTES   When you change mode to Indexed Color, you must specify the color depth of the converted image, the color palette to be used, and whether the colors of your image should be dithered (Diffusion or Pattern) or not (None). Figure 18-8 shows the mode changing dialog box from Photoshop, where the custom Netscape Navigator palette for Windows has been selected (this Photoshop custom palette is available for downloading at http://www.timestream.com/mmedia/graphics/).

One issue that seriously perplexed me when creating my first Web site was choosing the right palette for photographic or continuous tone images. Because images have to be small, you have to dither them to 8-bits. Well, what 8-bit palette do you dither down to...Macintosh, Windows, Netscape, Mosaic, MacWeb, etc., etc.?

Marlene Sinicki, Designer, San Francisco

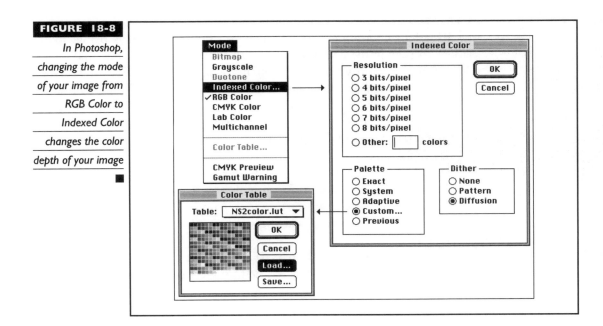

FIGURE 18-8

In Photoshop, changing the mode of your image from RGB Color to Indexed Color changes the color depth of your image

As Color Plate 10 describes, Netscape offers only 216 nondithering colors in its palette for the Windows version of Navigator running in 8-bit display mode (about 20 colors are reserved for the Windows desktop and 20 for Netscape's desktop and animated logo). Using this custom palette for your GIF image means that viewers using a Windows platform with a 256-color VGA monitor will see an image not further dithered by the Netscape application at run time—the 216 colors that make up the image are exactly those already in Navigator's palette. Running on Macintosh platforms, however, Navigator uses the full 256-color Macintosh system palette. So images saved in Photoshop's system palette will display without dithering on Macintoshes. Images dithered to the Macintosh system palette run the risk of using one or more of the 40 unavailable colors for Windows, which will then be dithered by Navigator on Windows platforms and may cause strange effects. Images saved with the Netscape custom palette will always display the same in Netscape Navigator on both platforms.

- -

http://www.netscape.com/assist/support/client/tn/windows/10117.html
http://www.onr.com/user/lights/netlinks.html
http://www.connect.hawaii.com/hc/webmasters/Netscape.colors.html
http://www.industrious.com/~industry/consider.html
http://mvassist.pair.com/Articles/NS2colors.html
http://www.timestream.com/mmedia/graphics/

More about the Netscape palette

INTERLACED AND PROGRESSIVE SCANS   Both GIF and JPEG images can be saved so that when your browser displays the image as it is being downloaded, you can immediately see a chunky approximation of the final image, with resolution improving as more and more data come in. While in *baseline*, or normal, configuration, image data are stored as a single top-to-bottom scan; in *interlaced* GIF and *progressive* JPEG files, the data are organized in a different sequence within the file. An interlaced GIF file, for example, is arranged into a series of four passes:

Pass 1 : Every 8th row, starting with row 0
Pass 2 : Every 8th row, starting with row 4
Pass 3 : Every 4th row, starting with row 2
Pass 4 : Every 2nd row, starting with row 1

Figure 18-9 shows Photoshop's GIF89a Export tool with its checkbox to enable saving an image as interlaced and four increasingly resolved interlaced passes of a GIF image.

18

FIGURE 18-9

Transparency allows an image to "float" on a document background; with interlacing, the image incrementally improves its resolution as it downloads

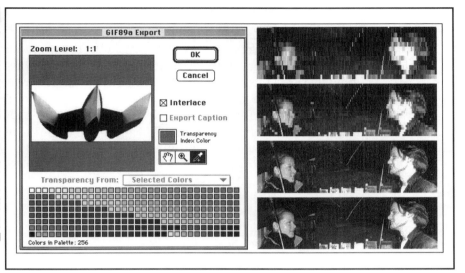

TRANSPARENCY The GIF89a specification allows for transparency: you can save your file with instructions to a browser to use the color that is in its own background for pixels that are your selected transparency color. In many cases, such as for company logos and inline illustrations, it is attractive to let an image float on top of the browser's background:

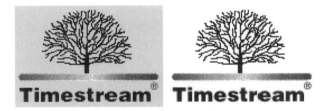

The background of the logo above is white and would (without transparency) be displayed as a rectangle showing white to its edges. To make the white background of the GIF image transparent so that the tree and lettering float on the background, choose white as the transparency index color, and then save the file. Tools that provide a palette from which you can select the transparency index color are available for saving transparent GIF files.

You cannot make a JPEG file transparent.

Backgrounds

Most browsers allow you to specify an image or color to place in the background of your page. Text and images will float on top of this layer.

Background Coloring

You can colorize your documents by choosing background, text, and URL link colors. Color controls are attributes of the <BODY> tag, so you can only set the colors of an *entire* document's background; you cannot change coloring partway through. The BGCOLOR attribute of the <BODY> tag supported by Netscape Navigator lets you change the color of the background without having to specify a graphic image to load. The format Navigator understands is

```
<BODY BGCOLOR="#rrggbb">Document here</BODY>
```

where "#rrggbb" is a hexadecimal red-green-blue triplet used to specify the background color (see Color Plate 10).

When you have chosen a background color, you will then want to set the color of your text and establish proper contrasts. Red on green can be pretty shimmery; black on black is invisible. So the four classes of text used in an HTML document are also attributes of Netscape's <BODY> tag.

The <TEXT> tag is used to control the color of all the normal text in a document—text that is not specially colored to indicate a link. The LINK, VLINK, and ALINK tags let you control the coloring of link text. LINK text displays a URL that you have not visited, VLINK text shows a visited link, and ALINK is an active link. The default coloring of these in Netscape Navigator is TEXT = very light gray, LINK = blue, VLINK = purple, and ALINK = red. If you placed these default colors into a <BODY> tag, the tag would read

```
<BODY BGCOLOR="#CDCDCD" TEXT="#000000" LINK="#0000FF"
VLINK="#FF00FF" ALINK="#FF0000">
```

Background Images

You can specify a special background image for your document. Fifty-five textures are publicly available at Netscape's home server and can add polish with little effort. By using background images served directly from Netscape, it is possible that the image will already be in the cache on your hard disk and will load more rapidly. A picker tool that shows a thumbnail of Netscape backgrounds and puts their URLs onto your system's Clipboard is shown in Figure 18-10. (These tools are available at http://www.timestream.com/mmedia/tools.)

Background images are automatically *tiled*, or repeated, across and down the page, so a randomly distributed "sandy" background image (see Color Plate 9) can easily be made up of a very small source image. None of your

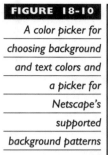

FIGURE 18-10

A color picker for choosing background and text colors and a picker for Netscape's supported background patterns

■

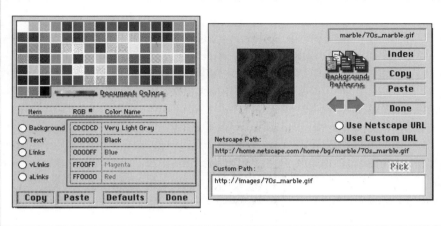

document can be displayed until the background image is loaded, so keep your background image small.

Load a background image into a document by specifying its URL in the BACKGROUND attribute of the <BODY> tag, for example:

```
<BODY BACKGROUND="http://home.netscape.com/home/bg/fabric/gray_fabric.gif">
```

---

tip   *It is a good idea, often overlooked, to specify a background color (BGCOLOR= "#rrggbb") similar to the prevailing color of the image in the <BODY> tag: if the user viewing your page has Image Loading turned off, or if your background image cannot be loaded for some reason, the page will still look close to the way you designed it. If the background image is not loaded for any reason by Navigator, and a BGCOLOR was not also specified, then any of the foreground controlling attributes (TEXT, LINK, VLINK, and ALINK) will be ignored. Netscape claims that the idea behind this is that if you didn't get your requested background image, setting your requested text colors on top of the default gray background could make your document unreadable. If the image you specify as a background has transparent areas, the BGCOLOR will show through.*

Sidebars

....

In the navigation map shown in Color Plate 9, a commonly seen graphic layout was used: a vertical bar containing the word "navmap" is displayed at the left of the screen and in the background. When users scroll up or down, this bar remains stationary.

Assuming that most users will have a viewing window about 640 pixels wide, but some may be wider on higher-resolution monitors, make the graphic bar at the left as wide as you wish (say 75 pixels), then set the full width of your image to 1,000 pixels. Fill the space to the right of your bar with plain color or a texture. When this background image tiles, it will repeat itself only when the user widens the viewing window to more than 1,000 pixels; but the image will tile vertically in increments of its height. Here is the basic setup; see Color Plate 9 for a full-page example.

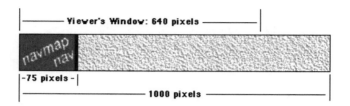

Clickable Buttons

To make a graphic image "clickable" so that it links to another document, simply include the image inside an HTML anchor that points to that document's URL:

```
<A HREF="documentToGoTo.html">
<IMG SRC="imageDisplayed.gif" BORDER=0>
</a>
```

You can also use the <A> tag to provide a link to a larger graphic from the small, thumbnail-sized image, or even to a video clip:

```
<A HREF="bigPicture.jpg"><IMG SRC="thumbnail.gif"></A>

<A HREF="videoClip.mpeg"><IMG SRC="thumbnail.gif"></A>
```

Be sure to include the BORDER=0 attribute in the <IMG> tag if you wish to avoid showing a default border around the button image (usually two blue pixels wide).

Image Maps

Image maps are pictures with defined hot spots that link to other documents when a user clicks on them. Until recently, using image maps at a Web site required a special CGI (Common Gateway Interface) program and a configuration or .map file containing the coordinates of the hot spots to be located on the server. It also required communication between client and server as well as processing time while the CGI program looked up the coordinates in the specified .map file on the server and associated them with a document. Depending upon Internet traffic and delays, performance could be sluggish. And setting up this kind of image map usually required help from a system administrator or the Internet Service Provider who owns the server. In this *server-side* system, the HTML <IMG> tag attribute, ISMAP, tells the server to launch the CGI program, look up the mouse coordinates in the referenced file, and deliver the specified document.

Netscape Navigator and Microsoft Explorer added support for *client-side* image maps so that mouse coordinates and their associated document URLs could be included in the client's own HTML document, thus avoiding the setup and communications hassles of the *server-side* system. This is managed by the USEMAP attribute of the <IMG> tag.

To make a client-side image map with USEMAP, you need three things: an image, a list of coordinates designating hot spots on the image, and the document URL associated with each hot spot. To program the image map into your HTML document, you use the USEMAP attribute of the <IMG> tag:

```
<IMG src="compas.gif" hspace=5 vspace=50 border="0" usemap="#compass">
<MAP name="compass">
    <AREA shape=circle coords="60,60,10" href="help.htm">
    <AREA shape=polygon coords="60,60,0,0,120,0" href="back.htm">
    <AREA shape=polygon coords="60,60,0,120,120,120" href="forward.htm">
    <AREA shape=polygon coords="60,60,0,0,0,120" href="navmap.htm">
    </MAP>
```

In the example above, which is illustrated in Figure 18-11, "compas.gif" is the transparent image, the hspace=5 and vspace=50 attributes provide space between the image and the text around it, and the border=0 attribute makes the image borderless. The usemap="#compass" attribute points to the <map> extension tag that contains the coordinates and URLs (the pound sign means the <MAP> tag is located in this same document). A <MAP> segment may be placed anywhere in the body of the HTML document and is related to the correct image by the name="compass" attribute. You can have more than one image map in an HTML document.

Within the <MAP> tag, the <AREA> tag defines the shape of the hot spot (as a circle, polygon, or rectangle) and anchors or links it to a URL. Areas are defined by x,y coordinates of the pixels in your bitmap: a circle by its center location and radius (60,60,10), a polygon by a sequence of x,y

18

FIGURE 18-11

This enlarged Photoshop image illustrates the coordinates used to define hot spots for image maps (the ruler is marked in pixels)

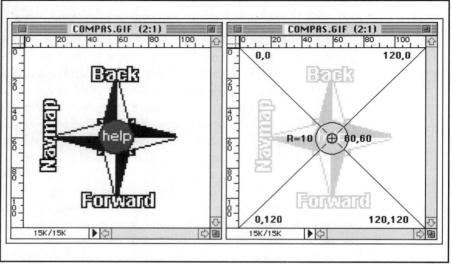

locations that close automatically (60,60,0,0,120,0 defines a triangle), or a rectangle (two x,y locations defining top left and bottom right).

http://wintermute.ncsa.uiuc.edu:8080/map-tutorial/image-maps.html
ftp://sunsite.unc.edu/pub/packages/infosystems/WWW/tools/mapedit
ftp://src.doc.ic.ac.uk/packages/WWW/mapedit

More information about image maps

∫ound for the Web

In the beginning, when the Internet was primarily a collection of Unix machines, sound files were sent from machine to machine in .AU format and, when downloaded, were played back using a sound application. Designing and making MIDI and digitized sound files is described in detail in Chapter 10.

As the Web has developed, sound has become more important, and plug-ins currently allow embedding of sounds into documents. Browsers have become sound capable: Microsoft Explorer offers the <BGSOUND> tag to play an .AU, .WAV, or MIDI sound track in a document background. Netscape 3.0 offers LiveAudio, a sound-playing plug-in for playing AIFF, MIDI, WAV, and AU formats. If your browser does not support sound, you can still launch an external "viewer" or helper application. Figure 18-12 shows a page with a link to the roar of a BMW roadster; in this figure, the sound is being played by the helper application, SoundMachine. These helper applications are available as freeware or shareware for most platforms, but you must download an entire sound file before you can play it.

Streaming audio is more useful for the Web, where a sound file can start playing as soon as data begin coming in—streaming is provided by the LiveAudio plug-in. Plug-ins such as StreamWorks, VocalTec, and RealAudio (see Chapter 15) feature streaming capability and high compression/good fidelity, but they also require special software at the server. The QuickTime plug-in for Navigator offers a fast-start feature to allow playing before a movie has been completely downloaded: MIDI files and digitized sound embedded in a QuickTime movie will play even without video, text, or image tracks. You can either embed HTML commands in a document to play a QuickTime movie automatically in the background, or you can display a controller providing stop, fast-forward, and rewind for the user.

With the Crescendo MIDI plug-in (which downloads and plays standard MIDI files of MIME-type .mid or .midi), you can automatically launch a background sound when a page opens by using the <EMBED> tag:

```
<EMBED SRC="theme.mid" height=2 width=0 autostart=true>
```

FIGURE 18-12

Helper applications can be used to play sounds downloaded from the Web

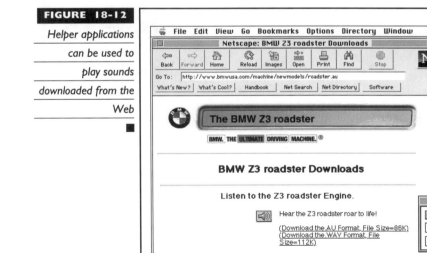

18

Or you can display a controller on the user's page by specifying a specific height and width in the tag:

```
<embed src="../music/anna.mid" width=200 height=55 autostart=false></embed>
```

Sound will become more fully integrated into the way people use the World Wide Web, and it can be included in Shockwave, PowerPoint, Persuasion, Astound, and other presentation tools that use plug-ins and players. CoolTalk is a real-time audio and information collaboration helper included in Netscape 3.0 to allow full-duplex audio conferencing and textual and graphical data conferencing using a shared whiteboard. Live3D, a VRML viewer and plug-in from Netscape, provides interactive 3-D spaces that include text, images, animation, sound, music, and video.

My eyes glaze over whenever someone rattles off a definition of multimedia. The glaze thickens when they focus on hardware speed or the merits of one platform or a multimedia authoring tool. The key is to become well versed in a tool—SuperCard, Toolbook, Director, Authorware, or whatever—so you can make it perform whatever your content requires...it's more important to be creative."

Alan Levine, Instructional Technologist, Maricopa
Community Colleges, Arizona

Making sound for the Web requires the basic tools and techniques described in Chapter 10. Always nibble at your sound elements and reduce them to the lowest file sizes that will play acceptably. Remember, they will move across the Internet and may be downloaded or played on machines with low-bandwidth connections.

Animation for the Web

HTML makes no provision for animation, by itself delivering only a static page of text and graphics. Boring, many people said, and programmers went to work devising methods to liven up the view. Netscape 1.0 offered the (annoying) <BLINK> tag; Microsoft's Explorer offered the (annoying)

<MARQUEE> tag to scroll text horizontally. JavaScript was applied to force (annoying) sliding text into the status bar. Arcane server-push/client-pull programming techniques refreshed images but loaded the network. Things were happening!

GIF89a

With Version 2.0 of Netscape Navigator, Netscape implemented a little-known animation feature of the final 1989 revision "a" of the GIF file format specification. It is possible to make simple animations by putting multiple images or *frames* into a single GIF89a file and display them with programmable delays (in 100ths of a second) between them. Figure 12-6 (in the chapter on animation) shows the individual parts of an animated GIF.

When you use the <IMG> tag to embed a GIF89a multiframe image, Netscape Navigator will download the file and store it in the cache folder of your local hard disk. Once fully downloaded, the image will play each frame quickly and smoothly. Limit animated GIFs to small images, and use a more capable plug-in for animations over larger areas.

Plug-ins and Players

When Macromedia introduced Shockwave to allow the animation and interactivity of its flagship tool, Director, to be embedded into pages viewed by Netscape Navigator, real animation and programmable power was available to Web page developers. Players and plug-ins were offered for other multimedia tools with animation capabilities (see Chapters 7, 8, and 15), and the view came alive. Read Chapter 12 to learn the basics of animation. Pick a tool or method and start creating. Visit http://www.hkkk.fi/mmedia/itp96/f02.htm to see Lokki, the Shockwaved seagull, created by a beginner in just a few hours:

---

t i p *When embedding a Shockwave, PowerPoint, Astound, or other plug-in- or player-supported animation file into a Web page, remember that cross-platform issues apply: if you use text fields, your fonts must properly map across platforms (see Chapter 9) unless you convert all text to bitmaps.*

Action	*http://www.open2u.com*
ASAP Webhow	*http://www.spco.com*
Astound Web Player	*http://www.golddisk.com*
CoolFusion	*http://www.iterated.com*
Expo	*http://www.pmace.com*
Maczilla	*http://maczilla.com*
mBed	*http://www.mbed.com*
MovieStar	*http://www.beingthere.com*
QuickTime VR	*http://www.apple.com*
Shockwave	*http://www.macromedia.com*
Sizzler	*http://www.totallyhip.com*
VDOlive	*http://www.vdolive.com*
ViewDirector	*http://www.tmsinc.com*
ViewMovie	*http://www.well.com/~ivanski*
WebAnimator	*http://www.deltapoint.com*
Whip!	*http://www.autodesk.com*

Tools for making and enabling animation on the Web

Figure 18-13 shows the QuickTime VR player—when you drag the mouse across this player's window, the scene tracks and rotates in a 360-degree panorama. Visit

http://www.bmwusa.com/ultimate/roadster/vrinterior.mov

to see what is going on in the back seat of this car. QuickTime, VRML browsers, MPEG, and other streaming technologies for animation, sound, and video still in development will bring the full power of multimedia to the World Wide Web.

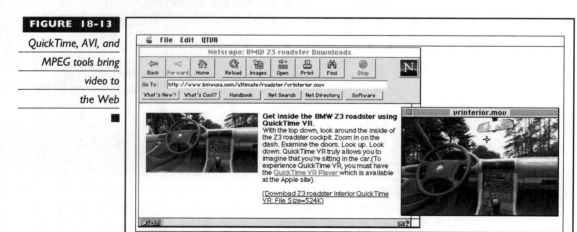

FIGURE 18-13

QuickTime, AVI, and MPEG tools bring video to the Web

Multi

Content is the information
and material that forms
the heart of your project...

Content comes from somewhere.

balance

media

chapter 19

Content and Talent

Either you make it or you acquire it.

EVERY multimedia project includes content. It is the "stuff" from which you fashion your messages. It is also the information and material that forms the heart of your project—that defines what your project is about.

Practically, content can be any and all of the elements of multimedia. You might use your collection of wedding photographs and videotapes to create a special multimedia newsletter for family and relatives. Or you might edit portions of the audio track from these videotapes and capture still images to build a multimedia database of aunts, uncles, and cousins. This material is your project's content.

Content can have low and high *production value*. If you hire a team of professionals to shoot your wedding video, and then they digitize images and audio clips at broadcast quality, your content will have high production value. If you persuade Hillary Rodham Clinton to record the voice-over and Garry Trudeau, the "Doonesbury" artist, to retouch the images, it will have yet higher production value.

You must always balance the production value of your project against your budget and the desired result. For aerial photographs of the wedding reception, you would not likely commission the private launch of a spy satellite from Kennedy Space Center to achieve highest production value. Instead, you could rent a helicopter with paparazzi and still achieve good production value. Or you could photograph the wedding yourself from a neighboring rooftop and be satisfied with the lower production value. The production value of your project is a question of balance (see Vaughan's Law of Multimedia Minimums in Chapter 10).

Content comes from somewhere—either you make it or you acquire it. Whether you make it, borrow it, or buy it depends upon your project's needs, your time constraints, and your pocketbook. Content that is destined for sale to the public is also wrapped in numerous legal issues. Who owns the content? Do you have the proper rights to use it? Copyright laws, for example, protect literary works; musical works; dramatic works; pictorial, graphic, and sculptural works; motion pictures and other audiovisual works; and sound recordings. Do you have licenses and signed releases?

When the Vatican recently made a collection of artwork available on the World Wide Web, they made certain there was a digital "watermark" for each image; they would then know if the artwork were ripped off, without recourse to even higher laws. The Vatican is aware (as you should be) of the nature of the electronic revolution:

> In accordance with international regulations on Intellectual Property and Author's Rights, we inform our readers that the news items contained in the Vatican Information Service may be used in part or in their entirety, but only if the source (V.I.S., Vatican Information Service) is quoted. In the case of electronic retransmission (Internet, telematic networks, via PC-modem, fax, etc.), prior authorization from the Vatican Information Service is always required.

http://www.vatican.va
http://www.christusrex.org/www1/icons/index.html

Collections of hundreds of classical images

This chapter discusses some of the legal issues surrounding content and the use of talent in multimedia projects. It provides examples of contract terms and introduces you to some of the sources and providers of content and talent. Needless to say, always consult an attorney versed in intellectual property law when you negotiate the rights and ownership of content.

Acquiring Content

Content acquisition can be one of the most expensive and time-consuming tasks in organizing a multimedia project. You must plan ahead, allocating sufficient time (and money) for this task.

- If your project describes the use of a new piece of robotics machinery, for example, will you need to send a photographer to the factory for the pictures? Or can you digitize existing photographs?

- Suppose you are working with 100 graphs and charts about the future of petroleum exploration. Will you begin by collecting the raw data from reports and memos, or start with an existing spreadsheet or database? Perhaps you have charts that have already been generated from the data and stored as TIFF or PICT files?

- You are developing an interactive guide to the trails in a national park, complete with video clips of the wildlife that hikers might encounter on the trails. Will you need to shoot original video footage, or are there existing tapes for you to edit?

---

t i p Be sure to specify in your project plan the format and quality of content and data to be supplied to you by third parties. Format conversion and editing takes real time.

This is how you do things on a shoestring. Almost ten years ago, we created a basketball product starring Dr. J and Larry Bird. The first thing we knew we had to do was sign a contract with Dr. J. So we found a guy that knew his agent and we made a side deal with him to pay him to convince Julius to do it. And then we went to Julius and we made a deal where we gave him some stock in the company, rather than writing a huge check. And we convinced him of the educational value of what we were doing, instead of just trying to get it to be an arms-length financial deal. So we were able to sign him up with an advance of only $20,000. And he was quite easily the biggest name in basketball and one of the top two or three regarded professional athletes at the time. We got him for a royalty rate of 2 1/2 percent (not what you hear today in a lot of cases), so you don't have to do things that have really high royalty rates and advances. By the way, he made a killing on the stock!

Trip Hawkins, Chairman & CEO, 3DO Company

Using Content Created by Others

Since the late 1980s, investors in the multimedia marketplace have been quietly purchasing electronic rights to the basic building blocks of content—films, videos, photographic collections, and textual information bases—knowing that in the future these elements can and perhaps will be converted from their traditional form to computer-based storage and delivery. This is smart, but not easy; the many union-supported contract restrictions and performer and producer rights are not only complicated and difficult to trace but also very expensive to acquire.

---

w a r n i n g *If you negotiate ownership or rights to someone else's content, be sure to get the advice of a skilled copyright and contracts attorney.*

Obtaining the rights to content is not, however, a hopeless undertaking. For example, Amaze, Inc., acquired rights from several sources to produce a series of computer-based daily planners with a cartoon-a-day from Gary Larson's "The Far Side" or Cathy Guisewite's "Cathy"; a word-a-day from Random House; or a question-a-day from the Trivial Pursuit game. Random House and Brøderbund's Living Books Division negotiated the rights to the Dr. Seuss books for multimedia use. Multimedia rights to Elvis Presley historical material, to the movie *Jurassic Park*, and to a myriad of other content have been acquired by multimedia developers and publishers.

Depending on the type and source of your content, the negotiations for usage rights can be simple and straightforward, or they may require complicated contracts and a stack of release forms. Each potential content provider you approach will likely have his or her own set of terms that you need to look at carefully so that the terms are broad enough not to constrain the scope of your multimedia project.

Locating Preexisting Content

Preexisting content can come from a variety of sources: from a trunk of old photographs in your neighbor's attic or from a stock house or image bank offering hundreds of thousands of hours of film and video or still images, available for licensing for a fee.

If your needs are simple and fairly flexible, you may be able to use material from collections of clip art. Such collections of photographs, graphics, sounds, music, animation, and video are becoming widely available from many sources, for anywhere from fifty to several hundred dollars. Part of the value of many of these packages is that you are granted unlimited use, and you can be comfortable creating derivative versions tailored to your specific application. Carefully read the license agreement that comes with the collection before assuming you can use the material in any manner. In the six-point italicized type on the back of the agreement, you may discover that the licensor offers no guarantee that the contents of the collection are original works. Thus, the licensor bears no responsibility to indemnify you for inadvertently infringing on the copyrights of a third party. You may also discover that the collection comes with severe restrictions on the way material can be used, or that a royalty is required for use.

If your content needs are more specific or complex, a good place to start your search for material might be at a still photo library, a sound library, or a stock footage house. These resources may be public or private and may contain copyrighted works as well as materials that are in the public domain, meaning that its copyright protection has expired over time and not been renewed; you can use the material without a license.

The National Archives in Washington D.C. is a rich source of content, both copyrighted and in the public domain. Other public sources include the Library of Congress, NASA, U.S. Information Agency, and the Smithsonian Institution, all in Washington D.C. You cannot, however, safely assume that all material acquired from a public source is in the public domain. You remain responsible for ensuring that you do not infringe on a copyright.

In addition to public sources, there are many other repositories of content material. Commercial stock houses offer millions of images, video and film clips, and sound clips, and they often own the works outright—so you don't have to worry about copyright infringement. Some stock sources also specialize in certain subjects. For example, if you want a video clip of a shark, you might contact a stock footage house that specializes in underwater videos, such as Images Unlimited in Bozeman, Montana, or Sea Studios in Monterey, California.

Copyrights

Copyright protection applies to "original works of authorship fixed in any tangible medium of expression." The Copyright Act of 1976, as amended (17 U.S.C.A. §101 et. seq.) protects the legal rights of the creator of an original work. Consequently, before you can use someone else's work in your multimedia project, you must first obtain permission from the owner of the copyright. If you do not do this, you may find yourself being sued for copyright infringement (unauthorized use of copyrighted material).

Works come under copyright protection as soon as they are created and presented in a fixed form. Works do not have to be registered with the U.S. Copyright Office to be protected. There are limited "fair use" exceptions in which copyrighted material can be used without permission, but you should consult an attorney before assuming this exception.

Owning a copy of a work does not entitle you to reproduce the work unless you have the permission of the copyright owner. If you buy a painting from an artist, the artist retains the copyright unless it is assigned to you. You do not have the right to reproduce the painting in any form, such as in postcards or a calendar, without permission.

. . . .

http://www.timestream.com/info/license.html
http://www.timestream.com/info/mmlaw.html

This white paper about Licensing Still Images and an intellectual property law primer for multimedia developers by Dianne Brinson and Mark Radcliffe provide useful insights into complex legal issues

For additional discussion about copyrights as they apply to original works created for a project, see "Using Content Created for a Project" later in this chapter, and visit the Library of Congress at http://lcweb.loc.gov/copyright/.

Obtaining Rights

19

You should license the rights to use copyrighted material before you develop a project around it. You may be able to negotiate outright ownership of copyrighted material. If the owner does not wish to give up or sell ownership rights, however, you may still be able to *license* the rights to use that material.

There are few guidelines for negotiating content rights for use in multimedia products. If you are dealing with content providers who are professionals familiar with electronic media, you may be given a standard rate card listing licensing fees for different uses, formats, and markets. Other content providers or owners may be less familiar with multimedia and electronic uses, and you will need to educate them.

Explaining multimedia technology to people can be a challenge. Michelle, an eighth-grader, wanted to scan some 1920s photographs to use in the San Rafael Community Express, a multimedia magazine done for kids by kids. When Michelle asked the 80-year-old docent at the local museum if she could use the photographs for a computer project, the woman responded in horror that these were priceless pictures and that they couldn't be put in a computer—they'd be ruined. The team spent another 15 minutes explaining scanning to the woman by comparing a scanner to a copy machine and assuring her that the original photographs would be returned unharmed.

John MacLeod, Publisher and Chief Pizza Provider for the San Rafael Community Express, a HyperStudio-based interactive magazine created by seventh- and eighth-graders at Davidson Middle School, San Rafael, California

Some licensing agreements may be as simple as a signed permission letter or release form describing how you may use the material. Other agreements will specify in minute detail how, where, when, and for what purpose the content may be used. Ideally, you would seek rights to use the content anytime, anywhere, and in any way you choose; more likely, however, the final license would contain restrictions about how the material may be used. Try to retain the option to renegotiate terms in case you want to broaden the scope of use at a later date.

The following items are but a few of the issues you need to consider when negotiating for rights to use preexisting content:

- How will the content be delivered? If you limit yourself to CD-ROMs, for example, you may not be able to distribute your product over cable or telephone lines without renegotiation.

- Is the license for a set period of time?

- Is the license exclusive or nonexclusive? In an exclusive use arrangement, no one else would be able to use the material in the manner stipulated.

- Where will your product be distributed? There may be different rates for domestic and international distribution.

- Do you intend to use the material in its entirety, or just a portion of it?

- What rights do you need? You need to be sure you have the right to reproduce and distribute the material. In addition, you may wish to use the material in promotions for your product.

- Does the content owner have the authority to assign rights to you? It is important to ensure you will not be held liable if a third party later sues for copyright infringement.

- Do you need to obtain any additional rights to use the content? For example, if you use a clip from a movie, do you need to get separate releases from actors appearing in the clip or from the director or producer of the movie?

- Will the copyright owner receive remuneration for the license? If so, what form will it take? A one-time fee? Royalty? Or a simple credit attribution?

- In what format do you wish to receive the content? Specifying formats is particularly important with video dubbed from a master.

Derivative Works

Any text taken verbatim, or any image or music perfectly copied, clearly requires permission from its owner to incorporate it into your work. But there are some other, less clear-cut issues. For example, as a starter for your work, you may wish to incorporate but a tiny portion of an image owned by someone else, altering the image until the original is no longer recognizable. Is this legal? Indeed, how much of the original must you change before the product becomes yours? There are no simple answers to these tough questions.

Figure 19-1 shows an original photograph taken by Mark Newman, along with some artwork derived from it. Newman sold certain rights to 21st Century Media, Inc., which packages and sells assortments of stock photographs on CD-ROM to computer graphics and multimedia developers. The CD-ROM product contains these instructions:

> You may make copies of the digitized images contained on the Product for use in advertisements, public or private presentations, business communications, multimedia presentations, and other uses as long as the images are not used to create a product for sale. For example, you may not use the images to create calendars, posters, greeting cards, or books of image collections for sale. You may not use, in whole or in part, or alter a digitized image in any manner for pornographic use.

19

FIGURE 19-1

The original photograph by Mark Newman was clipped and manipulated for use in a multimedia project. Who owns the resulting image?

Suppose, however, that the image in Figure 19-1 were scanned from the pages of *National Geographic* or *Time*—what then? If you change 51 percent of the pixels, is the image yours? These questions of ownership will undoubtedly be resolved eventually in the courts.

There is a serious issue facing multimedia developers. Now that they have tools to creatively modify things, how much of someone else's image, music, or video clip needs to be modified before ownership changes? This is up for grabs. There is a law called "fair use," which comes into play in a very limited way here. But I think there needs to be a law called "fair modification." We need something like that because otherwise multimedia is not going to get anywhere.

Trip Hawkins, Chairman & CEO, 3DO Company

Use of images, sounds, and other resources from stock houses such as PhotoDisc or Index Stock Photography is perhaps the safest way to go, because ownership and your rights to use the material are clearly stated.

warning *Beware of clip media claiming to be public domain (where no copyrights apply) that includes sounds from popular television shows or motion pictures.*

Permission must also be obtained to use copyrighted text. Figure 19-2 provides sample language for requesting permission to reprint copyrighted text material and sample terms that you might expect from the copyright owner.

Using Content Created for a Project

In the process of developing your multimedia project, interfaces will be designed, text written, lines of code programmed, and original artwork, photographs, animations, musical scores, sound effects, and video may be produced.Each of these elements is an original work. If you are creating a project single-handedly and for yourself, you own the copyright outright. If other persons who are not your employees also contribute to the final product, they may own copyright of the element created by them or may share joint ownership of the product unless they assign or license their ownership rights to you.

The ownership of a project created by employees in the course of their employment belongs solely to the employer if the work fits the requirements of a "work made for hire." To meet the definition of a work made for hire,

FIGURE 19-2

Sample permission

request and terms

from a publisher

for use of

copyrighted text

or images
■

Typical request to a large publishing company:

Dear Sirs:

I am currently producing a computer-based multimedia presentation with a working title of (Title). My publisher is (Publisher, Publisher's Address). The anticipated completion date of the work is (Month/Year). It will be used for (Use).

This letter is to request your permission to incorporate into this work a brief passage from: (Title, Author, Edition, ISBN, Page).

The text I wish to reproduce is: (Text).

Please process this request at your earliest convenience and use this letter or your own form to return your approval by mail or fax to: (Your Name/Address).

The undersigned, having full authority, hereby grants permission to (Your Name) to copy and reproduce the referenced text for use in the work cited above.

Signed: _____

Typical terms from a large publishing company:

1. To give full credit in every copy printed, on the copyright page or as a footnote on the page on which the quotation begins, or if in a magazine or a newspaper, on the first page of each quotation covered by the permission, exactly as "Reprinted with the permission of (Publisher) from (Title) by (Author). Copyright (Year) by (Publisher)."

2. To pay on publication of the work, or within 24 months of the date of granting the permission, whichever is earlier, a fee of: $_____.

3. To forward one copy of the work and payment on publication to the Permissions Department of (Publisher).

4. To make no deletions from, additions to, or changes in the text, without the written approval of (Publisher).

5. That the permission hereby granted applies only to the edition of the work specified in this agreement.

6. That permission granted herein is nonexclusive and not transferable.

7. That this permission applies, unless otherwise stated, solely to publication of the above-cited work in the English language in the United States, its territories and dependencies, and throughout the world. For translation rights, apply to the International Rights Department of (Publisher).

8. That unless the work is published within two years from the date of the applicant's signature (unless extended by written permission of (Publisher)) or, if published, it remains out of print for a period of six months, this permission shall automatically terminate.

9. This permission does not extend to any copyrighted material from other sources which may be incorporated in the books in question, nor to any illustrations or charts, nor to poetry, unless otherwise specified.

10. That the work containing our selection may be reproduced in Braille, large type, and sound recordings provided no charge is made to the visually handicapped.

11. That unless the agreement is signed and returned within six months from the date of issue, the permission shall automatically terminate.

19

several factors must be weighed to determine whether the individual is legally an employee or an independent contractor. Among these factors are where the work is done, the relationship between the parties, and who provides the tools and equipment.

If the individual contributing to a project is not an employee, the commissioned work must fall within one of the following "work made for hire" categories: a contribution to a collective work, a work that is part of a motion picture or other audiovisual work, a translation, a supplementary work, a compilation, an instructional text, a test, answer material for a test, or an atlas (1976 Copyright Act, 17 U.S.C. §201(b)). Even if the work falls within one of these categories, be sure to get an agreement in writing from every individual contributing to the work that it is being created as a work for hire. Figures 19-3 and 19-4 offer sample contracts with employees and contractors to precisely specify ownership issues.

The copyright ownership of works created in whole or in part by persons who fall under the definition of independent contractor may belong to that contractor unless the work is specially ordered or commissioned for use and qualifies as a work made for hire, in which case the copyright belongs to the entity commissioning the work.

A copyright can belong to a single individual or entity, or it may be shared jointly by several entities. Make sure that copyright ownership issues have been resolved, in writing, before people contribute to your project.

Using Talent

After you have tested everybody you know and you still have vacant seats in your project, you may need to turn to professional talent. Getting the perfect actor, model, or narrator's voice is critical. You don't want to settle for a voice or an actor who is not quite polished or is ill suited to the part, or your whole project may have an amateurish feel.

Professional voice-over talents and actors in the United States usually belong to a union or guild, either AFTRA (American Federation of Television and Radio Artists) or SAG (Screen Actors Guild). They are usually represented by a talent agent or agency that you can find in the Yellow Pages.

FIGURE 19-3	PROPRIETARY INFORMATION AND INVENTIONS AGREEMENT

Sample employer/employee agreement covering intellectual property and inventions; consult an attorney when preparing your own legal document

PROPRIETARY INFORMATION AND INVENTIONS AGREEMENT

NOTICE:

This agreement does not apply to an invention which qualifies fully under the provisions of Section 2870 of the Labor Code of California as an invention for which no equipment, supplies, facility, or trade secret information of (Company) was used and which was developed entirely on the employee's own time, and (a) which does not relate (1) to the business of (Company) or (2) to (Company's) actual or demonstrably anticipated research or development, or (b) which does not result from any work performed by the employee for (Company).

Employee's Name _____

Address _____

Date of Hire _____

In consideration of my employment by (Company) or any of its subsidiary or affiliated companies (all called "the Company") and the compensation paid me by the Company, I agree as follows:

1. I understand that my employment results in a confidential relationship between myself and the Company. It is expected that I will receive, during and for purposes of my employment, information about the Company's products, processes, business, plans, research programs, and like Company information (all called "the Company business"), which information is the property of the Company. I may also conceive of or develop ideas and inventions related to the Company business during or for purposes of my employment. The information received from the Company and information which I conceive or develop pertaining to the Company business are the sole property of the Company and are valuable trade secrets of the Company. I agree to preserve their value as Company property, by complying with the following requirements.

2. Except as required in the course of my employment, I shall not disclose to anyone or use at any time, either during or after my employment, any information about the Company business which is either received from the Company or conceived or developed by me, unless I have the prior written consent of the Company.

3. I agree to disclose promptly to the Company all inventions, ideas or conceptions, developments, and improvements (whether or not patentable or subject to copyright) which are made or conceived by me, either alone or together with others, during or as a result of my employment, provided that they pertain to the Company business. I will keep complete records of such matter and will and hereby do assign such matter to the Company, whether or not it has been tested or reduced to practice. Included are all data processing communications, computer software systems, programs, and procedures, which pertain to the Company business. All such records are and shall be the property of the Company alone.

4. Upon request of the Company, either during or after my employment, I will assist in applying for Letters Patent, or for copyright or Inventors Certificate or other appropriate legal form, on all such Inventions and Ideas, in this and in foreign countries, and will execute all papers necessary thereto, including assignments as may be requested by the Company, without further compensation to me. Such applications shall be filed at the expense of and under the control of the Company.

5. All unpublished data and information relating to the Company business, whether reduced to writing or not, are understood and agreed to be confidential and the sole property of the Company. This extends to all confidential information or data I may receive from or about any of the Company's licensees, customers, or others with whom the Company has a business relationship. I will maintain all such information in confidence and not use it other than as expressly requested by the Company, either during or after my employment with the Company, unless and until such information is published without fault on my part.

6. Upon termination of my employment, I will surrender all records and material relating to the Company business.

7. I am aware of no prior obligations which would prevent my compliance with the terms and spirit of this agreement.

8. This agreement shall be binding upon me and my heirs, executors, administrators, and assigns. The Company shall have the right to assign this agreement to any successor to the business in which I am employed.

Signed at _____ , on _____ , 19__

Employee (Signature)

Witness (Signature)

(Address of Witness)

FIGURE 19-4

Sample

employer/consultant

agreement in the

form of a letter;

hire an attorney

when preparing

your own legal

documents

Confidential

(Date)

(Name and Address of Consultant)

Dear (Consultant):

This document, when accepted and agreed to by you, will confirm our mutual understanding and agreement concerning your engagement as an independent contractor to render consulting services to (Employer Name). You will be engaged as an independent contractor to provide such advice, consultation, and other assistance as may, from time to time, be requested by (Employer Name) in furtherance of (Employer Name)'s business in general and particularly for:

(General Statement of Scope of Work)

During the term of this Consulting Agreement, you agree to provide consulting services to (Employer Name), on the terms and conditions contained in Attachment A, "Description of Services and Reimbursement." Twice monthly you will submit a statement, in a form satisfactory to (Employer Name), setting forth the milestone reached and any authorized expenses incurred to be reimbursed by (Employer Name). Payment will be made according to the schedule in Attachment A.

The consulting services that you will provide are to be rendered at such times and at such places as are mutually agreed upon by (Employer Name) and you. You agree that (Employer Name) shall own all intellectual property rights, including but not limited to copyrights, patents, trade secrets, and trademarks in any and all products of your work within the scope of this Agreement. Said products will be copyrighted by (Employer Name) or in such other name as (Employer Name) may designate. You further agree that any work provided hereunder shall be considered "work made for hire" within the meaning of 17 U.S.C. 2201(b). However, (Employer Name) will give proper credit to you in a manner to be mutually agreed upon as appropriate to the creative direction of the work.

In the performance of the consulting services herein contemplated, you are, and shall be deemed to be for all purposes, an independent contractor (and not an employee or agent of (Employer Name)) under any and all laws, whether existing or future, including without limitation, Social Security laws, state unemployment insurance laws, withholding tax laws, and the payments and reports of any taxes and/or contributions under such laws. You will not be entitled to participate in any employee benefits accruing to employees of (Employer Name). You will not be authorized to make any material representation, contract, or commitment on behalf of (Employer Name).

You agree to comply with applicable laws, rules, and regulations in respect to self-employment, including without limitation, the payment of all taxes required, and you agree to furnish (Employer Name) evidence of the payment of such taxes if requested. In addition, you agree to defend, indemnify, and hold (Employer Name) harmless against all losses, liabilities, claims, demands, actions and/or proceedings, and all costs and expenses in connection therewith, including attorney's fees, arising out of your failure to comply with this paragraph.

The term of this Consulting Agreement shall be for the period of time described in Attachment A, subject to the following limitations:

Upon five (5) days written notice, either you or (Employer Name) may terminate this Consulting Agreement. Such termination shall be effective at the conclusion of said five-day period.

This Consulting Agreement shall terminate on your death.

Notwithstanding anything herein to the contrary, (Employer Name) may, without liability, terminate this Consulting Agreement for cause at any time, and without notice, and thereafter (Employer Name)'s obligations hereunder shall cease and terminate. The term "cause" shall mean, by way of example, but not by way of limitation:

Misappropriating funds or property of (Employer Name);

Attempting to obtain any personal profit from any transaction related to THIS consulting work which is adverse to the interest of (Employer Name);

Unreasonable neglect or refusal to perform the consulting services agreed to be performed by you under this Consulting Agreement;

Being convicted of a felony;

Being adjudicated a bankrupt; or

A breach of any of the other provisions of this Consulting Agreement.

FIGURE 19-4

Sample

employer/consultant

agreement in the

form of a letter;

hire an attorney

when preparing

your own legal

documents

(continued)

Upon termination of this Consulting Agreement, for any reason, you will be paid your consulting fee on a pro rata basis, and you will be reimbursed for authorized expenses, to and including the effective date of such termination.

You agree to hold all Confidential Information in trust and confidence for (Employer Name), and except as may be authorized by (Employer Name) in writing, you shall not disclose to any person, and you shall take such reasonable precautions as may be necessary to prevent the disclosure of, any Confidential Information at all times during and after the term of this Consulting Agreement. For the purposes of this Consulting Agreement, "Confidential Information" shall mean all information obtained by you, or disclosed to you by (Employer Name), at any time before or during the term hereof, which relates to (Employer Name)'s or (Employer Name)'s clients' past, present, and future research, development, and business activities, and any other trade secrets, records, engineering notebooks, data, formulae, computer code, specifications, inventions, customer lists, and other proprietary information and data concerning (Employer Name) or any client, provided that Confidential Information shall not include information that becomes part of the public knowledge or literature (not as a result of any action or inaction on your part) either prior or subsequent to your receipt of such information.

Upon termination or expiration of this Consulting Agreement, you agree to return to (Employer Name) all written or descriptive matter, including but not limited to drawings, blueprints, descriptions, drafts, computer code, computer files, hardware, software, or other papers or documents that contain any Confidential Information.

(Employer Name) does not desire to receive information in confidence from you under this Consulting Agreement.

You represent and warrant that you are under no obligation or restriction nor will you assume any obligation or restriction which would in any way interfere or be inconsistent with the services to be furnished by you under this Consulting Agreement. In that regard, this Consulting Agreement will in no way restrict you from freely entering into other similar consulting agreements with other firms in the field as long as the provisions herein are honored.

(Employer Name) shall have sole discretion to make other consulting arrangements with other persons concerning any or all of the consulting services to be rendered by you under this Consulting Agreement.

(Employer Name) acknowledges and understands that he is the author of the work you are hired to consult on and that he is therefore responsible for its contents. In the event of a third party action against (Employer Name), (Employer Name) agrees to indemnify and hold you harmless if you are made a party to such action; provided however that (Employer Name) shall have no such responsibility to you if such suit arises due to your misconduct or gross negligence. You promise to provide (Employer Name) with all reasonable cooperation and assistance in any such action or proceedings.

If any action at law is necessary to enforce or interpret the terms of this Consulting Agreement, the prevailing party shall be entitled to reasonable attorneys' fees, costs, and necessary disbursements, in addition to any other relief to which such party shall be entitled.

This letter shall constitute the entire agreement between the parties hereto with respect to the subject matter hereof. In the event of any unresolved dispute in respect thereof, the matter shall be submitted to arbitration in accordance with the rules and regulations of the American Arbitration Association, and the decision of the arbitrator(s) shall be final and binding on both parties hereto.

The validity of this Consulting Agreement and any of its terms and conditions, as well as the rights and duties of the parties hereunder, shall be interpreted and construed pursuant to and in accordance with the laws of the State of California.

(Employer Name)

(Employer Signature)

Accepted and agreed to this _____ day of _____, 19__.

Consultant's Signature: _____

Consultant's Social Security Number or EIN: _____

Attachment A to the Consulting Agreement of (Date)

between (Employer Name) and (Consultant)

Description of Services and Reimbursement

First Person

We put out a call for a multimedia acting job (male, mid-30s, credible voice, earnest smile), and 18 men showed up for tryouts at a local studio—17 were nonunion and 1 belonged to AFTRA. We videotaped each applicant as he read a prepared script, chatted with all of them, and asked them to walk around and jump up and down. The best choice by far, we thought at the end of a long day, was Dave Kazanjian, the union member.

"Oooh," we said to ourselves, "real union talent! This is going to cost us." So we got together with the client and ran tapes of half a dozen of the better actors trying out, without saying which was our favorite. The client's choice was the same as ours, because Dave was very polished and professional and simply perfect for the part. Paying union-scale wages to the actor would double what we had estimated in our original budget; we had naively assumed we could quickly and easily find the right talent from the nonunion pool. We ran the new numbers past the client, implying that the second-choice actor was more affordable, even if he wasn't quite perfect. Then we showed Dave's clip next to the other guy, and repeated it a few times, until the difference was really apparent. The comparison was persuasive, and in the end, the client supported the extra cost.

We all learned again that you get what you pay for: Dave did a terrific job. In future proposals, we used union scale in estimating cost, whether we hired a union actor or not.

Locating the Professionals You Need

Before you can safely put a professional in front of a camera or a microphone, you have to find the talent first and then deal with hiring and union contracts.

Begin by calling a talent agency; explain what you need. The agency will probably suggest several clients who might fit your needs and send you a collection of videotapes or cassettes as samples of the actors' work. After reviewing the tapes, you can arrange auditions of the best candidates, at your office or at a studio. You can also get in touch with several agencies and put out a casting call for screen or audio auditions. Furthermore, you are not limited to using union talent, and if your call is posted on bulletin boards in public places (in the theater department of a local university, for example), you may find yourself with many applicants, both union and nonunion, who are eager for the work.

If you run your own audition, be sure you are organized for it. You will need sign-up sheets for names and phone numbers, a sample script for applicants to read, a video camera or tape recorder, tracking sheets so you can coordinate actors' names with their video or audio clips, and hospitable coffee and donuts.

Working with Union Contracts

The two unions, AFTRA and SAG, have similar contracts and terms for minimum pay and benefits. AFTRA recently approved an Interactive Media Agreement to cover on- and off-camera performers on all interactive media platforms. Figure 19-5 shows some AFTRA definitions related to interactive media.

The AFTRA and SAG contracts are lengthy and detailed. Both share language and job descriptions (such as principal, voice-over performer, extra, singer, and dancer). Also, both unions have approximately the same wage scales for these jobs. In 1998, AFTRA's minimum wage for an on-camera principal performer for interactive media was $522 for one eight-hour day, $1,321 for three days, or $1,813 for a week. The minimum wage for a voice-over performer doing up to three voices in a four-hour day was $522; each additional voice would be $174 more. Of course, an actor can always negotiate more than minimum wage.

If your talent needs are simple, you can usually get good contract advice directly from the union representative in your area or from the actors themselves. If your needs are elaborate or undefined, you may wish to consult an attorney or agent who specializes in this area and who can oversee the many required clauses and details of the contract.

Talent contracts are filled with quirky details and complicated formulas. Consider, for example, Article I.17.A.4(c)(i) of the AFTRA 1994-1998 Interactive Media Agreement, which reads:

> If a solo or duo is called upon to step out of a group to sing up to fifteen (15) cumulative bars during a session, the solo/duo shall be paid an adjustment of fifty percent (50%) of the solo/duo rate in addition to the appropriate group rate for that day.

FIGURE 19-5	
From the AFTRA	**DEFINITIONS**
Interactive Media	"Material": includes all products (audio or visual) derived from the recordation of the live-action performances of performers, whether or not such performances are incorporated into the final version of the fully-edited Interactive Program produced hereunder by Producer.
Agreement	
(reprinted courtesy	"Interactive": Interactive describes the attribute of products which enables the viewer to manipulate, affect or alter the presentation of the creative content of such product simultaneously with its use by the viewer.
of AFTRA, 260	
Madison Avenue,	"Interactive Media" means: any media on which interactive product operates and through which the user may interact with such product including but not limited to personal computers, games, machines, arcade games, all CD-interactive machines and any and all analogous, similar or dissimilar microprocessor-based units and the digitized, electronic or any other formats now known or hereinafter invented which may be utilized in connection therewith;
New York, NY	
10016)	
∎	"Performers": Persons whose performances are used as on or off-camera, including those who speak, act, sing, or in any other manner perform as talent in material for Interactive Media.

Although the concept of *stepping out* may be more in keeping with an MTV video project than with your own multimedia work, you need to keep an eye out for buried clauses that do apply to your project.

---

warning   *If you create a multimedia product that incorporates union talent under contract, you will be restricted to using the material only for its initial primary use. Later, if you wish to spin off bits and pieces for other purposes (such as a commercial or as part of a product for sale to the public), you must then negotiate again with the talent and the union and pay for this expanded and supplemental use.*

Acquiring Releases

A union talent contract explicitly states what rights you have to the still and motion images and voices you make and use. If, however, your talent is nonunion (a co-worker in your office, perhaps, or a neighbor's child, student actor, waitress, or tugboat captain), be sure to require the person to sign a release form. This form grants to you certain permissions and specifies the terms under which you can use the material you make during a recording session.

::::::::::::::::::::::::::::::::::

Sometimes it is very difficult to do certain things because of previous rights that have been given out. For example, not too long ago I asked an executive from a media company if it would be possible to take some of his film footage and put it into a copyright library, to have something available for multimedia software developers to freely use in their interactive products. He said, "Well, we couldn't use a single frame of any film that was ever shot by a director who was a member of the Directors Guild of America." The bottom line is that there are so many rights attached to so many of these things, with so many different people involved, that it is very complicated even to figure out if you have the right to use it in any way, and again that's too bad because again, that is just going to slow us down.

::::::::::::::::::::::::::::::::::

Trip Hawkins, Chairman & CEO, 3DO Company

Figure 19-6 is a sample release form that covers most situations in a multimedia project and provides nearly perfect rights to the producer. Because such forms are legal documents, always consult an attorney to be sure that the specific language of your own release document meets your requirements.

FIGURE 19-6

Sample release

form; consult an

attorney when

preparing your own

legal document

■

Release Form

This is a release and authorization to use the name, voice, sounds, image and likeness, and writings of the undersigned ("Model"), as obtained in the photography / filming / video / audio session / creative session taking place

_____ at, _____ ("the Session"), for commercial purposes by _____
and his respective successors and assigns (collectively, "Producer").

For valuable consideration, Model hereby authorizes the unlimited use in perpetuity by Producer of all recorded images, likenesses, voice and recorded sounds, and writings of Model obtained during the Session, and of Model's name in connection with such use. Model grants producer the rights to use such sounds, images, and likenesses in any and all media and forms now known or hereafter devised throughout the universe without limitation as to territory or term, including but not limited to advertising, literature, computer demonstrations, and packaging, whether in the form of photography, magnetic or electronic data storage, or any other form, both as obtained and as modified at Producer's sole discretion to suit business purposes of Producer. The compensation stated above shall be the sole compensation for all such use, and no further compensation, including but not limited to royalties, residuals, or use fees, shall be payable at any time.

Model further transfers and assigns all copyrights and all other rights in the recordings, sounds, images and likeness, and writings obtained at the Session to Producer. Producer shall have the right to register the copyright to these in the name of its choice and shall have the exclusive right to dispose of these in any manner whatsoever. This agreement constitutes the sole, complete, and exclusive agreement between Model and Producer.

Name: _____   SIGNATURE: _____

Address: _____   SOCIAL SECURITY NO.:_____

_____   DATE: _____

Phone: _____

19

w a r n i n g   *Do not include in your multimedia project any images or voices of people—even if you yourself recorded and edited the material—unless you have their written consent to use it; it is in the public domain; you are reporting it as news, commentary, or parody ("fair use"); or it is work unarguably made for hire.*

Multi

Test it, then test it again;
that's the unavoidable rule.

It's critical that you take the time
to thoroughly exercise your project
and fix both big and little problems...

test and review

media

Alpha...

20

Delivering

...in the end,
  you will save yourself
  a great deal of agony!

...Beta

T EST it, then test it again; that's the unavoidable rule. You must test and review your project or Web site to ensure that it is bug free, accurate, operationally and visually on target, and that the client's requirements have been met, even if that client is you.

Do this before the work is finalized and released for public or client consumption. A bad reputation earned by premature product release can destroy an otherwise excellent piece of work representing thousands of hours of effort. If you need to, delay the release of the work to be sure that it is as good as possible. It's critical that you take the time to thoroughly exercise your project and fix both big and little problems; in the end, you will save yourself a great deal of agony!

One of the major difficulties you face in testing the operation of your multimedia project is that its performance depends on specific hardware and system configurations and, in the case of the Internet, on end users' connection speeds. If you cannot control the end user's platform, or if the project is designed to be shown in many different environments, you must fully test your project on as many platforms as possible, including heavily loaded, highly expanded systems.

warning *Remember to budget for obtaining the hardware test platforms, as well as for the many hours of effort that testing will require.*

Few computer configurations are identical. Even identical hardware configurations may be running dissimilar software that can interact with your program in unexpected ways. The Macintosh environment is well known for its sensitivity to certain *extensions* (drivers and other parts of system software) that conflict with some software applications. Windows 95 uses its registry database to store configuration information and settings, and still uses the WIN.INI and SYS.INI files to hold custom information that may be different for each installation. If your project depends on the

Windows Multimedia Extensions, you will discover a great variety of options and implementations. If your project depends on QuickTime and will be delivered for Windows platforms, you will need to be sure the end user can install QuickTime from your CD or can download the QuickTime plug-in for use with Netscape's or Microsoft's Web browser.

---

tip   *If you are working for a client, clearly specify the intended delivery platform and its hardware and software configuration, and provide a clause in your agreement or contract that you will test only to that platform.*

Because any element of a computer's configuration may be the cause of a problem or a bug, you will spend a good portion of testing time configuring platforms and additional time reproducing reported problems and curing them. It is very difficult for even a well-equipped developer to test every possible configuration of computer, software, and third-party add-on boards. With this in mind, Apple Computer, for example, makes available to developers an elaborate testing facility at its corporate offices in Cupertino, California, where all of Apple's computer models and most variations of hardware and software are available.

20

---

warning   *Not everyone can test software. It takes a special personality to slog through this process. Every feature and function must be exercised, every button clicked. Then the same tests must be repeated again and again with different hardware and under various conditions.*

Testing

The terms *alpha* and *beta* are used by software developers to describe levels of product development when testing is done and feedback is sought. Alpha releases are typically for internal circulation only and are passed among a select group of mock users—often just the team working on the project. These versions of a product are often the very first working drafts of your project, and you can expect them to have problems or to be incomplete. Beta releases, on the other hand, are sent to a wider but still select audience with the same caveat: this software may contain errors, bugs, and unknown alligators that slither out of the swamp at day's end to bite startled designers from behind. Because your product is now being shown and used outside the privacy of its birth nest, its reputation will begin to take form during beta phase; thankfully, beta-level bugs are typically less virulent than alpha bugs.

Alpha Testing

Remain flexible and amenable to changes in both the design and the behavior of your project as you review the comments of your alpha testers. Beware of alpha testing groups made up of kindly friends who can provide positive criticism. Rather, you need to include aggressive people who will attack all aspects of your work. The meaner and nastier they are, the more likely they will sweat out errors or uncertainties in your product's design or navigation system. In the testing arena, learn to skillfully utilize friend and enemy alike. You will undoubtedly discover aspects of your work that, despite even the most insightful planning, you have overlooked.

Beta Testing

The beta testing group should be representative of real users and should not include persons who have been involved in the project's production. Beta testers must have no preconceived ideas. You want them to provide commentary and reports in exchange for getting to play with the latest software and for recognition as part of this "inside" process.

Managing beta test feedback is critical. If you ignore or overlook testers' comments, the testing effort is a waste. Ask your beta testers to include a very detailed description of the hardware and software configuration at the time the problem occurred, and a step-by-step recounting of the problem, so that you can re-create it, analyze it, and repair it. You should also solicit general comments and suggestions. Figure 20-1 presents a sample bug reporting form used for beta testing.

From a letter with enclosed disk, delivered by overnight courier to 240 testers around the world:

"We had a bit of a scare on this Beta. Here is the replacement copy for the infected B5 program disk. For your info, the virus that got past me was a strain of nVir. It was dormant and fooled Virus Detective, Virex, and Interferon. Virex 1.1 listed it as a harmless "Stub" that was left over from a previous cleanup. It wasn't until late yesterday that we discovered that it was real. I must apologize for letting this slip past me and thank the people in our tech support department for their help in calling all the members of the Beta test team and alerting them to this problem. If they didn't get hold of you, it was certainly not for lack of trying."

Ben Calica, letter author and SuperCard 1.5 product manager who claims this product shortened his life span by two years.

FIGURE 20-1

A typical bug reporting form for beta testing

Bug Reporting Form

Please fax or mail completed forms to:

Jane Researcher
Market Research Group
Large Computer Company
Industrial Park
Near A Major City, CA 94567
Phone: 555 - 555 - 1234
Fax: 555 - 555 - 5678

Beta program contact:

Name: _____
Title: _____
Company: _____
Address: _____
City: _____ State: ___ Zip: ___
Phone: _____
Fax: _____

System configuration:

CPU: ____ Clock speed: ____ MHz   Manufacturer: _____
Hard disk capacity: _____ Currently available: _____ RAM: _____
System software: _____ Monitor: _____

Summary of the problem:

_____
_____
_____
_____

Description of the bug:

_____
_____
_____
_____

Replication steps:
If the bug is reproducible, please describe how to do so:

_____
_____
_____
_____

20

Polishing to Gold

As you move through alpha and beta testing, then through the debugging process toward a final release, you may want to use terms that indicate the current version status of your project: *bronze* when you are close to being finished, *gold* when you have determined there is nothing left to change or correct and are ready to reproduce copies from your golden master. Some software developers also use the term *release candidate* (with a version number) as they continue to refine the product and approach a golden master. *Going gold*, or announcing that the job is finished, and then shipping, can be a scary thing. Indeed, if you examine the file creation time and date for many software programs, you will discover that many went gold at two o'clock in the morning.

First Person

We beat on the bronze version of the program right up to the last day, when we had to send a golden master to the duplicator by overnight courier. They were prepared to make 40,000 disks in a matter of hours and then hand-carry them directly to a trade show.

Like kids with sticks at a piñata birthday party, we did everything we could to make all the bugs tumble out of the program. Every time a bug appeared, we killed it. As we pounded and tested, fewer and fewer bugs fell out, until none appeared for about six hours straight, under every condition we could dream up. As the deadline for the courier's airport facility neared, we were ready to apply the finishing touches to the product and stamp it gold. One of the guys waited in his car with engine running, ready for the sprint through commuter traffic to the airport.

We were saving the program every three minutes and nervously backing it up on different media about every ten minutes. We had built in a hidden software routine for debugging this project, and when the product manager clicked Save for the last time, he forgot to reset the program for normal use—we didn't know the master was flawed. Handling the disk like a uranium fuel rod traveling through heavy water, we packed it up and got it to the waiting car. An hour later, our postpartum celebration was interrupted by a painful cry from down the hall—someone had discovered the flaw. By then the courier flight had departed.

We fixed it. Faced with the appalling possibility of 40,000 bad disks being invoiced to us instead of the client, we sent the exhausted product manager out on the midnight flight, without a chance even to go home and clean up. He had a golden master disk in his briefcase, one in his shirt pocket, one in his pants pocket, and one in a manila envelope that would never see an airport x-ray machine.

Preparing for Delivery

If your completed multimedia project will be delivered to consumers or to a client who will install the project on many computers, you will need to prepare your files so they can be easily transferred from your media to the user's platform. Simply copying a project's files to the user's hard disk is often not enough for proper installation; frequently, you will also need to install special system and run-time files.

So that end users can easily and automatically set up your project or application on their own computers, you may need to provide a single program that acts as an installation routine. Winstall for Windows, Install Wizard, and Borland's install routines for Windows, and Aladdin's InstallerMaker package for the Macintosh simplify the creation of an integrated, simple package.

http://www.aladdinsys.com
http://www.eschalon.com
http://www.top.net/qualsoft/instwiz.html
http://www.csusm.edu/cwis/winworld/install.html
http://www.blue-sky.com

Software and information about installer and help programs

w a r n i n g   *The task of writing a proper installation routine is not a trivial one. Be sure you set aside adequate time in your schedule and money in your programming budget for writing and testing the installation program for your project platforms.*

It is important to provide good written documentation about the installation process so that users have a clear step-by-step procedure to follow. That documentation must include a discussion of potential problems and constraints related to the full range of your target platforms. Because you likely will not have control over the specification and configuration of the user's platform, it is critical that you include appropriate warnings in your installation document, like these examples:

- Must have at least 8MB of RAM

- Will not run unless QuickTime is installed

- 3MB available disk drive space

- Disable all screen-savers before running

- On Macs, turn off extensions before installing

- Windows-compatible sound card

- Back up older versions before installing this update

Often a file named README.TXT or ReadMeFirst is a good thing to include on the distribution disk of your project. This file can be a simple ASCII text file accessible by any text editor or word processing application. It should contain a description of changes or bugs reported since the documentation was printed and may also contain a detailed description of the installation process.

The clearer and more detailed your installation instructions are, the fewer frustrated queries you will receive from your project's users. If your project is designed for wide distribution, installation problems can cause you many headaches and a great deal of time and expense in providing answers and service over the telephone. Set up a product-related Web site with pages for registering the software, bug reporting, technical support, and program upgrades.

::::::::::::::::::::::::::::::::::::

Date: Mon, 16 Jun 1997 13:09:12 +0200

From: Christopher Yavelow <Christopher@yav.com>

Subject: The case of the keyboardless kiosk

About ten days ago I posted an announcement to the list about our interactive kiosk installation at the new Netherlands Museum of Science and Technology (press release at: http://www.yav.com/docs/YMEMIMpr.html).

Now I've discovered that science museums at this level are the target of bands of teenage hackers that try to crash all the exhibits. Our exhibit fell prey to such a band last Friday.

Although the software is running inside of a kiosk built into a larger
"The Music is the Message" exhibit housing AND the museum visitor has only
a trackball and single push button to operate the exhibit AND there is
no way to quit the software without issuing a command-Q from a keyboard
which is double-locked inside the guts of the exhibit housing, some kids
were able to get back to the desktop and delete the 60 MB of files
associated with the exhibit...and they did so in such a way that Norton
Utils (3.5) could not find them for un-erasing (I had to bring over a
CD-ROM version and re-install the entire exhibit).

How did they do it? Is there a way to get back to the desktop in such a
scenario: a (for all practical purposes) keyboardless kiosk with only a
trackball and single button interface and no on-screen option to quit the
application? There are no menus, the menubar is hidden, there are no quit
buttons, AllowInterrupts is set to false, etc., etc.

20

Christopher Yavelow
YAV Interactive Media
Brederodestraat 47
2042 BB Zandvoort
The Netherlands
eMail: Christopher@yav.com
wSite: http://www.yav.com

— Scary message found at <supercard@list.allegiant.com>, an
Internet news group for multimedia programmers.

File Archives

Shareware and commercial utility programs for compressing and decompressing files have been in wide use in both the Macintosh and DOS environments for some time. These have been particularly popular with users of bulletin
boards (BBSs), the Internet, and on-line services such as CompuServe and
America Online because compressed files take less time to transmit by modem
than do uncompressed files. Most software that involves uploading and
downloading on-line files automatically handles compression/decompres-
sion. Netscape and Explorer, for example, use "helper" applications to
decompress documents downloaded from the World Wide Web:

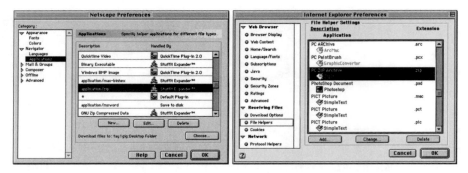

One or more of the files in your project can be compressed into a single file, called an archive. When that archive is then decompressed, or the files are expanded or extracted, each file in the archive is "reconstituted." Figure 20-2 shows the Translate menu of a StuffIt archive, which contains options for converting several archive types. Archives are usually identified by file name extensions representing the compression software that was used, as shown in Table 20-1.

Compression Software	Extension	Platform
PKZIP	.ZIP	DOS/Windows
ARC	.ARC	DOS/Windows
PAK	.PAK	DOS/Windows
Windows Install	.xx__	Windows
StuffIt	.SIT	Macintosh
PackIt	.PIT	Macintosh
DiskDoubler	.DD	Macintosh
CompactPro	.CPT	Macintosh
AppleLink	.PKG	Macintosh
Self-extracting	.SEA	Macintosh
Self-extracting	.EXE	DOS/Windows
BinHex	.hqx	Internet
Uuencode	.uu	Internet
Tar	.tar	Internet, Unix
Compress	.Z	Internet, Unix
Gzip	.gz	Internet, Unix

TABLE 20-1   *Common File Name Extensions for Compression Software* ■

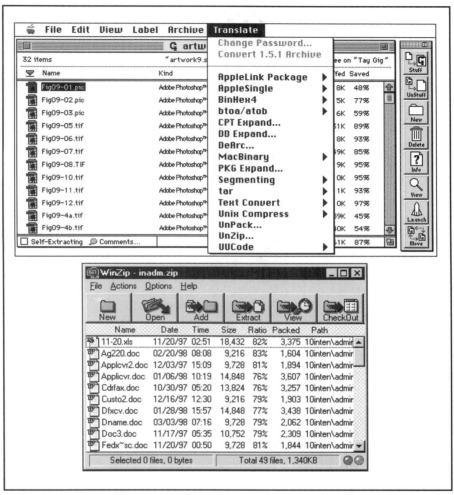

FIGURE 20-2

An archive can contain many compressed files

Self-extracting archives are useful for delivering projects on disks in compressed form. On the Mac, these files typically carry the DOS-like file name extension .SEA. On DOS platforms, these archives are executable files with an .EXE file name extender. With self-extracting archives, the user simply runs the executable archive, and the compressed files are automatically decompressed and placed on the hard disk. DiskDoubler and StuffIt Deluxe both create self-extracting archives on the Macintosh; WinZip creates them in Windows environments. StuffIt Deluxe, while running on the Macintosh (as shown in Figure 20-2), will also decompress .ARC, .PAK., .ZIP, and other files, and convert text that was originally created on a PC or a Unix system.

Some compression applications allow you to compress, split, and store large files on several disks; the segments from these disks are then automatically joined during installation.

Most compression utilities also provide an encryption or security feature, so that people who have access to disks containing private archive files cannot read them without authorization. This helps hide classified data.

For more information about applications for file compression and creating self-extracting archives, contact any of the publishers in the following list of URLs.

http://www.winzip.com
http://www.pkware.com
http://quest.jpl.nasa.gov/Info-Zip/Info-Zip.html
http://www.cis.ohio-state.edu/hypertext/faq/usenet/compression-faq/top.html
http://www.aksoft.com/
http://www.Symantec.com
ftp://ftp.iquest.com/pub/mac

Places to go for compression utilities

First Person

I recently discovered a group of computer scientists and programmers fully dedicated to exploring and improving the techniques and algorithms used for compression of digital data. These folks are from around the world and hang out on bulletin boards, where they have lengthy and arcane electronic conversations. Programmers and mathematicians such as Huffman, Lempel, and Ziv have been made famous on these services.

The greatest contribution this group has made to computer technology may not be in the area of information condensation, but in the creative spin-off of peculiar new words such as freshen, pack, crunch, squash, shrink, crush, implode, distill, squeeze, stuff, and garble. When you throw a few atoms and bestGuesses into this potpourri of words, the language of data compression joins that of modern physics, with its own quarks, gluons, and happy and sad particles. It's a creative and inventive place in the day-to-day forward motion of human endeavor, this place of strange and beautiful compression algorithms.

Delivering on CD-ROM

The majority of multimedia products sold into retail and business channels during the 1990s will be delivered on CD-ROM. By the end of 1991, more than 3 million CD-ROM players were installed around the world, and more than 3,000 commercial CD-ROM titles were published. By 1996, most computers sold included a CD-ROM player, and more than 6,000 titles were available. CD-ROM players are discussed in Chapter 5.

Over 600 million CD players and drives are installed worldwide, and over 10 billion discs have been sold. The majority of these 600 million is CD-audio, a product which by now can be regarded as a traditional consumer electronics product.

For CD-ROM, we expect...that the industry will sell more than 50 million units in 1996. The OEM price of a CD-ROM drive has gone down from $3,000 in 1984 to below $100 this year. We expect prices to stabilize after this year, but the products will have a higher performance. This year Philips will be market leader with the introduction of 8x drives, and we expect to step up to 10x-speed drives in the second half of this year.

20

In short, we expect the total optical drive market to grow from approximately 125 million drives per year in 1995 to 250 million drives in the year 2000, with or without DVD. And as the growth figure of CD-ROM drives in 1995, 1996, and 1997 shows, we expect PC-based multimedia products to generate the majority of this growth, with products offering a higher performance, both in drive speed and access time.

Jan Oosterveld, President, Philips Key Modules. From the opening speech at CeBIT, Hanover, Germany, March 13, 1996

CD-ROM players are the chickens, and the titles are the eggs—you can't have one without the other. As more chickens produce eggs, more chickens will emerge to produce even more eggs that yield yet greater numbers of chickens..., and so forth, in geometrically increasing progression.

The first users of CD-ROMs were owners of large databases: library catalogs, reference systems, and parts lists. In 1992, it was estimated that about 60 percent of existing CD-ROMs contained text-based databases. Some CD-ROM players are sold for dedicated business and special purposes and do not represent purchasers or consumers of CD-ROM-based multimedia titles, but with multimedia capability increasing (see Chapter 4), more new CD titles are being published for consumers in the areas of education, training, and entertainment.

In 1994, there were almost 12,000 CD-ROM titles in print, and that figure is expected to increase to as many as 40,000 titles by the year 2000. Also in 1994, about 100 million individual CD-ROM discs were sold worldwide; by the year 2000, some researchers predict that the number of CD-ROM title units sold may increase to a staggering 1.6 billion units!

Consumer-oriented CD-ROM titles fall into these categories:

Agriculture	Graphics
Bibliography	Health
Business	History
Dictionaries	Leisure
Directories	Life sciences
Education	Literature
Edutainment	Music and sound
Encyclopedias	Science and technology
Games	Travel
Geography	

Compact Disc Technology

A compact disc, or CD, is a thin wafer of clear polycarbonate plastic and metal measuring 4.75 inches (120 mm) in diameter, with a small hole, or hub, in its center. The metal layer is usually pure aluminum, sputtered onto the polycarbonate surface in a thickness measurable in molecules. As the disc spins in the CD player, the metal reflects light from a tiny infrared laser into a light-sensitive receiver diode. These reflections are transformed onto an electrical signal and then further converted to meaningful bits and bytes for use in digital equipment.

Pits on the CD, where the information is stored, are 1 to 3 microns long, about 1/2 micron wide, and 1/10 micron deep (by comparison, a human hair is about 18 microns in diameter). A CD can contain as many as 3 miles of these tiny pits wound in a spiral pattern from the hub to the edge. A layer of lacquer is applied to protect the surface, and artwork from the disc's author or publisher is usually silk-screened on the back side.

Compact discs are made in what is generally referred to as a *family* process. The glass master is made using the well-developed photolithographic techniques created by the microchip industry: First an optically ground glass disc is coated with a layer of photoresist material 1/10 micron thick. A laser exposes (*writes*) a pattern of pits onto the surface of the chemical layer of material. The disc is developed (the exposed areas are washed away) and is silvered, resulting in the actual pit structure of the finished master disc. The master is then electroplated with layers of nickel one molecule thick, one layer at a time, until the desired thickness is reached. The nickel layer is separated from the glass disc and forms a metal negative, or *father*.

In cases where low runs of just a few discs are required, the father is used to make the actual discs. Most projects, though, require several *mothers,* or positives, to be made by plating the surface of the father.

In a third plating stage, *sons* or stampers are made from the mother, and these are the parts that are used in the injection molding machines. Plastic pellets are heated and injected into the mold or stamper, forming the disc with the pits in it. The plastic disc is coated with a thin aluminum layer for reflectance and protective lacquer for protection, given a silk-screened label for marketing, and packaged for delivery. Most of these activities occur in a particle-free clean room, because one speck of dust larger than a pit can ruin many hours of work. The mastering process alone takes around 12 hours.

Compact Disc Standards

In 1979, Philips and Sony together launched CD technology as a digital method of delivering sound and music (audio) to consumers (see Chapter 10). This collaboration resulted in the Red Book standard (named for the color of the document's jacket), officially called the Compact Disc Digital Audio Standard. The Red Book standard defines the audio format for CDs available in music stores today; the Yellow Book is for CD-ROM; the Green Book is for CD-I (Interactive); the Orange Book is for write-once, read-only (WORM) CD-ROMs; and the White Book is for Video CD (Karaoke CD). These and other CD formats are discussed in the following sections.

The Red, Yellow, Green, Orange, and White Books

Red Book remains the basis for recent standards that define more elaborate digital data formats for computers and other digital devices. Audio CDs can provide up to 76 minutes of playing time, which is enough for a slow-tempo rendition of Beethoven's Ninth Symphony. This was reported to be Philips's and Sony's actual criterion during research and development for determining the size of sectors and ultimately the physical size of the CD itself.

A CD may contain one or more *tracks*. These are areas normally allocated for storing a single song in the Red Book format. CDs also contain lead-in information and a table of contents. Each track on the CD may use a different format; this allows you to create a mixed-mode disc that combines, for example, high-quality CD-Audio with Macintosh HFS CD-ROM or ISO 9660 data formats. Figure 20-3 illustrates the track layouts for Red Book, Yellow Book, Green Book, mixed mode, and for Kodak's PhotoCD Orange Book layout, discussed later.

cross platform *Macintosh and Windows support commands to access both Red Book Audio and data tracks on a CD, but you cannot access both at the same time.*

Though a CD contains tracks, the primary logical unit for data storage on a CD is a *sector,* which is 1/75 second in length. Each sector of a CD contains 2352 bytes of data. After every sector are another 882 bytes consisting of two layers of error-detecting and error-correcting information (EDC and ECC) and timing control data. A CD actually requires, then, 3234 bytes to store 2352 bytes of data. EDC and ECC allow a scratched or dirty data sector to be reconstructed by software fast enough to avoid dropout of music. Timing codes are used to display song-playing time on an audio CD player.

FIGURE 20-3

CD track layouts

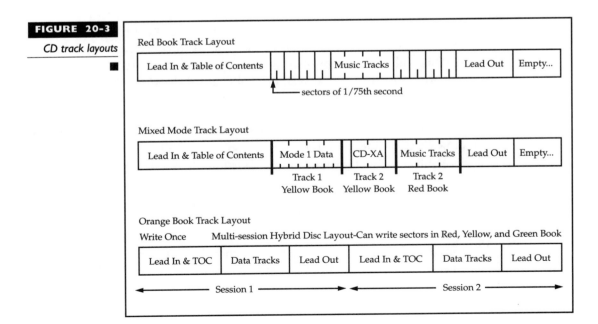

The disc spins at a constant linear velocity (CLV), so data can be read at a constant density and spacing. This means the rotational speed of the disc may vary from about 200 rpm when the read head is at the outer edge, to 530 rpm when it is reading near the hub. This translates to about 1.3 meters (51 inches) of travel along the data track each second. CD players use very sensitive motors so that no matter where the read head is on the disc, approximately the same amount of data are read in each second.

The CD's rotational speed and the density of the pits and lands on the CD allow data to be read at a sustained rate of 150K per second in a *single-speed* reader. This is sufficient for good audio, but it is very slow for large image files, motion video, and other multimedia resources, especially when compared to the high data-transfer rates of hard disk drives. New drives that spin many times faster when reading computer data, and slower for Red Book Audio, have been designed specifically for computers. In any case, CD access speed and transfer rate from CD-ROM is much slower than from a hard disk.

Philips and Sony developed the Yellow Book to provide an established standard for data storage and retrieval. Yellow Book adds yet another layer of error checking to accommodate the greater reliability required of computer data, and it provides two modes: one for computer data and the other for compressed audio and video/picture data.

The most common standard currently used for CD-ROM production evolved from the Yellow Book, with Microsoft joining the collaboration, and it was approved by the International Standards Organization as ISO 9660 (see the next section). Later, other standards were developed to deal with specific user requirements, such as synchronized interleaving of compressed audio and visual data in interactive digital movies (Green Book), and with formats for write-once and magneto-optical CD technologies (Orange Book).

The Red, Yellow, Green, and Orange books describe the types of compact discs listed in Table 20-2.

Within each standard, there are variations called modes, forms, and levels. These variations pertain to the method used to allocate the 2352 bytes available in a CD data sector and how the player reads them. Figure 20-4 shows the most common data layouts within sectors.

Each track on a CD can be one and only one of the following formats: CD-Audio, CD-ROM Mode 1, CD-ROM Mode 2, CD-ROM/XA, or CD-I. The whole track must be the same type. When you combine different types of tracks on the same disc, the disc is called a *mixed-mode* disc—for example, track 1 might be CD-ROM Mode 1 data, and all subsequent tracks might be audio data. This is the most common layout for CD-ROM Mode 2, CD-ROM/XA, or CD-I, but each whole track must be the same type.

Name	Description	Comment
CD-Audio or CD-DA	Digital audio	Consumer audio discs
CD-ROM High Sierra	Read-only memory	Vestigial standard, seldom used
CD-ROM ISO 9660	Read-only memory	MS-DOS and Macintosh files
CD-ROM HFS	Read-only memory	Macintosh HFS files
CD-ROM/XA	Read-only memory	Extended Architecture
CD-I or CD-RTOS	Interactive	Philips Interactive motion video
CD-I Ready	Interactive/Ready	Audio CD with features for CD-I player
CD-Bridge	Bridge	Allows XA track to play on CD-I player
CD-MO	Magneto optical	Premastered area readable on any CD player
CD-WO or CD-R	Write-once recordable	May use multiple sessions to fill disc
CD+G	Mixed mode	CD+Graphics, MTV on disc
CDTV	ISO 9660 variant	Commodore proprietary system
PhotoCD	Compressed images	Kodak multisession XA system
Video CD or Karaoke CD	Bridge	Karaoke full-motion MPEG video
DVD	Digital Versatile Disc	MPEG video, surround sound, and interactive multimedia

TABLE 20-2   *Compact Disc Formats* ■

tip *Because there is built-in error correction on CDs, small scratches may not affect playback, particularly when the scratch runs in a straight line from center to edge. To really wreck a CD, scratch it in an easy arc from the center to the rim; error correction won't keep up.*

Note that the CD-ROM/XA format uses an additional subheader that tells the reading software what type of data to expect in that sector: either computer data or compressed audio data interleaved with picture data. (CD-ROM/XA is discussed further in a later section.) Additional hardware is required to play a CD-ROM/XA disc, but these XA-capable players, and players that can read Kodak's PhotoCD multisession XA discs, have become standard. These players can also play Red Book and Yellow Book formats.

ISO 9660

The most widely used format for storing digital data in files on CDs is ISO 9660. This standard originated at a famous meeting of industry representatives at Del Webb's High Sierra Hotel & Casino in Reno, Nevada. At

FIGURE 20-4

The sectors on a

CD may store data

in various ways

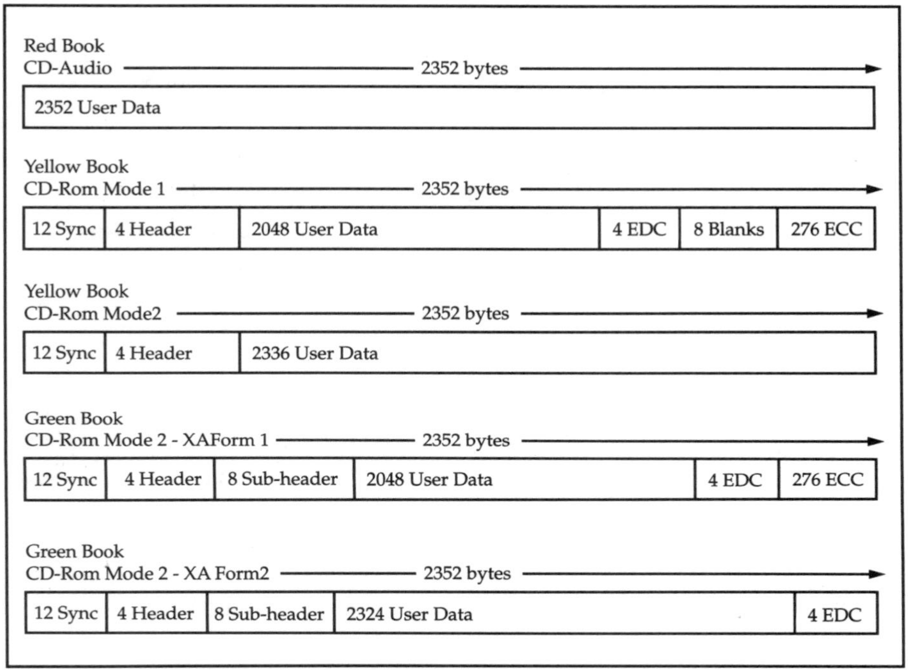

■

Red Book
CD-Audio ——————————————— 2352 bytes ———————————————→

2352 User Data

Yellow Book
CD-Rom Mode 1 ——————————————— 2352 bytes ———————————————→

12 Sync	4 Header	2048 User Data	4 EDC	8 Blanks	276 ECC

Yellow Book
CD-Rom Mode2 ——————————————— 2352 bytes ———————————————→

12 Sync	4 Header	2336 User Data

Green Book
CD-Rom Mode 2 - XAForm 1 ——————————— 2352 bytes ———————————→

12 Sync	4 Header	8 Sub-header	2048 User Data	4 EDC	276 ECC

Green Book
CD-Rom Mode 2 - XA Form2 ——————————— 2352 bytes ———————————→

12 Sync	4 Header	8 Sub-header	2324 User Data	4 EDC

20

that meeting, a common file structure for CDs specifically used by computers was defined. By the time it was processed as an international standard many months later, enhancements had been added, and the "High Sierra" format became outdated.

ISO 9660 file-naming conventions follow the MS-DOS style of eight characters, a period, and three extender characters. Directory names are limited to eight characters, and directories may not be nested more than eight deep. Acceptable characters for names are the capital letters A–Z, the digits 0–9, and the underscore character.

An executable program file designed for the PC will not run on a Macintosh (and vice versa). You can, however, access all files on the CD from either platform. On the Macintosh, you need the Apple CD-ROM extension, and the files named Foreign File Access and ISO 9660 File Access must be in the System folder. On MS-DOS or Windows computers, a device driver supplied by the player manufacturer must be called from the CON-FIG.SYS file, and the file MSCDEX.EXE (the Microsoft CD-ROM Extensions) or equivalent (such as Corel's CDX Extension) must be run during boot-up. The ISO 9660 CD-ROM is viewed by either operating system as just another storage device containing directories or folders, and files.

Many multimedia developers place both Macintosh files and PC files on the same CD in a *hybrid* format, letting the user launch the proper applications for the appropriate platform. You can hide the files of either platform when you make the hybrid disc so that users are not confused by the files belonging to the other platform.

---

cross platform   *Graphics, text, and data files written in common formats such as DOC, TIF, PIC, DBF, and WKS can be read from an ISO 9660 CD and imported into your application, whether the file was generated on a Macintosh or a PC.*

Macintosh HFS

The Hierarchical File System (HFS) is Apple's method for managing files and folders on the Macintosh desktop, although with System 8.1, a newer format was introduced to optimize hard disk space. Apple has developed its own drivers for Yellow Book Mode 1 CDs, and the HFS driver for CD-ROMs (the default driver built into Apple CD-ROM) provides Macintosh users with the expected comfort of the familiar Apple desktop, complete with 32-character, mixed-case file names. HFS does not, however, comply with the international ISO 9660 standard. If your project is destined only for Macintosh platforms, the HFS format is the preferred choice.

It is easy to produce a Macintosh HFS-formatted CD. Just organize all your files and folders on a hard disk or removable cartridge, test that all paths are correct and your software works, and submit the disk to a CD-ROM manufacturing house. They will copy your disk contents to an HFS CD-ROM with no muss or fuss. When you then mount the disk on a Macintosh, it will look just like the submitted hard disk. With the popularity of CD-R devices (see Chapter 5), most developers "burn" their own test CDs using software like Toast or Easy CD Creator and submit these directly to the manufacturer for mastering.

CD-ROM/XA (Sony)

A standard of great interest to multimedia developers is CD-ROM/XA (Extended Architecture), which is an extension to the Yellow Book standard. XA defines a new sector format to allow computer data (Form 1), as well as compressed audio data and video/image information (Form 2), to be read and played back apparently simultaneously. Computer data can be interleaved or mixed with audio and images. In effect, XA provides audio synchronization, similar to QuickTime or AVI.

Special enabling hardware is required onboard a CD-ROM/XA player because the audio must be separated from the interleaved data, decompressed, and then output to speakers—while the computer data are sent onward to the computer. XA audio can be digitized and played back at two quality levels; though it falls short of Red Book quality, it is still adequate. Production of a CD-ROM/XA disc requires extensive premastering, because the data and audio/video information must be properly interleaved from your original material. You can still have high-quality Red Book tracks on your XA disc.

PhotoCD

In the summer of 1992, Eastman Kodak Company pioneered a well-planned and heavily financed effort to establish early market share in worldwide electronic photo-imaging systems for consumers. Designed to protect Kodak's investment in the photoprocessing industry, its vast sales and technology infrastructure, and to allow gradual consumer transition from film-based cameras to digital cameras over the next decades, the new technology is a marriage of silver halide wet processing and digital processing and display techniques. Kodak has named this venture PhotoCD.

Customers present an exposed 35 mm roll of color film for wet processing and purchase a PhotoCD for an additional charge. The source images (negatives) are then processed by a technician who scans each image at an imaging workstation. The images (a *session*) are written onto PhotoCD write-once media, a color index of thumbnails of all the images is printed, and the PhotoCD is returned to the consumer in a CD jewel case with the printed thumbnails inserted as an attractive cover. The customer may return that same PhotoCD to have more images written onto it, creating a multi-session disc. A PhotoCD can contain 125 or more high-resolution images.

PhotoCD images may be viewed using a CD-ROM/XA-capable player (most CD players are XA capable) connected to a computer. In this way, desktop publishing and multimedia production houses have access to images and libraries of images distributed on PhotoCD. Kodak has also created a method for viewing PhotoCD images over the World Wide Web—with a PhotoCD-enabled browser, you can use options such as zoom in, zoom out, and enlarge to view images.

Philips CD-I

The Green Book, published in 1988, specifies an Extended Architecture format and operating system (CD-RTOS) for Philips's proprietary CD-I

(Interactive) environment. Like PhotoCD, CD-I discs are designed to play on a consumer-grade player connected to a television set. To prevent users from playing a CD-I track on an audio player (which produces maximum-volume noise and can damage eardrums), the CD-I tracks are not listed in the disc's table of contents. CD-I uses XA Form 1 and Form 2 data formats.

CD-I-ready discs are Red Book Audio discs with special information stored just ahead of track 1, in an area called the *pregap*. These discs are designed specifically to work with Philips CD-I players, allowing special pictures and text to be loaded into the player's memory before the Red Book Audio tracks begin to play. The disc can also be played on a standard CD-Audio player without interference from the additional information stored on the disc.

CD-Bridge discs are also designed to accommodate the Philips CD-I proprietary player system, and they conform to both the CD-I and CD-ROM/XA specifications. This format—which assigns two separate disc label locations, one for each format—allows a CD-ROM/XA track to be played on a CD-I player. Kodak PhotoCD discs are playable on Philips CD-I players because they are Bridge discs.

During the early 1990s, Philips, Kodak, Commodore, Tandy, Sega, NEC, Nintendo, Panasonic, and Sony entered the consumer electronics market-place with television-based systems that allow users to dynamically interact with sound and displayed graphical information. The Commodore CDTV and Tandy VIS ventures never caught on in the retail marketplace of the United States, however, and were abandoned by 1994.

Video CDD White Book

Originally called Karaoke CD, the White Book format was developed in a joint effort by Philips and the Victor Company of Japan, Ltd. (better known as JVC). It is also supported by Matsushita (Panasonic) and Sony. As a Bridge format CD, these discs can be played on most players using CD-ROM/XA. Specialized consumer players that hook up to television sets have been developed for the Karaoke market, and they take advantage of the Video CD format's implementation of MPEG.

warning *It is possible to damage your speakers if you play the digital track of a CD-ROM on your audio CD player. These digital data are decoded as full-volume noise by players that do not check for a data flag in the control field of the Q subchannel.*

DVD

Digital Video Disc (DVD) CDs employ a different (multilayer, high-density) manufacturing process than current 74-minute (about 640MB) audio and data CDs, and this technology provides 4.7 gigabytes of storage on a disc of the same diameter. The DVD format itself is a product of broad support from most of the industry's leading manufacturers. DVD is discussed in greater detail in Chapter 5.

Wrapping It Up

Packaging is an important area where sales and marketing issues extend the process of making multimedia into the real world of end users. Like the cover of a book, people will judge your work based upon the impression it makes.

If your project is for your own use, you may not need the pretty cover, cardboard box, and shrink-wrap that is required for over-the-counter software sold to consumers. If your project is for a client or for the Web, you may simply need to deliver it on any sufficient storage media or upload it to a server. But if your project is headed for wider distribution within a large company or organization or into retail channels, you will need to think about packaging.

If your project is destined to be sold into the consumer retail channel, then you have made a *title*. Software titles are most often distributed on CD-ROM. The software itself may, indeed, be only one item (the most important one) in a package that includes a user's manual, a registration card, quick reference guides, hardware adapters, and collateral marketing material from you or other parties with whom you have arrangements.

Retailers claim that consumers typically relate the finish of a package to quality and price of the product inside. The fancier, bigger, and heavier the package, the higher its perceived value. Software manufacturers juggle the elements of this equation when they determine the cost of goods and shipping/freight add-ons and set the product's price point. Many big software boxes are shipped with plenty of sailboat fuel inside, and with cardboard or open-cell foam to hold the thin CD and manuals in place.

The art for your cover should reflect the content and function of the enclosed product; it should also follow normal rules for good design layout. Your company's logo should be prominent, and if this is one of a series of titles, the artwork should conform to the coordinated look or style you are using throughout that series or product line.

20

When your product reaches the retail channel, it may be displayed on shelves or racks, in kiosks, or it may be hung on brackets. You should be sure to put the name of your title on the front face and on the spine of the package. Use photo-quality images and high-caliber artwork for the front, because this is the most visible face of your package. Many packages are shrink-wrapped with thin plastic to protect them from fingerprints and pilferage at the retail outlet. Even after the shrink-wrap is on your package, there is room for additional artwork: bright stickers can be effective eye-catchers. And some vendors apply specially made holographic stickers to identify their product and to prevent unauthorized bootleg copies from reaching the marketplace.

Some vendors have developed unique or special solutions to make their product stand out. Authorware, for example, was once shipped in a custom-designed briefcase with carry handle. An expensive software package, this briefcase was easily absorbed in the purchase price. Fractal Design Painter from MetaCreations is shipped in a metal paint can with a colorful paper wrapper, and AlienSkin's Eye Candy special effects for After Effects comes in a metal movie reel case (see Figure 20-5). But package size and shape options are, more often than not, limited by the common constraints of the floor and shelf space found in retailing outlets and by the expense of fabricating a nonstandard container.

FIGURE 20-5

Some software comes in interesting packages

Most industrial cities boast more than one packaging specialist with whom you can consult. These outfits can supply cardboard and plastic boxes, printing, cutting, folding, and wrapping services. Environmentally responsible packaging, especially for compact discs, is becoming popular, and special sleeves and cardboard containers are available. Be sure to consider the weight and bulk of your package—an ounce of extra weight that pushes you over a zone or destination boundary might increase your shipping costs significantly. The outside wrap for shipping should be plain because pilferage, especially for international destinations and customs zones, can be a problem. Look for volume discounts and price breaks.

The current trend in software packaging is toward simplification. Indeed, as the information revolution takes hold, more software and documentation will be available for purchase and downloading directly from the Web, and today's boxes and bright packages will become quaint collector's items.

Delivering on the World Wide Web

Delivering multimedia projects built for the World Wide Web can be as simple as renaming a directory or transferring a group of files to a Web server. Servers and networked systems are discussed in Chapters 5 and 14. On the face of it, the mechanics of actually putting a project on the Web are trivial, particularly because you have likely been designing, building, and testing within "Web space" throughout the development of your project, anyway. But delivery of your project and *activation* of your pages by making them available to your intended audience on the Web, whether to the general public or to an intranet of select users behind a fire wall, should be approached with caution. Here there are many technical considerations that, while outside the topic of multimedia per se, should be understood if you want your project to be a success.

If you own or *host* the delivery Web server yourself, you will have better security control, better integration of your project into your internal LAN or intranet, and you can fine-tune the server's configuration parameters and specify and install any special software you need. On the other hand, you will likely need a full-time webmaster to be in charge, and you will pay for a high bandwidth connection directly to the Internet. When you have control of the server, you can provide secure commerce services for credit card transactions, encryption and passwords, special databases, and custom CGI programming. Server-side setup for plug-ins is discussed in Chapter 15. For multimedia projects requiring streaming technologies such as RealAudio or video conferencing, you can purchase and install the necessary software on the server.

If your project will reside at a site hosted by an Internet Service Provider (ISP) or a service such as America Online or MSN, you must discover during the planning phase of your project what your service's limitations might be and design your project within those limitations. It does no good to include PhotoCD image pacs, ToolVox meta voice files, or complex Java scripts in your Web page, only to find that your ISP does not or will not support the MIME type or purchase and install the necessary server software for you.

Internet directories like Yahoo, and search engines like Lycos and AltaVista, are important components of the Web's functionality and power, and can be used in publicizing your project.

A few years ago I taught a student of mine about HTML, just before she went off to a summer internship working on a traditional book publisher's Web site. She returned to school three months later and demonstrated to me how one might use the Web to generate profit—at a time when many doubted it was easy to do. Working for the publisher, she was assigned the job of marketing a book to college students. She did her research and discovered how advertising in the search engines works. By "buying" the word "college" on a few of them, she was able to place an ad on search pages that were related to colleges; visitors who clicked on her ad were sent to the publisher's Web site where they could purchase the book online. While explaining the process she checked the online sales of her book: 5000 copies had been sold online within a month of publication—eight of them during the last hour!

Panagiotis Takis Metaxas, Assistant Professor of Computer Science, Wellesley College

Index

FreeHand 8

Step into the world of motion with FreeHand 8.

The world of design is in motion. Toward more powerful effects, animation, and the Web. FreeHand™ moves your print designs to a new level with tools like editable transparency, a customizable interface that streamlines integration with your other tools, and the industry's fastest redraws. Move into the world of Web design with vector graphics that download quickly with superior quality, anti-aliased text, and support for the leading Web animation tool, Macromedia Flash™. Get FreeHand 8 alone–or upgrade to the Design in Motion™ Suite, which also includes Flash and Insta.HTML 2 for turning FreeHand layouts into Web pages and save up to $300. Just call **1 800 457 1774**. Or visit http://www.macromedia/freehand for all the details.

macromedia®

Power, Productivity, and Platform Support!

macromedia
DIRECTOR® 6.5
The Most Powerful Tools for Multimedia and the Web

Create interactive applications for delivery on the web (via Shockwave Plug-in or Java), CD/DVD-ROM, or hybrid CD using the standard for multimedia and web development, Director 6.5 Multimedia Studio.

Director can import most standard formats, including PowerPoint, QuickTime, AVI, graphics and sounds to create richly interactive content. The power of Director can easily be extended though drag-and-drop behaviors, Lingo (the built-in Director scripting language), C, C++, and JavaScript.

Top Director 6.5 features:
• PowerPoint import
• QuickTime 3 import
• Save As Java
• Flash support
• AfterShock 2
• QuickTime VR import
• Custom cursors
• Insertion of Active X controls

For more information, visit **http://www.macromedia.com/ software/director** to order or call **800 457 1774**.

About the CD

This book's CD-ROM contains a variety of software demos for PC and Macintosh users from Macromedia®, Inc.

BY USING THE SOFTWARE ON THIS CD, YOU ARE AGREEING TO BECOME BOUND TO THE TERMS OF THE END-USER LICENSE AGREEMENT THAT IS INCLUDED ON THE CD.

To use the CD

Please follow the instructions below:
Insert the CD into your CD drive.

On a PC

Select File | Run from the Start Menu, type in the letter of your CD drive, and press Enter.

You will be presented with a window that shows different folders for each of the Macromedia product demos. Select the folder for the product you are interested in, and double-click on that folder's Setup file to run the installer Wizard. Follow the instructions on your screen to demo the products.

On a Macintosh

Double-click the CD icon on your desktop. You will be presented with a window that shows folders for each of the product demos. Select the folder for the product you are interested in, and double-click on that folder's Setup file to run the installer Wizard. Follow the instructions on your screen to demo the products.